The baby names almanac

2014

Emily Larson

sourcebooks

Copyright © 2011, 2012, 2013 by Sourcebooks, Inc.
Cover and internal design © 2010, 2013 by Sourcebooks, Inc.
Cover design by Dawn Adams/Sourcebooks, Inc.
Cover image © hannamariah/Shutterstock

Published by Sourcebooks, Inc.
P.O. Box 4410, Naperville, Illinois 60567-4410
(630) 961-3900
Fax: (630) 961-2168
www.sourcebooks.com

Library of Congress Cataloging-in-Publication data is on file with the publisher.

Printed and bound in the United States of America.
VP 10 9 8 7 6 5 4 3 2 1

Contents

So, you've got a baby to name.

As if preparing for the arrival of the baby isn't enough, you're dealing with all the pressure of figuring out what, exactly, to call the little bundle of joy. It can be stressful to find a name that will do justice to the hope you have for your child.

After all, names influence first impressions. They can trigger great—or unpleasant—nicknames. They can affect your child's self-esteem. They can be a tangible, lasting link to a family legacy.

But let's not forget that they can be fun. And that's what this book is all about.

Remember *The Old Farmer's Almanac*, which comes out annually as a guide to each year's trends, forecasts, and hot spots? Aimed at farmers, of course, the book provides a way to put the year into context, to navigate the shifting seasons, and to understand all the factors swirling in the atmosphere.

The 2014 Baby Names Almanac aims to be a similar lifeline for parents. With a finger on the pulse of pop culture and an ear to the ground of what's hip, new, and relevant, this book offers you an instant, idiosyncratic snapshot of how the world today is shaping what you may want to name your child tomorrow.

Jam-packed with information and ideas, plus thousands of names to browse, this book analyzes the most recent trends and fads in baby naming, offering up forecasts and predictions. You'll find our take on questions like these (and much more!):

Which cutting-edge names are on the rise?
Which popular names are on the decline?
What influence do celebrities have on names?

Names in music: Could you name your daughter **North** or **Nori**? Could **Hunter** or **Hayes** be your son's namesake?

Names in TV: Will **Arya** and **Tyrion** be in your child's kindergarten class? Or will you see more classic, Downton Abbey–inspired kids?

Names in royalty: With the arrival of Prince George of Cambridge, is **George** going to shoot up the charts? Will names like **Prince** and **King** continue to rise?

How many babies get the most popular name, anyway?

Which letter do most girls' names start with? How about boys' names?

What are the most popular "gender-neutral" names today—and which gender uses each name more often? (If you name your daughter **Emerson**, will she find herself playing with lots of other little girls named **Emerson**—or little boys instead?)

How can you take a trend and turn it into a name you love? (How about a little **Major** of your own?)

We understand that sometimes this information on trends and popularity is hard to digest, so we've created some easy-to-visualize graphics. Turn to page 4, for example, to see a map of the United States showing where **Sophia** reigns and where little **Mason** is king.

And what baby name book would be complete without the names? Flip to page 69 to begin browsing through more than 20,000 names, including entries for the most popular names for girls and boys as reported by the Social Security Administration (www.ssa.gov/OACT/babynames).

A little bit of a mishmash and a screenshot of the world today, *The 2014 Baby Names Almanac* is like no other book out there. Stuffed with ideas on what's hip and hot and how you can take a trend and turn it into a name you love, this book is your all-in-one guide to baby names now.

Inside the Popularity Charts

The Top 10

Let's start with the most popular names in the country. Ranked by the Social Security Administration (SSA), these names are released around Mother's Day each year. (The top 10 names get the most attention, but you may also hear about the top 100. The total number of names widely reported is 1,000.) In 2012 the top 10 names were similar to—but not identical to—the top 10 for 2011. For example, **Sophia** remained on top, but **Isabella** slid from second to third, while **Elizabeth** entered the top ten for the first time since 2008. On the boys' list, **Jacob** and **Mason** held on to the top two spots, while, for the first time ever, **Liam** stormed into the top ten at number six. Here's a quick comparison of 2011 and 2012:

2012 Girls	2011 Girls	2012 Boys	2011 Boys
1. Sophia	1. Sophia	1. Jacob	1. Jacob
2. Emma	2. Isabella	2. Mason	2. Mason
3. Isabella	3. Emma	3. Ethan	3. William
4. Olivia	4. Olivia	4. Noah	4. Jayden
5. Ava	5. Ava	5. William	5. Noah
6. Emily	6. Emily	6. Liam	6. Michael
7. Abigail	7. Abigail	7. Jayden	7. Ethan
8. Mia	8. Madison	8. Michael	8. Alexander
9. Madison	9. Mia	9. Alexander	9. Aiden
10. Elizabeth	10. Chloe	10. Aiden	10. Daniel

Just How Many Sophias Are There, Anyway?

Sure, these names are popular, but what does that mean? Well, it seems that new parents are increasingly looking for off-the-beaten-path names for their little ones, and it shows. According to the SSA, the top 1,000 names represent 72.85 percent of all babies born and named in the United States in 2012—a significant drop from the 77.84 percent recorded in 2000.

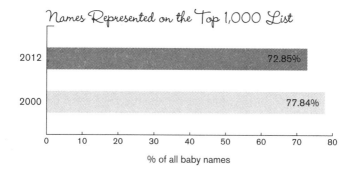

Names Represented on the Top 1,000 List

Although parents of either gender have always been looking beyond the top 1,000, parents of boys are more likely to pick a name in that mix—78.62 percent of boys' names are represented on the top 1,000 list, while only 66.82 percent of girls' names are.

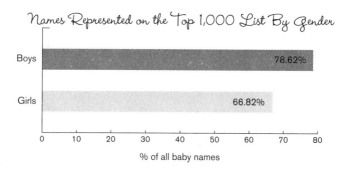

Names Represented on the Top 1,000 List By Gender

Plus, although it may seem like you know a zillion people with daughters named **Olivia** or **Abigail**, the most popular names are actually bestowed upon a relatively small number of babies each year. For example, in 2012 only 0.9404 percent of all male babies born in the United States (that's 18,899 little guys total) got the most popular name, **Jacob**. There are slightly more girls (22,158) with the most popular name, **Sophia**, but even that's only 1.153 percent of all girls born. Only a fifth of the Jacob total—3,781 babies—were given the 100th most popular name, **Ryder**. The number of babies with the number one name is dropping swiftly—back in 1999, the first year Jacob hit number one, more than 35,000 boys got that name,

> ### Mary, Mary Quite Contrary
>
> **Mary** has been the most popular girl's name in the last 100 years, with 3.6 million babies given the name since 1912. For boys, **James** reigns, with 4.8 million namesakes in the last century.

which is more than 16,000 additional babies compared to 2012. And back in 1970, 4.48 percent of all male babies (a staggering 85,298 tots) were named **Michael**, the most popular name of that year. So if you've got your heart set on naming your son **Ethan** but you're worried that he'll be surrounded by Ethans wherever he goes, take heart!

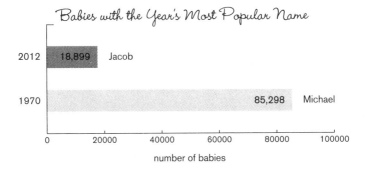

Babies with the Year's Most Popular Name

| 2012 | 18,899 Jacob |
| 1970 | 85,298 Michael |

0   20000   40000   60000   80000   100000

number of babies

What's Popular in My State?

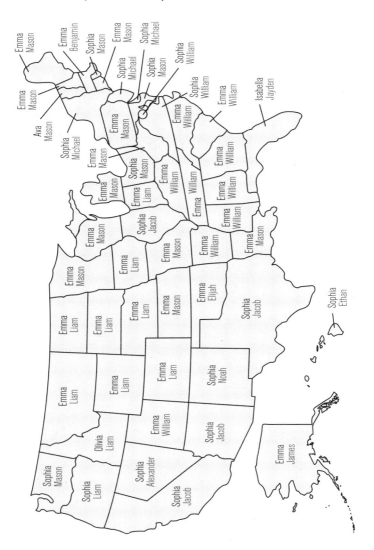

It's interesting to see how some names are more popular in certain states than in others. For example, **Benjamin** ranks 16th nationally for boys, but in Massachusetts it's the most popular name. Likewise, **Genesis** ranks fifth among Washington, D.C.'s baby girls, but only 56th in the nation.

The following chart lists the top five names for girls and boys for each of the 50 states, and it also shows the actual number of births for each of those names in each state. Check out how many girl babies got the number one name in Wyoming (**Emma**, 40) compared to the number of girl babies with the same name in California, where it was only the third most popular name (2,429):

Top Five Names by State

State	Girl	Births	Boy	Births
Alabama	Emma	317	William	436
	Ava	240	James	317
	Olivia	226	Mason	300
	Isabella	197	John	277
	Madison	191	Jacob	260
Alaska	Emma	57	James	51
	Sophia	55	Ethan	47
	Olivia	49	Liam	44
	Abigail	38	Gabriel	42
	Ava	32	Jacob	41
Arizona	Sophia	579	Jacob	390
	Isabella	483	Liam	376
	Emma	387	Daniel	374
	Mia	368	Ethan	372
	Olivia	348	Anthony	366

State	Girl	Births	Boy	Births
Arkansas	Emma	185	William	215
	Sophia	162	Mason	154
	Ava	138	James	153
	Isabella	135	Jacob	152
	Olivia	132	Elijah	151
California	Sophia	3,617	Jacob	2,955
	Isabella	3,087	Jayden	2,852
	Emma	2,429	Daniel	2,662
	Emily	2,409	Ethan	2,661
	Mia	2,311	Matthew	2,627
Colorado	Emma	337	Liam	353
	Sophia	331	Alexander	296
	Olivia	312	Jacob	287
	Isabella	258	William	283
	Ava	229	Noah	263
Connecticut	Emma	246	Mason	230
	Olivia	234	Jacob	213
	Isabella	232	Michael	207
	Sophia	226	Liam	203
	Ava	184	Ethan	191
Delaware	Sophia	67	Michael	60
	Emma	63	Anthony	55
	Isabella	63	Mason	53
	Ava	51	Liam	52
	Olivia	51	Alexander	51
District of Columbia	Sophia	50	William	94
	Emma	41	Alexander	67
	Olivia	40	Henry	65
	Charlotte	38	John	64
	Genesis	34	James	59

State	Girl	Births	Boy	Births
Florida	Isabella	1,578	Jayden	1,151
	Sophia	1,363	Jacob	1,068
	Emma	1,064	Ethan	1,023
	Olivia	905	Michael	1,018
	Mia	850	Mason	995
Georgia	Emma	613	William	776
	Ava	545	Mason	587
	Isabella	497	Jacob	555
	Madison	491	Michael	534
	Olivia	483	Jayden	527
Hawaii	Sophia	94	Ethan	85
	Emma	62	Noah	78
	Isabella	59	Mason	73
	Ava	54	Elijah	71
	Mia	52	Logan	63
Idaho	Olivia	116	Liam	130
	Sophia	112	William	90
	Emma	98	Mason	79
	Ava	72	Samuel	79
	Elizabeth	71	Logan	77
Illinois	Sophia	955	Jacob	758
	Olivia	814	Alexander	740
	Isabella	810	Noah	740
	Emma	771	Michael	701
	Ava	598	Ethan	678
Indiana	Emma	470	Liam	497
	Sophia	445	Mason	441
	Olivia	412	Elijah	416
	Ava	380	Noah	390
	Isabella	316	Jacob	389

State	Girl	Births	Boy	Births
Iowa	Emma	243	Liam	198
	Sophia	223	Mason	196
	Olivia	186	Carter	176
	Harper	159	William	164
	Ava	156	Owen	160
Kansas	Emma	238	Mason	202
	Sophia	190	Liam	198
	Olivia	177	William	186
	Isabella	167	Noah	173
	Ava	149	Jackson	164
Kentucky	Emma	352	William	347
	Isabella	280	Mason	335
	Sophia	262	James	301
	Ava	256	Jacob	269
	Abigail	221	Noah	265
Louisiana	Emma	318	Mason	312
	Ava	283	Jayden	256
	Isabella	229	William	248
	Olivia	218	Noah	240
	Chloe	209	Liam	227
Maine	Emma	101	Mason	100
	Sophia	78	Liam	98
	Abigail	74	Noah	74
	Ava	71	Owen	69
	Olivia	71	Jacob	67
Maryland	Sophia	358	Mason	362
	Emma	316	Michael	331
	Ava	309	Jacob	326
	Olivia	304	Noah	326
	Isabella	297	Ethan	315

State	Girl	Births	Boy	Births
Massachusetts	Emma	504	Benjamin	441
	Sophia	503	Mason	402
	Olivia	449	Ryan	402
	Isabella	405	William	400
	Ava	355	Jacob	388
Michigan	Emma	643	Mason	651
	Sophia	635	Liam	562
	Ava	557	Noah	560
	Olivia	523	Jacob	545
	Isabella	473	Carter	505
Minnesota	Emma	367	Mason	363
	Olivia	366	William	350
	Sophia	327	Ethan	330
	Ava	322	Liam	328
	Avery	281	Henry	314
Mississippi	Emma	159	William	225
	Madison	149	Mason	205
	Ava	148	John	169
	Olivia	118	James	167
	Chloe	111	Jayden	164
Missouri	Emma	469	Mason	436
	Sophia	416	William	421
	Olivia	340	Liam	408
	Ava	310	Jackson	343
	Isabella	299	Jacob	324
Montana	Emma	58	Liam	67
	Olivia	57	William	62
	Ava	53	Wyatt	58
	Harper	44	Mason	55
	Sophia	44	James	54

State	Girl	Births	Boy	Births
Nebraska	Emma	157	Liam	153
	Olivia	137	William	134
	Sophia	129	Mason	123
	Harper	105	Jackson	112
	Ava	88	Owen	106
Nevada	Sophia	195	Alexander	181
	Isabella	180	Anthony	179
	Emma	147	Daniel	169
	Olivia	144	Jayden	168
	Mia	138	Jacob	167
New Hampshire	Emma	100	Mason	99
	Sophia	100	Jackson	87
	Olivia	90	Jacob	80
	Isabella	74	Liam	79
	Ava	63	Noah	75
New Jersey	Sophia	641	Michael	643
	Isabella	578	Anthony	584
	Emma	526	Joseph	561
	Olivia	524	Jayden	554
	Ava	471	Matthew	545
New Mexico	Sophia	161	Noah	126
	Isabella	129	Jacob	125
	Emma	90	Elijah	112
	Mia	86	Jayden	105
	Aaliyah	76	Daniel	103
New York	Sophia	1,406	Michael	1,384
	Isabella	1,270	Jacob	1,335
	Emma	1,226	Jayden	1,270
	Olivia	1,135	Ethan	1,253
	Ava	968	Mason	1,219

State	Girl	Births	Boy	Births
North Carolina	Emma	654	William	706
	Sophia	591	Mason	683
	Ava	505	Jacob	576
	Olivia	469	Elijah	574
	Isabella	449	Noah	520
North Dakota	Emma	64	Liam	60
	Olivia	60	Mason	60
	Sophia	59	Ethan	56
	Harper	52	James	51
	Ava	51	Noah	51
Ohio	Sophia	830	Mason	847
	Emma	820	Liam	758
	Ava	778	William	672
	Olivia	631	Noah	657
	Isabella	601	Michael	629
Oklahoma	Emma	280	Elijah	215
	Sophia	207	Noah	195
	Isabella	194	Mason	193
	Olivia	175	Jacob	188
	Abigail	174	Aiden	186
Oregon	Sophia	263	Liam	241
	Emma	262	Mason	196
	Olivia	186	Alexander	195
	Isabella	169	William	184
	Abigail	161	Henry	179
Pennsylvania	Emma	869	Mason	861
	Sophia	856	Liam	779
	Ava	769	Jacob	757
	Olivia	762	Michael	726
	Isabella	707	Noah	694

State	Girl	Births	Boy	Births
Rhode Island	Sophia	105	Mason	95
	Ava	94	Michael	72
	Emma	90	Jacob	69
	Isabella	81	Ethan	65
	Olivia	78	Noah	63
South Carolina	Emma	254	William	401
	Madison	245	Mason	314
	Olivia	232	James	277
	Isabella	217	Elijah	268
	Ava	215	Jayden	240
South Dakota	Emma	62	Liam	72
	Harper	57	Mason	65
	Sophia	52	Jacob	59
	Olivia	49	Owen	54
	Ava	45	William	53
Tennessee	Emma	499	William	576
	Olivia	388	Mason	482
	Ava	385	Elijah	449
	Isabella	360	James	412
	Sophia	359	Jacob	384
Texas	Sophia	2,323	Jacob	1,944
	Isabella	2,083	Jayden	1,869
	Emma	1,951	Ethan	1,737
	Mia	1,595	Noah	1,676
	Emily	1,487	Daniel	1,631
Utah	Emma	265	William	278
	Olivia	240	Liam	260
	Sophia	207	Mason	221
	Ava	172	Ethan	215
	Lily	172	Jacob	212

State	Girl	Births	Boy	Births
	Ava	36	Mason	43
	Olivia	34	Noah	41
Vermont	Emma	33	Liam	40
	Sophia	32	Owen	37
	Ella	28	Logan	34
	Sophia	512	William	641
	Emma	511	Mason	543
Virginia	Olivia	493	Liam	497
	Abigail	398	Jacob	480
	Isabella	385	Elijah	476
	Sophia	473	Mason	410
	Emma	450	Liam	407
Washington	Olivia	429	Ethan	393
	Isabella	323	Alexander	350
	Ava	304	Benjamin	335
	Emma	170	Mason	155
	Sophia	120	Liam	143
West Virginia	Isabella	113	Bentley	126
	Ava	102	Jacob	124
	Olivia	99	Hunter	119
	Emma	363	Mason	426
	Sophia	322	Liam	350
Wisconsin	Olivia	313	Jackson	294
	Ava	311	Ethan	293
	Isabella	234	Owen	289
	Emma	40	Liam	41
	Sophia	32	Mason	36
Wyoming	Madison	29	Logan	33
	Elizabeth	26	William	33
	Olivia	23	Wyatt	29

What Joined—and Dropped Off—the Hot 100 in 2012?

One of the easiest ways to spot name trends is to watch what joins the Hot 100 and what drops off. For the (young) ladies, several new names joined in 2012: **Aria** (a variant of **Arya**, the biggest jumper in popularity for girls overall), **Annabelle**, **Piper**, **Reagan**, **Violet**, and **Skylar** (a 63-slot jump in popularity, from 145 in 2011 to 87 in 2012, though the same name for males dropped from 536 to 569).

Another bunch dropped off the list: **Brooke** and **Maria**, numbers 42 and 43 only ten years ago, lost their Hot 100 spots, as did **Destiny**, **Kaitlyn**, **Mariah**, and **Payton**. **Mary**, the girls' name that has been number one more often than any other name in the past 100 years, continued its slide, going from 112 in 2011 to 123 in 2012. **Jennifer**, which held the number-one spot from 1970 to 1984, continued to slide, dropping from 134 in 2011 to 163 in 2012. For the boys, a handful of newcomers joined the Hot 100. **Damian**, **Easton**, **Hudson**, **Jace**, **Ryder**, and **Kayden** all continued to rise, while **Cole**, **Diego**, **Jesus**, **Max**, and **Jaden** fell off (though variant **Jayden** stayed strong at number 7).

New to the Hot 100

Annabelle	Damian
Aria	Easton
Piper	Hudson
Reagan	Jace
Skylar	Kayden
Violet	Ryder

Off the Hot 100

Brooke	Cole
Destiny	Diego
Kaitlyn	Hayden
Maria	Jaden
Mariah	Jesus
Payton	Max

New to the Top 1,000 This Year

These names are fresh faces in the top 1,000 list this year. Some of them have never set foot on the list before, but odds are they'll keep moving up.

Girls

Cataleya:	479	Azalea:	906	Jazzlyn:	955
Litzy:	594	Everly:	907	Zahra:	957
Kenia:	642	Lillyana:	909	Collins:	960
Colette:	659	Emmalynn:	910	Azariah:	963
Paislee:	718	Annalee:	920	Milena:	965
Adley:	731	Evalyn:	927	Alisa:	967
Winter:	772	Raylee:	936	Kora:	975
Ariah:	817	Aubrielle:	938	Aubriana:	986
Coraline:	823	Bayleigh:	939	Aya:	989
Charlize:	846	Katrina:	942	Dalilah:	990
Emory:	881	Alaysia:	946	Devyn:	991
Estella:	882	Celine:	947	Landry:	995
Elissa:	888	Monroe:	949	Sofie:	996
Emmaline:	890	Estelle:	950	Jessa:	999
Dallas:	901	Harlee:	954	Katalina:	1000

Boys

Neymar:	699	Truman:	929	Maison:	979
Brentley:	750	Eliot:	935	Simeon:	980
Kyree:	804	Zaid:	937	Anton:	981
Thiago:	862	Leroy:	943	Emory:	983
Kyrie:	866	Sheldon:	944	Graeme:	987
Jionni:	870	Dariel:	945	Jael:	989
Yael:	878	Kaysen:	957	Karsen:	991
Oakley:	880	Mack:	958	Jarrett:	992
Yousef:	888	Titan:	961	Apollo:	993
Juelz:	896	Ameer:	963	Denzel:	994
Austyn:	898	Briggs:	966	Foster:	995
Axton:	917	Immanuel:	967	Kylen:	998
Lucca:	919	Kase:	972	Augustine:	999

Biggest Jumper: Arya and Major

The meteoric rise of the name **Major**, which rose 505 slots from 988 in 2011 to 483 in 2012, is likely a nod to the men and women serving their country in the U.S. military. On the other hand, **Arya**, which catapulted 298 slots from 711 to 413, probably owes its climb to the hit series *Game of Thrones*.

How Do You Spell Aydin?

When you take into account that the male name **Jayden** has nine spelling variations in the top 1,000 (see the list that follows), that means that this one name actually shows up on the list nine different times! We broke down the top 1,000 names for boys and girls this way, counting all the different spelling variations as one name, and we got some surprising results. Looking from that perspective, there aren't 1,000 unique names at all! We counted roughly 667 unique girls' names and approximately 773 unique boys' names. The girls have fewer unique names, spelled in more ways, whereas parents of boys reach into a bigger pool of names. Let's take a look at some of the names with the most (or most interesting!) variations in the top 1,000.

Note: Some of these names could be pronounced slightly differently from one another. Also, names are listed in order of popularity.

Boys

It's no surprise that the "-ayden" names (such as **Aiden**, **Jayden**, **Brayden**, and **Kaden**) offer lots of spelling variety, but the changes in **Tristan** and **Kason** struck us as a little more unusual.

Aiden
1. Aiden
2. Ayden
3. Aidan
4. Aden
5. Adan
6. Aydan
7. Aydin
8. Aidyn
9. Aaden

Jayden
1. Jaden
2. Jaiden
3. Jaydon
4. Jadon
5. Jaeden
6. Jaidyn

Cameron
1. Cameron
2. Kameron
3. Camron
4. Camren
5. Kamron
6. Kamryn
7. Camryn
8. Kamren

Kayden
1. Kayden
2. Kaden
3. Caden
4. Kaiden
5. Cayden
6. Caiden
7. Kaedan

Brayden
1. Brayden
2. Braden
3. Braydon
4. Braeden
5. Braiden
6. Bradyn

Devin
1. Devin
2. Devon
3. Davion
4. Davin
5. Davian
6. Davon
7. Devan

Kason
1. Kason
2. Cason
3. Kasen
4. Kayson
5. Casen
6. Cayson
7. Kaysen

Tristan
1. Tristan
2. Tristen
3. Tristian
4. Triston
5. Tristin
6. Trystan

Connor
1. Connor
2. Conner
3. Conor
4. Konnor
5. Konner

Jackson
1. Jackson
2. Jaxon
3. Jaxson
4. Jaxton
5. Jaxen

Girls

Some of these seemed more obvious—**Kailynn**, for one—but others, like **Leah**, surprised us with their robust variety. And quite a few new names popped up on our radar this year: **Annabelle**, **Kendall**, **Leah**, **Maya**, **Jayden**, and **Charlee**.

Kaelyn

1. Kaelyn
2. Kaylin
3. Kailyn
4. Kaylynn
5. Kaelynn
6. Kailynn
7. Kaylen
8. Kaylyn
9. Cailyn

Hailey

1. Hailey
2. Haley
3. Haylee
4. Hayley
5. Hallie
6. Halle
7. Hailee
8. Haylie
9. Haleigh
10. Hayleigh

Madelyn

1. Madelyn
2. Madeline
3. Madilyn
4. Madeleine
5. Madelynn
6. Madalyn
7. Madilynn
8. Madalynn

Carly

1. Carly
2. Karlee
3. Carlee
4. Carlie
5. Carley
6. Karlie
7. Carleigh

Kaitlyn

1. Kaitlyn
2. Katelyn
3. Caitlyn
4. Caitlin
5. Katelynn
6. Kaitlynn
7. Kaitlin

Kaylee

1. Kaylee
2. Callie
3. Kayleigh
4. Cali
5. Kailey
6. Kali
7. Kaylie
8. Caylee
9. Kallie
10. Kailee
11. Kaleigh

Aaliyah

1. Aaliyah
2. Aliyah
3. Aleah
4. Aliya
5. Alayah
6. Alia
7. Alaya
8. Aleigha

Adalyn

1. Adalyn
2. Adelyn
3. Adeline
4. Adalynn
5. Adelynn
6. Addilyn

Eliana

1. Eliana
2. Elliana
3. Aliana
4. Elianna
5. Iliana

Liliana

1. Liliana
2. Lilliana
3. Lilyana
4. Lilianna
5. Lillianna
6. Lilyanna
7. Lillyana

Laila

1. Layla
2. Laila
3. Leila
4. Laylah
5. Lailah
6. Leyla

Allison

1. Allison
2. Allyson
3. Alison
4. Alyson
5. Alisson

Emily	Annabelle	Charlee	Jaelyn
1. Emily	1. Annabelle	1. Charlie	1. Jaelyn
2. Emely	2. Anabelle	2. Charlee	2. Jaelynn
3. Emilee	3. Annabel	3. Charley	3. Jaylynn
4. Emilie	4. Anabel	4. Charleigh	4. Jaylin
5. Emmalee	5. Annabell	5. Charli	5. Jaylyn

Kendall	Maya	Makayla	Natalie
1. Kendall	1. Maya	1. Makayla	1. Natalie
2. Kyndall	2. Mya	2. Mikayla	2. Nataly
3. Kendal	3. Myah	3. Michaela	3. Nathalie
4. Kendyl	4. Maia	4. Mikaela	4. Natalee
5. Kyndal	5. Miya	5. Mckayla	5. Nathaly

Top 667 Names, Not Top 1,000

Only 67 percent of the top 1,000 girls' names are unique names.
Only 77 percent of the top 1,000 boys' names are unique names.
The rest of the names are spelling variations of those names.
Here are the three names with the most spelling variations:

Girls	Boys
1. Kaylee	1. Aiden
2. Hailey	2. Cameron
3. Kaelynn	3. Devin/Kason

What Do the Most Popular Names Start With?

You may find it surprising, but only five of the names in the top 1,000 girl baby names for 2012 start with a *W*: **Wendy**, **Whitney**, **Willa**, **Willow**, and **Winter**. At the same time, you probably won't find it surprising that the most popular letter that girls' names start with is *A* (173 of the top 1,000), with *M* as a close second with

96 names. Among the boys' names, 105 start with *J*, and *A* names comprise 93 of the total 1,000 names. In 2009, every single letter in the alphabet had at least one boy and girl name, as **Unique** hopped back on the chart (929) for the first time in four years. But in 2012, no *U* names made it on the girls' list (but the boys are covered, with **Uriah**, **Uriel**, **Urijah**, and **Ulises**). And only one Q (**Quinn**) or X (**Ximena**) for girls.

Gender-Neutral Options

Lots of names are popular for both boys and girls, but they're generally more popular for one gender than the other. Here's a list of names that appeared on both the boys' top 1,000 and the girls' top 1,000, plus how they ranked in 2012 for each gender. Some interesting finds here—the trend of names based on cities holds for both genders, but **London** is more popular for girls, while **Dallas** and **Phoenix** are more popular with boys. Also, the now unisex **Emory** is new to the top 1,000 for both boys and girls in 2012. And three names are roughly given to equal numbers of boys and girls: **Dakota**, **Jessie**, and **Justice**. We'd suggest that 2014 will be a great year for **Colby** (341 for boys in 2012) to hit the girls' list.

Spelling Matters!

If you're going to choose…
Cameron/Camryn/Kamryn: Camryn and Kamryn are the more popular choices for girls, Cameron for boys
Skylar/Skyler: Skylar is more popular for girls, while Skyler wins for boys
Jordan/Jordyn: Jordyn is more popular for girls, Jordan for boys

Nearly Equal

Name	Girl Rank	Boy Rank
Dakota	306	334
Jessie	641	698
Justice	518	519

More Popular for Girls

Name	Girl Rank	Boy Rank
Alexis	40	227
Ariel	181	772
Avery	13	187
Camryn	345	925
Eden	164	677
Emerson	244	364
Emery	211	655
Emory	881	983
Finley	349	547
Harley	415	632
Harper	24	605
Jamie	438	845
Jordyn	121	824
Kamryn	361	833
Kendall	116	648
London	94	537

Name	Girl Rank	Boy Rank
Lyric	295	830
Morgan	82	587
Payton	103	458
Peyton	53	183
Quinn	153	321
Reagan	97	893
Reese	128	549
Riley	47	133
Rylee	109	842
Sage	494	725
Sidney	831	921
Skylar	87	569
Tatum	330	597
Taylor	46	346
Teagan	258	755

More Popular for Boys

Name	Girl Rank	Boy Rank
Ali	865	352
Amari	483	309
Angel	227	57
Armani	690	432
Blake	694	71
Cameron	553	54
Casey	777	486
Charlie	305	233
Dallas	901	322
Dylan	512	31
Elliot	862	242
Hayden	196	109
Jayden	380	7
Jordan	222	48

Name	Girl Rank	Boy Rank
Kai	919	195
Kayden	585	99
Landry	995	669
Logan	456	21
Micah	873	103
Parker	315	80
Phoenix	573	381
River	686	407
Rowan	455	301
Ryan	607	26
Rylan	744	179
Sawyer	548	147
Skyler	372	290

Which Names are Moving Up—and Falling Down—the Fastest?

The SSA compiles a list of names that have made the biggest moves when compared to their rank the previous year (assuming the name has made the top 500 at least once in the last two years). Some of these jumpers have obvious triggers, while the reasons for other jumps and declines are more open to interpretation. Take a look and see what you think.

40 Girls' Names Heating Up

Name	Number of Spots It Moved Up	Name	Number of Spots It Moved Up
Arya	298	Myla	85
Perla	190	Skyler	84
Catalina	171	Ivy	80
Elisa	168	Rowan	78
Raelynn	155	Kali	77
Rosalie	141	Yaretzi	76
Haven	140	Miracle	75
Raelyn	136	Charlie	71
Briella	123	Baylee	69
Marilyn	119	Logan	68
Adelynn	116	Juliette	67
Hanna	106	Aria	66
Ayla	97	Paris	66
Averie	96	Athena	65
Arabella	92	Adelyn	64
Arielle	91	Jaylah	62
Paisley	91	Adelaide	61
Adalynn	88	Lucille	61
Elsie	86	Vivienne	60
Eloise	85	Emery	60

40 Girls' Names Cooling Down

Name	Number of Spots It Moved Down	Name	Number of Spots It Moved Down
Dulce	159	Jillian	65
Mikaela	141	Lindsey	64
Estrella	129	Marissa	63
Danna	125	Kennedi	63
Audrina	122	Courtney	63
Cameron	113	Briana	61
Kiera	108	Alyson	61
Savanna	101	Karla	58
Paola	98	Kailey	58
Tenley	96	Tiana	57
Kendra	94	Kaylin	56
Breanna	94	Jazmin	54
Kailyn	93	Jaelyn	54
Jasmin	93	Caylee	53
Joselyn	92	Lacey	52
Kiley	90	Camryn	51
Jayden	88	Jayda	50
Liana	82	Natasha	49
Sasha	77	Lexie	49
Karen	66	Haylee	49

40 Boys' Names Heating Up

Name	Number of Spots It Moved Up	Name	Number of Spots It Moved Up
Major	505	Orion	52
Gael	262	Abram	50
Jase	258	Leon	50
Messiah	246	Gunnar	49
Brantley	163	Ryker	49
Iker	149	Abel	46
King	133	Bruce	46
Rory	118	Lincoln	46
Ari	73	Waylon	46
Maverick	72	Kendrick	45
Armani	70	Archer	43
Gianni	66	Everett	43
Knox	66	Karter	43
Zayden	63	Cason	41
August	62	Cyrus	41
Barrett	61	Damian	41
Kasen	58	Graham	41
Remington	58	Gunner	40
Zaiden	56	Bennett	39
Atticus	52	Beau	39

40 Boys' Names Cooling Down

Name	Number of Spots It Moved Down	Name	Number of Spots It Moved Down
Braeden	105	Emanuel	45
Yahir	85	Braden	45
Kieran	82	Mitchell	44
Cullen	79	Raul	43
Brayan	73	Maurice	43
Jalen	70	Jimmy	42
Amare	70	Jaden	40
Trey	69	Ronald	38
Casey	62	Joe	38
Payton	60	Gary	38
Jakob	60	Corey	38
Randy	57	Jacoby	37
Zackary	56	Edwin	37
Eddie	56	Brenden	37
Jerry	53	Brendan	37
Jaylen	51	Uriel	36
Ernesto	50	Cesar	36
Devon	46	Bryant	36
Braylon	46	Danny	35
Reece	45	Fernando	34

What's Hot (or Not) Today (And What Will—and Won't!—Be Tomorrow)

Now that we've seen the state of baby names today, here's a snapshot of some interesting trends we've spotted, as well as some predictions of who you may be meeting on the playground sometime soon.

You'll notice that certain names are on the rise and others on the decline, showing how trends are morphing over time (for example, how religious names like **Mary** and **Rachel** are on the decline, while **Messiah** and **Genesis** are climbing the ranks). We've also included some offbeat and unique ways to take each of these trends and find a name that really fits you and your family.

Trends Today

SOLDIERING ON

An increasing number of parents are honoring military service members with the ultimate tribute—they're naming their kids after them! The name (and military rank) **Major**, which catapulted from 988 in 2011 to 483 in 2012, had the biggest jump in popularity of all top 1,000 names. **Marshall**, a variant of the army rank marshal, was number 402 only five years ago but now sits at 348. Other military-inspired names are also on the rise: **Gunner** shot up from 333 in 2011 to 293 in 2012 and **Crew** rose from 946 to 768, while **Knox** (like the military base Fort Knox) rose from 434 to 368. And **Justice** really is for all, rising to 518 (from 528) on the girls' list and sitting at 519 for boys.

As the trend continues, we wouldn't be at all surprised to see names like **General**, **Captain**, **Admiral**, and **Lieutenant** appear on the list in coming years.

UNDER HER SPELL-ING

Actress Tori Spelling documented three of her four pregnancies on her Oxygen-network reality show and has written extensively about parenthood in memoirs like *Mommywood* and *Uncharted TerriTORI*, so it's no surprise that fans take a cue from the star in naming their little ones. Spelling's oldest child, **Liam**, was born in 2007. That year, Liam was number 89 on the boys' list. In 2012, it broke into the top 10 for the first time ever, at number 6! In 2008, Spelling welcomed a daughter, **Stella**, and since then the name has jumped over 100 slots, up to 62 in 2012. Daughter **Hattie** arrived in 2011, and that same year the name entered the top 1,000 for the first time, at 994. In 2012, Hattie jumped to 709. Spelling's fourth child, son **Finn**, was born in 2012, the first year the name broke the 300 mark, landing at 291. Check out this brief history of the names of Tori Spelling's children. For fun, we've added **Tori**—which has taken a dive recently!—and her husband, **Dean** McDermott, as well.

Year	2006	2007	2008	2009	2010	2011	2012
Liam	98	89	75	49	30	15	6
Stella	242	244	184	126	85	73	62
Hattie	–	–	–	–	–	994	709
Finn	458	386	365	342	300	302	291
Tori	451	480	489	555	564	627	625
Dean	384	351	344	305	285	284	260

A dash means that the name did not make the list that year.

THE RISE OF IKER

The name **Iker** first debuted on the charts—it had never even been in the top 1,000!—in 2010, at number 646. A year later, Iker had the second-highest jump up the list, landing at 379. In

2012, it moved up another 149 spots to 230. The rise in popularity of the name is probably due to Spanish soccer team Real Madrid's talented (and extremely handsome!) goalkeeper, Iker Casillas, who led the Spanish national team to their first World Cup title in 2010 and the European Championship in 2012.

HISPANIC HERITAGE

Iker isn't the only rising name inspired by a Spanish-speaking culture. Hispanic Americans make up the second largest population group in the United States, and these demographics are reflected in a number of 2012's biggest jumpers. The second fast-rising name for boys (from 408 in 2011 to 146 in 2012) was **Gael**, perhaps inspired by Mexican actor Gael García Bernal, while the second-largest jumper for girls was **Perla** (from 642 to 452), the Hispanic version of Pearl. **Litzy**, the name of popular Mexican actress and singer Litzy Domínguez, burst onto the girls' list in 2012 at 594 for the first time since 2008, and entering the boys' list for the first time ever was **Neymar** at 699, likely a nod to rising Brazilian soccer star Neymar da Silva Santos Júnior.

Girls' Name	2011	2012
Perla	642	452
Catalina	648	477
Cataleya	–	479
Kamila	421	362
Ximena	216	214
Litzy	–	594
Luciana	565	555
Luna	279	223
Maritza	871	838

Ways to Make This Trend Your Own
Options still off the radar: Salome, Agustina, Romina, Manuela

Boys' Name	2011	2012
Gael	408	146
Neymar	–	699
Mateo	171	138
Gustavo	437	408
Thiago	–	862
Santiago	131	122
Ramon	503	497
Matias	566	563
Marcelo	824	789

Ways to Make This Trend Your Own
Options still off the radar: Facundo, Bautista, Patricio, Lautaro

THE BECKHAM EFFECT

Victoria and David Beckham added a fourth child, daughter **Harper**, to their brood in 2011, and as usual, the name struck a chord with many new parents and made big gains in popularity. Let's look at the history of the Beckham clan. Their first child, **Brooklyn**, was born in 1999. While Brooklyn Beckham is a boy, the name has been rising steadily on the girls' name chart for the past decade, getting as high as 21 in 2011. **Romeo**, the second Beckham son, was born in 2002, and that name started climbing in 2006 after years of sitting in the 600s. **Cruz**, the name of Beckham son number three, jumped into the top 500 in 2006, just after the Beckhams used it a year earlier. And finally daughter **Harper** arrived in 2011. That same year, the name made its first appearance in the top 100, shooting from number 118 in 2010 all the way to 54 in 2011. The name jumped another 30 slots in 2012, landing at number 24. Take a look at this chart, which tracks all the Beckham children's names (and their increasingly popular last name) through the decade.

Year	2003	2004	2005	2006	2007	2008	2009	2010	2011	2012
Brooklyn	118	101	78	67	57	47	37	34	21	29
Romeo	639	602	610	573	500	465	410	358	360	323
Cruz	597	561	516	496	429	367	346	321	300	284
Harper	–	887	745	508	439	296	172	118	54	24
Beckham	–	–	–	–	–	898	845	750	655	532

FIT FOR A KING

There is no monarchy on American soil, but that doesn't stop some parents from wishful thinking! Two boys' names on the rise this year? **King** and **Prince**. King jumped from 389 in 2011 to 256 in 2012, while Prince climbed from 480 to 457. Britain's Queen **Elizabeth** might be responsible for her name's ascent into the top 10, while the names of other British royalty also saw upticks in 2012: **Beatrice** rose from 701 to 691 and **Zara** went from 644 to 566. **Kate** and **Catherine** both slipped down the list, from 175 to 194 and 161 to 167 respectively, probably because they both saw a big jump after 2011's royal wedding. We're expecting the biggest royal influence to hit in years ahead. Now that Prince William and Kate Middleton have welcomed **George Alexander Louis**, expect to meet many of his namesakes on a playground near you!

GO WEST

Chalk it up to the popularity of FX's modern-day cowboy drama *Justified*. These days, names inspired by the Wild West are all the rage. The name of the show's main character, **Raylan**, made the top 1,000 for the first time in 2011, debuting at 699, and jumped another 164 spots to 535 in 2012. **Arlo**, another *Justified* character name, debuted in 2011 at 918 and is now 818. Names traditionally associated with cowboys and saloons are heating up across the board. Even the direction itself is inspiring popular names—**Weston** is up to number 171 and **Wesley** is 155! Check out these new popular names for the littlest cowboys and cowgirls.

Name	2010	2011	2012
Raylan	–	701	535
Arlo	–	918	818
Wyatt	57	48	41
Zeke	–	971	874
Amos	–	860	807
Levi	70	66	55
Maverick	505	425	356
Milo	422	361	330
Hattie	–	993	709
Elsie	645	480	397
Raelynn	629	496	341
Rose	337	291	261
Pearl	960	814	756
Emmalynn	–	–	910
Josephine	184	182	160
Charley	829	626	595
Annie	396	386	377
Mae	981	801	750

Way To Make This Trend Your Own
Options still off the radar: Boyd, Kirby, Buck, Nell, Clint, Peggy, Loretta, May

WE'RE KEEPING UP WITH THE KARDASHIANS!

There's no question that the oldest Kardashian sister, Kourtney, bears responsibility for the second most popular boys' name of 2012. Mason Dash Disick, Kourtney's son, was born December 14, 2009. Since his birth, the name **Mason** has shot up from number 34 in 2009 to number 12 in 2010 and then all the way to number 2 in 2011, where it holds steady in 2012. Kourtney's daughter, **Penelope** (also the name of comedian Tina Fey's second daughter), was born July 8, 2012. That year, Penelope climbed the name ranks from 169 in 2011 to 125 in 2012. (Just think, in 2001, Penelope was number 966!) With the 2013 arrival of Kim Kardashian's daughter with Kanye West, we can't wait to see where **North** ranks over the next few years.

COLORFUL KIDS

In January 2012, Beyonce and Jay-Z gave birth to their first child, a daughter named **Blue Ivy**. While the name Blue hasn't cracked the top 1,000 (yet!), **Ivy** shot up to 187 in 2012. And the superstar couple was clearly on trend—girl names that are also colors of the rainbow are becoming increasingly popular. Check out the chart below.

Name	2011	2012
Violet	101	89
Rose	291	261
Jade	113	112
Olive	416	368
Ruby	109	106
Hazel	209	175
Raven	591	543

Way To Make This Trend Your Own
Options still off the radar: Clementine, Coral, Goldie, Lavender, Silver, Azure, Cyan

THE BLOND BOMBSHELL

Interest in Marilyn Monroe reached a posthumous fever pitch in 2012, fifty years after the legendary icon died. *My Week with Marilyn* earned Oscar nominations, the TV show *Smash* featured a Marilyn-based musical, and the star was chosen as the poster girl for the prestigious Cannes Film Festival. Parents took note— **Marilyn** jumped from 545 to 426, while **Monroe** made its first ever appearance on the list at number 949 for girls.

LITERARY INSPIRATION

Been noticing a lot of Holdens and Eloises in the sandbox lately? Names from classic children's books and novels have been heating up, perhaps because parents have such fond memories and associations with these popular characters from their own youth. On the boys' side, **Holden** (for *Catcher in the Rye's* Holden Caulfield), **Atticus** (the heroic father and lawyer Atticus Finch in *To Kill a Mockingbird*), **Charlie** (from *Charlie and the Chocolate Factory*), **Rhett** (of *Gone with the Wind* fame), and **Sawyer** and **Finn** (the last names of popular Mark Twain heroes Tom Sawyer and Huckleberry Finn) have all been climbing the charts.

For girls, our eyes are on **Matilda** (from the Roald Dahl classic), **Eloise** (from Kay Thompson's popular series about a young girl who lives at the Plaza Hotel), **Josephine** (the full name of *Little Women's* Jo March), **Amelia** (from the children's series Amelia Bedelia), **Alice** (of Wonderland), and **Charlotte** (the kind spider in E. B. White's *Charlotte's Web*). Take a look at this chart to see

how these literary namesakes have been trending over the past
five years.

Year	2007	2008	2009	2010	2011	2012
Holden	377	357	333	316	299	296
Atticus	685	687	608	560	462	410
Charlie	334	306	274	244	236	233
Rhett	702	683	658	607	563	508
Sawyer	240	225	202	172	172	147
Finn	386	365	342	300	302	291
Matilda	–	825	757	799	769	658
Eloise	–	–	913	528	449	364
Josephine	223	208	201	185	182	160
Amelia	77	68	55	41	30	23
Alice	347	327	258	172	142	127
Charlotte	101	87	68	45	27	19

DESTINATION NAMES

Ten years ago, naming a child after a location was quite unusual.
Now, **Brooklyn** is number 29 on the list for girls! Naming tots
after places is a hot idea these days—it's even a big trend among
celebrities. Actress Reese Witherspoon named her son **Tennessee**
after the state where she grew up. Singer Shakira named her son
Milan, Rosie O'Donnell named her daughter **Dakota**, Kourtney
Kardashian used the middle name **Scotland** for her daughter,
and actress Jemima Kirke named her son **Memphis**. Here are
some place names on the rise.

Girls' Names	2000 Rank	2011 Rank
Brooklyn (New York)	177	20
Charlotte (North Carolina)	289	19

Girls' Names	2000 Rank	2011 Rank
London (England)	828	94
Paris (France)	473	274
Adelaide (Australia)	–	343
Aspen (Colorado)	570	504
Georgia	334	298

Ways to Make This Trend Your Own

Options still off the radar: Orleans (New Orleans, Louisiana), Helena (Montana), Olympia (Washington), Juneau (Alaska), Valletta (Malta), Dublin (Ireland), Pristina (Kosovo)

Boys' Names	2000 Rank	2012 Rank
Jackson (Mississippi)	72	22
Santiago (Chile)	359	122
Lincoln (Nebraska)	710	132
Kingston (Jamaica)	–	210
Phoenix (Arizona)	876	381
London (England)	895	537
Boston (Massachusetts)	–	538
Memphis (Tennessee)	–	751
Milan (Italy)	–	724

Ways to Make This Trend Your Own

Options still off the radar: Richmond (Virginia), Salem (Oregon), Montgomery (Alabama), Wellington (New Zealand), Dakar (Senegal), Cairo (Egypt)

NAMES FROM THE ANCIENT GREEKS AND ROMANS

When we say these names are old, we're not kidding. They have been around for a long, long time...and while many girls' names are becoming more popular (with some traditional exceptions—**Diana** and **Helen** are on the slide), the boys' names are surprisingly less popular (and perfect for someone looking for the cutting edge).

Girls' Names	1998 Rank	2012 Rank
Chloe	87	11
Athena	550	247
Phoebe	606	303
Paris	457	274
Daphne	757	420
Diana	83	251
Helen	349	402
Maeve	881	529

Ways to Make This Trend Your Own

Options still off the radar: Artemis, Antigone, Aphrodite, Ariadne, Calliope, Circe, Cleopatra, Echo, Electra, Eurydice, Euterpe, Gaia, Halcyone, Ione, Juno, Lavinia, Medea, Minerva, Persephone, Psyche, Rhea, Selene, Thalia, Venus

Boys' Names	1998 Rank	2012 Rank
Alexander	22	9
Cassius	–	928
Jason	40	76
Marcus	96	149
Hector	185	267

Boys' Names	1998 Rank	2012 Rank
Antony	832	955
Apollo	–	993
Titan	–	961

Ways to Make This Trend Your Own
Options still off the radar: Achilles, Aeneas, Cadmus, Dionysus, Endymion, Hercules, Hermes, Hyperion, Icarus, Janus, Mercury, Midas, Minos, Morpheus, Odysseus, Orpheus, Pegasus, Perseus, Prometheus, Ptolemy, Theseus, Vulcan, Zeus

A GIRL FOR ALL SEASONS

The name **Winter** made the girls' list for the first time in 2012, entering all the way at 772. (A nod to Gretchen Mol's daughter, Winter Morgan, and Nicole Richie's daughter, Harlowe Winter, perhaps?) **Autumn** is holding steady at 68, while **Summer** seems to be on the decline but still has a respectable rank of 176. Will baby **Spring** be next?

A CORNUCOPIA OF PURITAN NAMES

Many names have remained popular for hundreds of years, such as **Emily**, **Olivia**, **Michael**, and **Matthew**. However, in recent years, names with a Puritan bent in particular have become all the rage. You probably know at least one **Ethan** or **Emma**—names that would be equally at home in 1700s Salem, Massachusetts, and on today's playgrounds. In 2011, the name **Temperance** made its first ever appearance on the top 1,000, and in 2012 it shot up nearly 100 slots to 843. These names are ever hotter for boys. Here's a look at trends in Puritan names.

Girls' Names	2000 Rank	2012 Rank
Abigail	14	7
Leah	96	33
Emma	17	2
Grace	19	21
Charlotte	289	27

Ways to Make This Trend Your Own
Options still off the radar: Honor, Mercy, Providence, Constance, Verity, Prudence, Damaris

Boys' Names	2000 Rank	2012 Rank
Caleb	38	32
Levi	172	55
Asher	579	108
Silas	602	161
Tobias	589	516
Asa	655	562
Elias	242	114
Eli	235	44

Ways to Make This Trend Your Own
Options still off the radar: Ebenezer, Abner, Enoch, Sylas, Cyrus, Ariel, Abel

GETTING IN TOUCH WITH NATURE

Are you a nature lover? Are you planning to make your little one a part of your outdoorsy lifestyle? Perhaps the rise in eco-consciousness should get the credit for the explosion of nature names, especially for girls. Actress Poppy Montgomery, named for a flower herself (as are her siblings Lilly Belle, Rosie Thorn, Daisy Yellow, Jethro Tull, and Marigold Sun), was right on trend when she named her daughter, born in April 2013, Violet Grace.

Girls' Name	2011 Rank	2012 Rank
Azalea	–	906
Cataleya	–	479
Juniper	953	883
Willow	200	171
Iris	303	282
Ivy	267	187
Sky	984	856
Violet	101	89
Rose	291	261

Ways to Make This Trend Your Own
Options still off the radar: Blossom, Lake, Evergreen, Everest, Poppy, Petunia

Boys' Name	2011 Rank	2012 Rank
River	423	407
Hunter	55	45
Oakley	–	880
Fisher	853	831

Ways to Make This Trend Your Own
Options still off the radar: Forest, Ranger, Trail, Trek, Cliff, Scout, Summit

NAMES ENDING IN –LYNN

For girls, names that end in –*lynn* or –*lyn* have been on the rise for years. Many of the –*lynn* names in the top 1,000 weren't even on the list a decade ago! Perhaps because the syllable gives a feminine edge to almost any name, parents are choosing both traditional variants (**Jocelyn**) and some that are more unusual (**Jazzlyn**).

Girls' Names	2000 Rank	2012 Rank
Brooklynn	517	137
Evelynn	–	554
Adalynn	–	240
Madelyn	126	67
Kaylynn	750	624
Jaelyn	616	471
Braelynn	–	601
Gracelyn	–	506
Raelynn	–	341
Jocelyn	122	92
Emmalynn	–	910
Marilyn	510	426
Jazzlyn	–	955

Ways to Make This Trend Your Own
Options still off the radar: Lynn, Carlyn, Fallyn, Ugolyn, Newlyn

WHO'S RESPONSIBLE FOR BRANTLEY?

The biggest jumper for a boys' name in 2011 was **Brantley**, which first appeared in the top 1,000 in 2010 at 736. In 2012, the name shot up another 163, making it the fifth biggest riser of the year. A variation of the name, **Brentley**, appeared on the list for the first time in 2012 at 750. So what's responsible for the name's explosion? Probably country music chart-topper Brantley Gilbert, whose hit songs "Country Must Be Country Wide" and "You Don't Know Her Like I Do" hit number one in 2011 and 2012, respectively.

HAS *TWILIGHT* SEEN ITS END? WILL *HUNGER GAMES* TAKE ITS PLACE?

In 2009, names inspired by the *Twilight* series saw a huge bump in popularity. **Cullen** rose a stunning 71 spots in 2010 after another meteoric rise in 2009, accelerating from 782 in 2008 to 413 in 2010. It's a no-brainer why: the ladies get all swoony over *Twilight* vampire Edward Cullen, played by Robert Pattinson in the *Twilight* film series. (Not surprisingly, the Gaelic name means "good-looking boy.") But 2012 brought the final installments of the film franchise, and with it, a slowdown of the *Twilight* trend. In 2012, **Cullen** plummeted a whopping 79 spots to 551, making it the fourth biggest dropper overall. **Edward** fell 9 spots to 157; and **Esme**, which entered the list for the first time in 2010 at 923, dropped down to 977.

Then, of course, there's **Jacob**. The boys' name has been number one for fourteen years, starting long before the *Twilight* books. But Jacob is actually *declining*, even though it's still number one. As we mentioned earlier, more than 35,000 babies were named Jacob when it hit number one in 1999. In 2012, a mere 18,899 babies received the name.

The names of the Cullen siblings, though, are still enjoying a boom. The dowdyish name **Emmett** ranked at 740 in 2000 but is now at 186, up another 34 slots from 2011. **Alice** rose 15 spots to 127 in 2012, **Jasper** climbed from 281 to 264, and **Rosalie** shot up 141 slots to 406, making it 2012's fastest rising name of the Cullen clan.

While the *Twilight* movies wound down in 2012, *The Hunger Games* series was just getting started. The first film of the trilogy set opening-day records when it hit theaters that year, and the second film will only increase visibility for the series' unusual names. None of the unique monikers from the series have hit the top 1,000 yet, but we're thinking names like **Katniss**, **Gale**, **Peeta**, **Rue**, **Primrose**, **Effie**, and **Haymitch** might have banner years coming up!

LAST NAMES FIRST

We've already looked at gender-neutral names, and the surname-as-first-name fad is a deeper twist on that. In fact, perhaps due to women naming their children with their maiden names, using last names as first names is perhaps one of the biggest trends of the past ten years—especially for boys. One of the more unusual recent celebrity takes on this was Matthew McConaughey and Camila Alves's son, Livingston. Take a look at some of the more popular last-name choices for boys and girls.

Girls' Names	2012 Rank
Avery	13
Riley	47
Mackenzie	71
Bailey	79
Kennedy	83
Presley	203
Delaney	257
Kelsey	267
Parker	315
Sawyer	548
Monroe	949
Collins	960

Ways to Make This Trend Your Own

Options still off the radar: Golden, Kingsley, Sheridan, Easton, Curtis, Banfield, Robinson

Boys' Names	2012 Rank
Logan	21
Jackson	22
Carter	36
Landon	34
Hunter	45
Connor	59
Bentley	75
Chase	77
Parker	80
Cooper	83
Grayson	85
Carson	87
Brody	91
Easton	96
Braxton	125
Preston	129

Ways to Make This Trend Your Own

Options still off the radar: Ford, Albee, Burroughs, Pelham, Wilder, Barnes, Hopper

DOWNTON ABBEY

The British TV series about life on the fictional estate of Downton Abbey has taken America by storm, and its impact on names seems undeniable—even the name of the family dog, **Isis**, has risen in the ranks for girls! It jumped from 633 in 2011 to 610 in 2012.

Name	2011	2012
Cora	203	155
Violet	101	89
Edith	771	762
Elsie (Mrs. Hughes)	483	397
Branson	731	691
Anna	38	35
Isis	633	610

Ways to Make This Trend Your Own
Options still off the radar: Crawley, Sybil, Lavinia, Bates

RELIGIOUS NAMES

Religious names have become quite a bit more popular in recent years, and the trend is reflected in the different types of religious names that are popular now versus years ago. As a prime example, **Mary** is down nine slots from its 2011 rank, but **Nevaeh** (heaven backward) is holding strong at 39. In fact, **Messiah** had the fourth-largest rise in popularity for boys, jumping from 633 in 2011 to 387 in 2012, while **Genesis** rose from 82 to 56 to become the fifth most popular name in Washington, D.C. Here's a look at some religious names and how they've changed in popularity over the past fifteen years.

Girls' Names	1997 Rank	2012 Rank
Sarah	4	43
Nevaeh*	–	39

*Heaven spelled backward

Girls' Names	1997 Rank	2012 Rank
Trinity	544	93
Mary	46	123
Rebecca	26	157
Rachel	13	133
Heaven	474	321
Eve	–	558
Genesis	256	56
Eden	637	164
Miracle	556	416
Hadassah	–	832

Ways to Make This Trend Your Own
Options still off the radar: Khadija, Dinah, Seraphina

Boys' Names	1997 Rank	2012 Rank
Noah	38	4
Daniel	11	11
Joshua	5	17
Gabriel	57	24
Benjamin	29	16
Isaac	73	30
Isaiah	60	42
Adam	39	82
Zion	–	235
Moses	513	546
Muhammad	720	467
Messiah	–	387
Jesus	71	101

Boys' Names	1997 Rank	2012 Rank
Cain	950	779
Abel	353	192

Ways to Make This Trend Your Own
Options still off the radar: Aasif, Esau, Tabor

X MARKS THE SPOT

One hot fashion for boys is names with the letter *X*. Actress January Jones was right on trend in 2011 when she named her son **Xander**. But the names don't have to start with an *X* to have that something special the *X* adds. In 2013, Tom Arnold had baby **Jax**, and Hugh Grant welcomed **Felix**. Check these lists out.

Boys' Names	2002 Rank	2012 Rank
Xavier	87	81
Jaxon	310	66
Max	165	105
Axel	314	160
Braxton	328	125
Maddox	—	167
Xander	544	216
Maximus	313	206
Paxton	845	241
Felix	394	316
Jax	—	305
Dexter	756	362
Phoenix	876	381
Knox	—	368

Boys' Names	2002 Rank	2012 Rank
Xzavier	750	614
Rex	–	627
Daxton	–	620
Xavi	–	867
Lennox	–	776
Nixon	–	653

Ways to Make This Trend Your Own
Options still off the radar: Xesus, Xanthus, Xachary

PRESIDENTIAL PEDIGREES

One naming trend that has taken hold lately is that of presidential surnames, at least the ones that differ from already popular names (**Madison, Taylor**). Presidential options are popping up everywhere—**Truman** (for boys) and **Monroe** (for girls) entered the top 1,000 in 2012. **Nixon** appeared on the list for the first time in 2011 (it debuted at number 901) and shot up to 653 in 2012. The trend seems to be even hotter for girls than boys these days. Case in point: Actors Kristen Bell and Dax Shepard jumped on the presidential bandwagon in 2013 when they named their daughter **Lincoln**.

You might also want to consider changing the spelling to create your own spin on this trend. For example, if you don't want to name your darling **Reagan** because your politics are more to the left, consider **Regan** (2012 rank: 828) or even **Teagan** (2011 rank: 258). If you don't want your daughter to be a Kennedy, try **Kennedi** (2012 rank: 83).

Girls' Names	2000 Rank	2012 Rank
Madison (James)	3	9
Taylor (Zachary)	10	46
Kennedy (John F.)	139	83
Reagan (Ronald)	286	97
McKinley (William)	–	457
Monroe (James)	–	949

Ways to Make This Trend Your Own
Options still off the radar: Taft (William), Polk (James)

Boys' Names	2000 Rank	2012 Rank
Jackson (Andrew)	72	22
Tyler (John)	10	50
Grant (Ulysses)	123	163
Lincoln (Honest Abe)	710	132
Harrison (Benjamin or William Henry)	184	181
Pierce (Franklin)	498	479
Hayes (Rutherford)	–	689
Carter (Jimmy)	152	36
Truman (Harry S.)	–	994
Jefferson (Thomas)	717	615
Wilson (Woodrow)	526	599
Nixon (Richard)	–	653
Clinton (Bill)	632	906

Ways to Make This Trend Your Own
Options still off the radar: Buchanan (James), Fillmore (Millard), Garfield (James)

Crowdsourcing a Name

Yahoo CEO Marissa Mayer had a baby boy in September 2012 and immediately sent out an email asking for name suggestions. "Name TBD," she wrote. "Suggestions welcome!" The winning name? Macallister. Earlier that year, Kim Zolciak, star of *Don't Be Tardy*, took to Twitter for a baby-name guessing game. She tweeted: "Big Question?!! What do u think we are naming our son due in a couple months? Starts with a K of course?! #startguessing." **Kaden** was the most popular guess, though Zolciak said no one guessed the name they chose, which was Kash Kade. And if that's not taking technology far enough, rumor has it that one tech-savvy mom named her newborn Hashtag!

ERIN GO BRAGH!

Irish names have become quite popular for boys, but interestingly enough, traditional Irish girls' names are dropping in popularity. Poor **Colleen**, which consistently ranked in the top 200 names from 1948 to 1993, has dropped like a stone since then (from 207 in 1994 to falling off the top 1,000 list entirely in 2007). The counterpoint to this is **Malachi**, a name that first appeared on the top 1,000 in 1987 ranked at 992. Since then, it's taken off in popularity to be ranked at 168 in 2012.

Girls' Names	2000 Rank	2012 Rank
Erin	60	262
Kelly	111	354
Bridget	273	453
Kathleen	204	667
Eileen	627	824

Girls' Names	2000 Rank	2012 Rank
Colleen	455	–
Clare	536	727

Ways to Make This Trend Your Own
Options still off the radar: Deirdre, Saoirse, Siobhan, Nuala

Boys' Names	2000 Rank	2012 Rank
Liam	140	6
Riley	109	133
Malachi	351	168
Declan	545	143
Callum	–	810

Ways to Make This Trend Your Own
Options still off the radar: Conan, Daire, Lorcan

Predictions: Hot Names

Okay, so you've read about the trends. But what other names might be taking off in the near future? Here are some we think could be gaining ground.

BOYS AND GIRLS

Game of Thrones

The popular HBO series, based on the novels by George R. R. Martin, premiered in 2011. In 2012, the name **Arya**—also the name of one of the series' most popular characters—shot up from number 942 to 413, making it the biggest jumper for girls. While the series' other more unusual names haven't broken the top 1,000 yet, expect to meet little Tyrions and Cerseis soon!

Options for girls: Cersei, Melisandre, Sansa, Shae, Talisa, Daenerys
Options for boys: Tyrion, Jorah, Tywin, Bran, Eddard, Lanister

GIRLS

Daisy

It's been slipping over the last decade, but we see 2014 as a big year for **Daisy**, thanks to the resurgence of *The Great Gatsby*. The 3-D film version was a 2013 hit and shot the literary classic back onto bestseller lists. Daisy ranked 172 in 2012 and has never been in the top 100, but we expect it to make *great* gains next year!

Emerson

Celebrities are big fans of **Emerson** for their little girls—actress JoAnna Garcia Swisher and baseball player Nick Swisher welcomed their daughter Emerson Jay in 2013. *Grey's Anatomy* creator Shonda Rhimes named her daughter Emerson Pearl, and actress Teri Hatcher is mom to Emerson Rose. The name is on the rise (jumping from 833 in 2002 to 244 in 2012), probably because it has all the qualities of a girls' name that people love—it's unusual enough to stand out, bears a literary reference to Ralph Waldo Emerson, and lends itself to plenty of great nicknames.

Variants: Emersyn, Emme, Emmy

EMERSON RISING	
Year	**Rank**
2000	–
2001	–
2002	833
2003	766
2004	904

EMERSON RISING	
Year	**Rank**
2005	442
2006	308
2007	312
2008	290
2009	321
2010	315
2011	275
2012	244

Everly

"Sexiest Man Alive" Channing Tatum has had a stellar career, but his crowning achievement is daughter **Everly.** The name **Channing** has seen quite a boom in recent years—bursting onto the list at 645 in 2010 and rising to 513 in 2012—a testament to the actor's influence. Now that he's had a little girl, we expect to witness the Everly effect. The name entered the list for the first time in 2012 at 907. Watch for it to climb the ranks!

Variants: Eve, Evie, Evelyn, Evelyne

Marnie

This blast from the past fell off the list in 1977—it peaked at 427 in 1969 and fell to 982 before disappearing entirely—but has found its way back into the spotlight with the HBO hit *Girls.* The name **Marnie** has a lot going for it. It starts with the popular consonant *M*, has the coveted *–ie* ending, and feels like a throwback. Plus, music fans should note that singer Lily Allen welcomed her daughter Marnie Rose in 2013. You heard it here first!

Variants: Marina, Marion, Myrna

More 2013 Forecasts: Getting Hotter

Demi: Depending on who you ask, you'll get different explanations for the recent Demi comeback. Brat Pack lovers will credit the enduring influence of Demi Moore, while the younger generation will tell you it's an ode to singer and *X Factor* judge Demi Lovato. But everyone is in agreement that Demi is having a moment. After falling off the list entirely, Demi returned in 2009. In 2012, it sat at 795, and we're expecting a continued upward trend.

Mila: Could it be an Ashton Kutcher effect? Just as the name of his ex-wife, Demi, is rising, so too is Mila, the name of his current girlfriend, Mila Kunis. It's been a remarkable decade for the name—it first entered the list in 2006 at 747, and in 2012 it was 115. 2013 should be the year it breaks the top 100!

Haven: This name hits all the right notes—it has a hint of spirituality, is just unusual enough at number 432, and has a celebrity baby representative in Haven Garner, Jessica Alba's daughter. It's been a slow and steady climber for years, and we think Haven just might be the little name that could!

Raelynn/Raelyn: Names ending in *–lynn* are hugely popular for girls, and these were two of the biggest jumpers of 2012. (Raelynn jumped 155 spots and Raelyn moved up 136.) It could be due to singer-songwriter and 2012 *The Voice* contestant RaeLynn, who was the first contestant to land a song on the Billboard singles charts.

BOYS

George, Alexander, Louis

The name George has dropped in popularity over the past decade—it sat at 131 in 2002 and 166 in 2012—but the birth of Prince William and Kate Middleton's son Prince George of Cambridge is sure to inspire a climb up the charts. The Prince's full name is George Alexander Louis, so we expect to see all three names make big moves. Already at number 9, Alexander doesn't have far to climb, but Louis ranks at 312, while variant Luis sits at 90. We're thinking all three names will get the royal treatment in the years to come!

Cyrus

It rose 41 spots to 471 in 2012, and our bet is that **Cyrus** will keep heating up. Perhaps it's the popular character on the TV hit *Scandal*, or maybe it's because Claire Danes gave her first-born the moniker, or even the influence of names from ancient Greece...but whatever is influencing the name, it's working! We think the sky is the limit for Cyrus.

Zayden

It may sound unusual, but **Zayden** ranked respectably at 229 in 2012, after first entering the list in 2006 at number 881. Names that end in *–n* are extremely popular for boys, but the more typical variations—**Justin**, **Brian**, **Jaden**—dropped in 2012. Zayden is an offbeat option that's still on trend, and given its 63-slot rise in 2012, we anticipate meeting many more Zaydens in the future.

Variants: Zaiden, Zayne, Zane

Rory

Irish names, especially for boys, are having a moment, and professional golfer Rory McIlroy likely helped give this Celtic name a big-time boost. He won the U.S. Open in 2011, the same year his name jumped a stunning 151 spots from 750 in 2010 to 599 in 2011. In 2012, McIlroy won the PGA Championship—and **Rory** shot up another 118 slots to 481. This golfer continues to be a rising star—and so does his name!

Jase

The A&E reality show *Duck Dynasty* first aired in March 2012 and has set a number of ratings records in its three-season run. For its third season—which aired from February to April 2013—ratings increased an unbelievable 95 percent from the previous season. Wisecracking older brother **Jase** (short for **Jason**) likely deserves the credit for the speedy rise of his nickname. Jase had the third biggest increase of all boys' names in 2012—jumping a staggering 258 spots—and as long as these duck hunters keep calling, we expect Jase will be on the move.

Just Jase	
Year	**Rank**
2000	–
2001	–
2002	967
2003	971
2004	620
2005	570
2006	564
2007	560
2008	649
2009	634
2010	604
2011	562
2012	304

More 2013 Forecasts: Getting Hotter

Camden: We met two celebrity baby Camdens in 2012—Camden Cutler, son of Chicago Bears quarterback Jay Cutler and reality star Kristin Cavallari, and Camden Lachey, son of singer Nick Lachey and his wife, actress Vanessa Minnillo. Maryland parents might also like the name for its hometown flavor—Camden Yards is the home of the Baltimore Orioles. The name Camden has been hovering around the top 100 for a couple of years, so now might be the time it makes a run for the top.

Crosby: We love this last name as a first name, and we're not alone. It first made the list in 2011 at 740 and shot to 670 in 2012. It could be a nod to Pittsburgh Penguin Sidney Crosby or the lovable character on *Parenthood*...but no matter the reason. We can't wait to watch Crosby creep up!

Hayes: Rising country star Hunter Hayes has a double-threat name—his first and last are both on the rise! **Hunter** has been heating up for about five years, but we're more interested to see how **Hayes** climbs in the coming years. It broke into the top 1,000 in 2009 and shot to 689 in 2012.

Leo: Surely heartthrob Leonardo DiCaprio has something to do with the rise of his nickname Leo, but variations on the name are also on the move. Leo hit 134 in 2012. (Top 100, here he comes!) **Leon** made its first appearance in the 300s at 357, and **Leonardo** is sitting pretty at 150.

Hidden Climbers

These names aren't necessarily the biggest jumpers in popularity, and we've mentioned some of them already, but we wanted to bring them to your attention because they have steadily climbed the charts over the past few years. Look for them to gain even more ground in 2013.

Girls		Boys	
Adalyn	Hazel	Abel	Kai
Alana	Ivy	Asher	Kaiden
Alice	Jade	Avery	Leo
Alivia	Josephine	Bradley	Lincoln
Aliyah	Juliana	Brantley	Maddox
Allie	Kendall	Braxton	Mateo
Ariel	Kinley	Calvin	Maxwell
Aurora	Kinsley	Camden	Micah
Brielle	Londyn	Declan	Miles
Brynn	Melody	Elias	Preston
Clara	Mila	Emmett	Santiago
Cora	Nora	Ezra	Sawyer
Delilah	Paisley	Gael	Silas
Eden	Penelope	Greyson	Theodore
Eleanor	Quinn	Harrison	Tucker
Elena	Reese	Ivan	Vincent
Eliana	Ruby	Jaxson	Wesley
Elise	Ryleigh	Jayce	Weston
Hadley	Vivian	Jeremy	
Harmony	Willow	Jonah	

Predictions: The Coldest Baby Names

We think these names are over with a capital *O*. In some cases, they became really hot really fast, and now they're oh so out of style. Others are surprisingly low in popularity considering their perceived "commonality." Perhaps you might want to consider some of these options if you want your baby to stand out in a crowd. See if you agree.

BOYS

Amare: Perhaps because New York Knick Amar'e Stoudemire's basketball career is cooling down, so too is his name. Amare plummeted 70 slots in 2012, landing at 495.

Donald: Even Trump can't revive his first name, which has dropped nearly 200 slots since 2000.

Justin: With popular namesakes like Bieber and Timberlake, you'd think Justin would be a surefire hit. But the name hasn't seen the top 10 since 1990 and this year fell another 15 spots to 74.

Chandler: Thanks to *Friends*, Chandler saw a huge uptick from 1995 to 2000, peaking at 151. Now that Chandler Bing is only in reruns, the name continues to slide. In 2012 it fell to 455.

GIRLS

Audrina: Entering the list for the first time in 2007 (a nod to the popular MTV show *The Hills*, no doubt), Audrina had been on the rise for five years. But in 2012, the name dropped a severe 122 slots to 318.

Amanda: The trouble of one-time child star Amanda Bynes probably won't help her first name. Amanda ranked number 3 in 1992, but twenty years later it's 265.

Danica: Race-car driver Danica Patrick burst onto the scene in 2005, and so did her name. Entering the top 1,000 that year at

611, it rose all the way to 379 in 2009. Since then, Danica has been sliding down the charts, and we expect it to keep falling.

Chelsea: It peaked at 15 in 1992, perhaps because Chelsea Clinton became the First Daughter that same year. Now she's grown up, and the name has grown out of style—Chelsea was 233 in 2012, and the name shows no signs of revival.

Everything Old Is New Again

Names like **Rose**, **Louis**, **Alice**, and **Henry** might sound like old-fashioned monikers more fit for your grandparents than your kids, but these names—all of which were in the top 20 in 1913—were on the rise in 2012. If you like the idea of using a traditional name as a throwback to the greatest generation, check out these top 20 lists from 100, 90, and 80 years ago (and their corresponding 2012 ranks). Some of them aren't even in the top 1,000 anymore—perfect for parents looking for unique names!

1914 Rank	Boys' Name	2012 Rank
1	John	28
2	William	5
3	James	14
4	Robert	61
5	Joseph	20
6	George	166
7	Charles	62
8	Edward	157
9	Frank	319
10	Walter	376

1914 Rank	Boys' Name	2012 Rank
11	Thomas	63
12	Henry	43
13	Paul	193
14	Harold	836
15	Albert	401
16	Raymond	249
17	Richard	124
18	Arthur	355
19	Harry	718
20	Louis	312

1914 Rank	Girls' Name	2012 Rank
1	Mary	123
2	Helen	402
3	Dorothy	922
4	Margaret	178
5	Ruth	344
6	Anna	35
7	Mildred	–
8	Elizabeth	10
9	Frances	764
10	Marie	576
11	Evelyn	27
12	Alice	127
13	Florence	–

1914 Rank	Girls' Name	2012 Rank
14	Virginia	579
15	Rose	261
16	Lillian	25
17	Louise	–
18	Catherine	167
19	Edna	–
20	Gladys	–

1924 Rank	Boys' Name	2012 Rank
1	Robert	61
2	John	28
3	William	5
4	James	14
5	Charles	62
6	George	166
7	Joseph	20
8	Richard	124
9	Edward	157
10	Donald	400
11	Thomas	63
12	Frank	319
13	Harold	836
14	Paul	193
15	Raymond	249
16	Walter	376
17	Jack	46

1924 Rank	Boys' Name	2012 Rank
18	Henry	43
19	Kenneth	175
20	Arthur	355

1924 Rank	Girls' Name	2012 Rank
1	Mary	123
2	Dorothy	922
3	Helen	402
4	Betty	–
5	Margaret	178
6	Ruth	344
7	Virginia	579
8	Mildred	–
9	Doris	–
10	Frances	764
11	Elizabeth	10
12	Evelyn	27
13	Anna	35
14	Marie	576
15	Alice	127
16	Jean	–
17	Marjorie	–
18	Irene	655
19	Shirley	907
20	Florence	–

1934 Rank	Boys' Name	2012 Rank
1	Robert	61
2	James	14
3	John	28
4	William	5
5	Richard	124
6	Donald	400
7	Charles	62
8	George	166
9	Thomas	63
10	Joseph	20
11	Ronald	379
12	David	19
13	Edward	157
14	Paul	193
15	Kenneth	175
16	Frank	319
17	Jack	46
18	Harold	836
19	Raymond	249
20	Billy	662

1934 Rank	Girls' Name	2012 Rank
1	Mary	123
2	Betty	–
3	Barbara	900

1934 Rank	Girls' Name	2012 Rank
4	Shirley	907
5	Dorothy	922
6	Patricia	712
7	Joan	911
8	Margaret	178
9	Helen	402
10	Nancy	651
11	Doris	–
12	Joyce	892
13	Ruth	344
14	Carol	972
15	Virginia	579
16	Jean	–
17	Marilyn	426
18	Elizabeth	10
19	Frances	764
20	Lois	–

Celebrity-Inspired Names on the Rise

Kendrick (Lamar): Was 552 in 2005, now stands at 475.

Anderson (Cooper): Ranked 781 in 2000, now at 280.

Kellan (Lutz): Entered the list at 883 in 2007, now stands at 373.

Fiona (Apple): In 2000, ranked 460. Today, it's 209.

Norah (Jones): Debuted at 817 in 2003, now at 210.

Giuliana (Rancic): Entered the list at 902 in 2007, now at 296.

Ellie (Goulding): Ranked 360 in 2000, now ranks 84.

Kendall (Jenner): Debuted at 817 in 2003, now at 210.
Reese (Witherspoon): Sat at 886 in 2000. Today, it's 128.

Recent Celebrity Babies

Here's a quick overview of what the celebustork has dropped off.
Aden John Tanner (Tamera Mowry-Housley and Adam Housley)
Alexander John (Tom Ford and Richard Buckley)
Asher (Reina Capodici and Justin Guarini)
Asher James (Jamie Anne and Marshall Allman)
Ava Berlin (Sonni Pacheco and Jeremy Renner)
Ava Jaymes (Rochelle Karidis and A. J. McLean)
Calin (Samaire Armstrong and Jason Christopher)
Camden William (Emily and Eric Gunderson)
Cash Yun (Jennifer Birmingham Lee and Will Yun Lee)
Cyrus Michael Christopher (Claire Danes and Hugh Dancy)
Dakota (Rosie O'Donnell and Michelle Rounds)
Dashiell Max (Georgina Chapman and Harvey Weinstein)
Dean Turner (Bree Turner and Justin Saliman)
Delta Faye (Kasey and JT Hodges)
Dennis Ricardo (Kathryn Hernandez and Billy Smith)
Edward James (Eva Herzigová and Gregorio Marsiaj)
Elijah Joseph Daniel (Elton John and David Furnish)
Elizabeth Mae (Samantha Brown and Kevin O'Leary)
Ellis James (Samantha Brown and Kevin O'Leary)
Emerson Jay (JoAnna Garcia Swisher and Nick Swisher)
Everett Joseph (Chely Wright and Lauren Blitzer Wright)
Everly (Jenna Dewan-Tatum and Channing Tatum)
Felix Chang (Tinglan Hong and Hugh Grant)
Fiona Hepler (Kim and Chad Lowe)
Gavin Lee (Marisa Miller and Griffin Guess)
George Samuel (Chely Wright and Lauren Blitzer Wright)
Goldie Ryan (Wendy and Steve Madden)

Gracie James (Rosemarie DeWitt and Ron Livingston)
Greyson James (Kara DioGuardi and Mike McCuddy)
Hartley Eric (Veronica De La Cruz)
Holden John (Leigh Boniello and Howie Dorough)
Holiday Grace (Brittany and Harold Perrineau)
Hudson Lennon (Sarah and Jon Jones)
Jax Copeland (Ashley and Tom Arnold)
Jett Ling (Lisa Ling and Paul Song)
Justice Jay (Danneel Harris Ackles and Jensen Ackles)
Kenzie Lynne (Beverley Mitchell and Michael Cameron)
Knox Addison (Amanda Righetti and Jordan Alan)
Lincoln Bell (Kristen Bell and Dax Shepard)
Lion (Malia Jones and Alex O'Loughlin)
Livingston Alves (Camila and Matthew McConaughey)
Logan Phineas (Ryan Murphy and David Miller)
Lula Rosylea (Alicia Grimaldi and Bryan Adams)
Magnus Hamilton (Jennifer Nettles and Justin Miller)
Magnus Mitchell (Elizabeth Banks and Max Handelman)
Margaret "Mila" Laura (Jenna Bush Hager and Henry Hager)
Margot (Sophie Dahl and Jamie Cullum)
Marnie Rose (Lily Allen and Sam Cooper)
Memphis (Jemima Kirke and Michael Mosberg)
Milan Piqué (Shakira and Gerard Piqué)
Miller William (Kelley and Scott Wolf)
Miranda Scarlett (Patricia and Rob Schneider)
Natalie Bouader (Shiri Appleby and Jon Shook)
Noah Shannon (Megan Fox and Brian Austin Green)
Olive Barrymore (Drew Barrymore and Will Kopelman)
Oliver Charles (Jamie Anne and Marshall Allman)
Paisley Faye (Jennie Finch and Casey Daigle)
Penna Mae (Erin and Ian Ziering)
Pepper (Moon Bloodgood and Grady Hall)

Rainbow Aurora (Holly Madison and Pasquale Rotella)
Rekker Radley (Dominique Geisendorff and Cam Gigandet)
Riley Anne (Molly Malaney Mesnick and Jason Mesnick)
Rocky James (Sarah Michelle Gellar and Freddie Prinze Jr.)
Sage Lavinia (Shannan Click and Jack Huston)
Scout Margery (Kerri Walsh Jennings and Casey Jennings)
Sebastian (Malin Ackerman and Roberto Zincone)
Sebastian Taylor (Amber Rose and Wiz Khalifa)
Tennessee James (Reese Witherspoon and Jim Toth)
Talulah Rue (Sara Rue and Kevin Price)
Tucker McFadden (Melissa Joan Hart and Mark Wilkerson)
Vaunne Sydney (Mercedes McNab and Mark Henderson)
Violet Grace (Poppy Montgomery and Shawn Sanford)
Violet Marlowe (Jessie Baylin and Nathan Followill)
Vivian Lake (Gisele Bundchen and Tom Brady)
Wilhelmina Jane (Natalie and Taylor Hanson)
William Luca (Rose Costa and James Marsden)
Zander Jace (Linzi and Billy Martin)

Girls

★ — All names with a ★ in the text denote Top 100 Names of 2012.

^ — All names with a ^ in the text denote hot names rising in popularity in 2012.

A

Aadi (Hindi) Child of the beginning
Aadie, Aady, Aadey, Aadee, Aadea, Aadeah, Aadye

*Aaliyah (Arabic) An ascender, one having the highest social standing
Aaleyah, Aaliya, Aliyah, Alliyah, Alieya, Aliyiah, Alliyia, Aleeya, Alee, Aleiya, Alia, Aleah, Alea, Aliya

Aaralyn (American) Woman with song
Aaralynn, Aaralin, Aaralinn, Aaralinne, Aralyn, Aralynn

Aba (African) Born on a Thursday
Abah, Abba, Abbah

Abarrane (Hebrew) Feminine form of Abraham; mother of a multitude; mother of nations
Abarrayne, Abarraine, Abarane, Abarayne, Abaraine, Abame, Abrahana

Abena (African) Born on a Tuesday
Abenah, Abeena, Abyna, Abina, Abeenah, Abynah, Abinah

Abiela (Hebrew) My father is Lord
Abielah, Abiella, Abiellah, Abyela, Abyelah, Abyella, Abyellah

*Abigail (Hebrew) The source of a father's joy
Abagail, Abbigail, Abigael, Abigale, Abbygail, Abygail, Abygayle, Abbygayle, Abbegale, Abby, Abbagail, Abbey, Abbie, Abbi, Abigayle

Abijah (Hebrew) My father is Lord
Abija, Abisha, Abishah, Abiah, Abia, Aviah, Avia

Abila (Spanish) One who is beautiful
Abilah, Abyla, Abylah

Abilene (American / Hebrew) From a town in Texas / resembling grass
Abalene, Abalina, Abilena, Abiline, Abileene, Abileen, Abileena, Abilyn

Abir (Arabic) Having a fragrant scent
Abeer, Abyr, Abire, Abeere, Abbir, Abhir

Abira (Hebrew) A source of strength; one who is strong
Abera, Abyra, Abyrah, Abirah, Abbira, Abeerah

Abra (Hebrew / Arabic)
Feminine form of Abraham;
mother of a multitude;
mother of nations / lesson;
example
*Abri, Abrah, Abree, Abria,
Abbra, Abrah, Abbrah*

Abril (Spanish / Portuguese)
Form of April, meaning
opening buds of spring

Academia (Latin) From a com-
munity of higher learning
*Akademia, Academiah,
Akademiah*

Acantha (Greek) Thorny; in
mythology, a nymph who was
loved by Apollo
*Akantha, Ackantha, Acanthah,
Akanthah, Ackanthah*

Accalia (Latin) In mythology,
the foster mother of Romulus
and Remus
*Accaliah, Acalia, Accalya,
Acalya, Acca, Ackaliah, Ackalia*

Adah (Hebrew) Ornament;
beautiful addition to the
family
Adda, Adaya, Ada

Adanna (African) Her father's
daughter; a father's pride
*Adana, Adanah, Adannah,
Adanya, Adanyah*

Adanne (African) Her
mother's daughter; a
mother's pride
*Adane, Adayne, Adaine,
Adayn, Adain, Adaen, Adaene*

Adara (Greek / Arabic)
Beautiful girl / chaste one;
virgin
*Adair, Adare, Adaire, Adayre,
Adarah, Adarra, Adaora, Adar*

Addin (Hebrew) One who is
adorned; voluptuous
Addine, Addyn, Addyne

*Addison (English) Daughter
of Adam
*Addeson, Addyson, Adison,
Adisson, Addisyn, Adyson*

Adeen (Irish) Little fire shin-
ing brightly
*Adeene, Adean, Adeane, Adein,
Adeine, Adeyn, Adeyne*

Adela (German) Of the nobil-
ity; serene; of good humor
*Adele, Adelia, Adella, Adelle,
Adelie, Adelina, Adali*

^Adelaide (German) Of the
nobility; serene; of good
humor
Adelaid

^Adeline (German) Form of
Adela, meaning of the nobility
*Adalyn, **Adalynn**, Adelyn,
Adelynn*

Adianca (Native American)
One who brings peace
Adianka, Adyanca, Adyanka

Adira (Hebrew / Arabic)
Powerful, noble woman /
having great strength
*Adirah, Adeera, Adyra,
Adeerah, Adyrah, Adeira,
Adeirah, Adiera*

Admina (Hebrew) Daughter of
the red earth
*Adminah, Admeena, Admyna,
Admeenah, Admynah,
Admeina*

Adoración (Spanish) Having
the adoration of all

Adra (Arabic) One who is
chaste; a virgin

Adriana (Greek) Feminine
form of Adrian; from the
Adriatic Sea region; woman
with dark features
*Adria, Adriah, Adrea, Adreana,
Adreanna, Adrienna, Adriane,
Adriene, Adrie, Adrienne,
Adrianna, Adrianne, Adriel*

Adrina (Italian) Having great
happiness
*Adrinna, Adreena, Adrinah,
Adryna, Adreenah, Adrynah*

Aegea (Latin / Greek) From the
Aegean Sea / in mythology, a
daughter of the sun who was
known for her beauty

Aegina (Greek) In mythology,
a sea nymph
Aeginae, Aegyna, Aegynah

Aelwen (Welsh) Woman with
a fair brow
*Aelwenn, Aelwenne, Aelwin,
Aelwinn, Aelwinne, Aelwyn,
Aelwynn, Aelwynne*

Aerwyna (English) A friend of
the ocean

Afra (Hebrew / Arabic) Young
doe / white; an earth color
*Affra, Affrah, Afrah, Afrya,
Afryah, Afria, Affery, Affrie*

Afrodille (French) Daffodil;
showy and vivid
*Afrodill, Afrodil, Afrodile,
Afrodilla, Afrodila*

Afton (English) From the
Afton river

Agave (Greek) In mythology, a
queen of Thebes

Agnes (Greek) One who is
pure; chaste
*Agneis, Agnese, Agness, Agnies,
Agnus, Agna, Agne, Agnesa,
Nessa, Oona*

Agraciana (Spanish) One who
forgives
*Agracianna, Agracyanna,
Agracyana, Agraciann,
Agraciane, Agracyann,
Agracyane, Agracianne*

Agrona (Celtic) In mythology, the goddess of war and death
Agronna, Agronia, Agrone

Ahelia (Hebrew) Breath; a source of life
Ahelie, Ahelya, Aheli, Ahelee, Aheleigh, Ahelea, Aheleah, Ahely

Ahellona (Greek) Woman who has masculine qualities
Ahelona, Ahellonna, Ahelonna

Ahinoam (Hebrew) In the Bible, one of David's wives

Ahuva (Hebrew) One who is dearly loved
Ahuvah, Ahuda, Ahudah

Aida (English / French / Arabic) One who is wealthy; prosperous / one who is helpful / a returning visitor
Ayda, Aydah, Aidah, Aidee, Aidia, Aieeda, Aaida

Aidan (Gaelic) One who is fiery; little fire
Aiden, Adeen, Aden, Aideen, Adan, Aithne, Aithnea, Ajthne

Aiko (Japanese) Little one who is dearly loved

Ailbhe (Irish) Of noble character; one who is bright

Aileen (Irish / Scottish) Light bearer / from the green meadow
Ailean, Ailein, Ailene, Ailin, Aillen, Ailyn, Alean, Aleane

Ailis (Irish) One who is noble and kind
Ailish, Ailyse, Ailesh, Ailisa, Ailise

Ailna (German) One who is sweet and pleasant; of the nobility
Ailne

Ain (Irish / Arabic) In mythology, a woman who wrote laws to protect the rights of women / precious eye

Aine (Celtic) One who brings brightness and joy

Aingeal (Irish) Heaven's messenger; angel
Aingealag

Ainsley (Scottish) One's own meadow
Ainslie, Ainslee, Ainsly, Ainslei, Aynslie, Aynslee, Aynslie, Ansley

Aionia (Greek) Everlasting life
Aioniah, Aionea, Aioneah, Ayonia, Ayoniah, Ayonea, Ayoneah

Airic (Celtic) One who is pleasant and agreeable
Airick, Airik, Aeric, Aerick, Aerik

Aisha (Arabic / African) lively / womanly
Aiesha, Ayisha, Myisha

Aisling (Irish) A dream or vision; an inspiration
Aislin, Ayslin, Ayslinn, Ayslyn, Ayslynn, Aislyn, Aisylnn, Aislinn, Isleen

Aitheria (Greek) Of the wind
Aitheriah, Aitherea, Aithereah, Aytheria, Aytheriah, Aytherea, Aythereah

Ajaya (Hindi) One who is invincible; having the power of a god
Ajay

Aka (Maori / Turkish) Affectionate one / in mythology, a mother goddess
Akah, Akka, Akkah

Akili (Tanzanian) Having great wisdom
Akilea, Akilee, Akilie, Akylee, Akylie, Akyli, Akileah

Akilina (Latin) Resembling an eagle
Akilinah, Akileena, Akilyna, Akilinna, Ackilina, Acilina, Akylina, Akylyna

Akira (Scottish) One who acts as an anchor
Akera, Akerra, Akiera, Akirah, Akiria, Akyra, Akirrah, Akeri, Akeira, Akeara

Aksana (Russian) Form of Oksana, meaning "hospitality"
Aksanna, Aksanah, Aksannah

Alaia (Arabic / Basque) One who is majestic, of high worth joy
Alaya, Alayah, Alaiah

Alaina (French) Beautiful and fair woman; dear child
Alayna, Alaine, Alayne, Alainah, Alana, Alanah, Alanna, Alannah, Alanis, Alyn, Alani, Alanni, Alaney; Alanney; Alanie

Alair (French) One who has a cheerful disposition
Alaire, Allaire, Allair, Aulaire, Alayr, Alayre, Alaer

Alanza (Spanish) Feminine form of Alonzo; noble and ready for battle

Alarice (German) Feminine form of Alaric; ruler of all
Alarise, Allaryce, Alarica, Alarisa, Alaricia, Alrica

Alcina (Greek) One who is strong-willed and opinionated
Alceena, Alcyna, Alsina, Alsyna, Alzina, Alcine, Alcinia, Alcyne

Alda (German / Spanish) Long-lived, old / wise; an elder
Aldah, Aldine, Aldina, Aldinah, Aldene, Aldona

Aldis (English) From the ancient house
Aldys, Aldiss, Aldisse, Aldyss, Aldysse

Aldonsa (Spanish) One who is kind and gracious
Aldonza, Aldonsia, Aldonzia

Aleah (Arabic) Exalted
Alea, Alia, Aliah, Aliana, Aleana

Aleen (Celtic) Form of Helen, meaning "the shining light"
Aleena, Aleenia, Alene, Alyne, Alena, Alenka, Alynah, Aleine

Alegria (Spanish) One who is cheerful and brings happiness to others
Alegra, Aleggra, Allegra, Alleffra, Allecra

Alera (Latin) Resembling an eagle
Alerra, Aleria, Alerya, Alerah, Alerrah

Alethea (Greek) One who is truthful
Altheia, Lathea, Lathey, Olethea

*★**Alexa** (Greek) Form of Alexandra, meaning "helper and defender of mankind"
Aleka, Alexia

^★**Alexandra** (Greek) Feminine form of Alexander; a helper and defender of mankind
*Alexandria, Alexandrea, Alixandra, **Alessandra**, **Alexis**, Alondra, Aleksandra, Alejandra, Sandra, Sandrine, Sasha*

★**Alexis** (Greek) Form of Alexandra, meaning "helper and defender of mankind"
Alexus, Alexys, Alexia

Ali (English) Form of Allison or Alice, meaning "woman of the nobility"
Allie, Alie, Alli, Ally

Aliana (English) Form of Eliana, meaning "the Lord answers our prayers"
Alianna

^**Alice** (German) Woman of the nobility; truthful; having high moral character
Ally, Allie, Alyce, Alesia, Aleece

Alicia (Spanish) Form of Alice, meaning "woman of the nobility"
Alecia, Aleecia, Aliza, Aleesha, Alesha, Alisha, Alisa

Alika (Hawaiian) One who is honest
Alicka, Alicca, Alyka, Alycka, Alycca

Alina (Arabic / Polish) One who is noble / one who is beautiful and bright
Aline, Aleena, Alena, Alyna

Alivia (Spanish) Form of Olivia, meaning of the olive tree

★Allison (English) Form of Alice, meaning "woman of the nobility, truthful; having high moral character"
Alisanne, Alison, Alicen, Alisen, Alisyn, Allyson, Alyson, Allisson

Alma (Latin / Italian) One who is nurturing and kind / refers to the soul
Almah

Almira (English) A princess; daughter born to royalty
Almeera, Almeira, Almiera, Almyra, Almirah, Almeerah, Almeirah

Aloma (Spanish) Form of Paloma, meaning "dove-like"
Alomah, Alomma, Alommah

Alondra (Spanish) Form of Alexandra, meaning "helper and defender of mankind"

Alpha (Greek) The firstborn child; the first letter of the Greek alphabet

Alphonsine (French) Feminine form of Alphonse; one who is ready for battle
Alphonsina, Alphonsyne, Alphonsyna, Alphonseene, Alphonseena, Alphonseane, Alphonseana, Alphonsiene

Alura (English) A divine counselor
Allura, Alurea, Alhraed

Alvera (Spanish) Feminine of Alvaro; guardian of all; speaker of the truth
Alveria, Alvara, Alverna, Alvernia, Alvira, Alvyra, Alvarita, Alverra

★Alyssa (German) Form of Alice, meaning "woman of the nobility, truthful; having high moral character"
Alisa, Alissya, Alyssaya, Alishya, Alisia, Alissa, Allisa, Allyssa, Alysa, Alysse, Alyssia

Amada (Spanish) One who is loved by all
Amadia, Amadea, Amadita, Amadah

Amadea (Latin) Feminine form of Amedeo; loved by God
Amadya, Amadia, Amadine, Amadina, Amadika, Amadis

Amadi (African) One who rejoices
Amadie, Amady, Amadey, Amadye, Amadee, Amadea, Amadeah

Amalia (German) One who is industrious and hardworking
Amelia, Amalya, Amalie, Amalea, Amylia, Amyleah, Amilia, Neneca

Amalthea (Greek) One who soothes; in mythology, the foster mother of Zeus
Amaltheah, Amalthia, Amalthya

Amanda (Latin) One who is much loved
Amandi, Amandah, Amandea, Amandee, Amandey, Amande, Amandie, Amandy, Mandy

Amani (African / Arabic) One who is peaceful / one with wishes and dreams
Amanie, Amany, Amaney, Amanee, Amanye, Amanea, Amaneah

Amara (Greek) One who will be forever beautiful
Amarah, Amarya, Amaira, Amaria, Amar

Amari (African) Having great strength, a builder
Amaree, Amarie

Amaya (Japanese) Of the night rain
Amayah, Amaia, Amaiah

Amber (French) Resembling the jewel; a warm honey color
Ambur, Ambar, Amberly, Amberlyn, Amberli, Amberlee, Ambyr, Ambyre

Ambrosia (Greek) Immortal; in mythology, the food of the gods
Ambrosa, Ambrosiah, Ambrosyna, Ambrosina, Ambrosyn, Ambrosine, Ambrozin, Ambrozyn, Ambrozyna, Ambrozyne, Ambrozine, Ambrose, Ambrotosa, Ambruslne, Amhrosine

*Amelia (German) Form of Amalia or (Latin) form of Emily, meaning "one who is industrious and hardworking"
Amelie, Amelita, Amylia, Amely

America (Latin) A powerful ruler
Americus, Amerika, Amerikus

Amina (Arabic) A princess, one who commands; truthful, trustworthy
Amirah, Ameera, Amyra, Ameerah, Amyrah, Ameira, Ameirah, Amiera

Amissa (Hebrew) One who is honest; a friend
Amisa, Amise, Amisia, Amiza, Amysa, Amysia, Amysya, Amyza

Amiyah (American) Form of Amy, meaning "beloved"
Amiah, Amiya, Amya

Amrita (Hindi) Having immortality; full of ambrosia
Amritah, Amritta, Amryta, Amrytta, Amrytte, Amritte, Amryte, Amreeta

Amser (Welsh) A period of time

Amy (Latin) Dearly loved
Aimee, Aimie, Aimi, Aimy, Aimya, Aimey, Amice, Amicia

Anaba (Native American) A woman returning from battle
Anabah, Annaba, Annabah

Anabal (Gaelic) One who is joyful
Anaball, Annabal, Annaball

Anahi (Latin) Immortal

Analia (Spanish) Combination of Ana and Lea or Lucia
Annalee, Annali, Annalie, Annaleigh, Annalea, Analeigh, Anali, Analie, Annalina, Anneli, Annaleah, Annaliese, Annalise, Annalisa, Analise, Analiese, Analisa

Anarosa (Spanish) A graceful rose
Annarosa, Anarose, Annarose

Anastasia (Greek) One who shall rise again
Anastase, Anastascia, Anastasha, Anastasie, Stacia, Stasia, Stacy, Stacey

Ancina (Latin) Form of Ann, meaning "a woman graced with God's favor"
Ancyna, Anncina, Anncyna, Anceina, Annceina, Anciena, Annciena, Anceena

*Andrea (Greek / Latin) Courageous and strong / feminine form of Andrew; womanly
Andria, Andrianna, Andreia, Andreina, Andreya, Andriana, Andreana, Andera

Angel (Greek) A heavenly messenger

^**Angela** (Greek) A heavenly
messenger; an angel
*Angelica, **Angelina, Angelique,**
Anjela, Anjelika, Angella,
Angelita, Angeline, Angie, Angy*

Angelina (Greek) Form of
Angela, meaning "a heavenly
messenger, an angel"
*Angeline, Angelyn, Angelene,
Angelin*

Ani (Hawaiian) One who is
very beautiful
*Aneesa, Aney, Anie, Any, Aany,
Aanye, Anea, Aneah*

Aniceta (French) One who is
unconquerable
Anicetta, Anniceta, Annicetta

Aniya (American) Form of
Anna, meaning "a woman
graced with God's favor"
Aniyah, Anaya

*****Anna** (Latin) A woman graced
with God's favor
*Annah, Ana, Ann, Anne,
Anya, Ane, Annika, Anouche,
Annchen, Ancina, Annie, Anika*

^**Annabel** (Italian) Graceful
and beautiful woman
***Annabelle,** Annabell,
Annabella, Annabele, Anabel,
Anabell, Anabelle, Anabella*

Annabeth (English) Graced
with God's bounty
*Anabeth, Annabethe, Annebeth,
Anebeth, Anabethe*

Annalynn (English) From the
graceful lake
*Analynn, Annalyn, Annaline,
Annalin, Annalinn, Analyn,
Analine, Analin*

Annmarie (English) Filled with
bitter grace
*Annemarie, Annmaria,
Annemaria, Annamarie,
Annamaria, Anamarie,
Anamaria, Anamari*

Annora (Latin) Having great
honor
*Anora, Annorah, Anorah,
Anoria, Annore, Annorya,
Anorya, Annoria*

Anouhea (Hawaiian) Having a
soft, cool fragrance

Ansley (English) From the
noble's pastureland
*Ansly, Anslie, Ansli, Anslee,
Ansleigh, Anslea, Ansleah,
Anslye, Ainsley*

Antalya (Russian) Born with
the morning's first light
*Antaliya, Antalyah, Antaliyah,
Antalia, Antaliah*

Antea (Greek) In mythology, a woman who was scorned and committed suicide
Anteia, Anteah

Antje (German) A graceful woman

Antoinette (French) Praiseworthy
Toinette

Anwen (Welsh) A famed beauty
Anwin, Anwenne, Anwinne, Anwyn, Anwynn, Anwynne, Anwenn, Anwinn

Anya (Russian) Form of Anna, meaning "a woman graced with God's favor"

Aphrah (Hebrew) From the house of dust
Aphra

Aphrodite (Greek) Love; in mythology, the goddess of love and beauty
Afrodite, Afrodita, Aphrodita, Aphrodyte, Aphhrodyta, Aphrodytah

Aponi (Native American) Resembling a butterfly
Aponni, Apponni, Apponi

Apphia (Hebrew) One who is productive
Apphiah

Apple (American) Sweet fruit; one who is cherished
Appel, Aple, Apel

April (English) Opening buds of spring, born in the month of April
Avril, Averel, Averill, Avrill, Apryl, Apryle, Aprylle, Aprel, Aprele, Aprila, Aprile, Aprili, Aprilla, Aprille, Aprielle, Aprial, Abrielle, Avrielle, Avrial, Abrienda, Avriel, Averyl, Averil, Avryl, Apryll

Aquene (Native American) One who is peaceful
Aqueena, Aqueene, Aqueen

Arabella (Latin) An answered prayer; beautiful altar
Arabela, Arabel, Arabell

Araceli (Spanish) From the altar of heaven
Aracely, Aracelie, Areli, Arely

Aranka (Hungarian) The golden child

Ararinda (German) One who is tenacious
Ararindah, Ararynda, Araryndah

Arava (Hebrew) Resembling a willow; of an arid land
Aravah, Aravva, Aravvah

Arcadia (Greek / Spanish)
Feminine form of Arkadios;
woman from Arcadia / one
who is adventurous
*Arcadiah, Arkadia, Arcadya,
Arkadya, Arckadia, Arckadya*

Ardara (Gaelic) From the
stronghold on the hill
*Ardarah, Ardarra, Ardaria,
Ardarrah, Ardariah*

Ardel (Latin) Feminine form of
Ardos; industrious and eager
*Ardelle, Ardella, Ardele,
Ardelia, Ardelis, Ardela, Ardell*

Arden (Latin / English) One
who is passionate and enthusiastic / from the valley of the
eagles
*Ardin, Ardeen, Ardena, Ardene,
Ardan, Ardean, Ardine, Ardun*

Ardra (Celtic / Hindi) One
who is noble / the goddess of
bad luck and misfortune

Argea (Greek) In mythology,
the wife of Polynices
Argeia

^Aria (English) A beautiful
melody
Ariah

*Ariana (Welsh / Greek)
Resembling silver / one who
is holy
*Ariane, Arian, **Arianna**, Arianne,
Aerian, Aerion, Arianie,
Arieon, Aryana, Aryanna*

Ariel (Hebrew) A lionness of
God
*Arielle, Ariele, Airial, Ariela,
Ariella, Aryela, Arial, Ari,
Ariely, Arely, Arieli, Areli*

Arietta (Italian) A short but
beautiful melody
*Arieta, Ariete, Ariet, Ariett,
Aryet, Aryeta, Aryetta, Aryette*

Arin (English) Form of Erin,
meaning "woman of Ireland"
Aryn

Arisje (Danish) One who is
superior

Arissa (Greek) One who is
superior
Arisa, Aris, Aryssa, Arysa, Arys

Arizona (Native American)
From the little spring / from
the state of Arizona

Armani (Persian) One who is
desired
*Armanee, Armahni, Armaney,
Armanie, Armaney*

Arnette (English) A little eagle
*Arnett, Arnetta, Arnete, Arneta,
Arnet*

Aroha (Maori) One who loves and is loved

Arona (Maori) One who is colorful and vivacious
Aronah, Aronnah, Aronna

Arrosa (Basque) Sprinkled with dew from heaven; resembling a rose
Arrose

Artis (Irish / English / Icelandic) Lofy hill; noble / rock / follower of Thor
Artisa, Artise, Artys, Artysa, Artyse, Artiss, Arti, Artina

Arusi (African) A girl born during the time of a wedding
Arusie, Arusy, Arusey, Arusee, Arusea, Aruseah, Arusye

Arwa (Arabic) A female mountain goat

Arya (Indian) One who is noble and honored
Aryah, Aryana, Aryanna, Aryia

Ascención (Spanish) Refers to the Ascension

Ashby (English) Home of the ash tree
Ashbea, Ashbie, Ashbeah, Ashbey, Ashbi, Ashbee

Asherat (Syrian) In mythology, goddess of the sea

Ashima (Hebrew) In the Bible, a deity worshipped at Hamath
Ashimah, Ashyma, Asheema, Ashimia, Ashymah, Asheemah, Asheima, Asheimah

Ashira (Hebrew) One who is wealthy; prosperous
Ashyra, Ashyrah, Ashirah, Asheera, Asheerah, Ashiera, Ashierah, Asheira

*Ashley (English) From the meadow of ash trees
Ashlie, Ashlee, Ashleigh, Ashly, Ashleye, Ashlya, Ashala, Ashleay

Ashlyn (American) Combination of Ashley and Lynn
Ashlynn, Ashlynne

Asia (Greek / English) Resurrection / the rising sun; in the Koran, the woman who raised Moses; a woman from the east
Aysia, Asya, Asyah, Azia, Asianne

Asis (African) Of the sun
Asiss, Assis, Assiss

Asli (Turkish) One who is genuine and original
Aslie, Asly, Asley, Aslee, Asleigh, Aslea, Asleah, Alsye

Asma (Arabic) One of high status

Aspen (English) From the aspen tree
Aspin, Aspine, Aspina, Aspyn, Aspyna, Aspyne

Assana (Irish) From the waterfall
Assane, Assania, Assanna, Asanna, Asana

Astra (Latin) Of the stars; as bright as a star
Astera, Astrea, Asteria, Astrey, Astara, Astraea, Astrah, Astree

Astrid (Scandinavian / German) One with divine strength
Astryd, Estrid

Asunción (Spanish) Refers to the Virgin Mary's assumption into heaven

^**Athena** (Greek) One who is wise; in mythology, the goddess of war and wisdom
Athina, Atheena, Athene

^***Aubrey** (English) One who rules with elf-wisdom
Aubree, *Aubrie, Aubry, Aubri, Aubriana*

***Audrey** (English) Woman with noble strength
Audree, Audry, Audra, Audrea, Adrey, Audre, Audray, Audrin,
Audrina

Augusta (Latin) Feminine form of Augustus; venerable, majestic
Augustina, Agustina, Augustine, Agostina, Agostine, Augusteen, Augustyna, Agusta

Aulis (Greek) In mythology, a princess of Attica
Auliss, Aulisse, Aulys, Aulyss, Aulysse

Aurora (Latin) Morning's first light; in mythology, the goddess of the dawn
Aurore, Aurea, Aurorette

***Autumn** (English) Born in the fall
Autum

***Ava** (German / Iranian) A birdlike woman / from the water
Avah, Avalee, Avaleigh, Avali, Avalie, Avaley, Avelaine, Avelina

Avasa (Indian) One who is independent
Avasah, Avassa, Avasia, Avassah, Avasiah, Avasea, Avaseah

Avena (English) From the oat field
Avenah, Aviena, Avyna, Avina, Avinah, Avynah, Avienah, Aveinah

Avera (Hebrew) One who transgresses
Averah, Avyra, Avira

*Avery (English) One who is a wise ruler; of the nobility
Avrie, Averey, Averie, Averi, Averee, Averea, Avereah

Aviana (Latin) Blessed with a gracious life
Avianah, Avianna, Aviannah, Aviane, Avianne, Avyana, Avyanna, Avyane

Aviva (Hebrew) One who is innocent and joyful; resembling springtime
Avivi, Avivah, Aviv, Avivie, Avivice, Avni, Avri, Avyva

Awel (Welsh) One who is as refreshing as a breeze
Awell, Awele, Awela, Awella

Awen (Welsh) A fluid essence; a muse; a flowing spirit
Awenn, Awenne, Awin, Awinn, Awinne, Awyn, Awynn, Awynne

Axelle (German / Latin / Hebrew) Source of life; small oak / axe / peace
Axella, Axell, Axele, Axl, Axela, Axelia, Axellia

^**Ayala** (Hebrew) Resembling a gazelle
*Ayalah, Ayalla, Ayallah, **Aylin**, Ayleen, Ayline, Aileen*

Ayanna (Hindi / African) One who is innocent / resembling a beautiful flower
Ayana, Ayania, Ahyana, Ayna, Anyaniah, Ayannah, Aiyanna, Aiyana

Ayla (Hebrew) From the oak tree
Aylah, Aylana, Aylanna, Aylee, Aylea, Aylene, Ayleena, Aylena, Aylin, Ayleen, Ayline, Aileen

Aza (Arabic / African) One who provides comfort / powerful
Azia, Aiza, Aizia, Aizha

Azana (African) One who is superior
Azanah, Azanna, Azannah

Azar (Persian) One who is fiery; scarlet
Azara, Azaria, Azarah, Azarra, Azarrah, Azarr

Aznii (Chechen) A famed beauty
Azni, Aznie, Azny, Azney, Aznee, Aznea, Azneah

Azriel (Hebrew) God is my helper
Azrael, Azriell, Azrielle, Azriela, Azriella, Azraela

Azul (Spanish) Blue

B

Badia (Arabic) An elegant lady; one who is unique
Badiah, Badi'a, Badiya, Badea, Badya, Badeah

Bahija (Arabic) A cheerful woman
Bahijah, Bahiga, Bahigah, Bahyja, Bahyjah, Bahyga, Bahygah

*Bailey (English) From the courtyard within castle walls; a public official
Bailee, Bayley, Baylee, Baylie, Baili, Bailie, Baileigh, Bayleigh

Baka (Indian) Resembling a crane
Bakah, Bakka, Backa, Bacca

Baligha (Arabic) One who is forever eloquent
Balighah, Baleegha, Balygha, Baliegha, Baleagha, Baleigha

Banba (Irish) In mythology, a patron goddess of Ireland

Bansuri (Indian) One who is musical
Bansurie, Bansari, Banseri, Bansurri, Bansury, Bansurey, Bansuree

Bara (Hebrew) One who is chosen
Barah, Barra, Barrah

Barbara (Latin) A traveler from a foreign land; a stranger
Barbra, Barbarella, Barbarita, Baibin, Babette, Bairbre, Barbary, Barb

Barika (African) A flourishing woman; one who is successful
Barikah, Baryka, Barikka, Barykka, Baricka, Barycka, Baricca, Barycca

Barr (English) A lawyer
Barre, Bar

Barras (English) From among the trees

Beatrice (Latin) One who blesses others
Beatrix, Beatriz, Beatriss, Beatrisse, Bea, Beatrize, Beatricia, Beatrisa

Becky (English) Form of Rebecca, meaning "one who is bound to God"
Beckey, Becki, Beckie, Becca, Becka, Bekka, Beckee, Beckea

Bel (Indian) From the sacred wood

Belen (Spanish) Woman from Bethlehem

Belinda (English) A beautiful and tender woman
Belindah, Belynda, Balynda, Belienda, Bleiendah, Balyndah, Belyndah

Belisama (Celtic) In mythology, a goddess of rivers and lakes
Belisamah, Belisamma, Belysama, Belisma, Belysma, Belesama

*****Bella** (Italian) A woman famed for her beauty
Belle, Bela, Bell, Belita, Bellissa, Belia, Bellanca, Bellany

Bena (Native American) Resembling a pheasant
Benah, Benna, Bennah

Benigna (Spanish) Feminine form of Benigno; one who is kind; friendly

Bernice (Greek) One who brings victory
Berenisa, Berenise, Berenice, Bernicia, Bernisha, Berniss, Bernyce, Bernys

Bertha (German) One who is famously bright and beautiful
Berta, Berthe, Berth, Bertina, Bertyna, Bertine, Bertyne, Birte

Bertilda (English) A luminous battle maiden
Bertilde, Bertild

Beryl (English) Resembling the pale-green precious stone
Beryll, Berylle, Beril, Berill, Berille

Bess (English) Form of Elizabeth, meaning "my God is bountiful; God's promise"
Besse, Bessi, Bessie, Bessy, Bessey, Bessee, Bessea

Beth (English) Form of Elizabeth, meaning "my God is bountiful; God's promise"
Bethe

Bethany (Hebrew) From the house of figs
Bethan, Bethani, Bethanie, Bethanee, Bethaney, Bethane, Bethann, Bethanne

Beyonce (American) One who surpasses others
Beyoncay, Beyonsay, Beyonsai, Beyonsae, Beyonci, Beyoncie, Beyoncee, Beyoncea

Bianca (Italian) A shining, fair-skinned woman
Bianka, Byanca, Byanka

Bibiana (Italian) Form of Vivian, meaning "lively woman"
Bibiane, Bibianna

Bijou (French) As precious as a jewel

Billie (English) Feminine form of William; having a desire to protect
Billi, Billy, Billey, Billee, Billeigh, Billea, Billeah

Blaine (Scottish / Irish) A saint's servant / a thin woman
Blayne, Blane, Blain, Blayn, Blaen, Blaene

Blair (Scottish) From the field of battle
Blaire, Blare, Blayre, Blaer, Blaere, Blayr

Blake (English) A dark beauty
Blayk, Blayke, Blaik, Blaike, Blaek, Blaeke

Blue (English) A color, lighter than purple-indigo but darker than green

Blythe (English) Filled with happiness
Blyth, Blithe, Blith

Bonamy (French) A very good friend
Bonamey, Bonami, Bonamie, Bonamee, Bonamei, Bonamea, Bonameah

Bonnie (English) Pretty face
Boni, Bona, Bonea, Boneah, Bonee

Brady (Irish) A large-chested woman
Bradey, Bradee, Bradi, Bradie, Bradea, Bradeah

Braelyn (American) Combination of Braden and Lynn
Braylin, Braelin, Braylyn, Braelen, Braylen

Braima (African) Mother of multitudes
Braimah, Brayma, Braema, Braymah, Braemah

Brandy (English) A woman wielding a sword; an alcoholic drink
Brandey, Brandi, Brandie, Brandee, Branda, Brande, Brandelyn, Brandilyn

Brazil (Spanish) Of the ancient tree
Brasil, Brazile, Brazille, Brasille, Bresil, Brezil, Bresille, Brezille

Brencis (Slavic) Crowned with laurel

Brenda (Irish) Feminine form of Brendan; a princess; wielding a sword
Brynda, Brinda, Breandan, Brendalynn, Brendolyn, Brend, Brienda

Brenna (Welsh) A raven-like woman
Brinna, Brenn, Bren, Brennah, Brina, Brena, Brenah

*****Brianna** (Irish) Feminine form of Brian; from the high hill; one who ascends
Breanna, Breanne, Breana, Breann, Breeana, Breeanna, Breona, Breonna, Bryana, Bryanna, Briana

Brice (Welsh) One who is alert; ambitious
Bryce

Bridget (Irish) A strong and protective woman; in mythology, goddess of fire, wisdom, and poetry
Bridgett, Bridgette, Briget, Brigette, Bridgit, Bridgitte, Birgit, Birgitte

Brie (French) Type of cheese
Bree, Breeyah, Bria, Briya, Briah, Briyah, Brya

^**Briella** (Italian/Spanish) Form of Gabriella, meaning "heroine of God"

Brielle (French) Form of Brie, meaning "type of cheese"

Brilliant (American) A dazzling and sparkling woman

^**Brisa** (Spanish) Beloved
Brisia, Brisha, Brissa, Briza, Bryssa, Brysa

^**Bristol** (English) From the city in England
Brystol, Bristow, Brystow

Brittany (English) A woman from Great Britain
Britany, Brittanie, Brittaney, Brittani, Brittanee, Britney, Britnee, Britny

*****Brook** (English) From the running stream
Brooke, Brookie

*****Brooklyn** (American) Borough of New York City
Brooklin, Brooklynn, Brooklynne

Brylee (American) Variation of Riley
Brilee, Brylie, Briley, Bryli

^**Brynley** (English) From the burnt meadow
Brynlee, Brynly, Brinley, Brinli, Brynlie

^**Brynn** (Welsh) Hill
Brin, Brinn, Bryn, Brynlee, Brynly, Brinley, Brinli, Brynlie

Bryony (English) Of the healing place
Briony, Brionee

Cabrina (American) Form of Sabrina, meaning "a legendary princess"
Cabrinah, Cabrinna

Cabriole (French) An adorable girl
Cabriolle, Cabrioll, Cabriol, Cabryole, Cabryolle, Cabryoll, Cabryol, Cabriola

Cacalia (Latin) Resembling the flowering plant
Cacaliah, Cacalea, Cacaleah

Caden (English) A battle maiden
Cadan, Cadin, Cadon

Cadence (Latin) Rhythmic and melodious; a musical woman
Cadena, Cadenza, Cadian, Cadienne, Cadianne, Cadiene, Caydence, Cadencia, Kadence, Kaydence

Caia (Latin) One who rejoices
Cai, Cais

Cailyn (Gaelic) A young woman
Cailin

Cainwen (Welsh) A beautiful treasure
Cainwenn, Cainwenne, Cainwin, Cainwinn, Cainwinne, Cainwyn, Cainwynn, Cainwynne

Cairo (African) From the city in Egypt

Caitlin (English) Form of Catherine, meaning one who is pure, virginal
Caitlyn, Catlin, Catline, Catlyn, Caitlan, Caitlinn, Caitlynn

Calais (French) From the city in France

Cale (Latin) A respected woman
Cayl, Cayle, Cael, Caele, Cail, Caile

Caledonia (Latin) Woman of Scotland
Caledoniah, Caledoniya, Caledona, Caledonya, Calydona

California (Spanish) From paradise; from the state of California
Califia

Calise (Greek) A gorgeous woman
Calyse, Calice, Calyce

Calista (Greek) Most beautiful; in mythology, a nymph who changed into a bear and then into the Great Bear constellation
Calissa, Calisto, Callista, Calyssa, Calysta, Calixte, Colista, Collista

Calla (Greek) Resembling a lily; a beautiful woman
Callah

Callie (Greek) A beautiful girl
Cali, Callee, Kali, Kallie

Calypso (Greek) A woman with secrets; in mythology, a nymph who captivated Odysseus for seven years

Camassia (American) One who is aloof
Camassiah, Camasia, Camasiah, Camassea, Camasseah, Camasea, Camaseah

Cambay (English) From the town in India
Cambaye, Cambai, Cambae

Cambria (Latin) A woman of Wales
Cambriah, Cambrea, Cambree, Cambre, Cambry, Cambrey, Cambri, Cambrie, Cambreah

Camdyn (English) Of the enclosed valley
Camden, Camdan, Camdon, Camdin

Cameron (Scottish) Having a crooked nose
Cameryn, Camryn, Camerin, Camren, Camrin, Camron

*Camila (Italian) Feminine form of Camillus; a ceremonial attendant; a noble virgin
Camile, Camille, Camilla, Camillia, Caimile, Camillei, Cam, Camelai

Campbell (Scottish) Having a crooked mouth
Campbel, Campbelle, Campbele

Candace (Ethiopian / Greek) A queen / one who is white and glowing
Candice, Candiss, Candyce, Candance, Candys, Candyss, Candy

Candida (Latin) White-skinned

Candra (Latin) One who is glowing

Candy (English) A sweet girl; form of Candida, meaning "white-skinned"; form of Candace, meaning "a queen / one who is white and glowing"
Candey, Candi, Candie, Candee, Candea, Candeah

Caneadea (Native American) From the horizon
Caneadeah, Caneadia, Caneadiah

Canika (American) A woman shining with grace
Canikah, Caneeka, Canicka, Canyka, Canycka, Caneekah, Canickah, Canykah

Canisa (Greek) One who is very much loved
Canisah, Canissa, Canysa, Caneesa, Canyssa

Cannes (French) A woman from Cannes

Cantabria (Latin) From the mountains
Cantabriah, Cantebria, Cantabrea, Cantebrea

Caprina (Italian) Woman of the island Capri
Caprinah, Caprinna, Capryna, Capreena, Caprena, Capreenah, Caprynah, Capriena

Cara (Italian / Gaelic) One who is dearly loved / a good friend
Carah, Caralee, Caralie, Caralyn, Caralynn, Carrah, Carra, Chara

Carina (Latin) Little darling
Carinna, Cariana, Carine, Cariena, Caryna, Carinna, Carynna

Carissa (Greek) A woman of grace
Carisa, Carrisa, Carrissa, Carissima

Carla (Latin) Feminine form of Carl; a free woman
Carlah, Carlana, Carleen, Carlena, Carlene, Carletta

Carlessa (American) One who is restless
Carlessah, Carlesa, Carlesah

Carly (American) Form of Carla, meaning "a free woman"
Carlee, Carleigh, Carli, Carlie, Carley

Carmel (Hebrew) Of the fruitful orchid
Carmela, Carmella, Karmel

Carmen (Latin) A beautiful song
Carma, Carmelita, Carmencita, Carmia, Carmie, Carmina, Carmine, Carmita

Carna (Latin) In mythology, a goddess who ruled the heart

Carni (Latin) One who is vocal
Carnie, Carny, Carney, Carnee, Carnea, Carneah, Carnia, Carniah

Carol (English) Form of Caroline, meaning "joyous song"; feminine form of Charles; a small, strong woman
Carola, Carole, Carolle, Carolla, Caroly, Caroli, Carolie, Carolee

*Caroline (Latin) Joyous song; feminine form of Charles; a small, strong woman
Carol, Carolina, Carolyn, Carolann, Carolanne, Carolena, Carolene, Carolena, Caroliana

Carrington (English) A beautiful woman; a woman of Carrington
Carington, Carryngton, Caryngton

Carson (Scottish) Son of the marshland
Carsan, Carsen, Carsin, Carsyn

Carys (Welsh) One who loves and is loved
Caryss, Carysse, Caris, Cariss, Carisse, Cerys, Ceryss, Cerysse

Casey (Greek / Irish) A vigilant woman
Casie, Casy, Caysie, Kasey

Cason (Greek) A seer
Cayson, Caison, Caeson

Cassandra (Greek) An unheeded prophetess; in mythology, King Priam's daughter who foretold the fall of Troy
Casandra, Cassandrea, Cassaundra, Cassondra, Cass, Cassy, Cassey, Cassi, Cassie

Cassidy (Irish) Curly-haired girl
Cassady, Cassidey, Cassidi, Cassidie, Cassidee, Cassadi, Cassadie, Cassadee, Casidhe, Cassidea, Cassadea

Casta (Spanish) One who is pure; chaste
Castah, Castalina, Castaleena, Castaleina, Castaliena, Castaleana, Castalyna, Castara

Catherine (English) One who is pure; virginal
Catharine, Cathrine, Cathryn, Catherin, Catheryn, Catheryna, Cathi, Cathy, Katherine, Catalina

Catrice (Greek) A wholesome woman
Catrise, Catryce, Catryse, Catreece, Catreese, Catriece

Cayenne (French) Resembling the hot and spicy pepper

Cayla (American) Form of Kaila, meaning "crowned with laurel"
Caila, Caylah, Cailah

Caylee (American) Form of Kayla, meaning "crowned with laurel"
Caleigh, Caley, Cayley, Cailey, Caili, Cayli

Cecilia (Latin) Feminine form of Cecil; one who is blind; patron saint of music
Cecelia, Cecile, Cecilee, Cicely, Cecily, Cecille, Cecilie, Cicilia, Sheila, Silka, Sissy, Celia

Celand (Latin) One who is meant for heaven
Celanda, Celande, Celandia, Celandea

Celandine (English) Resembling a swallow
Celandyne, Celandina, Celandyna, Celandeena, Celandena, Celandia

Celeste (Latin) A heavenly daughter
Celesta, Celestia, Celisse, Celestina, Celestyna, Celestine

Celia (Latin) Form of Cecelia, meaning patron saint of music

Celina (Latin) In mythology, one of the daughters of Atlas who was turned into a star of the Pleiades constellation; of the heavens; form of Selena, meaning "of the moon"
Celena, Celinna, Celene, Celenia, Celenne, Celicia

Celosia (Greek) A fiery woman; burning; aflame
Celosiah, Celosea, Celoseah

Cera (French) A colorful woman
Cerah, Cerrah, Cerra

Cerina (Latin) Form of Serena, meaning "having a peaceful disposition"
Cerinah, Ceryna, Cerynah, Cerena, Cerenah, Ceriena

Cerise (French) Resembling the cherry
Cerisa

Chadee (French) A divine woman; a goddess
Chadea, Chadeah, Chady, Chadey, Chadi, Chadie

Chai (Hebrew) One who gives life
Chae, Chaili, Chailie, Chailee, Chaileigh, Chaily, Chailey, Chailea

Chailyn (American)
Resembling a waterfall
Chailynn, Chailynne, Chaelyn,
Chaelynn, Chaelynne, Chaylyn

Chakra (Arabic) A center of
spiritual energy

Chalette (American) Having
good taste
Chalett, Chalet, Chalete,
Chaletta, Chaleta

Chalina (Spanish) Form
of Rosalina, meaning
"resembling a gentle horse /
resembling the beautiful and
meaningful flower"
Chalinah, Chalyna, Chaleena,
Chalena, Charo, Chaliena,
Chaleina, Chaleana

Chameli (Hindi) Resembling
jasmine
Chamelie, Chamely, Chameley,
Chamelee

Chan (Sanskrit) A shining
woman

Chana (Hebrew) Form of
Hannah, meaning "having
favor and grace"
Chanah, Channa, Chaanach,
Chaanah, Chanach, Channah

Chance (American) One who
takes risks
Chanci, Chancie, Chancee,
Chancea, Chanceah, Chancy,
Chancey

Chanda (Sanskrit) An enemy
of evil
Chandy, Chaand, Chand,
Chandey, Chandee, Chandi,
Chandie, Chandea

Chandra (Hindi) Of the moon;
another name for the goddess
Devi
Chandara, Chandria,
Chaundra, Chandrea,
Chandreah

Chanel (French) From the
canal; a channel
Chanell, Chanelle, Channelle,
Chenelle, Chenel, Chenell

Channary (Cambodian) Of the
full moon
Channarie, Channari, Channarey,
Channaree, Chantrea, Chantria

Chantrice (French) A singer
Chantryce, Chantrise, Chantryse

Charisma (Greek) Blessed with
charm
Charismah, Charizma,
Charysma, Karisma

Charity (Latin) A woman of
generous love
Charitey, Chariti, Charitie,
Charitee

Charlesia (American)
Feminine form of Charles;
small, strong woman
*Charlesiah, Charlesea,
Charleseah, Charlsie, Charlsi*

^**Charlie** (English) Form of
Charles, meaning "one who is
strong"
*Charlee, Charli, Charley,
Charlize, Charlene, Charlyn,
Charlaine, Charlisa, Charlena*

Charlotte (French) Form of
Charles, meaning "a small,
strong woman"
Charlize, Charlot, Charlotta

Charlshea (American) Filled
with happiness
*Charlsheah, Charlshia,
Charlshiah*

Charnee (American) Filled
with joy
*Charny, Charney, Charnea,
Charneah, Charni, Charnie*

Charnesa (American) One who
gets attention
Charnessa, Charnessah

Charsetta (American) An emo-
tional woman
*Charsett, Charsette, Charset,
Charsete, Charseta*

Chartra (American) A classy
lady
Chartrah

Charu (Hindi) One who is
gorgeous
Charoo, Charou

Chasia (Hebrew) One who is
protected; sheltered
*Chasiah, Chasea, Chaseah,
Chasya, Chasyah*

Chasidah (Hebrew) A religious
woman; pious
Chasida, Chasyda, Chasydah

Chavi (Egyptian) A precious
daughter
*Chavie, Chavy, Chavey,
Chavee, Chavea, Chaveah*

Chaya (Hebrew) Life
Chaia

Chedra (Hebrew) Filled with
happiness
Chedrah

Cheer (American) Filled with
joy
Cheere

Chekia (American) A saucy
woman
*Cheekie, Checki, Checkie,
Checky, Checkey, Checkee,
Checkea, Checkeah*

Chelone (English) Resembling
a flowering plant

Chelsea (English) From the
landing place for chalk
*Chelcie, Chelsa, Chelsee,
Chelseigh, Chelsey, Chelsi,
Chelsie, Chelsy*

Chemarin (French) A dark
beauty
*Chemarine, Chemaryn,
Chemareen, Chemarein,
Chemarien*

Chemda (Hebrew) A charismatic woman
Chemdah

Chenille (American) A soft-
skinned woman
*Chenill, Chenil, Chenile,
Chenilla, Chenila*

Cherika (French) One who is
dear
*Chericka, Cheryka, Cherycka,
Cherieka, Cheriecka, Chereika,
Chereicka, Cheryka*

Cherish (English) To be held
dear, valued

Cherry (English) Resembling a
fruit-bearing tree
*Cherrie, Cherri, Cherrey,
Cherree, Cherrea, Cherreah*

Chesney (English) One who
promotes peace
*Chesny, Chesni, Chesnie,
Chesnea, Chesneah, Chesnee*

Cheyenne (Native American)
Unintelligible speaker
*Chayanne, Cheyane, Cheyene,
Shayan, Shyann*

Chiante (Italian) Resembling
the wine
*Chianti, Chiantie, Chiantee,
Chianty, Chiantey, Chiantea*

Chiara (Italian) Daughter of
the light
Chiarah, Chiarra, Chiarrah

Chiba (Hebrew) One who
loves and is loved
*Chibah, Cheeba, Cheebah,
Cheiba, Cheibah, Chieba,
Chiebah, Cheaba*

Chidi (Spanish) One who is
cheerful
*Chidie, Chidy, Chidey, Chidee,
Chidea, Chideah*

Chidori (Japanese) Resembling
a shorebird
*Chidorie, Chidory, Chidorey,
Chidorea, Chidoreah, Chidoree*

Chikira (Spanish) A talented
dancer
*Chikirah, Chikiera, Chikierah,
Chikeira, Chikeirah, Chikeera,
Chikeerah, Chikyra*

Chiku (African) A talkative girl

Chinara (African) God receives
*Chinarah, Chinarra,
Chinarrah*

Chinue (African) God's own blessing
Chinoo, Chynue, Chynoo

Chiriga (African) One who is triumphant
Chyriga, Chyryga, Chiryga

Chislaine (French) A faithful woman
Chislain, Chislayn, Chislayne, Chislaen, Chislaene, Chyslaine, Chyslain, Chyslayn

Chitsa (Native American) One who is fair
Chitsah, Chytsa, Chytsah

Chizoba (African) One who is well-protected
Chizobah, Chyzoba, Chyzobah

*****Chloe** (Greek) A flourishing woman; blooming
Clo, Cloe, Cloey, Chloë

Christina (English) Follower of Christ
Christinah, Cairistiona, Christine, Christin, Christian, Christiana, Christiane, Christianna, Kristina, Cristine, Christal, Crystal, Chrystal, Cristal

Chula (Native American) Resembling a colorful flower
Chulah, Chulla, Chullah

Chulda (Hebrew) One who can tell fortunes
Chuldah

Chun (Chinese) Born during the spring

Chyou (Chinese) Born during autumn

Ciara (Irish) A dark beauty
Ceara, Ciaran, Ciarra, Ciera, Cierra, Ciere, Ciar, Ciarda

Cidrah (American) One who is unlike others
Cidra, Cydrah, Cydra

Cinnamon (American) Resembling the reddish-brown spice
Cinnia, Cinnie

Ciona (American) One who is steadfast
Cionah, Cyona, Cyonah

Claennis (Anglo-Saxon) One who is pure
Claenis, Claennys, Claenys, Claynnis, Claynnys, Claynys, Claynyss

*****Claire** (French) Form of Clara, meaning "famously bright"
Clare, Clair

Clancey (American) A light-hearted woman
Clancy, Clanci, Clancie, Clancee, Clancea, Clanceah

*Clara (Latin) One who is famously bright
Clarie, Clarinda, Clarine, Clarita, Claritza, Clarrie, Clarry, Clarabelle, Claire, Clarice

Clarice (French) A famous woman; also a form of Clara, meaning "one who is famously bright"
Claressa, Claris, Clarisa, Clarise, Clarisse, Claryce, Clerissa, Clerisse, Clarissa

Claudia (Latin / German / Italian) One who is lame
Claudelle, Gladys

Clelia (Latin) A glorious woman
Cloelia, Cleliah, Clelea, Cleleah, Cloeliah, Cloelea, Cloeleah

Clementine (French) Feminine form of Clement; one who is merciful
Clem, Clemence, Clemency, Clementia, Clementina, Clementya, Clementyna, Clementyn

Cleodal (Latin) A glorious woman
Cleodall, Cleodale, Cleodel, Cleodell, Cleodelle

Cleopatra (Greek) A father's glory; of the royal family
Clea, Cleo, Cleona, Cleone, Cleonie, Cleora, Cleta, Cleoni

Clever (American) One who is quick-witted and smart

Cloris (Greek) A flourishing woman; in mythology, the goddess of flowers
Clores, Clorys, Cloriss, Clorisse, Cloryss, Clorysse

Cloud (American) A light-hearted woman
Cloude, Cloudy, Cloudey, Cloudee, Cloudea, Cloudeah, Cloudi, Cloudie

Clydette (American) Feminine form of Clyde, meaning "from the river"
Clydett, Clydet, Clydete, Clydetta, Clydeta

Clymene (Greek) In mythology, the mother of Atlas and Prometheus
Clymena, Clymyne, Clymyn, Clymyna, Clymeena, Clymeina, Clymiena, Clymeana

Clytie (Greek) The lovely one; in mythology, a nymph who was changed into a sunflower
Clyti, Clytee, Clyty, Clytey, Clyte, Clytea, Clyteah

Coby (Hebrew) Feminine form of Jacob; the supplanter
Cobey, Cobi, Cobie, Cobee, Cobea, Cobeah

Coffey (American) A lovely woman
Coffy, Coffe, Coffee, Coffea, Coffeah, Coffi, Coffie

Coira (Scottish) Of the churning waters
Coirah, Coyra, Coyrah

Colanda (American) Form of Yolanda, meaning "resembling the violet flower; modest"
Colande, Coland, Colana, Colain, Colaine, Colane, Colanna, Corlanda, Calanda, Calando, Calonda, Colantha, Colanthe, Culanda, Culonda, Coulanda, Colonda

Cole (English) A swarthy woman; having coal-black hair
Col, Coal, Coale, Coli, Colie, Coly, Coley, Colee

Colette (French) Victory of the people
Collette, Kolette

Coligny (French) Woman from Cologne
Coligney, Colignie, Coligni, Colignee, Colignea, Coligneah

Colisa (English) A delightful young woman
Colisah, Colissa, Colissah, Colysa, Colysah, Colyssa, Colyssah

Colola (American) A victorious woman
Colo, Cola

Comfort (English) One who strengthens or soothes others
Comforte, Comfortyne, Comfortyna, Comforteene, Comforteena, Comfortene, Comfortena, Comfortiene

Conary (Gaelic) A wise woman
Conarey, Conarie, Conari, Conaree, Conarea, Conareah

Concordia (Latin) Peace and harmony; in mythology, goddess of peace
Concordiah, Concordea, Concord, Concorde, Concordeah

Constanza (American) One who is strong-willed
Constanzia, Constanzea

Consuela (Spanish) One who provides consolation
Consuelia, Consolata, Consolacion, Chela, Conswela, Conswelia, Conswelea, Consuella

Contessa (Italian) A titled woman; a countess
Countess, Contesse, Countessa, Countesa, Contesa

Cooper (English) One who makes barrels
Couper

Copper (American) A red-headed woman
Coper, Coppar, Copar

^**Cora** (English) A young maiden
Corah, Coraline, Corra

Coral (English) Resembling the semiprecious sea growth; from the reef
Coralee, Coralena, Coralie, Coraline, Corallina, Coralline, Coraly, Coralyn

Corazon (Spanish) Of the heart
Corazana, Corazone, Corazona

Cordelia (Latin) A good-hearted woman; a woman of honesty
Cordella, Cordelea, Cordilia, Cordilea, Cordy, Cordie, Cordi, Cordee

Corey (Irish) From the hollow; of the churning waters
Cory, Cori, Coriann, Corianne, Corie, Corri, Corrianna, Corrie

Corgie (American) A humorous woman
Corgy, Corgey, Corgi, Corgee, Corgea, Corgeah

Coriander (Greek) A romantic woman; resembling the spice
Coryander, Coriender, Coryender

Corina (Latin) A spear-wielding woman
Corinne, Corine, Corinna, Corrinne, Corryn, Corienne, Coryn, Corynna

Corinthia (Greek) A woman of Corinth
Corinthiah, Corinthe, Corinthea, Corintheah, Corynthia, Corynthea, Corynthe

Cornelia (Latin) Feminine form of Cornelius; referring to a horn
Cornalia, Corneelija, Cornela, Cornelija, Cornelya, Cornella, Cornelle, Cornie

Cota (Spanish) A lively woman
Cotah, Cotta, Cottah

Coty (French) From the river-bank
Cotey, Coti, Cotie, Cotee, Cotea, Coteah

Courtney (English) A courteous woman; courtly
Cordney, Cordni, Cortenay, Corteney, Cortland, Cortnee, Cortneigh, Cortney, Courteney

Covin (American) An unpredictable woman
Covan, Coven, Covyn, Covon

Coy (English) From the woods, the quiet place
Coye, Coi

Cree (Native American) A tribal name
Crei, Crey, Crea, Creigh

Cressida (Greek) The golden girl; in mythology, a woman of Troy
Cressa, Criseyde, Cressyda, Crissyda

Cristos (Greek) A dedicated and faithful woman
Crystos, Christos, Chrystos

Cwen (English) A royal woman; queenly
Cwene, Cwenn, Cwenne, Cwyn, Cwynn, Cwynne, Cwin, Cwinn

Cylee (American) A darling daughter
Cyleigh, Cyli, Cylie, Cylea, Cyleah, Cyly, Cyley

Cynthia (Greek) Moon goddess
Cinda, Cindy, Cinthia, Cindia, Cinthea

Cyrene (Greek) In mythology, a maiden-huntress loved by Apollo
Cyrina, Cyrena, Cyrine, Cyreane, Cyreana, Cyreene, Cyreena

Czigany (Hungarian) A gypsy girl; one who moves from place to place
Cziganey, Czigani, Cziganie, Cziganee

D

Dacey (Irish) Woman from the south
Daicey, Dacee, Dacia, Dacie, Dacy, Daicee, Daicy, Daci

Daffodil (French) Resembling the yellow flower
Daffodill, Daffodille, Dafodil, Dafodill, Dafodille, Daff, Daffodyl, Dafodyl

Dagmar (Scandinavian) Born
on a glorious day
*Dagmara, Dagmaria,
Dagmarie, Dagomar,
Dagomara, Dagomaria,
Dagmarr, Dagomarr*

Dahlia (Swedish) From the val-
ley; resembling the flower
*Dahlea, Dahl, Dahiana,
Dayha, Daleia, Dalia*

Daira (Greek) One who is well-
informed
Daeira, Danira, Dayeera

Daisy (English) Of the day's
eye; resembling a flower
*Daisee, Daisey, Daisi, Daisie,
Dasie, Daizy, Daysi, Deysi*

Dakota (Native American) A
friend to all
*Dakotah, Dakotta, Dakoda,
Dakodah*

Damali (Arabic) A beautiful
vision
*Damalie, Damaly, Damaley,
Damalee, Damaleigh, Damalea*

Damani (American) Of a
bright tomorrow
*Damanie, Damany, Damaney,
Damanee, Damanea,
Damaneah*

Damaris (Latin) A gentle woman
*Damara, Damaress, Damariss,
Damariz, Dameris, Damerys,
Dameryss, Damiris*

Dana (English) Woman from
Denmark
*Danna, Daena, Daina,
Danaca, Danah, Dane, Danet,
Daney, Dania*

Danica (Slavic) Of the morning
star
Danika

Daniela (Spanish) Form of
Danielle, meaning "God is
my judge"
Daniella

Danielle (Hebrew) Feminine
form of Daniel; God is my
judge
*Daanelle, Danee, Danele,
Danella, Danelle, Danelley,
Danette, Daney*

^Danna (American) Variation
of Dana, meaning woman
from Denmark
Dannah

Daphne (Greek) Of the laurel
tree; in mythology, a virtuous
woman transformed into a
laurel tree to protect her from
Apollo
*Daphna, Daphney, Daphni,
Daphnie, Daffi, Daffie, Daffy,
Dafna*

Darby (English) Of the deer park
Darb, Darbee, Darbey, Darbie, Darrbey, Darrbie, Darrby, Derby, Larby

Daria (Greek) Feminine form of Darius; possessing good fortune; wealthy
Dari, Darian, Dariane, Darianna, Dariele, Darielle, Darien, Darienne

Daring (American) One who takes risks; a bold woman
Daryng, Derring, Dering, Deryng

Darlene (English) Our little darling
Dareen, Darla, Darleane, Darleen, Darleena, Darlena, Darlenny, Darlina

Daryn (Greek) Feminine form of Darin; a gift of God
Darynn, Darynne, Darinne, Daren, Darenn, Darene

Dawn (English) Born at daybreak; of the day's first light
Dawna, Dawne, Dawnelle, Dawnetta, Dawnette, Dawnielle, Dawnika, Dawnita

Day (American) A father's hope for tomorrow
Daye, Dai, Dae

Daya (Hebrew) Resembling a bird of prey
Dayah, Dayana, Dayanara, Dayania, Dayaniah, Dayanea, Dayaneah

Dayton (English) From the sunny town
Dayten, Daytan

Dea (Greek) Resembling a goddess
Deah, Diya, Diyah

Deborah (Hebrew) Resembling a bee; in the Bible, a prophetess
Debbera, Debbey, Debbi, Debbie, Debbra, Debby

Deidre (Gaelic) A brokenhearted or raging woman
Deadra, Dede, Dedra, Deedra, Deedre, Deidra, Deirdre, Deidrie

Deiondre (American) From the lush valley
Deiondra, Deiondria, Deiondrea, Deiondriya

Deja (French) One of remembrance
Dayja, Dejah, Daejah, Daijia, Daija, Daijah, Deijah, Deija

Dekla (Latvian) In mythology, a trinity goddess
Decla, Deckla, Deklah, Decklah, Declah

Delaney (Irish / French) The dark challenger / from the elder-tree grove
Delaina, Delaine, Delainey, Delainy, Delane, Delanie, Delany, Delayna

Delaware (English) From the state of Delaware
Delawair, Delaweir, Delwayr, Delawayre, Delawaire, Delawaer, Delawaere

Delilah (Hebrew) A seductive woman
Delila, Delyla, Delylah

Delta (Greek) From the mouth of the river; the fourth letter of the Greek alphabet
Dellta, Deltah, Delltah

Delyth (Welsh) A pretty young woman
Delythe, Delith, Delithe

Demeter (Greek) In mythology, the goddess of the harvest
Demetra, Demitra, Demitras, Dimetria, Demetre, Demetria, Dimitra, Dimitre

Demi (Greek) A petite woman
Demie, Demee, Demy, Demiana, Demianne, Demianna, Demea

Denali (Indian) A superior woman
Denalie, Denaly, Denally, Denalli, Denaley, Denalee, Denallee, Denallie

Dendara (Egyptian) From the town on the river
Dendera, Dendaria, Denderia, Dendarra

Denise (French) Feminine form of Dennis; a follower of Dionysus
Denese, Denyse, Denice, Deniece, Denisa, Denissa, Denize, Denyce, Denys

Denver (English) From the green valley

Derora (Hebrew) As free as a bird
Derorah, Derorra, Derorit, Drora, Drorah, Drorit, Drorlya, Derorice

Derry (Irish) From the oak grove
Derrey, Derri, Derrie, Derree, Derrea, Derreah

Deryn (Welsh) A birdlike woman
Derran, Deren, Derhyn, Deron, Derrin, Derrine, Derron, Derrynne

Desiree (French) One who is desired
Desaree, Desirae, Desarae, Desire, Desyre, Dezirae, Deziree, Desirat

*Destiny (English) Recognizing one's certain fortune; fate
Destanee, Destinee, Destiney, Destini, Destinie, Destine, Destina, Destyni

Deva (Hindi) A divine being
Devi, Daeva

Devera (Latin) In mythology, goddess of brooms
Deverah

Devon (English) From the beautiful farmland; of the divine
Devan, Deven, Devenne, Devin, Devona, Devondra, Devonna, Devonne, Devyn

Dextra (Latin) Feminine form of Dexter; one who is skillful
Dex

Dharma (Hindi) The universal law of order
Darma

Dhisana (Hindi) In Hinduism, goddess of prosperity
Dhisanna, Disana, Disanna, Dhysana

Dhyana (Hindi) One who meditates

Diamond (French) Woman of high value
Diamanta, Diamonique, Diamante

Diana (Latin) Of the divine; in mythology, goddess of the moon and the hunt
Dianna, Dayanna, Dayana, Deanna

Diane (Latin) Form of Diana, meaning "of the divine"
Dayann, Dayanne, Deana, Deane, Deandra, Deann

Diata (African) Resembling a lioness
Diatah, Dyata, Diatta, Dyatah, Dyatta, Diattah, Dyattah

Dido (Latin) In mythology, the queen of Carthage who committed suicide
Dydo

Dielle (Latin) One who worships God
Diele, Diell, Diella, Diela, Diel

Dimity (English) Resembling a sheer cotton fabric
Dimitee, Dimitey, Dimitie, Dimitea, Dimiteah, Dimiti

Dimona (Hebrew) Woman
from the south
*Dimonah, Dymona, Demona,
Demonah, Dymonah*

Disa (English) Resembling an
orchid

Discordia (Latin) In mythol-
ogy, goddess of strife
*Dyscordia, Diskordia,
Dyskordia*

Diti (Hindi) In Hinduism, an
earth goddess
*Dyti, Ditie, Dytie, Dity, Dyty,
Ditey, Dytey, Ditee*

Dixie (English) Woman from
the South
Dixi, Dixy, Dixey, Dixee

Dolores (Spanish) Woman of
sorrow; refers to the Virgin
Mary
*Dalores, Delora, Delores,
Deloria, Deloris, Dolorcita,
Dolorcitas, Dolorita*

Domina (Latin) An elegant
lady
Dominah, Domyna, Domynah

Dominique (French) Feminine
form of Dominic; born on the
Lord's day
*Domaneke, Domanique,
Domenica, Domeniga,
Domenique, Dominee,
Domineek, Domineke*

Doreen (French / Gaelic)
The golden one / a brooding
woman
*Dorene, Doreyn, Dorine, Dorreen,
Doryne, Doreena, Dore,
Doirean, Doireann, Doireanne,
Doireana, Doireanna*

Dorothy (Greek) A gift of God
*Dasha, Dasya, Dodie, Dody,
Doe, Doll, Dolley, Dolli*

Dove (American) Resembling
a bird of peace
Duv

Drisana (Indian) Daughter of
the sun
*Dhrisana, Drisanna, Drysana,
Drysanna, Dhrysana,
Dhrisanna, Dhrysanna*

Drury (French) One who is
greatly loved
*Drurey, Druri, Drurie, Druree,
Drurea, Drureah*

Duana (Irish) Feminine form
of Dwayne; little, dark one
*Duane, Duayna, Duna,
Dwana, Dwayna, Dubhain,
Dubheasa*

Duena (Spanish) One who acts
as a chaperone

Dulce (Latin) A very sweet
woman
Dulcina, Dulcee, Dulcie

Dumia (Hebrew) One who is silent
Dumiya, Dumiah, Dumiyah, Dumea, Dumeah

Duvessa (Irish) A dark beauty
Duvessah, Duvesa, Dubheasa, Duvesah

^Dylan (Welsh) Daughter of the waves
Dylana, Dylane, Dyllan, Dyllana, Dillon, Dillan, Dillen, Dillian

Dympna (Irish) Fawn; the patron saint of the insane
Dymphna, Dimpna, Dimphna

Dyre (Scandinavian) One who is dear to the heart

Dysis (Greek) Born at sunset
Dysiss, Dysisse, Dysys, Dysyss, Dysysse

E

Eadlin (Anglo-Saxon) Born into royalty
Eadlinn, Eadlinne, Eadline, Eadlyn, Eadlynn, Eadlynne, Eadlina, Eadlyna

Eadrianne (American) One who stands out
Eadrian, Eadriann, Edriane, Edriana, Edrianna

Eara (Scottish) Woman from the east
Earah, Earra, Earrah, Earia, Earea, Earie, Eari, Earee

Earla (English) A great leader
Earlah

Earna (English) Resembling an eagle
Earnah, Earnia, Earnea, Earniah, Earneah

Easter (American) Born during the religious holiday
Eastere, Eastre, Eastir, Eastar, Eastor, Eastera, Easteria, Easterea

Easton (American) A wholesome woman
Eastan, Easten, Eastun, Eastyn

Eathelin (English) Noble woman of the waterfall
Eathelyn, Eathelinn, Eathelynn, Eathelina, Eathelyna, Ethelin, Ethelyn, Eathelen

Eber (Hebrew) One who moves beyond

Ebere (African) One who shows mercy
Eberre, Ebera, Eberia, Eberea, Eberria, Eberrea, Ebiere, Ebierre

Ebony (Egyptian) A dark
beauty
*Eboni, Ebonee, Ebonie,
Ebonique, Eboney, Ebonea,
Eboneah*

Ebrill (Welsh) Born in April
*Ebrille, Ebril, Evril, Evrill,
Evrille*

Edana (Irish) Feminine form
of Aidan; a fiery woman
*Edanah, Edanna, Ena,
Eideann, Eidana*

Eden (Hebrew) Place of pleasure
Edan, Edin, Edon

Edith (English) The spoils of
war; one who is joyous; a
treasure
*Edyth, Eda, Edee, Edie, Edita,
Edelina, Edeline, Edelyne,
Edelynn, Edalyn, Edalynn,
Edita, Edyta, Eydie*

Edna (Hebrew) One who
brings pleasure; a delight
Ednah, Edena, Edenah

Edra (English) A powerful and
mighty woman
*Edrah, Edrea, Edreah, Edria,
Edriah*

Eduarda (Portugese) Feminine
form of Edward; a wealthy
protector
*Eduardia, Eduardea, Edwarda,
Edwardia, Edwardea,
Eduardina, Eduardyna,
Edwardina*

Edurne (Basque) Feminine form
of Edur; woman of the snow
*Edurna, Edurnia, Edurnea,
Edurniya*

Egan (American) A wholesome
woman
Egann, Egen, Egun, Egon

Egeria (Latin) A wise counselor; in mythology, a water
nymph
*Egeriah, Egerea, Egereah,
Egeriya, Egeriyah*

Eileen (Gaelic) Form of Evelyn,
meaning "a birdlike woman"
*Eila, Eileene, Eilena, Eilene,
Eilin, Eilleen, Eily, Eilean*

Eiluned (Welsh) An idol wor-
shipper
Luned

Eilwen (Welsh) One with a fair
brow
*Eilwenne, Eilwin, Eilwinne,
Eilwyn, Eilwynne*

Eirene (Greek) Form of Irene, meaning "a peaceful woman"
Eireen, Eireene, Eiren, Eir, Eireine, Eirein, Eirien, Eiriene

Eires (Greek) A peaceful woman
Eiress, Eiris, Eiriss, Eirys, Eiryss

Eirian (Welsh) One who is bright and beautiful
Eiriann, Eiriane, Eiriana, Eirianne, Eirianna

Ekron (Hebrew) One who is firmly rooted
Eckron, Ecron

Elaine (French) Form of Helen, meaning "the shining light"
Ellaine, Ellayne, Elaina, Elayna, Elayne, Elaene, Elaena, Ellaina

Elana (Hebrew) From the oak tree
Elanna, Elanah, Elanie, Elani, Elany, Elaney, Elanee, Elan

Elata (Latin) A high-spirited woman
Elatah, Elatta, Elattah, Elatia, Elatea, Elatiah, Elateah

Elath (Hebrew) From the grove of trees
Elathe, Elatha, Elathia, Elathea

Eldora (Greek) A gift of the sun
Eleadora, Eldorah, Eldorra, Eldoria, Eldorea

Eldoris (Greek) Woman of the sea
Eldorise, Eldoriss, Eldorisse, Eldorys, Eldoryss, Eldorysse

Eleacie (American) One who is forthright
Eleaci, Eleacy, Eleacey, Eleacee, Eleacea

Eleanor (Greek) Form of Helen, meaning "the shining light"
Eleanora, Eleni, Eleonora, Eleonore, Elinor, Elnora, Eleanore, Elinora, Nora

Elena (Spanish) Form of Helen, meaning "the shining light"
Elenah, Eleena, Eleenah, Elyna, Elynah, Elina, Elinah, Eleni, Eliana

Eliana (Hebrew) The Lord answers our prayers
Eleana, Elia, Eliane, Elianna, Elianne, Eliann, Elyana, Elyanna, Elyann, Elyan, Elyanne

Elica (German) One who is noble
Elicah, Elicka, Elika, Elyca, Elycka, Elyka, Elsha, Elsje

Elida (English) Resembling a winged creature
Elidah, Elyda, Eleeda, Eleda, Elieda, Eleida, Eleada

Elika (Hebrew) God will judge
Elikah, Elyka, Elicka, Elycka, Elica, Elyca

^**Elisa** (English) Form of Elizabeth, meaning "my God is bountiful"
Elisha, Elishia, Elissa, Elisia, Elysa, Elysha, Elysia, Elyssa

Elise (English) Form of Elizabeth, meaning "my God is bountiful"
Elle, Elice, Elisse, Elyse, Elysse, Ilyse

Elita (Latin) The chosen one
Elitah, Elyta, Elytah, Eleta, Eletah, Elitia, Elitea, Electa

*****Elizabeth** (Hebrew) My God is bountiful; God's promise
Liz, Elisabet, Elisabeth, Elisabetta, Elissa, Eliza, Elizabel, Elizabet, Elsa, Beth, Babette, Libby, Lisa, Itzel, Ilsabeth, Ilsabet

*****Ella** (German) From a foreign land
Elle, Ellee, Ellesse, Elli, Ellia, Ellie, Elly, Ela

Ellen (English) Form of Helen, meaning "the shining light"
Elin, Elleen, Ellena, Ellene, Ellyn, Elynn, Elen, Ellin

Ellery (English) Form of Hilary, meaning "a cheerful woman"
Ellerey, Elleri, Ellerie, Elleree, Ellerea, Ellereah

Elliana (Hebrew) The Lord answers our prayers
Eliana

*****Ellie** (English) Form of Eleanor, meaning "the shining light"
Elli, Elly, Elley, Elleigh

^**Ellyanne** (American) A shining and gracious woman
*Ellianne, Ellyanna, **Ellianna**, Ellyann, Elliann, Ellyan, Ellian*

Elma (German) Having God's protection
Elmah

^**Eloisa** (Latin) Form of Louise, meaning "a famous warrior"
***Eloise**, Eloiza, Eloisee, Eloize, Eloizee, Aloisa, Aloise*

Elrica (German) A great ruler
Elricah, Elrika, Elrikah, Elryca, Elrycah, Elryka, Elrykah, Elrick

^**Elsie** (English) Form of Elizabeth, meaning "my god is bountiful"

Elvia (Irish) A friend of the elves
Elva, Elvie, Elvina, Elvinia, Elviah, Elvea, Elveah, Elvyna

Elvira (Latin) A truthful woman; one who can be trusted
Elvera, Elvita, Elvyra

Ema (Polynesian / German) One who is greatly loved / a serious woman

Ember (English) A low-burning fire
Embar, Embir, Embyr

Emerson (German) Offspring of Emery
Emmerson, Emyrson

Emery (German) Industrious
Emeri, Emerie, Emori, Emorie, Emory

*Emily** (Latin) An industrious and hardworking woman
Emilee, Emilie, Emilia, Emelia, Emileigh, Emeleigh, Emeli, Emelie, Emely, Emmalee

*Emma** (German) One who is complete; a universal woman
Emmy, Emmajean, Emmalee, Emmi, Emmie, Emmaline, Emelina, Emeline

Emmylou (American) A universal ruler
Emmilou, Emmielou, Emylou, Emilou, Emielou

Ena (Irish) A fiery and passionate woman
Enah, Enat, Eny, Enya

Encarnación (Spanish) Refers to the Incarnation festival

Engracia (Spanish) A graceful woman
Engraciah, Engracea, Engraceah

Enslie (American) An emotional woman
Ensli, Ensley, Ensly, Enslee, Enslea, Ensleigh

Eranthe (Greek) As delicate as a spring flower
Erantha, Eranth, Eranthia, Eranthea

Erasta (African) A peaceful woman

Ercilia (American) One who is frank
Erciliah, Ercilea, Ercileah, Ercilya, Ercilyah, Erciliya, Erciliyah

Erendira (Spanish) Daughter born into royalty
Erendirah, Erendiria, Erendirea, Erendyra, Erendyria, Erendyrea, Erendeera, Erendiera

Erica (Scandinavian / Latin) Feminine form of Eric; ever the ruler / resembling heather
Erika, Ericka, Erikka, Eryka, Erike, Ericca, Erics, Eiric, Rica

Erimentha (Greek) A devoted protector
Erimenthe, Erimenthia, Erimenthea

Erin (Gaelic) Woman from Ireland
Erienne, Erina, Erinn, Erinna, Erinne, Eryn, Eryna, Erynn, Arin

Ernestina (German) Feminine form of Ernest; one who is determined; serious
Ernesta, Ernestine, Ernesha

Esdey (American) A warm and caring woman
Essdey, Esdee, Esdea, Esdy, Esdey, Esdi, Esdie, Esday

Eshah (African) An exuberant woman
Esha

Eshe (African) Giver of life
Eshey, Eshay, Esh, Eshae, Eshai

Esme (French) An esteemed woman
Esmai, Esmae, Esmay, Esmaye, Esmee

Esmeralda (Spanish) Resembling a prized emerald
Esmerald, Emerald, Emeralda, Emelda, Esma

Esne (English) Filled with happiness
Esnee, Esney, Esnea, Esni, Esnie, Esny

Essence (American) A perfumed woman
Essince, Esense, Esince, Essynce, Esynce

Esthelia (Spanish) A shining woman
Estheliah, Esthelea, Estheleah, Esthelya, Esthelyah, Estheliya, Estheliyah

Esther (Persian) Resembling the myrtle leaf
Ester, Eszter, Eistir, Eszti

Estrella (Spanish) Star
Estrela

Estrid (Norse) Form of Astrid, meaning "one with divine strength"
Estread, Estreed, Estrad, Estri, Estrod, Estrud, Estryd, Estrida

Etana (Hebrew) A strong and dedicated woman
Etanah, Etanna, Etannah, Etania, Etanea, Ethana, Ethanah, Ethania

Etaney (Hebrew) One who is focused
Etany, Etanie, Etani, Etanee, Etanea

Eternity (American) Lasting forever
Eternitie, Eterniti, Eternitey, Eternitee, Eternyty, Eternyti, Eternytie, Eternytee

Ethna (Irish) A graceful woman
Ethnah, Eithne, Ethne, Eithna, Eithnah

Eudlina (Slavic) A generous woman
Eudlinah, Eudleena, Eudleenah

Eudocia (Greek) One who is esteemed
Eudociah, Eudocea, Eudoceah

Eugenia (Greek) A well-born woman
Eugenie, Gina, Zenechka

Eulanda (American) A fair woman
Eulande, Euland, Eulandia, Eulandea

Eunice (Greek) One who conquers
Eunise, Eunyce, Eunis, Euniss, Eunyss, Eunysse

Eurybia (Greek) In mythology, a sea goddess and mother of Pallas, Perses, and Astraios
Eurybiah, Eurybea, Eurybeah

Eurynome (Greek) In mythology, the mother of the Graces
Eurynomie, Eurynomi

Euvenia (American) A hardworking woman

*Eva** (Hebrew) Giver of life; a lively woman
Eve, Evetta, Evette, Evia, Eviana, Evie, Evita, Eeva

^**Evangeline** (Greek) A bringer of good news
Evangelina, Evangelyn

*Evelyn** (German) A bird-like woman
Evaleen, Evalina, Evaline, Evalyn, Evelin, Evelina, Eveline, Evelyne, Eileen, Evelynn

Evline (French) One who loves nature
Evleen, Evleene, Evlean, Evleane, Evlene, Evlyn, Evlyne

F

Faillace (French) A delicate and beautiful woman
Faillase, Faillaise, Falace, Falase, Fallase, Fallace

Fairly (English) From the far meadow
Fairley, Fairlee, Fairleigh, Fairli, Fairlie, Faerly, Faerli, Faerlie

Faith (English) Having a belief and trust in God
Faythe, Faithe, Faithful, Fayana, Fayanna, Fayanne, Fayane, Fayth

Fakhira (Arabic) A magnificent woman
Fakhirah, Fakhyra, Fakhyrah, Fakheera, Fakira, Fakirah, Fakeera, Fakyra

Fala (Native American) Resembling a crow
Falah, Falla, Fallah

Fallon (Irish) A commanding woman
Fallyn, Faline, Falinne, Faleen, Faleene, Falynne, Falyn, Falina

Fantasia (Latin) From the fantasy land
Fantasiah, Fantasea, Fantasiya, Fantazia, Fantazea, Fantaziya

Farley (English) From the fern clearing
Farly, Farli, Farlie, Farlee, Farleigh, Farlea, Farleah

Fate (Greek) One's destiny
Fayte, Faite, Faete, Faet, Fait, Fayt

Fatima (Arabic) The perfect woman
Fatimah, Fahima, Fahimah

Fatinah (Arabic) A captivating woman
Fatina, Fateena, Fateenah, Fatyna, Fatynah, Fatin, Fatine, Faatinah, Fateana, Fateanah, Fatiena, Fatienah, Fateina, Fateinah

Favor (English) One who grants her approval
Faver, Favar, Favorre

Fay (English) From the fairy kingdom; a fairy or an elf
Faye, Fai, Faie, Fae, Fayette, Faylinn, Faylyn, Faylynn

Fayina (Russian) An independent woman
Fayinah, Fayena, Fayeena, Fayeana, Fayiena, Fayeina

February (American) Born in the month of February
Februari, Februarie, Februarey, Februaree, Februarea

Feechi (African) A woman who worships God
Feechie, Feechy, Feechey, Feechee, Fychi, Fychie, Fychey, Fychy

Felicity (Latin) Form of Felicia, meaning "happy"
Felicy, Felicie, Felisa

Femi (African) God loves me
Femmi, Femie, Femy, Femey, Femee, Femea, Femeah

Fenia (Scandinavian) A gold worker
Feniah, Fenea, Feneah, Feniya, Feniyah, Fenya, Fenyah, Fenja

Fernanda (Spanish) Feminine form of Fernando; an adventurous woman

Fernilia (American) A successful woman
Ferniliah, Fernilea, Fernileah, Fernilya, Fernilyah

Fia (Portuguese / Italian / Scottish) A weaver / from the flickering fire / arising from the dark of peace
Fiah, Fea, Feah, Fya, Fiya, Fyah, Fiyah

Fianna (Irish) A warrior huntress
Fiannah, Fiana, Fianne, Fiane, Fiann, Fian

Fielda (English) From the field
Fieldah, Felda, Feldah

Fife (American) Having dancing eyes
Fyfe, Fifer, Fify, Fifey, Fifee, Fifea, Fifi, Fifie

Fifia (African) Born on a Friday
Fifiah, Fifea, Fifeah, Fifeea, Fifeeah

Filipa (Spanish) Feminine form of Phillip; a friend of horses
Filipah, Filipina, Filipeena, Filipyna, Filippa, Fillipa, Fillippa

Fina (English) Feminine form of Joseph; God will add
Finah, Feena, Fyna, Fifine, Fifna, Fifne, Fini, Feana

^**Finley** (Gaelic) A fair-haired hero
Finlay, Finly, Finlee, Finli, Finlie, Finnley, Finnlee, Finnli, Finn, Fin

Finnea (Gaelic) From the stream of the wood
Finneah, Finnia, Fynnea, Finniah, Fynnia

Fiona (Gaelic) One who is fair; a white-shouldered woman
Fionna, Fione, Fionn, Finna, Fionavar, Fionnghuala, Fionnuala, Fynballa

Firdaus (Arabic) From the garden in paradise

Flair (English) An elegant woman of natural talent
Flaire, Flare, Flayr, Flayre, Flaer, Flaere

Flame (American) A passionate and fiery woman
Flaym, Flayme, Flaime, Flaim, Flaem, Flaeme

Flannery (Gaelic) From the flatlands
Flanery, Flanneri, Flannerie, Flannerey, Flannaree, Flannerea

Fleming (English) Woman from Belgium
Flemyng, Flemming, Flemmyng

Fleta (English) One who is swift
Fletah, Flete, Fleda, Flita, Flyta

Florence (Latin) A flourishing woman; a blooming flower
Florencia, Florentina, Florenza, Florentine, Florentyna, Florenteena, Florenteene, Florentyne

Florizel (English) A young woman in bloom
Florizell, Florizelle, Florizele, Florizel, Florizella, Florizela, Florazel, Florazell

Fola (African) Woman of honor
Folah, Folla, Follah

Fontenot (French) One who is special

Forest (English) A woodland dweller
Forrest

Forever (American) Everlasting

Francesca (Italian) Form of Frances, meaning "one who is free"
Francia, Francina, Francisca, Franchesca, Francie, Frances

Frederica (German) Peaceful ruler
Freda, Freida, Freddie, Rica

Freira (Spanish) A sister
Freirah, Freyira, Freyirah

Freya (Norse) A lady
Freyah, Freyja, Freja

Freydis (Norse) Woman born into the nobility
Freydiss, Freydisse, Freydys, Fredyss, Fraidis, Fradis, Fraydis, Fraedis

Frida (German) Peaceful
Frieda, Fryda

Fuchsia (Latin) Resembling the flower
Fusha, Fushia, Fushea, Fewsha, Fewshia, Fewshea

Fury (Greek) An enraged woman; in mythology, a winged goddess who punished wrongdoers
Furey, Furi, Furie, Furee

G

*Gabriella (Italian / Spanish) Feminine form of Gabriel; heroine of God
Gabriela, Gabriellia, Gabrila, Gabryela, Gabryella

Gabrielle (Hebrew) Feminine form of Gabriel; heroine of God
Gabriel, Gabriela, Gabriele, Gabriell, Gabriellen, Gabriellia, Gabrila

Galena (Greek) Feminine form of Galen; one who is calm and peaceful
Galene, Galenah, Galenia, Galenea

Galiana (Arabic) The name of a Moorish princess
Galianah, Galianna, Galianne, Galiane, Galian, Galyana, Galyanna, Galyann

Galila (Hebrew) From the rolling hills
Galilah, Gelila, Gelilah, Gelilia, Gelilya, Glila, Glilah, Galyla

Galilee (Hebrew) From the sacred sea
Galileigh, Galilea, Galiley, Galily, Galili, Galilie

Galina (Russian) Form of Helen, meaning "the shining light"
Galinah, Galyna, Galynah, Galeena, Galeenah, Galine, Galyne, Galeene

Garbi (Basque) One who is pure; clean
Garbie, Garby, Garbey, Garbee, Garbea, Garbeah

Gardenia (English) Resembling the sweet-smelling flower
Gardeniah, Gardenea, Gardyna

Garima (Indian) A woman of importance
Garimah, Garyma, Gareema

Garnet (English) Resembling the dark-red gem
Garnette, Granata, Grenata, Grenatta

Gasha (Russian) One who is well-behaved
Gashah, Gashia, Gashea, Gashiah, Gasheah

Gavina (Latin) Feminine form of Gavin; resembling the white falcon; woman from Gabio

Gaza (Hebrew) Having great strength
Gazah, Gazza, Gazzah

Geila (Hebrew) One who brings joy to others
Geela, Geelah, Geelan, Geilah, Geiliya, Geiliyah, Gelisa, Gellah

^**Gemma** (Latin) As precious as a jewel
Gemmalyn, Gemmalynn, Gem, Gema, Gemmaline, Jemma

***Genesis** (Hebrew) Of the beginning; the first book of the Bible
Genesies, Genesiss, Genessa, Genisis

Genevieve (French) White wave; fair-skinned
Genavieve, Geneve, Genevie, Genivee, Genivieve, Genoveva, Gennie, Genny

Georgia (Greek) Feminine form of George; one who works the earth; a farmer; from the state of Georgia
Georgeann, Georgeanne, Georgina, Georgena, Georgene, Georgetta, Georgette, Georgiana, Jeorjia

Gerardine (English) Feminine form of Gerard; one who is mighty with a spear
Gerarda, Gerardina, Gerardyne, Gererdina, Gerardyna, Gerrardene, Gerhardina, Gerhardine

Gertrude (German) Adored warrior
Geertruide, Geltruda, Geltrudis, Gert, Gerta, Gerte, Gertie, Gertina, Trudy

^**Gia** (Italian) Form of Gianna, meaning "God is Gracious"
Giah

Giada (Italian) Jade
Giadda

***Gianna** (Italian) Feminine form of John, meaning "God is gracious"
Gia, Giana, Giovana

Gillian (Latin) One who is youthful
Gilian, Giliana, Gillianne, Ghilian

Gina (Japanese / English) A silvery woman / form of Eugenia, meaning "a well-born woman"; form of Jean, meaning "God is gracious"
Geana, Geanndra, Geena, Geina, Gena, Genalyn, Geneene, Genelle

Ginger (English) A lively woman; resembling the spice
Gingee, Gingie, Ginjer, Gingea, Gingy, Gingey, Gingi

Ginny (English) Form of Virginia, meaning "one who is chaste; virginal"
Ginnee, Ginnelle, Ginnette, Ginnie, Ginnilee, Ginna, Ginney, Ginni

Giona (Italian) Resembling the bird of peace
Gionah, Gionna, Gyona, Gyonna, Gionnah, Gyonah, Gyonnah

Giovanna (Italian) Feminine form of Giovanni; God is gracious
Geovana, Geovanna, Giavanna, Giovana, Giovani, Giovanni, Giovanie, Giovanee

Giselle (French) One who offers her pledge
Gisel, Gisela, Gisella, Jiselle

Gita (Hindi / Hebrew) A beautiful song / a good woman
Gitah, Geeta, Geetah, Gitika, Gatha, Gayatri, Gitel, Gittel

Gitana (Spanish) A gypsy woman
Gitanah, Gitanna, Gitannah, Gitane

Githa (Anglo-Saxon) A gift from God
Githah, Gytha

^**Giulia** (Italian) Form of Julia, meaning "one who is youthful, daughter of the sky"
Giuliana, Giulie, Giulietta, Giuliette

Gladys (Welsh) Form of Claudia, meaning "one who is lame"
Gladdis, Gladdys, Gladi, Gladis, Gladyss, Gwladys, Gwyladyss, Gleda

Glenna (Gaelic) From the valley between the hills
Gleana, Gleneen, Glenene, Glenine, Glen, Glenn, Glenne, Glennene

Glenys (Welsh) A holy woman
Glenice, Glenis, Glennice, Glennis, Glennys, Glynis

Gloria (Latin) A renowned and highly praised woman
Gloriana, Glorianna, Glorya, Glorie, Gloree, Gloriane

Golda (English) Resembling the precious metal
Goldarina, Goldarine, Goldee, Goldi, Goldie, Goldina, Goldy, Goldia

Gordana (Serbian / Scottish) A proud woman / one who is heroic
Gordanah, Gordanna, Gordania, Gordaniya, Gordanea, Gordannah, Gordaniah, Gordaniyah

*****Grace** (Latin) Having God's favor; in mythology, the Graces were the personification of beauty, charm, and grace
Gracee, Gracella, Gracelynn, Gracelynne, Gracey, Gracia, Graciana, Gracie, Gracelyn

Gracie (Latin) Form of Grace, meaning "having God's favor"
Gracee, Gracey, Graci

Granada (Spanish) From the Moorish kingdom
Granadda, Grenada, Grenadda

Greer (Scottish) Feminine form of Gregory; one who is alert and watchful
Grear, Grier, Gryer

Gregoria (Latin) Feminine form of Gregory; one who is alert and watchful
Gregoriana, Gregorijana, Gregorina, Gregorine, Gregorya, Gregoryna, Gregorea, Gregoriya

Greta (German) Resembling a pearl
Greeta, Gretal, Grete, Gretel, Gretha, Grethe, Grethel, Gretna, Gretchen

Guadalupe (Spanish) From the valley of wolves
Guadelupe, Lupe, Lupita

Gudny (Swedish) One who is unspoiled
Gudney, Gudni, Gudnie, Gudne, Gudnee, Gudnea, Gudneah

Guinevere (Welsh) One who is fair; of the white wave; in mythology, King Arthur's queen
Guenever, Guenevere, Gueniver, Guenna, Guennola, Guinever, Guinna, Gwen

Guiseppina (Italian) Feminine
form of Guiseppe; the Lord
will add
*Giuseppyna, Giuseppa,
Giuseppia, Giuseppea,
Guiseppie, Guiseppia,
Guiseppa, Giuseppina*

Gulielma (German) Feminine
form of Wilhelm; determined
protector
*Guglielma, Guillelmina,
Guillielma, Gulielmina,
Guillermina*

Gulinar (Arabic) Resembling
the pomegranate
*Gulinare, Gulinear, Gulineir,
Gulinara, Gulinaria,
Gulinarea*

Gwendolyn (Welsh) One who
is fair; of the white ring
*Guendolen, Guendolin,
Guendolinn, Guendolynn,
Guenna, Gwen, Gwenda,
Gwendaline, Wendy*

Gwyneth (Welsh) One who is
blessed with happiness
*Gweneth, Gwenith, Gwenyth,
Gwineth, Gwinneth, Gwinyth,
Gwynith, Gwynna*

Gytha (English) One who is
treasured
Gythah

H

Habbai (Arabic) One who is
much loved
Habbae, Habbay, Habbaye

Habiba (Arabic) Feminine
form of Habib; one who is
dearly loved; sweetheart
Habibah, Habeeba, Habyba

Hachi (Native American /
Japanese) From the river /
having good fortune
*Hachie, Hachee, Hachiko,
Hachiyo, Hachy, Hachey,
Hachikka*

Hadara (Hebrew) A spectacu-
lar ornament; adorned with
beauty
*Hadarah, Hadarit, Haduraq,
Hadarra, Hadarrah*

Hadassah (Hebrew) From the
myrtle tree
Hadassa, Hadasah, Hadasa

Hadiya (Arabic) A gift from
God; a righteous woman
*Hadiyah, Hadiyyah,
Haadiyah, Haadiya, Hadeeya,
Hadeeyah, Hadieya, Hadieyah*

Hadlai (Hebrew) In a resting state; one who hinders
Hadlae, Hadlay, Hadlaye

^**Hadley** (English) From the field of heather
Hadlea, Hadleigh, Hadly, Hedlea, Hedleigh, Hedley, Hedlie, Hadlee

Hadria (Latin) From the town in northern Italy
Hadrea, Hadriana, Hadriane, Hadrianna, Hadrien, Hadrienne, Hadriah, Hadreah

Hafthah (Arabic) One who is protected by God
Haftha

Hagab (Hebrew) Resembling a grasshopper
Hagabah, Hagaba, Hagabe

Hagai (Hebrew) One who has been abandoned
Hagae, Hagay, Hagaye, Haggai, Haggae, Hagie, Haggie, Hagi

Hagen (Irish) A youthful woman
Hagan, Haggen, Haggan

Haggith (Hebrew) One who rejoices; the dancer
Haggithe, Haggyth, Haggythe, Hagith, Hagithe, Hagyth, Hagythe

Haidee (Greek) A modest woman; one who is well-behaved
Hadee, Haydee, Haydy, Haidi, Haidie, Haydi, Haydie, Haidy

***Hailey** (English) from the field of hay
*Haley, Hayle, Hailee, **Haylee**, Haylie, Haleigh, Hayley, Haeleigh*

Haimati (Indian) A queen of the snow-covered mountains
Haimatie, Haimaty, Haimatey, Haimatee, Haymati, Haymatie, Haymatee, Haimatea

Haimi (Hawaiian) One who searches for the truth
Haimie, Haimy, Haimey, Haimee, Haymi, Haymie, Haymee, Haimea

Hakana (Turkish) Feminine form of Hakan; ruler of the people; an empress
Hakanah, Hakanna, Hakane, Hakann, Hakanne

Hakkoz (Hebrew) One who has the qualities of a thorn
Hakoz, Hakkoze, Hakoze, Hakkoza, Hakoza

Halak (Hebrew) One who is bald; smooth

Haleigha (Hawaiian) Born with the rising sun
Haleea, Haleya, Halya

Hall (American) One who is distinguished
Haul

Hallie (Scandinavian / Greek / English) From the hall / woman of the sea / from the field of hay
Halley, Hallie, Halle, Hallee, Hally, Halleigh, Hallea, Halleah

Halo (Latin) Having a blessed aura
Haylo, Haelo, Hailo

Halsey (American) A playful woman
Halsy, Halsee, Halsea, Halsi, Halsie, Halcie, Halcy, Halcey

Halyn (American) A unique young woman
Halynn, Halynne, Halin, Halinn, Halinne

Hammon (Hebrew) Of the warm springs

Hamula (Hebrew) Feminine form of Hamul; spared by God
Hamulah, Hamulla, Hamullah

Hana (Japanese / Arabic) Resembling a flower blossom / a blissful woman
Hanah, Hanako

Hanan (Arabic) One who shows mercy and compassion

Hang (Vietnamese) Of the moon

Hanika (Hebrew) A graceful woman
Hanikah, Haneeka, Haneekah, Hanyka, Hanykah, Haneika, Haneikah, Hanieka

Hanita (Indian) Favored with divine grace
Hanitah, Hanyta, Haneeta, Hanytah, Haneetah, Haneita, Haneitah, Hanieta

Haniyah (Arabic) One who is pleased; happy
Haniya, Haniyyah, Haniyya, Hani, Hanie, Hanee, Hany, Haney

*Hannah (Hebrew) Having favor and grace; in the Bible, mother of Samuel
Hanalee, Hanalise, Hanna, Hanne, Hannele, Hannelore, Hannie, Hanny, Chana

Hanya (Aboriginal) As solid as a stone

Happy (American) A joyful woman
Happey, Happi, Happie, Happee, Happea

Hara (Hebrew) From the mountainous land
Harah, Harra, Harrah

Haradah (Hebrew) One who is filled with fear
Harada

Harika (Turkish) A superior woman
Harikah, Haryka, Hareeka, Harykah, Hareekah, Hareaka, Hareakah

Hariti (Indian) In mythology, the goddess for the protection of children
Haritie, Haryti, Harytie, Haritee, Harytee, Haritea, Harytea

Harley (English) From the meadow of the hares
Harlea, Harlee, Harleen, Harleigh, Harlene, Harlie, Harli, Harly

Harlow (American) An impetuous woman

Harmony (English / Latin) Unity / musically in tune
Harmonie, Harmoni, Harmonee

*Harper (English) One who plays or makes harps

Harriet (German) Feminine form of Henry; ruler of the house
Harriett, Hanriette, Hanrietta, Harriette, Harrietta, Harrette

Harva (English) A warrior of the army

Hasibah (Arabic) Feminine form of Hasib; one who is noble and respected
Hasiba, Hasyba, Hasybah, Haseeba, Haseebah

Hasina (African) One who is good and beautiful
Hasinah, Hasyna, Hasynah

Haurana (Hebrew) Feminine form of Hauran; woman from the caves
Hauranna, Hauranah, Haurann, Hauranne

Haven (English) One who provides a safe haven
Hayven, Havan, Hayvan, Havon, Hayvon, Havin, Hayvin, Havyn, Hayvyn, Haeven, Haevin, Haevan

Havva (Turkish) A giver of the breath of life
Havvah, Havvia, Havviah

Hayden (English) From the hedged valley
Haden, Haydan, Haydn, Haydon, Haeden, Haedyn, Hadyn

Hayud (Arabic) From the mountain
Hayuda, Hayudah, Hayood, Hayooda

Hazel (English) From the
hazel tree
*Hazell, Hazelle, Haesel, Hazle,
Hazal, Hayzel, Haezel, Haizel*

Heartha (Teutonic) A gift from
Mother Earth

Heather (English) Resembling
the evergreen flowering plant
Hether, Heatha, Heath, Heathe

Heaven (American) From
paradise; from the sky
*Heavely, Heavenly, Hevean,
Hevan, Heavynne, Heavenli,
Heavenlie, Heavenleigh,
Heavenlee, Heavenley,
Heavenlea, Heavyn*

Hecate (Greek) In mythology, a goddess of fertility and
witchcraft
Hekate

Heidi (German) Of the nobility,
serene
Heidy, Heide, Hydie

Heirnine (Greek) Form of
Helen, meaning "the shining
light"
*Heirnyne, Heirneine,
Heirniene, Heirneene,
Heirneane*

Helen (Greek) The shining
light; in mythology, Helen
was the most beautiful
woman in the world
*Helene, Halina, Helaine,
Helana, Heleena, Helena,
Helenna, Hellen, Aleen, Elaine,
Eleanor, Elena, Ellen, Galina,
Heirnine, Helice, Leanna,
Yalena*

Helia (Greek) Daughter of the
sun
*Heliah, Helea, Heleah, Heliya,
Heliyah, Heller, Hellar*

Helice (Greek) Form of Helen,
meaning "the shining light"
*Helyce, Heleece, Heliece,
Heleace*

Helike (Greek) In mythology, a
willow nymph who nurtured
Zeus
*Helica, Helyke, Helika, Helyka,
Helyca*

Helle (Greek) In mythology,
the daughter of Athamas who
escaped sacrifice on the back
of a golden ram

Helma (German) Form of
Wilhelmina, meaning "deter-
mined protector"
*Helmah, Helmia, Helmea,
Helmina, Helmyna, Helmeena,
Helmine, Helmyne*

Heloise (French) One who is famous in battle
Helois, Heloisa, Helewidis

Hen (English) Resembling the mothering bird

Henrietta (German) Feminine form of Henry; ruler of the house
Henretta, Henrieta, Henriette, Henrika, Henryetta, Hetta, Hette, Hettie

Hephzibah (Hebrew) She is my delight
Hepsiba, Hepzibeth, Hepsey

Herdis (Scandinavian) A battle maiden
Herdiss, Herdisse, Herdys

Hermelinda (Spanish) Bearing a powerful shield
Hermelynda, Hermalinda, Hermalynda, Hermelenda

Hermia (Greek) Feminine form of Hermes; a messenger of the gods
Hermiah, Hermea, Hermila

Hermona (Hebrew) From the mountain peak
Hermonah, Hermonna

Hernanda (Spanish) One who is daring
Hernandia, Hernandea, Hernandiya

Herra (Greek) Daughter of the earth
Herrah

Hersala (Spanish) A lovely woman
Hersalah, Hersalla, Hersallah, Hersalia, Hersaliah, Hersalea, Hersaleah

Hesiena (African) The first-born of twins
Hesienna, Hesienah, Heseina

Hesione (Greek) In mythology, a Trojan princess saved by Hercules from a sea monster

Hester (Greek) A starlike woman
Hestere, Hesther, Hesta, Hestar

Heven (American) A pretty young woman
Hevin, Hevon, Hevun, Hevven, Hevvin, Hevvon, Hevvun

Hezer (Hebrew) A woman of great strength
Hezir, Hezyr, Hezire, Hezyre, Hezere

Hiah (Korean) A bright woman
Heija, Heijah, Hia

Hibiscus (Latin) Resembling the showy flower
Hibiskus, Hibyscus, Hibyskus, Hybiscus, Hybiskus, Hybyscus, Hybyskus

Hikmah (Arabic) Having great wisdom
Hikmat, Hikma

Hilan (Greek) Filled with happiness
Hylan, Hilane, Hilann, Hilanne, Hylane, Hylann, Hylanne

Hilary (Latin) A cheerful woman
Hillary, Hillery, Ellery

Hina (Polynesian) In mythology, a dual goddess symbolizing day and night
Hinna, Henna, Hinaa, Hinah, Heena, Hena

Hind (Arabic) Owning a group of camels; a wife of Muhammed
Hynd, Hinde, Hynde

Hinda (Hebrew) Resembling a doe
Hindah, Hindy, Hindey, Hindee, Hindi, Hindie, Hynda, Hyndy

Hiriwa (Polynesian) A silvery woman

Hitomi (Japanese) One who has beautiful eyes
Hitomie, Hitomee, Hitomea, Hitomy, Hitomey

Holda (German) A secretive woman; one who is hidden
Holde

Hollander (Dutch) A woman from Holland
Hollynder, Hollender, Holander, Holynder, Holender, Hollande, Hollanda

Holly (English) Of the holly tree
Holli, Hollie, Hollee, Holley, Hollye, Hollyanne, Holle, Hollea

Holton (American) One who is whimsical
Holten, Holtan, Holtin, Holtyn, Holtun

Holy (American) One who is pious or sacred
Holey, Holee, Holeigh, Holi, Holie, Holye, Holea, Holeah

Hope (English) One who has high expectations through faith

Hortensia (Latin) Woman of the garden
Hartencia, Hartinsia, Hortencia, Hortense, Hortenspa, Hortenxia, Hortinzia, Hortendana

Hova (African) Born into the middle class

Hoyden (American) A spirited woman
Hoiden, Hoydan, Hoidan, Hoydyn, Hoidyn, Hoydin, Hoidin

Hudson (English) One who is adventurous; an explorer
Hudsen, Hudsan, Hudsun, Hudsyn, Hudsin

Hueline (German) An intelligent woman
Huelene, Huelyne, Hueleine, Hueliene, Hueleene, Huleane

Huhana (Maori) Form of Susannah, meaning "white lily"
Huhanah, Huhanna, Huhanne, Huhann, Huhane

Humita (Native American) One who shells corn
Humitah, Humyta, Humeeta, Humieta, Humeita, Humeata, Humytah, Humeetah

Hutena (Hurrian) In mythology, the goddess of fate
Hutenah, Hutenna, Hutyna, Hutina

Huwaidah (Arabic) One who is gentle
Huwaydah, Huwaida

Huyen (Vietnamese) A woman with jet-black hair

Hypatia (Greek) An intellectually superior woman
Hypasia, Hypacia, Hypate

Hypermnestra (Greek) In mythology, the mother of Amphiareos

I

Ianthe (Greek) Resembling the violet flower; in mythology, a sea nymph, a daughter of Oceanus
Iantha, Ianthia, Ianthina

Ibtesam (Arabic) One who smiles often
Ibtisam, Ibtysam

Ibtihaj (Arabic) A delight; bringer of joy
Ibtehaj, Ibtyhaj

Ida (Greek) One who is diligent; hardworking; in mythology, the nymph who cared for Zeus on Mount Ida
Idania, Idaea, Idalee, Idaia, Idania, Idalia, Idalie, Idana

Idil (Latin) A pleasant woman
Idyl, Idill, Idyll

Idoia (Spanish) Refers to the Virgin Mary
Idoea, Idurre, Iratze, Izazkun

Idona (Scandinavian) A fresh-faced woman
Idonah, Idonna, Idonnah

Ife (African) One who loves and is loved
Ifeh, Iffe

Ignatia (Latin) A fiery woman; burning brightly
Igantiah, Ignacia, Ignazia

Iheoma (Hawaiian) Lifted up by God

Ikeida (American) A spontaneous woman
Ikeidah, Ikeyda, Ikeydah

Ilamay (French) From the island
Ilamaye, Ilamai, Ilamae

Ilandere (American) Moon woman
Ilander, Ilanderre, Ilandera, Ilanderra

Ilia (Greek) From the ancient city
Iliah, Ilea, Ileah, Iliya, Iliyah, Ilya, Ilyah

Iliana (English) Form of Aileen, meaning, "the light-bearer"
Ilianna, Ilyana, Ilyanna, Ilene, Iline, Ilyne

Ilithyia (Greek) In mythology, goddess of childbirth
Ilithya, Ilithiya, Ilithyiah

Ilma (German) Form of Wilhelmina, meaning "determined protector"
Ilmah, Illma, Illmah

Ilori (African) A special child; one who is treasured
Illori, Ilorie, Illorie, Ilory, Illory, Ilorey, Illorey, Iloree

Ilta (Finnish) Born at night
Iltah, Illta

Ilyse (German / Greek) Born into the nobility / form of Elyse, meaning "blissful"
Ilysea, Ilysia, Ilysse, Ilysea

Imala (Native American) One who disciplines others
Imalah, Imalla, Imallah, Immala, Immalla

Iman (Arabic) Having great faith
Imani, Imanie, Imania, Imaan, Imany, Imaney, Imanee, Imanea, Imain, Imaine, Imayn

Imanuela (Spanish) A faithful
woman
*Imanuella, Imanuel, Imanuele,
Imanuell*

Imari (Japanese) Daughter of
today
*Imarie, Imaree, Imarea, Imary,
Imarey*

Imelda (Italian) Warrior in the
universal battle
Imeldah, Imalda, Imaldah

Imperia (Latin) A majestic
woman
*Imperiah, Imperea, Impereah,
Imperial, Imperiel, Imperielle,
Imperialle*

Ina (Polynesian) In mythology,
a moon goddess
Inah, Inna, Innah

Inaki (Asian) Having a gener-
ous nature
*Inakie, Inaky, Inakey, Inakea,
Inakee*

Inanna (Sumerian) A lady
of the sky; in mythology,
goddess of love, fertility,
war, and the earth
*Inannah, Inana, Inanah,
Inann, Inanne, Inane*

Inara (Arabic) A heaven-sent
daughter; one who shines
with light
Inarah, Innara, Inarra, Innarra

Inari (Finnish / Japanese)
Woman from the lake / one
who is successful
*Inarie, Inaree, Inary, Inarey,
Inarea, Inareah*

Inaya (Arabic) One who cares
for the well-being of others
Inayah, Inayat

Inca (Indian) An adventurer
*Incah, Inka, Inkah, Incka,
Inckah*

India (English) From the river;
woman from India
*Indea, Indiah, Indeah, Indya,
Indiya, Indee, Inda, Indy*

Indiana (English) From the
land of the Indians; from the
state of Indiana
Indianna, Indyana, Indyanna

Indiece (American) A capable
woman
*Indeice, Indeace, Indeece,
Indiese, Indeise, Indeese,
Indease*

Indigo (English) Resembling
the plant; a purplish-blue dye
Indygo, Indeego

Ineesha (American) A
sparkling woman
*Ineeshah, Ineisha, Ineishah,
Iniesha, Inieshah, Ineasha,
Ineashah, Ineysha*

Ingalls (American) A peaceful woman

Ingelise (Danish) Having the grace of the god Ing
Ingelisse, Ingeliss, Ingelyse, Ingelisa, Ingelissa, Ingelysa, Ingelyssa

Inghean (Scottish) Her father's daughter
Ingheane, Inghinn, Ingheene, Ingheen, Inghynn

Ingrid (Scandinavian) Having the beauty of the God Ing
Ingred, Ingrad, Inga, Inge, Inger, Ingmar, Ingrida, Ingria, Ingrit, Inkeri

Inis (Irish) Woman from Ennis
Iniss, Inisse, Innis, Inys, Innys, Inyss, Inysse

Intisar (Arabic) One who is victorious; triumphant
Intisara, Intisarah, Intizar, Intizara, Intizarah, Intisarr, Intysarr, Intysar

Iolanthe (Greek) Resembling a violet flower
Iolanda, Iolanta, Iolantha, Iolante, Iolande, Iolanthia, Iolanthea

Iona (Greek) Woman from the island
Ionna, Ioane, Ioann, Ioanne

Ionanna (Hebrew) Filled with grace
Ionannah, Ionana, Ionann, Ionane, Ionanne

Ionia (Greek) Of the sea and islands
Ionya, Ionija, Ioniah, Ionea, Ionessa, Ioneah, Ioniya

Iosepine (Hawaiian) Form of Josephine, meaning "God will add"
Iosephine, Iosefa, Iosefena, Iosefene, Iosefina, Iosefine, Iosepha, Iosephe

Iowa (Native American) Of the Iowa tribe; from the state of Iowa

Iphedeiah (Hebrew) One who is saved by the Lord

Iphigenia (Greek) One who is born strong; in mythology, daughter of Agamemnon
Iphigeneia, Iphigenie

Ipsa (Indian) One who is desired
Ipsita, Ipsyta, Ipseeta, Ipseata, Ipsah

Iratze (Basque) Refers to the Virgin Mary
Iratza, Iratzia, Iratzea, Iratzi, Iratzie, Iratzy, Iratzey, Iratzee

Ireland (Celtic) The country of the Irish
Irelan, Irelann

Irem (Turkish) From the heavenly gardens
Irema, Ireme, Iremia, Iremea

Irene (Greek) A peaceful woman; in mythology, the goddess of peace
Ira, Irayna, Ireen, Iren, Irena, Irenea, Irenee, Irenka, Eirene

Ireta (Greek) One who is serene
Iretah, Iretta, Irettah, Irete, Iret, Irett, Ireta

Iris (Greek) Of the rainbow; a flower; a messenger goddess
Irida, Iridiana, Iridianny, Irisa, Irisha, Irita, Iria, Irea, Iridian, Iriss, Irys, Iryss

Irma (German) A universal woman

Irta (Greek) Resembling a pearl
Irtah

Irune (Basque) Refers to the Holy Trinity
Iroon, Iroone, Iroun, Iroune

*Isabel (Spanish) Form of Elizabeth, meaning "my God is bountiful; God's promise"
Isabeau, Isabela, Isabele, Isabelita, Isabell, Isabelle, Ishbel, Ysabel

*Isabella (Italian / Spanish) Form of Isabel, meaning consecrated to God
Isabela, Isabelita, Isobella, Izabella, Isibella, Isibela

Isadore (Greek) A gift from the goddess Isis
Isadora, Isador, Isadoria, Isidor, Isidoro, Isidorus, Isidro, Isidora

Isana (German) A strong-willed woman
Isanah, Isanna, Isane, Isann

Isela (American) A giving woman
Iselah, Isella, Isellah

Isis (Egyptian) In mythology, the most powerful of all goddesses

Isla (Gaelic) From the island
Islae, Islai, Isleta

Isleen (Gaelic) Form of Aisling, meaning "a dream or vision; an inspiration"
Isleene, Islyne, Islyn, Isline, Isleine, Isliene, Islene, Isleyne

Isolde (Celtic) A woman known for her beauty; in mythology, the lover of Tristan
Iseult, Iseut, Isold, Isolda, Isolt, Isolte, Isota, Isotta

Isra (Arabic) One who travels in the evening
Israh, Isria, Isrea, Israt

Itiah (Hebrew) One who is comforted by God
Itia, Iteah, Itea, Itiyah, Itiya, Ityah, Itya

Itidal (Arabic) One who is cautious
Itidalle, Itidall, Itidale

Itsaso (Basque) Woman of the ocean
Itasasso, Itassaso, Itassasso

Iudita (Hawaiian) An affectionate woman
Iuditah, Iudyta, Iudytah, Iudeta, Iudetah

Iuginia (Hawaiian) A high-born woman
Iuginiah, Iuginea, Iugineah, Iugynia

Ivana (Slavic) Feminine form of Ivan; God is gracious
Iva, Ivah, Ivania, Ivanka, Ivanna, Ivanya, Ivanea, Ivane, Ivanne

Ivory (English) Having a creamy-white complexion; as precious as elephant tusks
Ivorie, Ivorine, Ivoreen, Ivorey, Ivoree, Ivori, Ivoryne, Ivorea

Ivy (English) Resembling the evergreen vining plant
Ivie, Ivi, Ivea

Iwilla (American) She shall rise
Iwillah, Iwilah, Iwila, Iwylla, Iwyllah, Iwyla, Iwylah

Ixchel (Mayan) The rainbow lady; in mythology, the goddess of the earth, moon, and healing
Ixchell, Ixchelle, Ixchela, Ixchella, Ixchal, Ixchall, Ixchalle, Ixchala

Iyabo (African) The mother is home

Izanne (American) One who calms others
Izann, Izane, Izana, Izan, Izanna

Izolde (Greek) One who is philosophical
Izold, Izolda

J

Jacey (American) Form of Jacinda, meaning "resembling the hyacinth"
Jacee, Jacelyn, Jaci, Jacine, Jacy, Jaicee, Jaycee, Jacie

Jacinda (Spanish) Resembling the hyacinth
Jacenda, Jacenia, Jacenta, Jacindia, Jacinna, Jacinta, Jacinth, Jacintha, Jacinthe, Jacinthia, Jacynth, Jacyntha, Jacynthe, Jacynthia, Jakinda, Jakinta, Jaikinda, Jaekinda

Jacqueline (French) Feminine form of Jacques; the supplanter
Jackie, Xaquelina, Jacalin, Jacalyn, Jacalynn, Jackalin, Jackalinne, Jackelyn, Jacquelyn

Jade (Spanish) Resembling the green gemstone
Jadeana, Jadee, Jadine, Jadira, Jadrian, Jadrienne, Jady

Jaden (Hebrew / English) One who is thankful to God / form of Jade, meaning "resembling the green gemstone"
Jadine, Jadyn, Jadon, Jayden, Jadyne, Jaydyn, Jaydon, Jaidyn

Jadzia (Polish) A princess; born into royalty
Jadziah, Jadzea, Jadzeah

Jae (English) Feminine form of Jay; resembling a jaybird
Jai, Jaelana, Jaeleah, Jaelyn, Jaenelle, Jaya

Jael (Hebrew) Resembling a mountain goat
Jaella, Jaelle, Jayel, Jaele, Jayil

Jaen (Hebrew) Resembling an ostrich
Jaena, Jaenia, Jaenea, Jaenne

Jaffa (Hebrew) A beautiful woman
Jaffah, Jafit, Jafita

Jalila (Arabic) An important woman; one who is exalted
Jalilah, Jalyla, Jalylah, Jaleela

Jamaica (American) From the island of springs
Jamaeca, Jamaika, Jemaica, Jamika, Jamieka

Jamie (Hebrew) Feminine form of James; she who supplants
Jaima, Jaime, Jaimee, Jaimelynn, Jaimey, Jaimi, Jaimie, Jaimy

Janan (Arabic) Of the heart and soul

Jane (Hebrew) Feminine form of John; God is gracious
Jaina, Jaine, Jainee, Janey, Jana, Janae, Janaye, Jandy, Sine, Janel, Janelle

Janet (Scottish) Feminine form of John, meaning "God is gracious"
Janetta, Jenetta, Janeta, Janette, Janit

Janis (English) Feminine form of John; God is gracious
Janice, Janeece, Janess, Janessa, Janesse, Janessia, Janicia, Janiece

Janiyah (American) Form of Jana, meaning gracious, merciful
Janiya, Janiah

Jarah (Hebrew) A sweet and kind woman

Jasher (Hebrew) One who is righteous; upright
Jashiere, Jasheria, Jasherea

Jaslene (American) Form of Jocelyn, meaning joy
Jaslin, Jaslyn, Jazlyn, Jazlynn

*****Jasmine** (Persian) Resembling the climbing plant with fragrant flowers
Jaslyn, Jaslynn, Jasmin, Jasmyn, Jazmin, Jazmine, Jazmyn

Javiera (Spanish) Feminine form of Xavier; one who is bright; the owner of a new home
Javierah, Javyera, Javyerah, Javeira, Javeirah

Jayda (English) Resembling the green gemstone
***Jada**, Jaydah, Jaida, Jaidah*

^**Jayla** (Arabic) One who is charitable
*Jaela, Jaila, Jaylah, Jaylee, Jaylen, Jaylene, **Jayleen**, Jaylin, Jaylyn, Jaylynn*

Jean (Hebrew) Feminine form of John; God is gracious
Jeanae, Jeanay, Jeane, Jeanee, Jeanelle, Jeanetta, Jeanette, Jeanice, Gina

Jemima (Hebrew) Our little dove; in the Bible, the eldest of Job's daughters
Jemimah, Jamina, Jeminah, Jemmimah, Jemmie, Jemmy, Jem, Jemmi, Jemmey, Jemmee, Jemmea

Jemma (English) Form of Gemma, meaning "as precious as a jewel"
Jemmah, Jema, Jemah, Jemmalyn, Jemalyn

Jena (Arabic) Our little bird
Jenna, Jenah

Jendayi (Egyptian) One who is thankful
Jendayie, Jendayey, Jendayee

Jennifer (Welsh) One who is fair; a beautiful girl
Jenefer, Jeni, Jenifer, Jeniffer, Jenn, Jennee, Jenni, Jen, **Jenna,** *Jenny*

Jeorjia (American) Form of Georgia, meaning "one who works the earth; a farmer"
Jeorgia, Jeorja, Jorja, Jorjette, Jorgette, Jorjeta, Jorjetta, Jorgete

Jereni (Slavic) One who is peaceful
Jerenie, Jereny, Jereney, Jerenee

Jermaine (French) Woman from Germany
Jermainaa, Jermane, Jermayne, Jermina, Jermana, Jermayna

Jessica (Hebrew) The Lord sees all
Jess, Jessa, Jessaca, Jessaka, Jessalin, Jessalyn, Jesse, Jesseca, Yessica, Jessie

Jetta (Danish) Resembling the jet-black lustrous gemstone
Jette, Jett, Jeta, Jete, Jettie, Jetty, Jetti, Jettey

Jewel (French) One who is playful; resembling a precious gem
Jewell, Jewelle, Jewelyn, Jewelene, Jewelisa, Jule, Jewella, Juelline

Jezebel (Hebrew) One who is not exalted; in the Bible, the queen of Israel punished by God
Jessabell, Jetzabel, Jezabel, Jezabella, Jezebelle, Jezibel, Jezibelle, Jezybell

Jie (Chinese) One who is pure; chaste

Jiera (Lithuanian) A lively woman
Jierah, Jyera, Jyerah, Jierra, Jyerra

Jillian (English) Form of Gillian, meaning "one who is youthful"
Jilian, Jiliana, Jillaine, Jillan, Jillana, Jillane, Jillanne, Jillayne, Jillene, Jillesa, Jilliana, Jilliane, Jilliann, Jillianna, Jill

Jimena (Spanish) One who is heard

Jinelle (Welsh) Form of Genevieve, meaning "white wave; fair-skinned"
Jinell, Jinele, Jinel, Jynelle, Jynell, Jynele, Jynel

Jiselle (American) Form of Giselle, meaning "one who offers her pledge"
Jisell, Jisele, Jisela, Jizelle, Joselle, Jisella, Jizella, Jozelle

Jo (English) Feminine form of Joseph; God will add
Jobelle, Jobeth, Jodean, Jodelle, Joetta, Joette, Jolinda, Jolisa

Joanna (French) Feminine form of John, meaning "God is Gracious"
Joana

*Jocelyn (German / Latin) From the tribe of Gauts / one who is cheerful, happy
Jocelin, Jocelina, Jocelinda, Joceline, Jocelyne, Jocelynn, Jocelynne, Josalind, Joslyn, Joslynn, Joselyn

Joda (Hebrew) An ancestor of Christ

Jolan (Greek) Resembling a violet flower
Jola, Jolaine, Jolande, Jolanne, Jolanta, Jolantha, Jolandi, Jolanka

Jolene (English) Feminine form of Joseph; God will add
Joeline, Joeleen, Joeline, Jolaine, Jolean, Joleen, Jolena, Jolina

Jolie (French) A pretty young woman
Joly, Joely, Jolee, Joleigh, Joley, Joli

Jonina (Israeli) Resembling a little dove
Joninah, Jonyna, Jonynah, Joneena, Joneenah, Jonine, Jonyne, Joneene

Jorah (Hebrew) Resembling an autumn rose
Jora

Jord (Norse) In mythology, goddess of the earth
Jorde

Jordan (Hebrew) Of the down-flowing river; in the Bible, the river where Jesus was baptized
Jardena, Johrdan, Jordain, Jordaine, Jordana, Jordane, Jordanka, Jordyn, Jordin

Josephine (French) Feminine form of Joseph; God will add
Josefina, Josephene, Jo, Josie, Iosepine

Journey (American) One who likes to travel
Journy, Journi, Journie, Journee

Jovana (Spanish) Feminine form of Jovian; daughter of the sky
Jeovana, Jeovanna, Jovanna, Jovena, Jovianne, Jovina, Jovita, Joviana

Joy (Latin) A delight; one who brings pleasure to others
Jioia, Jioya, Joi, Joia, Joie, Joya, Joyann, Joyanna

Joyce (English) One who brings joy to others
Joice, Joyceanne, Joycelyn, Joycelynn, Joyse, Joyceta

Judith (Hebrew) Woman from Judea
Judithe, Juditha, Judeena, Judeana, Judyth, Judit, Judytha, Judita, Hudes

*Julia (Latin) One who is youthful; daughter of the sky
Jiulia, Joleta, Joletta, Jolette, Julaine, Julayna, Julee, Juleen, Julie, Julianne

Juliana (Spanish) Form of Julia, meaning "one who is youthful"
Julianna

Juliet (French) Form of Julia, meaning one who is youthful
Juliette, Julitta, Julissa

July (Latin) Form of Julia, meaning "one who is youthful; daughter of the sky"; born during the month of July
Julye

^June (Latin) One who is youthful; born during the month of June
Junae, Junel, Junelle, Junette, Junita, Junia

Justice (English) One who upholds moral rightness and fairness
Justyce, Justiss, Justyss, Justis, Justus, Justise

Kachina (Native American) A spiritual dancer
Kachine, Kachinah, Kachineh, Kachyna, Kacheena, Kachynah, Kacheenah, Kacheana

Kadin (Arabic) A beloved companion
Kadyn, Kadan, Kaden, Kadon, Kadun, Kaedin, Kaeden, Kaydin

Kaelyn (English) A beautiful girl from the meadow
Kaelynn, Kaelynne, Kaelin, Kailyn, Kaylyn, Kaelinn, Kaelinne

Kagami (Japanese) Displaying one's true image
Kagamie, Kagamy, Kagamey, Kagamee, Kagamea

Kailasa (Indian) From the silver mountain
Kailasah, Kailassa, Kaylasa, Kaelasa, Kailas, Kailase

*Kaitlyn (Greek) Form of Katherine, meaning "one who is pure, virginal"
*Kaitlin, Kaitlan, Kaitleen, Kaitlynn, Katalin, Katalina, Katalyn, Katelin, Kateline, Katelinn, **Katelyn**, Katelynn, Katilyn, Katlin*

Kakra (Egyptian) The younger of twins
Kakrah

Kala (Arabic / Hawaiian) A moment in time / form of Sarah, meaning "a princess; lady"
Kalah, Kalla, Kallah

Kalifa (Somali) A chaste and holy woman
Kalifah, Kalyfa, Kalyfah, Kaleefa, Kaleefah, Kalipha, Kalypha, Kaleepha, Kaleafa, Kaleafah, Kaleapha

Kalinda (Indian) Of the sun
Kalindah, Kalynda, Kalinde, Kalindeh, Kalindi, Kalindie, Kalyndi, Kalyndie

Kallie (English) Form of Callie, meaning "a beautiful girl"
Kalli, Kallita, Kally, Kalley, Kallee, Kalleigh, Kallea, Kalleah

Kalma (Finnish) In mythology, goddess of the dead

Kalyan (Indian) A beautiful and auspicious woman
Kalyane, Kalyanne, Kalyann, Kaylana, Kaylanna, Kalliyan, Kaliyan, Kaliyane

Kama (Indian) One who loves and is loved
Kamah, Kamma, Kammah

Kamala (Arabic) A woman of perfection
Kamalah, Kammala, Kamalla

Kamaria (African) Of the moon
Kamariah, Kamarea, Kamareah, Kamariya, Kamariyah

Kambiri (African) Newest addition to the family
Kambirie, Kambiry, Kambyry

Kamea (Hawaiian) The one and only; precious one
Kameo

^**Kamila** (Spanish) Form of Camilla, meaning ceremonial attendant
Kamilah

Kamyra (American) Surrounded by light
Kamira, Kamera, Kamiera, Kameira, Kameera, Kameara

Kanda (Native American) A magical woman
Kandah

Kanika (African) A dark, beautiful woman
Kanikah, Kanyka, Kanicka

Kantha (Indian) A delicate woman
Kanthah, Kanthe, Kantheh

Kanya (Thai) A young girl; a virgin

Kaoru (Japanese) A fragrant girl
Kaori

Kara (Greek / Italian / Gaelic) One who is pure / dearly loved / a good friend
Karah, Karalee, Karalie, Karalyn, Karalynn, Karrah, Karra, Khara

Karcsi (French) A joyful singer
Karcsie, Karcsy, Karcsey, Karcsee, Karcsea

Karen (Greek) Form of Katherine, meaning "one who is pure; virginal"
Karan, Karena, Kariana, Kariann, Karianna, Karianne, Karin, Karina

Karina (Scandinavian / Russian) One who is dear and pure
Karinah, Kareena, Karyna

Karisma (English) Form of Charisma, meaning "blessed with charm"
Kharisma, Karizma, Kharizma

Karissa (Greek) Filled with grace and kindness; very dear
Karisa, Karyssa, Karysa, Karessa, Karesa, Karis, Karise

Karla (German) Feminine form of Karl; a small strong, woman
Karly, Karli, Karlie, Karleigh, Karlee, Karley, Karlin, Karlyn, Karlina, Karleen

Karmel (Latin) Form of Carmel, meaning "of the fruitful orchard"
Karmelle, Karmell, Karmele, Karmela, Karmella

Karoline (English) A small and strong woman
Karolina, Karolinah, Karolyne, Karrie, Karie, Karri, Kari, Karry

Karsen (American) Variation of the Scottish Carson, meaning "from the swamp"
Karsyn, Karsin

Karsten (Greek) The anointed one
Karstin, Karstine, Karstyn, Karston, Karstan, Kiersten, Keirsten

Kasey (Irish) Form of Casey, meaning "a vigilant woman"
Kacie, Kaci, Kacy, KC, Kacee, Kacey, Kasie, Kasi

Kasi (Indian) From the holy city; shining

Kasmira (Slavic) A peacemaker
Kasmirah, Kasmeera

Kate (English) Form of Katherine, meaning "one who is pure, virginal"
Katie, Katey, Kati

*Katherine (Greek) Form of Catherine, meaning "one who is pure; virginal"
Katharine, Katharyn, Kathy, Kathleen, Katheryn, Kathie, Kathrine, Kathryn, Karen, Kay

Katniss (American) From the young adult novel series *The Hunger Games*

Katriel (Hebrew) Crowned by God
Katriele, Katrielle, Katriell

Kaveri (Indian) From the sacred river
Kaverie, Kauveri, Kauverie, Kavery, Kaverey, Kaveree, Kaverea, Kauvery

Kay (English / Greek) The keeper of the keys / form of Katherine, meaning "one who is pure; virginal"
Kaye, Kae, Kai, Kaie, Kaya, Kayana, Kayane, Kayanna

Kayden (American) Form of Kaden, meaning "a beloved companion"

*Kayla (Arabic / Hebrew) Crowned with laurel
Kaylah, Kalan, Kalen, Kalin, Kalyn, Kalynn, Kaylan, Kaylana, Kaylin, Kaylen, Kaylynn, Kaylyn, Kayle

*Kaylee (American) Form of Kayla, meaning "crowned with laurel"
Kaleigh, Kaley, Kaelee, Kaeley, Kaeli, Kailee, Kailey, Kalee, Kayleigh, Kayley, Kayli, Kaylie

Kearney (Irish) The winner
Kearny, Kearni, Kearnie, Kearnee, Kearnea

Keaton (English) From a shed town
Keatan, Keatyn, Keatin, Keatun

Keavy (Irish) A lovely and graceful girl
Keavey, Keavi, Keavie, Keavee, Keavea

Keeya (African) Resembling a flower
Keeyah, Kieya, Keiya, Keyya

Kefira (Hebrew) Resembling a young lioness
Kefirah, Kefiera, Kefeira

Keira (Irish) Form of Kiera, meaning "little dark-haired one"
Kierra, Kyera, Kyerra, Keiranne, Kyra, Kyrie, Kira, Kiran

Keisha (American) The favorite child; form of Kezia, meaning "of the spice tree"
Keishla, Keishah, Kecia, Kesha, Keysha, Keesha, Kiesha, Keshia

Kelly (Irish) A lively and bright-headed woman
Kelley, Kelli, Kellie, Kellee, Kelliegh, Kellye, Keely, Keelie, Keeley, Keelyn

Kelsey (English) From the island of ships
Kelsie, Kelcey, Kelcie, Kelcy, Kellsie, Kelsa, Kelsea, Kelsee, Kelsi, Kelsy, Kellsey

Kendall (Welsh) From the royal valley
Kendal, Kendyl, Kendahl, Kindall, Kyndal, Kenley

Kendra (English) Feminine form of Kendrick; having royal power; from the high hill
Kendrah, Kendria, Kendrea, Kindra, Kindria

^**Kenley** (American) Variation of Kinley and McKinley

****Kennedy** (Gaelic) A helmeted chief
Kennedi, Kennedie, Kennedey, Kennedee, Kenadia, Kenadie, Kenadi, Kenady, Kenadey

Kensington (English) A brash lady
Kensyngton, Kensingtyn, Kinsington, Kinsyngton, Kinsingtyn

^**Kenzie** (American) Diminutive of McKenzie

Kerensa (Cornish) One who loves and is loved
Kerinsa, Keransa, Kerensia, Kerensea, Kerensya, Kerenz, Kerenza, Keranz

Kerr (Scottish) From the marshland

Keshon (American) Filled with happiness
Keyshon, Keshawn, Keyshawn, Kesean, Keysean, Keshaun, Keyshaun, Keshonna

Kevina (Gaelic) Feminine form of Kevin; a beautiful and beloved child
Kevinah, Keva, Kevia, Kevinne, Kevyn, Kevynn

Keyla (English) A wise daughter

Kezia (Hebrew) Of the spice tree
Keziah, Kesia, Kesiah, Kesi, Kessie, Ketzia, Keisha

Khai (American) Unlike the others; unusual
Khae, Khay, Khaye

Khalida (Arabic) Feminine form of Khalid; an immortal woman
Khalidah, Khaleeda, Khalyda

Khaliqa (Arabic) Feminine form of Khaliq; a creator; one who is well-behaved
Khaliqah, Khalyqa, Khaleeqa

Khayriyyah (Arabic) A charitable woman
Khayriyah, Khariyyah, Khariya, Khareeya

Khepri (Egyptian) Born of the morning sun
Kheprie, Kepri, Keprie, Khepry, Kepry, Khepree, Kepree, Kheprea

Khiana (American) One who is different
Khianna, Khiane, Khianne, Khian, Khyana, Khyanna, Kheana, Kheanna

*Khloe (Greek) Form of Chloe, meaning "a flourishing woman, blooming"

Kiara (American) Form of Chiara, meaning "daughter of the light"

Kichi (Japanese) The fortunate one

Kidre (American) A loyal woman
Kidrea, Kidreah, Kidria, Kidriah, Kidri, Kidrie, Kidry, Kidrey

Kiele (Hawaiian) Resembling the gardenia
Kielle, Kiel, Kiell, Kiela, Kiella

Kikka (German) The mistress of all
Kika, Kykka, Kyka

Kiley (American) Form of Kylie, meaning "a boomerang"
Kylie

Kimana (American) Girl from the meadow
Kimanah, Kimanna

Kimball (English) Chief of the warriors; possessing royal boldness
Kimbal, Kimbell, Kimbel, Kymball, Kymbal

*****Kimberly** (English) Of the royal fortress
Kimberley, Kimberli, Kimberlee, Kimberleigh, Kimberlin, Kimberlyn, Kymberlie, Kymberly

Kimeo (American) Filled with happiness
Kimeyo

Kimetha (American) Filled with joy
Kimethah, Kymetha

Kimiko (Japanese) A noble child; without equal

Kimora (American) Form of Kimberly, meaning "royal"

Kina (Hawaiian) Woman of China

Kinley (American) Variation of McKinley, Scottish, meaning offspring of the fair hero

Kinsey (English) The king's victory
Kinnsee, Kinnsey, Kinnsie, Kinsee, Kinsie, Kinzee, Kinzie, Kinzey

^**Kinsley** (English) From the king's meadow
Kinsly, Kinslee, Kinsleigh, Kinsli, Kinslie, Kingsley, Kingslee, Kingslie

Kioko (Japanese) A daughter born with happiness

Kirima (Eskimo) From the hill
Kirimah, Kiryma, Kirymah, Kirema, Kiremah, Kireema, Kireemah, Kireama

Kismet (English) One's destiny; fate

Kiss (American) A caring and compassionate woman
Kyss, Kissi, Kyssi, Kissie, Kyssie, Kissy, Kyssy, Kissey

Kobi (American) Woman from California
Kobie, Koby, Kobee, Kobey, Kobea

Kolette (English) Form of Colette, meaning "victory of the people"
Kolete, Kolett, Koleta, Koletta, Kolet

Komala (Indian) A delicate and tender woman
Komalah, Komalla, Komal, Komali, Komalie, Komalee

Kona (Hawaiian) A girly woman
Konah, Konia, Koniah, Konea, Koneah, Koni, Konie, Koney

Konane (Hawaiian) Daughter of the moonlight

Kreeli (American) A charming and kind girl
Kreelie, Krieli, Krielie, Kryli, Krylie, Kreely, Kriely, Kryly

Krenie (American) A capable woman
Kreni, Kreny, Kreney, Krenee

Kristina (English) Form of Christina, meaning "follower of Christ"
Kristena, Kristine, Kristyne, Kristyna, Krystina, Krystine

Kumi (Japanese) An everlasting beauty
Kumie, Kumy, Kumey, Kumee

Kyla (English) Feminine form of Kyle; from the narrow channel
Kylah, Kylar, Kyle

*Kylie (Australian) A boomerang
Kylee, Kyleigh, Kyley, Kyli, Kyleen, Kyleen, Kyler, Kily, Kileigh, Kilee, Kilie, Kili, Kilea, Kylea

Kyra (Greek) Form of Cyrus, meaning "noble"
Kyrah, Kyria, Kyriah, Kyrra, Kyrrah

L

Lacey (French) Woman from Normandy; as delicate as lace
Lace, Lacee, Lacene, Laci, Laciann, Lacie, Lacina, Lacy

Lael (Hebrew) One who belongs to God
Laele, Laelle

*Laila (Arabic) A beauty of the night, born at nightfall
Layla, Laylah

Lainil (American) A soft-hearted woman
Lainill, Lainyl, Lainyll, Laenil, Laenill, Laenyl, Laenyll, Laynil

Lais (Greek) A legendary courtesan
Laise, Lays, Layse, Laisa, Laes, Laese

Lajita (Indian) A truthful woman
Lajyta, Lajeeta, Lajeata

Lake (American) From the still waters
Laken, Laiken, Layken, Layk, Layke, Laik, Laike, Laeken

Lala (Slavic) Resembling a tulip
Lalah, Lalla, Lallah, Laleh

Lalaine (American) A hard-working woman
Lalain, Lalaina, Lalayn, Lalayne, Lalayna, Lalaen, Lalaene, Lalaena

Lalia (Greek) One who is well-spoken
Lali, Lallia, Lalya, Lalea, Lalie, Lalee, Laly, Laley

Lalita (Indian) A playful and charming woman
Lalitah, Laleeta, Laleetah, Lalyta, Lalytah, Laleita, Laleitah, Lalieta

Lamia (Greek) In mythology, a female vampire
Lamiah, Lamiya, Lamiyah, Lamea, Lameah

Lamya (Arabic) Having lovely dark lips
Lamyah, Lamyia, Lama

Lanassa (Russian) A light-hearted woman; cheerful
Lanasa, Lanassia, Lanasia, Lanassiya, Lanasiya

Landon (English) From the long hill
Landyn, Landen

Lang (Scandinavian) Woman of great height

Lani (Hawaiian) From the sky; one who is heavenly
Lanikai

Lanza (Italian) One who is noble and willing
Lanzah, Lanzia, Lanziah, Lanzea, Lanzeah

Lapis (Egyptian) Resembling the dark-blue gemstone
Lapiss, Lapisse, Lapys, Lapyss, Lapysse

Laquinta (American) The fifth-born child

Laramie (French) Shedding tears of love
Larami, Laramy, Laramey, Laramee, Laramea

Larby (American) Form of Darby, meaning "of the deer park"
Larbey, Larbi, Larbie, Larbee, Larbea

Larch (American) One who is full of life
Larche

Lark (English) Resembling the songbird
Larke

Larue (American) Form of Rue, meaning "a medicinal herb"
LaRue, Laroo, Larou

Lashawna (American) Filled with happiness
Lashauna, Laseana, Lashona, Lashawn, Lasean, Lashone, Lashaun

Lata (Indian) Of the lovely vine
Latah

Latanya (American) Daughter of the fairy queen
Latanyah, Latonya, Latania, Latanja, Latonia, Latanea

LaTeasa (Spanish) A flirtatious woman
Lateasa, Lateaza

Latona (Latin) In mythology, the Roman equivalent of Leto, the mother of Artemis and Apollo
Latonah, Latonia, Latonea, Lantoniah, Latoneah

Latrelle (American) One who laughs a lot
Latrell, Latrel, Latrele, Latrella, Latrela

Laudonia (Italian) Praises the house
Laudonea, Laudoniya, Laudomia, Laudomea, Laudomiya

Laura (Latin) Crowned with laurel; from the laurel tree
Lauraine, Lauralee, Laralyn, Laranca, Larea, Lari, Lauralee, Lauren, Loretta

*Lauren (French) Form of Laura, meaning "crowned with laurel; from the laurel tree"
Laren, Larentia, Larentina, Larenzina, Larren, Laryn, Larryn, Larrynn

*Leah (Hebrew) One who is weary; in the Bible, Jacob's first wife
Leia, Leigha, Lia, Liah, Leeya

Leanna (Gaelic) Form of Helen, meaning "the shining light"
Leana, Leann, Leanne, Lee-Ann, Leeann, Leeanne, Leianne, Leyanne

Lecia (English) Form of Alice, meaning "woman of the nobility; truthful; having high moral character"
Licia, Lecea, Licea, Lisha, Lysha, Lesha

Ledell (Greek) One who is queenly
Ledelle, Ledele, Ledella, Ledela, Ledel

Legend (American) One who is memorable
Legende, Legund, Legunde

Legia (Spanish) A bright woman
Legiah, Legea, Legeah, Legiya, Legiyah, Legya, Legyah

Leila (Persian) Night, dark beauty
Leela, Lela

Lenis (Latin) One who has soft and silky skin
Lene, Leneta, Lenice, Lenita, Lennice, Lenos, Lenys, Lenisse

Leona (Latin) Feminine form of Leon; having the strength of a lion
Leeona, Leeowna, Leoine, Leola, Leone, Leonelle, Leonia, Leonie

Lequoia (Native American) Form of Sequoia, meaning "of the giant redwood tree"
Lequoya, Lequoiya, Lekoya

Lerola (Latin) Resembling a blackbird
Lerolla, Lerolah, Lerolia, Lerolea

Leslie (Gaelic) From the holly garden; of the gray fortress
Leslea, Leslee, Lesleigh, Lesley, Lesli, Lesly, Lezlee, Lezley

Leucippe (Greek) In mythology, a nymph
Lucippe, Leucipe, Lucipe

Leucothea (Greek) In mythology, a sea nymph
Leucothia, Leucothiah, Leucotheah

Levora (American) A homebody
Levorah, Levorra, Levorrah, Levoria, Levoriah, Levorea, Levoreah, Levorya

Lewa (African) A very beautiful woman
Lewah

Lewana (Hebrew) Of the white moon
Lewanah, Lewanna, Lewannah

Lia (Italian) Form of Leah, meaning "one who is weary"

Libby (English) Form of Elizabeth, meaning "my God is bountiful; God's promise"
Libba, Libbee, Libbey, Libbie, Libet, Liby, Lilibet, Lilibeth

Liberty (English) An independent woman; having freedom
Libertey, Libertee, Libertea, Liberti, Libertie, Libertas, Libera, Liber

Libra (Latin) One who is balanced; the seventh sign of the zodiac
Leebra, Leibra, Liebra, Leabra, Leighbra, Lybra

Librada (Spanish) One who is free
Libradah, Lybrada, Lybradah

Lieu (Vietnamese) Of the willow tree

Ligia (Greek) One who is musically talented
Ligiah, Ligya, Ligiya, Lygia, Ligea, Lygea, Lygya, Lygiya

^Lila (Arabic / Greek) Born at night / resembling a lily
Lilah, *Lyla, Lylah*

Lilac (Latin) Resembling the bluish-purple flower
Lilack, Lilak, Lylac, Lylack, Lylak, Lilach

Lilette (Latin) Resembling a budding lily
Lilett, Lilete, Lilet, Lileta, Liletta, Lylette, Lylett, Lylete

Liliana (Italian, Spanish) Form of Lillian, meaning "resembling the lily"
Lilliana, Lillianna, Liliannia, Lilyana, Lilia

Lilith (Babylonian) Woman of the night
Lilyth, Lillith, Lillyth, Lylith, Lyllith, Lylyth, Lyllyth, Lilithe

*Lillian (Latin) Resembling the lily
Lilian, Liliane, Lilianne, Lilias, Lilas, Lillas, Lillias

Lilo (Hawaiian) One who is generous
Lylo, Leelo, Lealo, Leylo, Lielo, Leilo

*Lily (English) Resembling the flower; one who is innocent and beautiful
Leelee, Lil, Lili, Lilie, Lilla, Lilley, Lilli, Lillie, Lilly

Limor (Hebrew) Refers to myrrh
Limora, Limoria, Limorea, Leemor, Leemora, Leemoria, Leemorea

Lin (Chinese) Resembling jade; from the woodland

Linda (Spanish) One who is soft and beautiful
Lindalee, Lindee, Lindey, Lindi, Lindie, Lindira, Lindka, Lindy, Lynn

Linden (English) From the hill
of lime trees
*Lindenn, Lindon, Lindynn,
Lynden, Lyndon, Lyndyn,
Lyndin, Lindin*

Lindley (English) From the
pastureland
*Lindly, Lindlee, Lindleigh,
Lindli, Lindlie, Leland, Lindlea*

Lindsay (English) From the
island of linden trees; from
Lincoln's wetland
*Lind, Lindsea, Lindsee,
Lindseigh, Lindsey, Lindsy,
Linsay, Linsey*

Lisa (English) Form of
Elizabeth, meaning "my God
is bountiful; God's promise"
*Leesa, Liesa, Lisebet, Lise,
Liseta, Lisette, Liszka, Lisebeth*

Lishan (African) One who is
awarded a medal
*Lishana, Lishanna, Lyshan,
Lyshana, Lyshanna*

Lissie (American) Resembling
a flower
Lissi, Lissy, Lissey, Lissee, Lissea

Liv (Scandinavian / Latin) One
who protects others / from
the olive tree
*Livia, Livea, Liviya, Livija,
Livvy, Livy, Livya, Lyvia*

Liya (Hebrew) The Lord's
daughter
*Liyah, Leeya, Leeyah, Leaya,
Leayah*

Lo (American) A fiesty woman
Loe, Low, Lowe

Loicy (American) A delightful
woman
*Loicey, Loicee, Loicea, Loici,
Loicie, Loyce, Loice, Loyci*

Lokelani (Hawaiian)
Resembling a small red rose
*Lokelanie, Lokelany, Lokelaney,
Lokelanee, Lokelanea*

Loki (Norse) In mythology, a
trickster god
*Lokie, Lokee, Lokey, Loky,
Lokea, Lokeah, Lokia, Lokiah*

Lola (Spanish) Form of
Dolores, meaning "woman
of sorrow"
Lolah, Loe, Lolo

^***London** (English) From the
capital of England
Londyn

Lorelei (German) From the
rocky cliff; in mythology, a
siren who lured sailors to
their deaths
*Laurelei, Laurelie, Loralee,
Loralei, Loralie, Loralyn*

Loretta (Italian) Form of Laura, meaning "crowned with laurel; from the laurel tree"
Laretta, Larretta, Lauretta, Laurette, Leretta, Loreta, Lorette, Lorretta

Lorraine (French) From the kingdom of Lothair
Laraine, Larayne, Laurraine, Leraine, Lerayne, Lorain, Loraina, Loraine

Love (English) One who is full of affection
Lovey, Loveday, Lovette, Lovi, Lovie, Lov, Luv, Luvey

Lovely (American) An attractive and pleasant woman
Loveli, Loveley, Lovelie, Lovelee, Loveleigh, Lovelea

Luana (Hawaiian) One who is content and enjoys life
Lewanna, Lou-Ann, Louann, Louanna, Louanne, Luanda, Luane, Luann

Lucretia (Latin) A bringer of light; a successful woman; in mythology, a maiden who was raped by the prince of Rome
Lacretia, Loucrecia, Loucrezia, Loucresha, Loucretia, Lucrece, Lucrecia, Lucreecia

^***Lucy** (Latin) Feminine form of Lucius; one who is illuminated
*Luce, Lucetta, Lucette, Luci, Lucia, Luciana, Lucianna, Lucida, **Lucille***

Lucylynn (American) A light-hearted woman
Lucylyn, Lucylynne, Lucilynn, Lucilyn, Lucilynne

^**Luna** (Latin) Of the moon
Lunah

Lunet (English) Of the crescent moon
Lunett, Lunette, Luneta, Lunete, Lunetta

Lupita (Spanish) Form of Guadalupe, meaning "from the valley of wolves"
Lupe, Lupyta, Lupelina, Lupeeta, Lupieta, Lupeita, Lupeata

Lurissa (American) A beguiling woman
Lurisa, Luryssa, Lurysa, Luressa, Luresa

Luyu (Native American) Resembling the dove

***Lydia** (Greek) A beautiful woman from Lydia
Lidia, Lidie, Lidija, Lyda, Lydie, Lydea, Liddy, Lidiy

Lyla (Arabic) Form of Lila, meaning "born at night, resembling a lily"
Lylah

Lynn (English) Woman of the lake; form of Linda, meaning "one who is soft and beautiful"
Linell, Linnell, Lyn, Lynae, Lyndel, Lyndell, Lynell, Lynelle

^**Lyric** (French) Of the lyre; the words of a song
Lyrica, Lyricia, Lyrik, Lyrick, Lyrika, Lyricka

Lytanisha (American) A scintillating woman
Lytanesha, Lytaniesha, Lytaneisha, Lytanysha, Lytaneesha, Lytaneasha

M

Macanta (Gaelic) A kind and gentle woman
Macan, Macantia, Macantea, Macantah

Machi (Taiwanese) A good friend
Machie, Machy, Machey, Machee, Machea

Mackenna (Gaelic) Daughter of the handsome man
Mackendra, Mackennah, McKenna, McKendra, Makenna, Makennah

***Mackenzie** (Gaelic) Daughter of a wise leader; a fiery woman; one who is fair
Mckenzie, Mackenzey, Makensie, Makenzie, M'Kenzie, McKenzie, Meckenzie, Mackenzee, Mackenzy

^**McKinley** (English) Offspring of the fair hero

^**Macy** (French) One who wields a weapon
Macee, Macey, Maci, Macie, Maicey, Maicy, Macea, Maicea

Madana (Ethiopian) One who heals others
Madayna, Madaina, Madania, Madaynia, Madainia

Maddox (English) Born into wealth and prosperity
Madox, Madoxx, Maddoxx

***Madeline** (Hebrew) Woman from Magdala
Mada, Madalaina, Madaleine, Madalena, Madalene, Madelyn, Madalyn, Madelynn, Madilyn

Madhavi (Indian) Feminine form of Madhav; born in the springtime
Madhavie, Madhavee, Madhavey, Madhavy, Madhavea

Madini (Swahili) As precious as a gemstone
Madinie, Madiny, Madiney, Madinee, Madyny, Madyni, Madinea, Madynie

*Madison (English) Daughter of a mighty warrior
Maddison, Madisen, Madisson, Madisyn, Madyson

Madonna (Italian) My lady; refers to the Virgin Mary
Madonnah, Madona, Madonah

Maeve (Irish) An intoxicating woman
Mave, Meave, Medb, Meabh

Maggie (English) Form of Margaret, meaning "resembling a pearl"
Maggi

Magnolia (French) Resembling the flower
Magnoliya, Magnoliah, Magnolea, Magnoleah, Magnoliyah, Magnolya, Magnolyah

Mahal (Native American) A tender and loving woman
Mahall, Mahale, Mahalle

Mahari (African) One who offers forgiveness
Maharie, Mahary, Maharey

Mahesa (Indian) A powerful and great lady
Maheshvari

Mahira (Arabic) A clever and adroit woman
Mahirah, Mahir, Mahire

Maia (Latin / Maori) The great one; in mythology, the goddess of spring / a brave warrior
Maiah, Mya, Maja

Maida (English) A maiden; a virgin
Maidel, Maidie, Mayda, Maydena, Maydey, Mady, Maegth, Magd

Maiki (Japanese) Resembling the dancing flower
Maikie, Maikei, Maikki, Maikee

Maimun (Arabic) One who is lucky; fortunate
Maimoon, Maimoun

Maine (French) From the mainland; from the state of Maine

Maiolaine (French) As delicate as a flower
Maiolainie, Maiolani

Maisha (African) Giver of life
Maysha, Maishah, Mayshah, Maesha, Maeshah

Maisie (Scottish) Form of Margaret, meaning "resembling a pearl"
Maisee, Maisey, Maisy, Maizie, Mazey, Mazie, Maisi, Maizi

Majaya (Indian) A victorious woman
Majayah

Makala (Hawaiian) Resembling myrtle
Makalah, Makalla, Makallah

*Makayla (Celtic / Hebrew / English) Form of Michaela, meaning "who is like God?"
Macaela, MacKayla, Mak, Mechaela, Meeskaela, Mekea, Mekelle

Makani (Hawaiian) Of the wind
Makanie, Makaney, Makany, Makanee

Makareta (Maori) Form of Margaret, meaning "resembling a pearl / the child of light"
Makaretah, Makarita

Makea (Finnish) One who is sweet
Makeah, Makia, Makiah

Makelina (Hawaiian) Form of Madeline, meaning "woman from Magdala"
Makelinah, Makeleena, Makelyna, Makeleana

Makena (African) One who is filled with happiness
Makenah, Makeena, Makeenah, Makeana, Makeanah, Makyna, Makynah, Mackena

Makenna (Irish) Form of McKenna, meaning "of the Irish one"
Makennah

Malak (Arabic) A heavenly messenger; an angel
Malaka, Malaika, Malayka, Malaeka, Malake, Malayk, Malaek, Malakia

Malati (Indian) Resembling a fragrant flower
Malatie, Malaty, Malatey, Malatee, Malatea

Mali (Thai / Welsh) Resembling a flower / form of Molly, meaning "star of the sea / from the sea of bitterness"
Malie, Malee, Maleigh, Maly, Maley

Malia (Hawaiian) Form of Mary, meaning "star of the sea / from the sea of bitterness"
Maliah, Maliyah, Maleah

Malika (Arabic) Destined to be queen
Malikah, Malyka, Maleeka, Maleika, Malieka, Maliika, Maleaka

Malina (Hawaiian) A peaceful woman
Malinah, Maleena, Maleenah, Malyna, Malynah, Maleina, Maliena, Maleana

Malinka (Russian) As sweet as a little berry
Malinkah, Malynka, Maleenka, Malienka, Maleinka, Maleanka

Mana (Polynesian) A charismatic and prestigious woman
Manah

Manal (Arabic) An accomplished woman
Manala, Manall, Manalle, Manalla, Manali

Mandoline (English) One who is accomplished with the stringed instrument
Mandalin, Mandalyn, Mandalynn, Mandelin, Mandellin, Mandellyn, Mandolin, Mandolyn

Mangena (Hebrew) As sweet as a melody
Mangenah, Mangenna, Mangennah

Manyara (African) A humble woman
Manyarah

Maola (Irish) A handmaiden
Maoli, Maole, Maolie, Maolia, Maoly, Maoley, Maolee, Maolea

Mapenzi (African) One who is dearly loved
Mpenzi, Mapenzie, Mapenze, Mapenzy, Mapenzee, Mapenzea

Maram (Arabic) One who is wished for
Marame, Marama, Marami, Maramie, Maramee, Maramy, Maramey, Maramea

Marcella (Latin) Dedicated to Mars, the God of war
Marcela, Marsela, Marsella, Maricela, Maricel

Marcia (Latin) Feminine form of Marcus; dedicated to Mars, the god of war
Marcena, Marcene, Marchita, Marciana, Marciane, Marcianne, Marcilyn, Marcilynn

Marely (American) form of Marley, "meaning of the marshy meadow"

Margaret (Greek / Persian) Resembling a pearl / the child of light
Maighread, Mairead, Mag, Maggi, Maggie, Maggy, Maiga, Malgorzata, Megan, Marwarid, Marjorie, Marged, Makareta

Marged (Welsh) Form of Margaret, meaning "resembling a pearl / the child of light"
Margred, Margeda, Margreda

*Maria (Spanish) Form of Mary, meaning "star of the sea / from the sea of bitterness"
Mariah, Marialena, Marialinda, Marialisa, Maaria, Mayria, Maeria, Mariabella

*Mariah (Latin) Form of Mary, meaning "star of the sea"

Mariana (Spanish / Italian) Form of Mary, meaning "star of the sea"
Marianna

Mariane (French) Blend of Mary, meaning "star of the sea / from the sea of bitterness," and Ann, meaning "a woman graced with God's favor"
Mariam, Mariana, Marian, Marion, Maryann, Maryanne, Maryanna, Maryane

Marietta (French) Form of Mary, meaning "star of the sea / from the sea of bitterness"
Mariette, Maretta, Mariet, Maryetta, Maryette, Marieta

Marika (Danish) Form of Mary, meaning "star of the sea / from the sea of bitterness"

Mariko (Japanese) Daughter of Mari; a ball or sphere
Maryko, Mareeko, Marieko, Mareiko

Marilyn (English) Form of Mary, meaning "star of the sea / from the sea of bitterness"
Maralin, Maralyn, Maralynn, Marelyn, Marilee, Marilin

Marissa (Latin) Woman of the sea
Maressa, Maricia, Marisabel, Marisha, Marisse, Maritza, Mariza, Marrissa

Marjam (Slavic) One who is merry
Marjama, Marjamah, Marjami, Marjamie, Marjamy, Marjamey, Marjamee, Marjamea

Marjani (African) Of the coral reef
Marjanie, Marjany, Marjaney, Marjanee, Marjean, Marjeani, Marjeanie, Marijani

Marjorie (English) Form of Margaret, meaning "resembling a pearl / the child of light"
Marcharie, Marge, Margeree, Margerie, Margery, Margey, Margi

Marlene (German) Blend of Mary, meaning "star of the sea / from the sea of bitterness," and Magdalene, meaning "woman from Magdala"
Marlaina, Marlana, Marlane, Marlayna

Marley (English) Of the marshy meadow
Marlee, Marleigh, Marli, Marlie, Marly

Marlis (German) Form of Mary, meaning "star of the sea / from the sea of bitterness"
Marlisa, Marliss, Marlise, Marlisse, Marlissa, Marlys, Marlyss, Marlysa

Marlo (English) One who resembles driftwood
Marloe, Marlow, Marlowe, Marlon

Marsala (Italian) From the place of sweet wine
Marsalah, Marsalla, Marsallah

Martha (Aramaic) Mistress of the house; in the Bible, the sister of Lazarus and Mary
Maarva, Marfa, Marhta, Mariet, Marit, Mart, Marta, Marte

Mary (Latin / Hebrew) Star of the sea / from the sea of bitterness
Mair, Mal, Mallie, Manette, Manon, Manya, Mare, Maren, Maria, Marietta, Marika, Marilyn, Marlis, Maureen, May, Mindel, Miriam, Molly, Mia

Masami (African / Japanese) A commanding woman / one who is truthful
Masamie, Masamee, Masamy, Masamey, Masamea

Mashaka (African) A troublemaker; a mischievous woman
Mashakah, Mashakia

Massachusetts (Native American) From the big hill; from the state of Massachusetts
Massachusets, Massachusette, Massachusetta, Massa, Massachute, Massachusta

Matana (Hebrew) A gift from God
Matanah, Matanna, Matannah, Matai

Matangi (Hindi) In Hinduism, the patron of inner thought
Matangy, Matangie, Matangee, Matangey, Matangea

Matsuko (Japanese) Child of the pine tree

Maureen (Irish) Form of Mary, meaning "star of the sea / from the sea of bitterness"
Maura, Maurene, Maurianne, Maurine, Maurya, Mavra, Maure, Mo

Mauve (French) Of the mallow plant
Mawve

Maven (English) Having great knowledge
Mavin, Mavyn

Maverick (American) One who is wild and free
Maverik, Maveryck, Maveryk, Mavarick, Mavarik

Mavis (French) Resembling a songbird
Mavise, Maviss, Mavisse, Mavys, Mavyss, Mavysse

May (Latin) Born during the month of May; form of Mary, meaning "star of the sea / from the sea of bitterness"
Mae, Mai, Maelynn, Maelee, Maj, Mala, Mayana, Maye

*Maya (Indian / Hebrew) An illusion, a dream / woman of the water
Mya

Mayumi (Japanese) One who embodies truth, wisdom, and beauty

Mazarine (French) Having deep-blue eyes
Mazareen, Mazareene, Mazaryn, Mazaryne, Mazine, Mazyne, Mazeene

Mazhira (Hebrew) A shining woman
Mazhirah, Mazheera

McKayla (Gaelic) A fiery woman
McKale, McKaylee, McKaleigh, McKay, McKaye, McKaela

Meara (Gaelic) One who is filled with happiness
Mearah

Medea (Greek) A cunning ruler; in mythology, a sorceress
Madora, Medeia, Media, Medeah, Mediah, Mediya, Mediyah

Medini (Indian) Daughter of the earth
Medinie, Mediny, Mediney, Medinee, Medinea

Meditrina (Latin) The healer; in mythology, goddess of health and wine
Meditreena, Meditryna, Meditriena

Medora (Greek) A wise ruler
Medoria, Medorah, Medorra, Medorea

Medusa (Greek) In mythology, a Gorgon with snakes for hair
Medoosa, Medusah, Medoosah, Medousa, Medousah

Meenakshi (Indian) Having beautiful eyes

Megan (Welsh) Form of Margaret, meaning "resembling a pearl / the child of light"
Maegan, Meg, Magan, Magen, Megin, Maygan, Meagan, Meaghan, Meghan

Mehalia (Hebrew) An affectionate woman
Mehaliah, Mehalea, Mehaleah, Mehaliya, Mehaliyah

Melangell (Welsh) A sweet messenger from heaven
Melangelle, Melangela, Melangella, Melangele, Melangel

*Melanie (Greek) A dark-skinned beauty
Malaney, Malanie, Mel, Mela, Melaina, Melaine, Melainey, Melany

Meli (Native American) One who is bitter
Melie, Melee, Melea, Meleigh, Mely, Meley

Melia (Hawaiian / Greek) Resembling the plumeria / of the ash tree; in mythology, a nymph
Melidice, Melitine, Meliah, Meelia, Melya

Melika (Turkish) A great beauty
Melikah, Melicka, Melicca, Melyka, Melycka, Meleeka, Meleaka

Melinda (Latin) One who is sweet and gentle
Melynda, Malinda, Malinde, Mallie, Mally, Malynda, Melinde, Mellinda, Mindy

Melisande (French) Having the strength of an animal
Malisande, Malissande, Malyssandre, Melesande, Melisandra, Melisandre

Melissa (Greek) Resembling a honeybee; in mythology, a nymph
Malissa, Mallissa, Mel, Melesa, Melessa, Melisa, Melise, Melisse

Melita (Greek) As sweet as honey
Malita, Malitta, Melida, Melitta, Melyta, Malyta, Meleeta, Meleata

Melody (Greek) A beautiful song
Melodee, Melodey, Melodi, Melodia, Melodie, Melodea

Merana (American) Woman of the waters
Meranah, Meranna, Merannah

Mercer (English) A prosperous merchant

Meredith (Welsh) A great ruler; protector of the sea
Maredud, Meridel, Meredithe, Meredyth, Meridith, Merridie, Meradith, Meredydd

Meribah (Hebrew) A quarrelsome woman
Meriba

Meroz (Hebrew) From the cursed plains
Meroza, Merozia, Meroze

Merry (English) One who is lighthearted and joyful
Merree, Merri, Merrie, Merrielle, Merrile, Merrilee, Merrili, Merrily

Mertice (English) A well-known lady

Merton (English) From the village near the pond
Mertan, Mertin, Mertun

Metea (Greek) A gentle woman
Meteah, Metia, Metiah

Metin (Greek) A wise counselor
Metine, Metyn, Metyne

Metis (Greek) One who is industrious
Metiss, Metisse, Metys, Metyss, Metysse

Mettalise (Danish) As graceful as a pearl
Metalise, Mettalisse, Mettalisa, Mettalissa

*Mia (Israeli / Latin) Who is like God? / form of Mary, meaning "star of the sea / from the sea of bitterness"
Miah, Mea, Meah, Meya

^Michaela (Celtic, Gaelic, Hebrew, English, Irish) Feminine form of Michael; who is like God?
*Macaela, MacKayla, Mak, Mechaela, Meeskaela, Mekea, Micaela, **Mikaela***

Michelle (French) Feminine form of Michael; who is like God?
Machelle, Mashelle, M'chelle, Mechelle, Meechelle, Me'Shell, Meshella, Mischa

Michewa (Tibetan) Sent from heaven
Michewah

Mide (Irish) One who is thirsty
Meeda, Mida

Midori (Japanese) Having green eyes
Midorie, Midory, Midorey, Midoree, Midorea

Mignon (French) One who is cute and petite

Mikayla (English) Feminine form of Michael, meaning "who is like God?"

^**Mila** (Slavic) One who is industrious and hardworking
Milaia, Milaka, Milla, Milia

Milan (Latin) From the city in Italy; one who is gracious
Milaana

Milena (Slavic) The favored one
Mileena, Milana, Miladena, Milanka, Mlada, Mladena

Miley (American) Form of Mili, meaning "a virtuous woman"
Milee, Mylee, Mareli

Miliana (Latin) Feminine of Emeliano; one who is eager and willing
Milianah, Milianna, Miliane, Miliann, Milianne

Milima (Swahili) Woman from the mountains
Milimah, Mileema, Milyma

Millo (Hebrew) Defender of the sacred city
Milloh, Millowe, Milloe

Mima (Hebrew) Form of Jemima, meaning "our little dove"
Mimah, Mymah, Myma

Minda (Native American / Hindi) Having great knowledge
Mindah, Mynda, Myndah, Menda, Mendah

Mindel (Hebrew) Form of Mary, meaning "star of the sea / from the sea of bitterness"
Mindell, Mindelle, Mindele, Mindela, Mindella

Mindy (English) Form of Melinda, meaning "one who is sweet and gentle"
Minda, Mindee, Mindi, Mindie, Mindey, Mindea

Ming Yue (Chinese) Born beneath the bright moon

Minka (Teutonic) One who is resolute; having great strength
Minkah, Mynka, Mynkah, Minna, Minne

Minowa (Native American) One who has a moving voice
Minowah, Mynowa, Mynowah

Minuit (French) Born at midnight
Minueet

Miracle (American) An act of God's hand
Mirakle, Mirakel, Myracle, Myrakle

Mirai (Basque / Japanese) A miracle child / future
Miraya, Mirari, Mirarie, Miraree, Mirae

Miranda (Latin) Worthy of admiration
Maranda, Myranda, Randi

Miremba (Ugandan) A promoter of peace
Mirembe, Mirem, Mirembah, Mirembeh, Mirema

Miriam (Hebrew) Form of Mary, meaning "star of the sea / from the sea of bitterness"
Mariam, Maryam, Meriam, Meryam, Mirham, Mirjam, Mirjana, Mirriam

Mirinesse (English) Filled with joy
Miriness, Mirinese, Mirines, Mirinessa, Mirinesa

Mirit (Hebrew) One who is strong-willed

Mischa (Russian) Form of Michelle, meaning "who is like God?"
Misha

Mistico (Italian) A mystical woman
Mistica, Mystico, Mystica, Mistiko, Mystiko

Mitali (Indian) A friendly and sweet woman
Mitalie, Mitalee, Mitaleigh, Mitaly, Mitaley, Meeta, Mitalea

Miya (Japanese) From the sacred temple
Miyah

Miyo (Japanese) A beautiful daughter
Miyoko

Mizar (Hebrew) A little
woman; petite
*Mizarr, Mizarre, Mizare,
Mizara, Mizaria, Mizarra*

Mliss (Cambodian) Resembling
a flower
*Mlissa, Mlisse, Mlyss, Mlysse,
Mlyssa*

Mocha (Arabic) As sweet as
chocolate
Mochah

Modesty (Latin) One who is
without conceit
*Modesti, Modestie, Modestee,
Modestus, Modestey, Modesta,
Modestia, Modestina*

Moesha (American) Drawn
from the water
*Moisha, Moysha, Moeesha,
Moeasha, Moeysha*

Mohini (Indian) The most
beautiful
Mohinie, Mohinee, Mohiny

Moladah (Hebrew) A giver of
life
Molada

*Molly (Irish) Form of Mary,
meaning "star of the sea /
from the sea of bitterness"
*Moll, Mollee, Molley, Molli,
Mollie, Molle, Mollea, Mali*

Mona (Gaelic) One who is
born into the nobility
*Moina, Monah, Monalisa,
Monalissa, Monna, Moyna,
Monalysa, Monalyssa*

Moncha (Irish) A solitary
woman
Monchah

Monica (Greek / Latin) A
solitary woman / one who
advises others
*Monnica, Monca, Monicka,
Monika, Monike*

Monique (French) One who
provides wise counsel
*Moniqua, Moneeque,
Moneequa, Moneeke, Moeneek,
Moneaque, Moneaqua, Moneake*

Monisha (Hindi) Having great
intelligence
*Monishah, Monesha,
Moneisha, Moniesha,
Moneysha, Moneasha*

Monroe (Gaelic) Woman from
the river
Monrow, Monrowe, Monro

Monserrat (Latin) From the
jagged mountain
Montserrat

Montana (Latin) Woman of the mountains; from the state of Montana
Montanna, Montina, Monteene, Montese

Morcan (Welsh) Of the bright sea
Morcane, Morcana, Morcania, Morcanea

Moreh (Hebrew) A great archer; a teacher

*****Morgan** (Welsh) Circling the bright sea; a sea dweller
Morgaine, Morgana, Morgance, Morgane, Morganica, Morgann, Morganne, Morgayne

Morguase (English) In Arthurian legend, the mother of Gawain
Marguase, Margawse, Morgawse, Morgause, Margause

Morina (Japanese) From the woodland town
Morinah, Moreena, Moryna, Moriena, Moreina, Moreana

Mubarika (Arabic) One who is blessed
Mubaarika, Mubaricka, Mubaryka, Mubaricca, Mubarycca

Mubina (Arabic) One who displays her true image
Mubeena, Mubinah, Mubyna, Mubeana, Mubiena

Mudan (Mandarin) Daughter of a harmonious family
Mudane, Mudana, Mudann, Mudaen, Mudaena

Mufidah (Arabic) One who is helpful to others
Mufeeda, Mufeyda, Mufyda, Mufeida, Mufieda, Mufeada

Mugain (Irish) In mythology, the wife of the king of Ulster
Mugayne, Mugaine, Mugane

Muirne (Irish) One who is dearly loved
Muirna

Munay (African) One who loves and is loved
Manay, Munaye, Munae, Munai

Munazza (Arabic) An independent woman; one who is free
Munazzah, Munaza, Munazah

Muriel (Irish) Of the shining sea
Merial, Meriel, Merrill

Murphy (Celtic) Daughter of a great sea warrior
Murphi, Murphie, Murphey

Musoke (African) Having the beauty of a rainbow

Mya (American) Form of Maya, meaning "an illusion, woman of the water"
Myah

Myisha (Arabic) Form of Aisha, meaning "lively; womanly"
Myesha, Myeisha, Myeshia, Myiesha, Myeasha

Myka (Hebrew) Feminine of Micah, meaning "who is like God?"
Micah, Mika

Myrina (Latin) In mythology, an Amazon
Myrinah, Myreena, Myreina, Myriena, Myreana

Myrrh (Egyptian) Resembling the fragrant oil

N

Naama (Hebrew) Feminine form of Noam; an attractive woman; good-looking
Naamah

Naava (Hebrew) A lovely and pleasant woman
Naavah, Nava, Navah, Navit

Nabila (Arabic) Daughter born into nobility; a highborn daughter
Nabilah, Nabeela, Nabyla, Nabeelah, Nabylah, Nabeala, Nabealah

Nadda (Arabic) A very generous woman
Naddah, Nada, Nadah

Nadia (Slavic) One who is full of hope
Nadja, Nadya, Naadiya, Nadine, Nadie, Nadiyah, Nadea, Nadija

Nadirah (Arabic) One who is precious; rare
Nadira, Nadyra, Nadyrah, Nadeera, Nadeerah, Nadra

Naeva (French) Born in the evening
Naevah, Naevia, Naevea, Nayva, Nayvah

Nagge (Hebrew) A radiant woman

Nailah (Arabic) Feminine form of Nail; a successful woman; the acquirer
Na'ila, Na'ilah, Naa'ilah, Naila, Nayla, Naylah, Naela, Naelah

Najia (Arabic) An independent
woman; one who is free
Naajia

Najja (African) The second-
born child
Najjah

Namid (Native American) A
star dancer
Namide, Namyd, Namyde

Namita (Papuan) In mythology, a mother goddess
Namitah, Nameeta, Namyta

Nana (Hawaiian / English)
Born during the spring; a
star / a grandmother or one
who watches over children

Nancy (English) Form of
Anna, meaning "a woman
graced with God's favor"
*Nainsey, Nainsi, Nance,
Nancee, Nancey, Nanci,
Nancie, Nancsi*

Nandalia (Australian) A fiery
woman
*Nandaliah, Nandalea,
Nandaleah, Nandali, Nandalie,
Nandalei, Nandalee, Nandaleigh*

Nandita (Indian) A delightful
daughter
Nanditah, Nanditia, Nanditea

*Naomi** (Hebrew / Japanese)
One who is pleasant / a beauty
above all others
Namoie, Nayomi, Naomee

Narella (Greek) A bright
woman; intelligent
*Narellah, Narela, Narelah,
Narelle, Narell, Narele*

Nascio (Latin) In mythology,
goddess of childbirth

Natalia (Spanish / Latin) form
of Natalie; born on Christmas
day
Natalya, Natalja

*Natalie** (Latin) Refers to
Christ's birthday; born on
Christmas Day
*Natala, Natalee, Nathalie,
Nataline, Nataly, Natasha*

Natane (Native American) Her
father's daughter
Natanne

Natasha (Russian) Form of
Natalie, meaning "born on
Christmas Day"
*Nastaliya, Nastalya, Natacha,
Natascha, Natashenka,
Natashia, Natasia, Natosha*

Navida (Iranian) Feminine form of Navid; bringer of good news
Navyda, Navidah, Navyda, Naveeda, Naveedah, Naveada, Naveadah

Navya (Indian) One who is youthful
Navyah, Naviya, Naviyah

Nawal (Arabic) A gift of God
Nawall, Nawalle, Nawala, Nawalla

Nawar (Arabic) Resembling a flower
Nawaar

Nazahah (Arabic) One who is pure and honest
Nazaha, Nazihah, Naziha

Nechama (Hebrew) One who provides comfort
Nehama, Nehamah, Nachmanit, Nachuma, Nechamah, Nechamit

Neda (Slavic) Born on a Sunday
Nedda, Nedah, Nedi, Nedie, Neddi, Neddie, Nedaa

Neena (Hindi) A woman who has beautiful eyes
Neenah, Neanah, Neana, Neyna, Neynah

Nefertiti (Egyptian) A queenly woman
Nefertari, Nefertyty, Nefertity, Nefertitie, Nefertitee, Nefertytie, Nefertitea

Neith (Egyptian) In mythology, goddess of war and hunting
Neitha, Neytha, Neyth, Neit, Neita, Neitia, Neitea, Neithe, Neythe

Nekana (Spanish) Woman of sorrow
Nekane, Nekania, Nekanea

Neo (African) A gift from God

Nerissa (Italian / Greek) A black-haired beauty / sea nymph
Narissa, Naryssa, Nericcia, Neryssa, Narice, Nerice, Neris

Nessa (Hebrew / Greek) A miracle child / form of Agnes, meaning "one who is pure; chaste"
Nesha, Nessah, Nessia, Nessya, Nesta, Neta, Netia, Nessie

Netis (Native American) One who is trustworthy
Netiss, Netisse, Netys, Netyss, Netysse

*****Nevaeh** (American) Child from heaven

Nevina (Scottish) Feminine form of Nevin; daughter of a saint
Nevinah, Neveena, Nevyna, Nevinne, Nevynne, Neveene, Neveana, Neveane

Newlyn (Gaelic) Born during the spring
Newlynn, Newlynne, Newlin, Newlinn, Newlinne, Newlen, Newlenn, Newlenne

Neziah (Hebrew) One who is pure; a victorious woman
Nezia, Nezea, Nezeah, Neza, Nezah, Neziya, Neziyah

Niabi (Native American) Resembling a fawn
Niabie, Niabee, Niabey, Niaby

Niagara (English) From the famous waterfall
Niagarah, Niagarra, Niagarrah, Nyagara, Nyagarra

Nicole (Greek) Feminine form of Nicholas; of the victorious people
Necole, Niccole, Nichol, Nichole, Nicholle, Nickol, Nickole, Nicol

Nicosia (English) Woman from the capital of Cyprus
Nicosiah, Nicosea, Nicoseah, Nicotia, Nicotea

Nidia (Spanish) One who is gracious
Nydia, Nidiah, Nydiah, Nidea, Nideah, Nibia, Nibiah, Nibea

Nike (Greek) One who brings victory; in mythology, goddess of victory
Nikee, Nikey, Nykee, Nyke

Nilam (Arabic) Resembling a precious blue stone
Neelam, Nylam, Nilima, Nilyma, Nylyma, Nylima, Nealam, Nealama

Nilsine (Scandinavian) Feminine form of Neil; a champion

Nimeesha (African) A princess; daughter born to royalty
Nimeeshah, Nimiesha

Nini (African) As solid as a stone
Ninie, Niny, Niney, Ninee, Ninea

Nishan (African) One who wins awards
Nishann, Nishanne, Nishana, Nishanna, Nyshan, Nyshana

Nitya (Indian) An eternal beauty
Nithya, Nithyah, Nityah

Nixie (German) A beautiful water sprite
Nixi, Nixy, Nixey, Nixee, Nixea

Noelle (French) Born at Christmastime
Noel, Noela, Noele, Noe

Nolcha (Native American) Of the sun
Nolchia, Nolchea

Nomusa (African) One who is merciful
Nomusah, Nomusha, Nomusia, Nomusea, Nomushia, Nomushea

Nora (English) Form of Eleanor, meaning "the shining light"
Norah, Noora, Norella, Norelle, Norissa, Norri, Norrie, Norry

Nordica (German) Woman from the north
Nordika, Nordicka, Nordyca, Nordyka, Nordycka, Norda, Norell, Norelle

Nosiwe (African) Mother of the homeland

Noura (Arabic) Having an inner light
Nureh, Nourah, Nure

Nyala (African) Resembling an antelope
Nyalah, Nyalla, Nyallah

^**Nylah** (Gaelic) Cloud or champion

Nyneve (English) In Arthurian legend, another name for the lady of the lake
Nineve, Niniane, Ninyane, Nyniane, Ninieve, Niniveve

O

Oaisara (Arabic) A great ruler; an empress
Oaisarah, Oaisarra, Oaisarrah

Oamra (Arabic) Daughter of the moon
Oamrah, Oamira, Oamyra, Oameera

Oba (African) In mythology, the goddess of rivers
Obah, Obba, Obbah

Octavia (Latin) Feminine form of Octavius; the eighth-born child
Octaviana, Octavianne, Octavie, Octiana, Octoviana, Ottavia, Octavi, Octavy

Ode (Egyptian / Greek) Traveler of the road / a lyric poem
Odea

Odessa (Greek) Feminine form of Odysseus; one who wanders; an angry woman
Odissa, Odyssa, Odessia, Odissia, Odyssia, Odysseia

Odina (Latin / Scandinavian) From the mountain / feminine form of Odin, the highest of the gods
Odinah, Odeena, Odeene, Odeen, Odyna, Odyne, Odynn, Odeana

Ogin (Native American) Resembling the wild rose

Oheo (Native American) A beautiful woman

Oira (Latin) One who prays to God
Oyra, Oirah, Oyrah

Okalani (Hawaiian) Form of Kalani, meaning "from the heavens"
Okalanie, Okalany, Okalaney, Okalanee, Okaloni, Okalonie, Okalonee, Okalony, Okaloney, Okeilana, Okelani, Okelani, Okelanie, Okelany, Okelaney, Okelanee, Okalanea, Okalonea, Okelanea

Okei (Japanese) Woman of the ocean

Oksana (Russian) Hospitality
Oksanah, Oksie, Aksana

Ola (Nigerian / Hawaiian / Norse) One who is precious / giver of life; well-being / a relic of one's ancestors
Olah, Olla, Ollah

Olaide (American) A thoughtful woman
Olaid, Olaida, Olayd, Olayde, Olayda, Olaed, Olaede, Olaeda

Olathe (Native American) A lovely young woman

Olayinka (Yoruban) Surrounded by wealth and honor
Olayenka, Olayanka

Oleda (English) Resembling a winged creature
Oldedah, Oleta, Olita, Olida, Oletah, Olitah, Olidah

Olethea (Latin) Form of Alethea, meaning "one who is truthful"
Oletheia, Olethia, Oletha, Oletea, Olthaia, Olithea, Olathea, Oletia

Olina (Hawaiian) One who is joyous
Oline, Oleen, Oleene, Olyne, Oleena, Olyna, Olin

^***Olivia** (Latin) Feminine form of Oliver; of the olive tree; one who is peaceful
*Oliviah, Oliva, **Olive**, Oliveea, Olivet, Olivetta, Olivette, Olivija*

Olwen (Welsh) One who leaves a white footprint
Olwynn, Olvyen, Olvyin

Olympia (Greek) From Mount Olympus; a goddess
Olympiah, Olimpe, Olimpia, Olimpiada, Olimpiana, Olypme, Olympie, Olympi

Omri (Arabic) A red-haired woman
Omrie, Omree, Omrea, Omry, Omrey

Ona (Hebrew) Filled with grace
Onit, Onat, Onah

Ondrea (Slavic) Form of Andrea, meaning "courageous and strong / womanly"
Ondria, Ondrianna, Ondreia, Ondreina, Ondreya, Ondriana, Ondreana, Ondera

Oneida (Native American) Our long-awaited daughter
Onieda, Oneyda, Onida, Onyda

Onida (Native American) The one who has been expected
Onidah, Onyda, Onydah

Ontina (American) An open-minded woman
Ontinah, Onteena, Onteenah, Onteana, Onteanah, Ontiena, Ontienah, Onteina

Oona (Gaelic) Form of Agnes, meaning "one who is pure; chaste"

Opal (Sanskrit) A treasured jewel; resembling the iridescent gemstone
Opall, Opalle, Opale, Opalla, Opala, Opalina, Opaline, Opaleena

Ophelia (Greek) One who offers help to others
Ofelia, Ofilia, OphÈlie, Ophelya, Ophilia, Ovalia, Ovelia, Opheliah

Ophrah (Hebrew) Resembling a fawn; from the place of dust
Ofra, Ofrit, Ophra, Oprah, Orpa, Orpah, Ofrat, Ofrah

Orange (Latin) Resembling the sweet fruit
Orangetta, Orangia, Orangina, Orangea

Orbelina (American) One who brings excitement
Orbelinah, Orbeleena

Orea (Greek) From the mountains
Oreah

Orenda (Iroquois) A woman with magical powers

Oriana (Latin) Born at sunrise
Oreana, Orianna, Oriane, Oriann, Orianne

Oribel (Latin) A beautiful golden child
Orabel, Orabelle, Orabell, Orabela, Orabella, Oribell, Oribelle, Oribele

Orin (Irish) A dark-haired beauty
Orine, Orina, Oryna, Oryn, Oryne

Orinthia (Hebrew / Gaelic) Of the pine tree / a fair lady
Orrinthia, Orenthia, Orna, Ornina, Orinthea, Orenthea, Orynthia, Orynthea

Oriole (Latin) Resembling the gold-speckled bird
Oreolle, Oriolle, Oreole, Oriola, Oriolla, Oriol, Oreola, Oreolla

Orion (Greek) The huntress; a constellation

Orithna (Greek) One who is natural
Orithne, Orythna, Orythne, Orithnia, Orythnia, Orithnea, Orythnea

Orla (Gaelic) The golden queen
Orlah, Orrla, Orrlah, Orlagh, Orlaith, Orlaithe, Orghlaith, Orghlaithe

Orna (Irish / Hebrew) One who is pale-skinned / of the cedar tree
Ornah, Ornette, Ornetta, Ornete, Orneta, Obharnait, Ornat

Ornella (Italian) Of the flowering ash tree

Ornice (Irish) A pale-skinned woman
Ornyce, Ornise, Orynse, Orneice, Orneise, Orniece, Orniese, Orneece

Orva (Anglo-Saxon / French) A courageous friend / as precious as gold

Orynko (Ukrainian) A peaceful woman
Orinko, Orynka, Orinka

Osaka (Japanese) From the city of industry
Osaki, Osakie, Osakee, Osaky, Osakey, Osakea

Osma (English) Feminine form of Osmond; protected by God
Osmah, Ozma, Ozmah

Otina (American) A fortunate woman
Otinah, Otyna, Otynah, Oteena, Oteenah, Oteana, Oteanah, Otiena

Overton (English) From the upper side of town
Overtown

Owena (Welsh) A high-born woman
Owenah, Owenna, Owennah, Owenia, Owenea

Ozora (Hebrew) One who is wealthy
Ozorah, Ozorra, Ozorrah

P

Pace (American) A charismatic young woman
Paice, Payce, Paece, Pase, Paise, Payse, Paese

Pacifica (Spanish) A peaceful woman
Pacifika, Pacyfyca, Pacyfyka, Pacifyca, Pacifyka, Pacyfica, Pacyfika

Pageant (American) A dramatic woman
Pagent, Padgeant, Padgent

Paige (English) A young assistant
Page, Payge, Paege

Paisley (English) Woman of the church

Paki (African) A witness of God
Pakki, Packi, Pacci, Pakie, Pakkie, Paky, Pakky, Pakey

Palba (Spanish) A fair-haired woman

Palemon (Spanish) A kind-hearted woman
Palemond, Palemona, Palemonda

Palesa (African) Resembling a flower
Palessa, Palesah, Palysa, Palisa, Paleesa

Paloma (Spanish) Dove-like
Palloma, Palomita, Palometa, Peloma, Aloma

Pamela (English) A woman who is as sweet as honey
Pamelah, Pamella, Pammeli, Pammelie, Pameli, Pamelie, Pamelia, Pamelea

Panagiota (Greek) Feminine form of Panagiotis; a holy woman

Panchali (Indian) A princess; a high-born woman
Panchalie, Panchaly, Panchalli

Panda (English) Resembling the bamboo-eating animal
Pandah

Pandara (Indian) A good wife
Pandarah, Pandarra, Pandaria, Pandarea

Pandora (Greek) A gifted, talented woman; in mythology, the first mortal woman, who unleashed evil upon the world
Pandorah, Pandorra, Pandoria, Pandorea, Pandoriya

Pantxike (Latin) A woman who is free
Pantxikey, Pantxikye, Pantxeke, Pantxyke

Paras (Indian) A woman against whom others are measured

^**Paris** (English) Woman of the city in France
Pariss, Parisse, Parys, Paryss, Parysse

^**Parker** (English) The keeper of the park
Parkyr

Parry (Welsh) Daughter of Harry
Parri, Parrie, Parrey, Parree, Parrea

Parvani (Indian) Born during a full moon
Parvanie, Parvany, Parvaney, Parvanee, Parvanea

Parvati (Hindi) Daughter of the mountain; in Hinduism, a name for the wife of Shiva
Parvatie, Parvaty, Parvatey, Parvatee, Pauravi, Parvatea, Pauravie, Pauravy

Paterekia (Hawaiian) An upper-class woman
Paterekea, Pakelekia, Pakelekea

Patience (English) One who is patient; an enduring woman
Patiencia, Paciencia, Pacencia, Pacyncia, Pacincia, Pacienca

Patricia (English) Feminine form of Patrick; of noble descent
Patrisha, Patrycia, Patrisia, Patsy, Patti, Patty, Patrizia, Pattie, Trisha

Patrina (American) Born into the nobility
Patreena, Patriena, Patreina, Patryna, Patreana

Paula (English) Feminine form of Paul; a petite woman
Paulina, Pauline, Paulette, Paola, Pauleta, Pauletta, Pauli, Paulete

Pausha (Hindi) Resembling the moon
Paushah

Pax (Latin) One who is peaceful; in mythology, the goddess of peace
Paxi, Paxie, Paxton, Paxten, Paxtan, Paxy, Paxey, Paxee

^***Payton** (English) From the warrior's village
Paton, Paeton, Paiton, Payten, Paiten

Pearl (Latin) A precious gem of the sea
Pearla, Pearle, Pearlie, Pearly, Pearline, Pearlina, Pearli, Pearley

Pelopia (Greek) In mythology, the wife of Thyestes and mother of Aegisthus
Pelopiah, Pelopea, Pelopeah, Pelopiya

Pembroke (English) From the broken hill
Pembrook, Pembrok, Pembrooke

Pendant (French) A decorated woman
Pendent, Pendante, Pendente

Penelope (Greek) Resembling a duck; in mythology, the faithful wife of Odysseus
Peneloppe, Penelopy, Penelopey, Penelopi, Penelopie, Penelopee, Penella, Penelia

Penia (Greek) In mythology, the personification of poverty
Peniah, Penea, Peniya, Peneah, Peniyah

Penthesilea (Greek) In mythology, a queen of the Amazons

Peony (Greek) Resembling the flower
Peoney, Peoni, Peonie, Peonee, Peonea

Pepin (French) An awe-inspiring woman
Peppin, Pepine, Peppine, Pipin, Pippin, Pepen, Pepan, Peppen

Pepita (Spanish) Feminine form of Joseph; God will add
Pepitah, Pepitta, Pepitia, Pepitina

Perdita (Latin) A lost woman
Perditah, Perditta, Perdy, Perdie, Perdi, Perdee, Perdea, Perdeeta

Perdix (Latin) Resembling a partridge
Perdixx, Perdyx, Perdyxx

Peri (Persian / English) In mythology, a fairy / from the pear tree
Perry, Perri, Perie, Perrie, Pery, Perrey, Perey, Peree

Perpetua (Latin) One who is constant; steadfast

Persephone (Greek) In mythology, the daughter of Demeter and Zeus who was abducted to the underworld
Persephoni, Persephonie, Persephony, Persephoney, Persephonee, Persefone, Persefoni, Persefonie

Persis (Greek) Woman of Persia
Persiss, Persisse, Persys, Persyss, Persysse

Pesha (Hebrew) A flourishing woman
Peshah, Peshia, Peshiah, Peshea, Pesheah, Peshe

Petronela (Latin) Feminine form of Peter, as solid and strong as a rock
Petronella, Petronelle, Petronia, Petronilla, Petronille, Petrona, Petronia, Petronel

Petunia (English) Resembling the flower
Petuniah, Petuniya, Petunea, Petoonia, Petounia

***Peyton** (English) From the warrior's village
Peyten

Phaedra (Greek) A bright woman; in mythology, the wife of Theseus
Phadra, Phaidra, Phedra, Phaydra, Phedre, Phaedre

Phailin (Thai) Resembling a sapphire
Phaylin, Phaelin, Phalin

Phashestha (American) One who is decorated
Phashesthea, Phashesthia, Phashesthiya

Pheakkley (Vietnamese) A faithful woman
Pheakkly, Pheakkli, Pheakklie, Pheakklee, Pheakkleigh, Pheakklea

Pheodora (Greek) A supreme gift
Pheodorah, Phedora, Phedorah

Phernita (American) A well-spoken woman
Pherneeta, Phernyta, Phernieta, Pherneita, Pherneata

Phia (Italian) A saintly woman
Phiah, Phea, Pheah

Philippa (English) Feminine form of Phillip; a friend of horses
Phillippa, Philipa, Phillipa, Philipinna, Philippine, Phillipina, Phillipine, Pilis

Philomena (Greek) A friend of strength
Filomena, Philomina, Mena

Phoebe (Greek) A bright, shining woman; in mythology, another name for the goddess of the moon
Phebe, Phoebi, Phebi, Phoebie, Phebie, Pheobe, Phoebee, Phoebea

Phoena (Greek) Resembling a mystical bird
Phoenah, Phoenna, Phena, Phenna

Phoenix (Greek) A dark-red color; in mythology, an immortal bird
Phuong, Phoenyx

Phyllis (Greek) Of the foliage; in mythology, a girl who was turned into an almond tree
Phylis, Phillis, Philis, Phylys, Phyllida, Phylida, Phillida, Philida

Pili (Egyptian) The second-born child
Pilie, Pily, Piley, Pilee, Pilea, Pileigh

Pililani (Hawaiian) Having great strength
Pililanie, Pililany, Pililaney, Pililanee, Pililanea

Piluki (Hawaiian) Resembling a small leaf
Pilukie, Piluky, Pilukey, Pilukee, Pilukea

Pineki (Hawaiian) Resembling a peanut
Pinekie, Pineky, Pinekey, Pinekee, Pinekea

Ping (Chinese) One who is peaceful
Pyng

Pinga (Inuit) In mythology, goddess of the hunt, fertility, and healing
Pingah, Pyngah, Pyngah

Pinquana (Native American) Having a pleasant fragrance
Pinquan, Pinquann, Pinquanne, Pinquanna, Pinquane

Piper (English) One who plays the flute
Pipere, Piperel, Piperell, Piperele, Piperelle, Piperela, Piperella, Pyper

Pippi (French / English) A friend of horses / a blushing young woman
Pippie, Pippy, Pippey, Pippee, Pippea

Pirouette (French) A ballet dancer
Piroette, Pirouett, Piroett, Piroueta, Piroeta, Pirouetta, Piroetta, Pirouet

Pisces (Latin) The twelfth sign of the zodiac; the fishes
Pysces, Piscees, Pyscees, Piscez, Pisceez

Pithasthana (Hindi) In Hinduism, a name for the wife of Shiva

Platinum (English) As precious as the metal
Platynum, Platnum, Platie, Plati, Platee, Platy, Platey, Platea

Platt (French) From the plains
Platte

Pleshette (American) An extravagent woman
Pleshett, Pleshet, Pleshete, Plesheta, Pleshetta

Pleun (American) One who is good with words
Pleune

Po (Italian) A lively woman

Podarge (Greek) In mythology, one of the Harpies

Poetry (American) A romantic woman
Poetrey, Poetri, Poetrie, Poetree, Poetrea

Polete (Hawaiian) A kind young woman
Polet, Polett, Polette, Poleta, Poletta

Polina (Russian) A small woman
Polinah, Poleena, Poleenah, Poleana, Poleanah, Poliena, Polienah, Poleina

Polyxena (Greek) In mythology, a daughter of Priam and loved by Achilles
Polyxenah, Polyxenia, Polyxenna, Polyxene, Polyxenea

Pomona (Latin) In mythology, goddess of fruit trees
Pomonah, Pomonia, Pomonea, Pamona, Pamonia, Pamonea

Poni (African) The second-born daughter
Ponni, Ponie, Ponnie, Pony, Ponny, Poney, Ponney, Ponee

Poodle (American) Resembling the dog; one with curly hair
Poudle, Poodel, Poudel

Poonam (Hindi) A kind and caring woman
Pounam

Porter (Latin) The doorkeeper

Posala (Native American) Born at the end of spring
Posalah, Posalla, Posallah

Posh (American) A fancy young woman
Poshe, Posha

Potina (Latin) In mythology, goddess of children's food and drink
Potinah, Potyna, Potena, Poteena, Potiena, Poteina, Poteana

Powder (American) A light-hearted woman
Powdar, Powdir, Powdur, Powdor, Powdi, Powdie, Powdy, Powdey

Praise (Latin) One who expresses admiration
Prayse, Praize, Prayze, Praze, Praese, Praeze

Pramada (Indian) One who is indifferent

Pramlocha (Hindi) In Hinduism, a celestial nymph

Precious (American) One who is treasured
Preshis, Preshys

Presley (English) Of the priest's town
Presly, Preslie, Presli, Preslee

Primola (Latin) Resembling a primrose
Primolah, Primolia, Primoliah, Primolea, Primoleah

Princess (English) A high-born daughter; born to royalty
Princessa, Princesa, Princie, Princi, Princy, Princee, Princey, Princea

Prisca (Latin) From an ancient family
Priscilla, Priscella, Precilla, Presilla, Prescilla, Prisilla, Prisella, Prissy, Prissi

Promise (American) A faithful woman
Promice, Promyse, Promyce, Promis, Promiss, Promys, Promyss

Prudence (English) One who is cautious and exercises good judgment
Prudencia, Prudensa, Prudensia, Prudentia, Predencia, Predentia, Prue, Pru

Pryce (American / Welsh) One who is very dear / an enthusiastic child
Price, Prise, Pryse

Pulcheria (Italian) A chubby baby
Pulcheriah, Pulcherea, Pulchereah, Pulcherya, Pulcheryah, Pulcheriya

Pulika (African) An obedient and well-behaved girl
Pulikah, Pulicca, Pulicka, Pulyka, Puleeka, Puleaka

Pyrena (Greek) A fiery woman
Pyrenah, Pyrina, Pyrinah, Pyryna, Pyrynah, Pyreena, Pyreenah, Pyriena

Pyria (American) One who is cherished
Pyriah, Pyrea, Pyreah, Pyriya, Pyriyah, Pyra

Qadesh (Syrian) In mythology, goddess of love and sensuality
Quedesh, Qadesha, Quedesha, Qadeshia, Quedeshia, Quedeshiya

Qamra (Arabic) Of the moon
Qamrah, Qamar, Qamara, Qamrra, Qamaria, Qamrea, Qamria

Qimat (Indian) A valuable woman
Qimate, Qimatte, Qimata, Qimatta

Qitarah (Arabic) Having a nice fragrance
Qitara, Qytarah, Qytara, Qitaria, Qitarra, Qitarria, Qytarra, Qytarria

Qoqa (Chechen) Resembling a dove

Quana (Native American) One who is aromatic; sweet-smelling
Quanah, Quanna, Quannah, Quania, Quaniya, Quanniya, Quannia, Quanea

Querida (Spanish) One who is dearly loved; beloved
Queridah, Queryda, Querydah, Querrida, Queridda, Querridda, Quereeda, Quereada

Queta (Spanish) Head of the household
Quetah, Quetta, Quettah

Quiana (American) Living with grace; heavenly
Quianah, Quianna, Quiane, Quian, Quianne, Quianda, Quiani, Quianita

Quincy (English) The fifth-born child
Quincey, Quinci, Quincie, Quincee, Quincia, Quinncy, Quinnci, Quyncy

^Quinn (English / Irish) Woman who is queenly
Quin, Quinne

Quintana (Latin / English) The fifth girl / queen's lawn
Quintanah, Quinella, Quinta, Quintina, Quintanna, Quintann, Quintara, Quintona

Quintessa (Latin) Of the essence
Quintessah, Quintesa, Quintesha, Quintisha, Quintessia, Quyntessa, Quintosha, Quinticia

Quinyette (American) The fifth-born child
Quinyett, Quinyet, Quinyeta, Quinyette, Quinyete

Quirina (Latin) One who is contentious
Quirinah, Quiryna, Quirynah, Quireena, Quireenah, Quireina, Quireinah, Quiriena

Quiritis (Latin) In mythology, goddess of motherhood
Quiritiss, Quiritisse, Quirytis, Quirytys, Quiritys, Quirityss

R

Rabiah (Egyptian / Arabic) Born in the springtime / of the gentle wind
Rabia, Raabia, Rabi'ah, Rabi

Rachana (Hindi) Born of the creation
Rachanna, Rashana, Rashanda, Rachna

Rachel (Hebrew) The innocent lamb; in the Bible, Jacob's wife
Rachael, Racheal, Rachelanne, Rachelce, Rachele, Racheli, Rachell, Rachelle, Raquel

Radcliffe (English) Of the red cliffs
Radcleff, Radclef, Radclif, Radclife, Radclyffe, Radclyf, Radcliphe, Radclyphe

Radella (English) An elfin counselor
Radell, Radel, Radele, Radela, Raedself, Radself, Raidself

Radmilla (Slavic) Hard-working for the people
Radilla, Radinka, Radmila, Redmilla, Radilu

Rafi'a (Arabic) An exalted
woman
*Rafia, Rafi'ah, Rafee'a, Rafeea,
Rafeeah, Rafiya, Rafiyah*

Ragnara (Swedish) Feminine
form of Ragnar; one who pro-
vides counsel to the army
*Ragnarah, Ragnarra,
Ragnaria, Ragnarea, Ragnari,
Ragnarie, Ragnary, Ragnarey*

Rahi (Arabic) Born during the
springtime
*Rahii, Rahy, Rahey, Rahee,
Rahea, Rahie*

Rahimah (Arabic) A compas-
sionate woman; one who is
merciful
*Rahima, Raheema, Raheemah,
Raheima, Rahiema, Rahyma,
Rahymah, Raheama*

Raina (Polish) Form of Regina,
meaning "a queenly woman"
*Raenah, Raene, Rainah, Raine,
Rainee, Rainey, Rainelle, Rainy*

Raja (Arabic) One who is filled
with hope
Rajah

Raleigh (English) From the
clearing of roe deer
*Raileigh, Railey, Raley, Rawleigh,
Rawley, Raly, Rali, Ralie*

Ramona (Spanish) Feminine
form of Ramon; a wise pro-
tector
*Ramee, Ramie, Ramoena,
Ramohna, Ramonda,
Ramonde, Ramonita,
Ramonna*

Randi (English) Feminine
form of Randall; shielded
by wolves; form of Miranda,
meaning "worthy of admiration"
*Randa, Randee, Randelle,
Randene, Randie, Randy,
Randey, Randilyn*

Raquel (Spanish) Form of
Rachel, meaning "the inno-
cent lamb"
*Racquel, Racquell, Raquela,
Raquelle, Roquel, Roquela,
Rakel, Rakell*

Rasha (Arabic) Resembling a
young gazelle
*Rashah, Raisha, Raysha,
Rashia, Raesha*

Ratana (Thai) Resembling a
crystal
*Ratanah, Ratanna, Ratannah,
Rathana, Rathanna*

Rati (Hindi) In Hinduism,
goddess of passion and lust
*Ratie, Ratea, Ratee, Raty,
Ratey*

Ratri (Indian) Born in the evening
Ratrie, Ratry, Ratrey, Ratree, Ratrea

Rawiyah (Arabic) One who recites ancient poetry
Rawiya, Rawiyya, Rawiyyah

Rawnie (English) An elegant lady
Rawni, Rawny, Rawney, Rawnee, Rawnea

Raya (Israeli) A beloved friend
Rayah

Raymonde (German) Feminine form of Raymond; one who offers wise protection
Raymondi, Raymondie, Raymondee, Raymondea, Raymonda, Raymunde, Raymunda

Rayna (Hebrew / Scandinavian) One who is pure / one who provides wise counsel
Raynah, Raynee, Rayni, Rayne, Raynea, Raynie

Reba (Hebrew) Form of Rebecca, meaning "one who is bound to God"
Rebah, Reeba, Rheba, Rebba, Ree, Reyba, Reaba

Rebecca (Hebrew) One who is bound to God; in the Bible, the wife of Isaac
Rebakah, Rebbeca, Rebbecca, Rebbecka, Rebeca, Rebeccah, Rebeccea, Becky, Reba

Reese (American) Form of Rhys, meaning "having great enthusiasm for life"
Rhyss, Rhysse, Reece, Reice, Reise, Reace, Rease, Riece

Reagan (Gaelic) Born into royalty; the little ruler
Raegan, Ragan, Raygan, Reganne, Regann, Regane, Reghan, Regan

Regina (Latin) A queenly woman
Regeena, Regena, Reggi, Reggie, Régine, Regine, Reginette, Reginia, Raina

Rehan (Armenian) Resembling a flower
Rehane, Rehann, Rehanne, Rehana, Rehanna, Rehanan, Rehannan, Rehania

Rehoboth (Hebrew) From the city by the river
Rehobothe, Rehobotha, Rehobothia

Rekha (Indian) One who walks a straight line
Rekhah, Reka, Rekah

Remy (French) Woman from the town of Rheims
Remi, Remie, Remmy, Remmi, Remmie, Remmey, Remey

Ren (Japanese) Resembling a water lily

Renée (French) One who has been reborn
Ranae, Ranay, Ranée, Renae, Renata, Renay, Renaye, René

Reseda (Latin) Resembling the mignonette flower
Resedah, Reselda, Resedia, Reseldia

Resen (Hebrew) From the head of the stream; refers to a bridle

Reshma (Arabic) Having silky skin
Reshmah, Reshman, Reshmane, Reshmann, Reshmanne, Reshmana, Reshmanna, Reshmaan

Reya (Spanish) A queenly woman
Reyah, Reyeh, Reye, Reyia, Reyiah, Reyea, Reyeah

Reza (Hungarian) Form of Theresa, meaning "a harvester"
Rezah, Rezia, Reziah, Rezi, Rezie, Rezy, Rezee, Resi

Rezeph (Hebrew) As solid as a stone
Rezepha, Rezephe, Rezephia, Rezephah, Rezephiah

Rhea (Greek) Of the flowing stream; in mythology, the wife of Cronus and mother of gods and goddesses
Rea, Rhae, Rhaya, Rhia, Rhiah, Rhiya, Rheya

Rheda (Anglo-Saxon) A divine woman; a goddess
Rhedah

Rhiannon (Welsh) The great and sacred queen
Rheanna, Rheanne, Rhiana, Rhiann, Rhianna, Rhiannan, Rhianon, Rhyan

Rhonda (Welsh) Wielding a good spear
Rhondelle, Rhondene, Rhondiesha, Rhonette, Rhonnda, Ronda, Rondel, Rondelle

Rhys (Welsh) Having great enthusiasm for life
Rhyss, Rhysse, Reece, Reese, Reice, Reise, Reace, Rease

Ria (Spanish) From the river's mouth
Riah

Riane (Gaelic) Feminine form of Ryan; little ruler
Riana, Rianna, Rianne, Ryann, Ryanne, Ryana, Ryanna, Riann

Rica (English) Form of Frederica, meaning "peaceful ruler"; form of Erica, meaning "ever the ruler / resembling heather"
Rhica, Ricca, Ricah, Rieca, Riecka, Rieka, Riqua, Ryca

Riddhi (Indian) A prosperous woman
Riddhie, Riddhy, Riddhey, Riddhee, Riddhea

Rihanna (Arabic) Resembling sweet basil
Rihana

*Riley (Gaelic) From the rye clearing; a courageous woman
Reilley, Reilly, Rilee, Rileigh, Ryley, Rylee, Ryleigh, Rylie

Rini (Japanese) Resembling a young rabbit
Rinie, Rinee, Rinea, Riny, Riney

Rio (Spanish) Woman of the river
Rhio

Risa (Latin) One who laughs often
Risah, Reesa, Riesa, Rise, Rysa, Rysah, Riseh, Risako

Rita (Greek) Precious pearl
Ritta, Reeta, Reita, Rheeta, Riet, Rieta, Ritah, Reta

Roberta (English) Feminine form of Robert; one who is bright with fame
Robertah, Robbie, Robin

Rochelle (French) From the little rock
Rochel, Rochele, Rochell, Rochella, Rochette, Roschella, Roschelle, Roshelle

Roja (Spanish) A red-haired lady
Rojah

Rolanda (German) Feminine form of Roland; well-known throughout the land
Rolandah, Rolandia, Roldandea, Rolande, Rolando, Rollanda, Rollande

Romhilda (German) A glorious battle maiden
Romhilde, Romhild, Romeld, Romelde, Romelda, Romilda, Romild, Romilde

Ronli (Hebrew) My joy is the Lord
Ronlie, Ronlee, Ronleigh, Ronly, Ronley, Ronlea, Ronia, Roniya

Ronni (English) Form of Veronica, meaning "displaying her true image"
Ronnie, Ronae, Ronay, Ronee, Ronelle, Ronette, Roni, Ronica, Ronika

Rosalind (German / English) Resembling a gentle horse / form of Rose, meaning "resembling the beautiful and meaningful flower"
Ros, Rosaleen, Rosalen, Rosalin, Rosalina, Rosalinda, Rosalinde, Rosaline, Chalina

Rose (Latin) Resembling the beautiful and meaningful flower
Rosa, Rosie, Rosalind

Roseanne (English) Resembling the graceful rose
Ranna, Rosana, Rosanagh, Rosanna, Rosannah, Rosanne, Roseann, Roseanna

Rosemary (Latin / English) The dew of the sea / resembling a bitter rose
Rosemaree, Rosemarey, Rosemaria, Rosemarie, Rosmarie, Rozmary, Rosamaria, Rosamarie

Rowan (Gaelic) Of the red-berry tree
Rowann, Rowane, Rowanne, Rowana, Rowanna

Rowena (Welsh / German) One who is fair and slender / having much fame and happiness
Rhowena, Roweena, Roweina, Rowenna, Rowina, Rowinna, Rhonwen, Rhonwyn

Ruana (Indian) One who is musically inclined
Ruanah, Ruanna, Ruannah, Ruane, Ruann, Ruanne

Ruby (English) As precious as the red gemstone
Rubee, Rubi, Rubie, Rubyna, Rubea

Rudella (German) A well-known woman
Rudela, Rudelah, Rudell, Rudelle, Rudel, Rudele, Rudy, Rudie

Rue (English, German) A medicinal herb
Ru, Larue

Rufina (Latin) A red-haired woman
Rufeena, Rufeine, Ruffina, Rufine, Ruffine, Rufyna, Ruffyna, Rufyne

Ruhi (Arabic) A spiritual woman
Roohee, Ruhee, Ruhie, Ruhy, Ruhey, Roohi, Roohie, Ruhea

Rukmini (Hindi) Adorned with gold; in Hinduism, the first wife of Krishna
Rukminie, Rukminy, Rukminey, Rukminee, Rukminea, Rukminni, Rukminii

Rumah (Hebrew) One who has been exalted
Ruma, Rumia, Rumea, Rumiah, Rumeah, Rumma, Rummah

Rumina (Latin) In mythology, a protector goddess of mothers and babies
Ruminah, Rumeena, Rumeenah, Rumeina, Rumiena, Rumyna, Rumeinah, Rumienah

Rupali (Indian) A beautiful woman
Rupalli, Rupalie, Rupalee, Rupallee, Rupal, Rupa, Rupaly, Rupaley

Ruqayyah (Arabic) A gentle woman; a daughter of Muhammad
Ruqayya, Ruqayah, Ruqaya

Ruth (Hebrew) A beloved companion
Ruthe, Ruthelle, Ruthellen, Ruthetta, Ruthi, Ruthie, Ruthina, Ruthine

Ryba (Slavic) Resembling a fish
Rybah, Rybba, Rybbah

Ryder (American) An accomplished horsewoman
Rider

Rylee (American) Form of Riley, meaning "from the rye clearing / a courageous woman"

S

Saba (Greek / Arabic) Woman from Sheba / born in the morning
Sabah, Sabaa, Sabba, Sabbah, Sabaah

Sabana (Spanish) From the open plain
Sabanah, Sabanna, Sabann, Sabanne, Sabane, Saban

Sabi (Arabic) A lovely young lady
Sabie, Saby, Sabey, Sabee, Sabbi, Sabbee, Sabea

Sabirah (Arabic) Having great patience
Sabira, Saabira, Sabeera, Sabiera, Sabeira, Sabyra, Sabirra, Sabyrra

Sabra (Hebrew) Resembling the cactus fruit; to rest
Sabrah, Sebra, Sebrah, Sabrette, Sabbra, Sabraa, Sabarah, Sabarra

Sabrina (English) A legendary princess
Sabrinah, Sabrinna, Sabreena, Sabriena, Sabreina, Sabryna, Sabrine, Sabryne, Cabrina, Zabrina

Sachet (Hindi) Having consciousness
Sachett, Sachette

Sada (Japanese) The pure one
Sadda, Sadaa, Sadako, Saddaa

Sadella (American) A beautiful fairylike princess
Sadel, Sadela, Sadelah, Sadele, Sadell, Sadellah, Sadelle, Sydel

Sadhana (Hindi) A devoted woman
Sadhanah, Sadhanna, Sadhannah, Sadhane, Sadhanne, Sadhann, Sadhan

Sadhbba (Irish) A wise woman
Sadhbh, Sadhba

Sadie (English) Form of Sarah, meaning "a princess; lady"
Sadi, Sady, Sadey, Sadee, Saddi, Saddee, Sadiey, Sadye

Sadiya (Arabic) One who is fortunate; lucky
Sadiyah, Sadiyyah, Sadya, Sadyah

Sadzi (American) Having a sunny disposition
Sadzee, Sadzey, Sadzia, Sadziah, Sadzie, Sadzya, Sadzyah, Sadzy

Safa (Arabic) One who is innocent and pure
Safah, Saffa, Sapha, Saffah, Saphah

Saffron (English) Resembling the yellow flower
Saffrone, Saffronn, Saffronne, Safron, Safronn, Safronne, Saffronah, Safrona

Saheli (Indian) A beloved friend
Sahelie, Sahely, Saheley, Sahelee, Saheleigh, Sahyli, Sahelea

Sahila (Indian) One who provides guidance
Sahilah, Saheela, Sahyla, Sahiela, Saheila, Sahela, Sahilla, Sahylla

Sahkyo (Native American) Resembling the mink
Sakyo

Saida (Arabic) Fortunate one; one who is happy
Saidah, Sa'ida, Sayida, Saeida, Saedah, Said, Sayide, Sayidea

Saihah (Arabic) One who is useful; good
Saiha, Sayiha

Sailor (American) One who sails the seas
Sailer, Sailar, Saylor, Sayler, Saylar, Saelor, Saeler, Saelar

Saima (Arabic) A fasting woman
Saimah, Saimma, Sayima

Sajni (Indian) One who is dearly loved
Sajnie, Sajny, Sajney, Sajnee, Sajnea

Sakae (Japanese) One who is prosperous
Sakai, Sakaie, Sakay, Sakaye

Sakari (Native American) A sweet girl
Sakarie, Sakary, Sakarri, Sakarey, Sakaree, Sakarree, Sakarah, Sakarrie

Sakina (Indian / Arabic) A beloved friend / having God-inspired peace of mind
Sakinah, Sakeena, Sakiena, Sakeina, Sakyna, Sakeyna, Sakinna, Sakeana

Sakti (Hindi) In Hinduism, the divine energy
Saktie, Sakty, Sakkti, Sackti, Saktee, Saktey, Saktia, Saktiah

Saku (Japanese) Remembrance of the Lord
Sakuko

Sakura (Japanese) Resembling a cherry blossom
Sakurah, Sakurako, Sakurra

Sala (Hindi) From the sacred sala tree
Salah, Salla, Sallah

Salal (English) An evergreen shrub with flowers and berries
Sallal, Salall, Sallall, Salalle, Salale, Sallale

Salamasina (Samoan) A princess; born to royalty
Salamaseena, Salamasyna, Salamaseana, Salamaseina, Salamasiena

Salina (French) One of a solemn, dignified character
Salin, Salinah, Salinda, Salinee, Sallin, Sallina, Sallinah, Salline

Saloma (Hebrew) One who offers peace and tranquility
Salomah, Salome, Salomia, Salomiah, Schlomit, Shulamit, Salomeaexl, Salomma

Salus (Latin) In mythology, goddess of health and prosperity; salvation
Saluus, Salusse, Saluss

Salwa (Arabic) One who provides comfort; solace
Salwah

Samah (Arabic) A generous, forgiving woman
Sama, Samma, Sammah

*Samantha (Aramaic) One who listens well
Samanthah, Samanthia, Samanthea, Samantheya, Samanath, Samanatha, Samana, Samanitha

Sameh (Arabic) One who forgives
Sammeh, Samaya, Samaiya

Samina (Arabic) A healthy woman
Saminah, Samine, Sameena, Samyna, Sameana, Sameina, Samynah

Samone (Hebrew) Form of Simone, meaning "one who listens well"
Samoan, Samoane, Samon, Samona, Samonia

Samuela (Hebrew) Feminine form of Samuel; asked of God
Samuelah, Samuella, Samuell, Samuelle, Sammila, Sammile, Samella, Samielle

Sana (Persian / Arabic) One who emanates light / brilliance; splendor
Sanah, Sanna, Sanako, Sanaah, Sane, Saneh

Sanaa (Swahili) Beautiful work of art
Sanae, Sannaa

Sandeep (Punjabi) One who is enlightened
Sandeepe, Sandip, Sandipp, Sandippe, Sandeyp, Sandeype

Sandhya (Hindi) Born at twilight; name of the daughter of the god Brahma
Sandhiya, Sandhyah, Sandya, Sandyah

Sandra (Greek) Form of Alexandra, meaning "a helper and defender of mankind"
Sandrah, Sandrine, Sandy, Sandi, Sandie, Sandey, Sandee, Sanda, Sandrica

Sandrica (Greek) Form of Alexandra, meaning "a helper and defender of mankind"
Sandricca, Sandricah, Sandricka, Sandrickah, Sandrika, Sandrikah, Sandryca, Sandrycah

Sandrine (Greek) Form of Alexandra, meaning "a helper and defender of mankind"
Sandrin, Sandreana, Sandreanah, Sandreane, Sandreen, Sandreena, Sandreenah, Sandreene

Sangita (Indian) One who is musical
Sangitah, Sangeeta, Sangeita, Sangyta, Sangieta, Sangeata

Saniya (Indian) A moment in time preserved
Saniyah, Sanya, Sanea, Sania

Sanjna (Indian) A conscientious woman

Santana (Spanish) A saintly woman
Santa, Santah, Santania, Santaniah, Santaniata, Santena, Santenah, Santenna

Saoirse (Gaelic) An independent woman; having freedom
Saoyrse

Sapna (Hindi) A dream come true
Sapnah, Sapnia, Sapniah, Sapnea, Sapneah, Sapniya, Sapniyah

*Sarah (Hebrew) A princess; lady; in the Bible, wife of Abraham
Sara, Sari, Sariah, Sarika, Saaraa, Sarita, Sarina, Sarra, Kala, Sadie

Saraid (Irish) One who is excellent; superior
Saraide, Saraed, Saraede, Sarayd, Sarayde

Sarama (African / Hindi) A kind woman / in Hinduism, Indra's dog
Saramah, Saramma, Sarrama, Sarramma

Saran (African) One who brings joy to others
Sarane, Sarran, Saranne, Saranna, Sarana, Sarann

Sarasvati (Hindi) In Hinduism, goddess of learning and the arts
Sarasvatti, Sarasvatie, Sarasvaty, Sarasvatey, Sarasvatee, Sarasvatea

Saraswati (Hindi) Owning water; in Hinduism, a river goddess
Saraswatti, Saraswatie, Saraswaty, Saraswatey, Saraswatee, Saraswatea

Sardinia (Italian) Woman from a mountainous island
Sardiniah, Sardinea, Sardineah, Sardynia, Sardyniah, Sardynea, Sardyneah

Sasa (Japanese) One who is helpful; gives aid
Sasah

Sasha (Russian) Form of Alexandra, meaning "a helper and defender of mankind"
Sascha, Sashenka, Saskia

Sauda (Swahili) A dark beauty
Saudaa, Sawda, Saudda

*Savannah** (English) From the open grassy plain
Savanna, Savana, Savanne, Savann, Savane, Savanneh

Savarna (Hindi) Daughter of the ocean
Savarnia, Savarnea, Savarniya, Savarneia

Savitri (Hindi) In Hinduism, the daughter of the god of the sun
Savitari, Savitrie, Savitry, Savitarri, Savitarie, Savitree, Savitrea, Savitrey

Savvy (American) Smart and perceptive woman
Savy, Savvi, Savvie, Savvey, Savee, Savvee, Savvea, Savea

Sayyida (Arabic) A mistress
Sayyidah, Sayida, Sayyda, Seyyada, Seyyida, Seyada, Seyida

^*Scarlett** (English) Vibrant red color; a vivacious woman
Scarlet, *Scarlette, Skarlet*

Scota (Irish) Woman of Scotland
Scotta, Scotah, Skota, Skotta, Skotah

Sea'iqa (Arabic) Thunder and lightning
Seaqa, Seaqua

Season (Latin) A fertile woman; one who embraces change
Seazon, Seeson, Seezon, Seizon, Seasen, Seasan, Seizen, Seizan

Sebille (English) In Arthurian legend, a fairy
Sebylle, Sebill, Sebile, Sebyle, Sebyl

Secunda (Latin) The second-born child
Secundah, Secuba, Secundus, Segunda, Sekunda

Seda (Armenian) Voices of the forest
Sedda, Sedah, Seddah

Sedona (American) Woman from a city in Arizona
Sedonah, Sedonna, Sedonnah, Sedonia, Sedonea

Seema (Greek) A symbol; a sign
Seyma, Syma, Seama, Seima, Siema

Sefarina (Greek) Of a gentle wind
Sefarinah, Sefareena, Sefareenah, Sefaryna, Sefarynah, Sefareana, Sefareanah

Seiko (Japanese) The force of truth

Selene (Greek) Of the moon
Sela, Selena, Selina, Celina, Zalina

Sema (Arabic) A divine omen; a known symbol
Semah

Senalda (Spanish) A sign; a symbol
Senaldah, Senaldia, Senaldiya, Senaldea, Senaldya

September (American) Born in the month of September
Septimber, Septymber, Septemberia, Septemberea

Sequoia (Native American) Of the giant redwood tree
Sekwoya, Lequoia

Serafina (Latin) A seraph; a heavenly winged angel
Serafinah, Serafine, Seraphina, Serefina, Seraphine, Sera

Serena (Latin) Having a peaceful disposition
Serenah, Serene, Sereena, Seryna, Serenity, Serenitie, Serenitee, Serepta, Cerina, Xerena

Serendipity (American) A fateful meeting; having good fortune
Serendipitey, Serendipitee, Serendipiti, Serendipitie, Serendypyty

*Serenity (Latin) Peaceful

Sevati (Indian) Resembling the white rose
Sevatie, Sevatti, Sevate, Sevatee, Sevatea, Sevaty, Sevatey, Sevti

Shabana (Arabic) A maiden belonging to the night
Shabanah, Shabanna, Shabaana, Shabanne, Shabane

Shabnan (Persian) A falling raindrop
Shabnane, Shabnann, Shabnanne

Shadha (Arabic) An aromatic fragrance
Shadhah

Shafiqa (Arabic) A compassionate woman
Shafiqah, Shafiqua, Shafeeqa, Shafeequa

Shai (Gaelic) A gift of God
Shay, Shae, Shayla, Shea, Shaye

Sha'ista (Arabic) One who is polite and well-behaved
Shaistah, Shaista, Shaa'ista, Shayista, Shaysta

Shakila (Arabic) Feminine form of Shakil; beautiful one
Shakilah, Shakela, Shakeela, Shakeyla, Shakyla, Shakeila, Shakiela, Shakina

Shakira (Arabic) Feminine form of Shakir; grateful; thankful
Shakirah, Shakiera, Shaakira, Shakeira, Shakyra, Shakeyra, Shakura, Shakirra

Shakti (Indian) A divine woman; having power
Shaktie, Shakty, Shaktey, Shaktee, Shaktye, Shaktea

Shaliqa (Arabic) One who is sisterly
Shaliqah, Shaliqua, Shaleeqa, Shaleequa, Shalyqa, Shalyqua

Shamima (Arabic) A woman full of flavor
Shamimah, Shameema, Shamiema, Shameima, Shamyma, Shameama

Shandy (English) One who is rambunctious; boisterous
Shandey, Shandee, Shandi, Shandie, Shandye, Shandea

Shani (African) A marvelous woman
Shanie, Shany, Shaney, Shanee, Shanni, Shanea, Shannie, Shanny

Shanley (Gaelic) Small and ancient woman
Shanleigh, Shanlee, Shanly, Shanli, Shanlie, Shanlea

Shannon (Gaelic) Having ancient wisdom; river name
Shanon, Shannen, Shannan, Shannin, Shanna, Shannae, Shannun, Shannyn

Shaquana (American) Truth in life
Shaqana, Shaquanah, Shaquanna, Shaqanna, Shaqania

Sharifah (Arabic) Feminine form of Sharif; noble; respected; virtuous
Sharifa, Shareefa, Sharufa, Sharufah, Sharyfa, Sharefa, Shareafa, Shariefa

Sharik (African) One who is a child of God
Shareek, Shareake, Sharicke, Sharick, Sharike, Shareak, Sharique, Sharyk

Sharikah (Arabic) One who is a good companion
Sharika, Shareeka, Sharyka, Shareka, Shariqua, Shareaka

Sharlene (French) Feminine form of Charles; petite and womanly
Sharleene, Sharleen, Sharla, Sharlyne, Sharline, Sharlyn, Sharlean, Sharleane

Sharon (Hebrew) From the plains; a flowering shrub
Sharron, Sharone, Sharona, Shari, Sharis, Sharne, Sherine, Sharun

Shasta (Native American) From the triple-peaked mountain
Shastah, Shastia, Shastiya, Shastea, Shasteya

Shawnee (Native American) A tribal name
Shawni, Shawnie, Shawnea, Shawny, Shawney, Shawnea

Shayla (Irish) Of the fairy palace; form of Shai, meaning "a gift of God"
Shaylah, Shaylagh, Shaylain, Shaylan, Shaylea, Shayleah, Shaylla, Sheyla

Shaylee (Gaelic) From the fairy palace; a fairy princess
Shalee, Shayleigh, Shailee, Shaileigh, Shaelee, Shaeleigh, Shayli, Shaylie

Sheehan (Celtic) Little peaceful one; peacemaker
Shehan, Sheyhan, Shihan, Shiehan, Shyhan, Sheahan

Sheela (Indian) One of cool conduct and character
Sheelah, Sheetal

Sheena (Gaelic) God's gracious gift
Sheenah, Shena, Shiena, Sheyna, Shyna, Sheana, Sheina

Sheherezade (Arabic) One who is a city dweller

Sheila (Irish) Form of Cecilia, meaning "one who is blind"
Sheilah, Sheelagh, Shelagh, Shiela, Shyla, Selia, Sighle, Sheiletta

Shelby (English) From the willow farm
Shelbi, Shelbey, Shelbie, Shelbee, Shelbye, Shelbea

Sheridan (Gaelic) One who is wild and untamed; a searcher
Sheridann, Sheridanne, Sherydan, Sherridan, Sheriden, Sheridon, Sherrerd, Sherida

Sheshebens (Native American) Resembling a small duck

Shifra (Hebrew) A beautiful midwife
Shifrah, Shiphrah, Shiphra, Shifria, Shifriya, Shifrea

Shikha (Indian) Flame burning brightly
Shikhah, Shikkha, Shekha, Shykha

Shima (Native American) Little mother
Shimah, Shimma, Shyma, Shymah

Shina (Japanese) A virtuous woman; having goodness
Shinah, Shinna, Shyna, Shynna

Shobha (Indian) An attractive woman
Shobhah, Shobbha, Shoba, Shobhan, Shobhane

Shoshana (Arabic) Form of Susannah, meaning "white lily"
Shosha, Shoshan, Shoshanah, Shoshane, Shoshanha, Shoshann, Shoshanna, Shoshannah

Shradhdha (Indian) One who is faithful; trusting
Shraddha, Shradha, Shradhan, Shradhane

Shruti (Indian) Having good hearing
Shrutie, Shruty, Shrutey, Shrutee, Shrutye, Shrutea

Shunnareh (Arabic) Pleasing in manner and behavior
Shunnaraya, Shunareh, Shunarreh

Shyann (English) Form of Cheyenne, meaning "unintelligible speaker"
Shyanne, Shyane, Sheyann, Sheyanne, Sheyenne, Sheyene

Shysie (Native American) A quiet child
Shysi, Shysy, Shysey, Shysee, Shycie, Shyci, Shysea, Shycy

Sibyl (English) A prophetess; a seer
Sybil, Sibyla, Sybella, Sibil, Sibella, Sibilla, Sibley, Sibylla

Siddhi (Hindi) Having spiritual power
Sidhi, Syddhi, Sydhi

Sidero (Greek) In mythology, stepmother of Pelias and Neleus
Siderro, Sydero, Sideriyo

Sieglinde (German) Winning a gentle victory

Sienna (Italian) Woman with reddish-brown hair
Siena, Siennya, Sienya, Syenna, Syinna

Sierra (Spanish) From the jagged mountain range
Siera, Syerra, Syera, Seyera, Seeara

Sigfreda (German) A woman who is victorious
Sigfreeda, Sigfrida, Sigfryda, Sigfreyda, Sigfrieda, Sigfriede, Sigfrede

Sigismonda (Teutonic) A victorious defender
Sigismunda

Signia (Latin) A distinguishing sign
Signiya, Signea, Signeia, Signeya, Signa

Sigyn (Norse) In mythology, the wife of Loki

Sihu (Native American) As delicate as a flower

Silka (Latin) Form of Cecelia, meaning "one who is blind"
Silke, Silkia, Silkea, Silkie, Silky, Silkee, Sylka, Sylke

Sima (Arabic) One who is treasured; a prize
Simma, Syma, Simah, Simia, Simiya

Simone (French) One who listens well
Sim, Simonie, Symone, Samone

Sine (Scottish) Form of Jane, meaning "God is gracious"
Sinead, Sineidin, Sioned, Sionet, Sion, Siubhan, Siwan, Sineh

Sinobia (Greek) Form of Zenobia, meaning "child of Zeus"
Sinobiah, Sinobya, Sinobe, Sinobie, Sinovia, Senobia, Senobya, Senobe

Sinopa (Native American) Resembling a fox

Sinope (Greek) In mythology, one of the daughters of Asopus

Siran (Armenian) An alluring and lovely woman

Siren (Greek) In mythology, a sea nymph whose beautiful singing lured sailors to their deaths; refers to a seductive and beautiful woman
Sirene, Sirena, Siryne, Siryn, Syren, Syrena, Sirine, Sirina

Siria (Spanish / Persian) Bright like the sun / a glowing woman
Siriah, Sirea, Sireah, Siriya, Siriyah, Sirya, Siryah

Siroun (Armenian) A lovely woman
Sirune

Sirpuhi (Armenian) One who is holy; pious
Sirpuhie, Sirpuhy, Sirpuhey, Sirpuhea, Sirpuhee

Sissy (English) Form of Cecilia, meaning "one who is blind"
Sissey, Sissie, Sisley, Sisli, Sislee, Sissel, Sissle, Syssy

Sita (Hindi) In Hinduism, goddess of the harvest and wife of Rama

Sive (Irish) A good and sweet girl
Sivney, Sivny, Sivni, Sivnie, Sivnee, Sivnea

Skylar (English) One who is learned, a scholar
Skylare, Skylarr, Skyler, Skylor, Skylir

Sloane (Irish) A strong protector; a woman warrior
Sloan, Slone

Smita (Indian) One who smiles a lot

Snow (American) Frozen rain
Snowy, Snowie, Snowi, Snowey, Snowee, Snowea, Sno

Snowdrop (English) Resembling a small white flower

Solana (Latin / Spanish) Wind from the east / of the sunshine
Solanah, Solanna, Solann, Solanne

Solange (French) One who is religious and dignified

Solaris (Greek) Of the sun
Solarise, Solariss, Solarisse, Solarys, Solaryss, Solarysse, Sol, Soleil

Solita (Latin) One who is solitary
Solitah, Solida, Soledad, Soledada, Soledade

Somatra (Indian) Of the excellent moon

Sona (Arabic) The golden one
Sonika, Sonna

Sonora (Spanish) A pleasant-sounding woman
Sonorah, Sonoria, Sonorya, Sonoriya

Soo (Korean) Having an excellent long life

*****Sophia** (Greek) Form of Sophie, meaning great wisdom and foresight
Sofia, Sofiya

*****Sophie** (Greek) Wisdom
Sophia, Sofiya, Sofie, Sofia, Sofi, Sofiyko, Sofronia, Sophronia, Zofia

Sorina (Romanian) Feminine form of Sorin; of the sun
Sorinah, Sorinna, Sorinia, Soriniya, Sorinya, Soryna, Sorynia, Sorine

Sorrel (French) From the surele plant
Sorrell, Sorrelle, Sorrele, Sorrela, Sorrella

Sparrow (English) Resembling a small songbird
Sparro, Sparroe, Sparo, Sparow, Sparowe, Sparoe

Sslama (Egyptian) One who is peaceful

Stacey (English) Form of Anastasia, meaning "one who shall rise again"
Stacy, Staci, Stacie, Stacee, Stacia, Stasia, Stasy, Stasey

*****Stella** (English) Star of the sea
Stela, Stelle, Stele, Stellah, Stelah

Stephanie (Greek) Feminine form of Stephen; crowned in victory
Stephani, Stephany, Stephaney, Stephanee, Stephene, Stephana, Stefanie, Stefani

Stevonna (Greek) A crowned lady
Stevonnah, Stevona, Stevonah, Stevonia, Stevonea, Stevoniya

Styx (Greek) In mythology, the river of the underworld
Stixx, Styxx, Stix

Suave (American) A smooth and courteous woman
Swave

Subhadra (Hindi) In Hinduism, the sister of Krishna

Subhaga (Indian) A fortunate person

Subhuja (Hindi) An auspicious celestial damsel

Subira (African) One who is patient
Subirah, Subirra, Subyra, Subyrra, Subeera, Subeara, Subeira, Subiera

Suhaila (Arabic) Feminine form of Suhail; the second brightest star
Suhayla, Suhaela, Suhala, Suhailah, Suhaylah, Suhaelah, Suhalah

Sulwyn (Welsh) One who shines as bright as the sun
Sulwynne, Sulwynn, Sulwinne, Sulwin, Sulwen, Sulwenn, Sulwenne

Sumana (Indian) A good-natured woman
Sumanah, Sumanna, Sumane, Sumanne, Sumann

Sumi (Japanese) One who is elegant and refined
Sumie

Sumitra (Indian) A beloved friend
Sumitrah, Sumita, Sumytra, Sumyta, Sumeetra, Sumeitra, Sumietra, Sumeatra

Summer (American) Refers to the season; born in summer
Sommer, Sumer, Somer, Somers

Suna (Turkish) A swan-like woman

Sunanda (Indian) Having a sweet character
Sunandah, Sunandia, Sunandiya, Sunandea, Sunandya

Sunila (Indian) Feminine form of Sunil; very blue
Sunilah, Sunilla, Sunilya, Suniliya

Sunniva (English) Gift of the sun
Synnove, Synne, Synnove, Sunn

Surabhi (Indian) Having a lovely fragrance
Surbhii, Surabhie, Surabhy, Surabhey, Surabhee, Surabhea

Susannah (Hebrew) White lily
*Susanna, Susanne, Susana,
Susane, Susan, Suzanna,
Suzannah, Suzanne,
Shoshana, Huhana*

Sushanti (Indian) A peaceful
woman; tranquil
*Sushantie, Sushanty,
Sushantey, Sushantee,
Sushantea*

Suzu (Japanese) One who is
long-lived
Suzue, Suzuko

Swanhilda (Norse) A woman
warrior; in mythology, the
daughter of Sigurd
*Swanhild, Swanhilde,
Svanhilde, Svanhild, Svenhilde,
Svenhilda*

Swarupa (Indian) One who is
devoted to the truth

*Sydney (English) Of the wide
meadow
*Sydny, Sydni, Sydnie, Sydnea,
Sydnee, Sidney, Sidne, Sidnee*

T

Taariq (Swahili) Resembling
the morning star
Tariq, Taarique, Tarique

Tabia (African / Egyptian) One
who makes incantations / a
talented woman
*Tabiah, Tabya, Tabea, Tabeah,
Tabiya*

Tabita (African) A graceful
woman
*Tabitah, Tabyta, Tabytah,
Tabeeta, Tabeata, Tabieta,
Tabeita*

Tabitha (Greek) Resembling a
gazelle; known for beauty and
grace
*Tabithah, Tabbitha, Tabetha,
Tabbetha, Tabatha, Tabbatha,
Tabotha, Tabbotha*

Tabora (Spanish) One who
plays a small drum
*Taborah, Taborra, Taboria,
Taborya*

Tacincala (Native American)
Resembling a deer
*Tacincalah, Tacyncala,
Tacyncalah, Tacincalla,
Tacyncalla*

Tahsin (Arabic) Beautification;
one who is praised
*Tahseen, Tahsene, Tahsyne,
Tasine, Tahseene, Tahsean,
Tahseane*

Tahzib (Arabic) One who is
educated and cultured
*Tahzeeb, Tahzebe, Tahzybe,
Tazib, Tazyb, Tazeeb,
Tahzeab, Tazeab*

Taithleach (Gaelic) A quiet and
calm young lady

Takako (Japanese) A lofty child

Takoda (Native American)
Friend to everyone
*Takodah, Takodia, Takodya,
Takota*

Tala (Native American) A
stalking wolf
Talah, Talla

Talia (Hebrew / Greek)
Morning dew from heaven /
blooming
*Taliah, Talea, Taleah, Taleya,
Tallia, Talieya, Taleea, Taleia*

Talihah (Arabic) One who
seeks knowledge
*Taliha, Talibah, Taliba,
Talyha, Taleehah, Taleahah*

Taline (Armenian) Of the
monestary
*Talene, Taleen, Taleene, Talyne,
Talinia, Talinya, Taliniya*

Talisa (American) Consecrated
to God
*Talisah, Talysa, Taleesa,
Talissa, Talise, Taleese, Talisia,
Talisya*

Talisha (American) A damsel;
an innocent
*Talesha, Taleisha, Talysha,
Taleesha, Tylesha, Taleysha,
Taleshia, Talishia*

Talitha (Arabic) A maiden;
young girl
*Talithah, Taletha, Taleetha,
Talytha, Talithia, Talethia,
Tiletha, Talith*

Tamanna (Indian) One who is
desired
*Tamannah, Tamana,
Tamanah, Tammana,
Tammanna*

Tamasha (African) Pageant
winner
*Tamasha, Tomosha, Tomasha,
Tamashia, Tamashya*

Tamesis (Celtic) In mythology,
the goddess of water; source
of the name for the river
Thames
Tamesiss, Tamesys, Tamesyss

Tangia (American) The angel
*Tangiah, Tangya, Tangiya,
Tangeah*

Tani (Japanese / Melanesian / Tonkinese) From the valley / a sweetheart / a young woman
Tanie, Tany, Taney, Tanee, Tanni, Tanye, Tannie, Tanny

Tania (Russian) Queen of the fairies
Tanya, Tannie, Tanny, Tanika

Tanner (English) One who tans hides
Taner, Tannar, Tannor, Tannis

Tansy (English / Greek) An aromatic yellow flower / having immortality
Tansey, Tansi, Tansie, Tansee, Tansye, Tansea, Tancy, Tanzy

Tanushri (Indian) One who is beautiful; attractive
Tanushrie, Tanushry, Tanushrey, Tanushree, Tanushrea

Tanvi (Indian) Slender and beautiful woman
Tanvie, Tanvy, Tanvey, Tanvee, Tanvye, Tannvi, Tanvea

Tapati (Indian) In mythology, the daughter of the sun god
Tapatie, Tapaty, Tapatey, Tapatee, Tapatye, Tapatea

Taphath (Hebrew) In the Bible, Solomon's daughter
Tafath, Taphathe, Tafathe

Tara (Gaelic / Indian) Of the tower; rocky hill / star; in mythology, an astral goddess
Tarah, Tarra, Tayra, Taraea, Tarai, Taralee, Tarali, Taraya

Tarachand (Indian) Silver star
Tarachande, Tarachanda, Tarachandia, Tarachandea, Tarachandiya, Tarachandya

Taree (Japanese) A bending branch
Tarea, Tareya

Taregan (Native American) Resembling a crane
Tareganne, Taregann

Tareva-chine(shanay) (Native American) One with beautiful eyes

Tariana (American) From the holy hillside
Tarianna, Taryana, Taryanna

Tarika (Indian) A starlet
Tarikah, Taryka, Tarykah, Taricka, Tarickah

Tarisai (African) One to behold; to look at
Tarysai

Tasanee (Thai) A beautiful view
Tasane, Tasani, Tasanie, Tasany, Tasaney, Tasanye, Tasanea

Taskin (Arabic) One who provides peace; satisfaction
Taskine, Taskeen, Taskeene, Taskyne, Takseen, Taksin, Taksyn

Tasnim (Arabic) From the fountain of paradise
Tasnime, Tasneem, Tasneeme, Tasnyme, Tasnym, Tasneam, Tasneame

Tatum (English) Bringer of joy; spirited
Tatom, Tatim, Tatem, Tatam, Tatym

Tavi (Aramaic) One who is well-behaved
Tavie, Tavee, Tavy, Tavey, Tavea

*Taylor (English) Cutter of cloth; one who alters garments
Tailor, Taylore, Taylar, Tayler, Talour, Taylre, Tailore, Tailar

Teagan (Gaelic) One who is attractive
Teegan

Tehya (Native American) One who is precious
Tehyah, Tehiya, Tehiyah

Teigra (Greek) Resembling a tiger
Teigre

Telephassa (Latin) In mythology, the queen of Tyre
Telephasa, Telefassa, Telefasa

Temperance (English) Having self-restraint
Temperence, Temperince, Temperancia, Temperanse, Temperense, Temperinse

Tendai (African) Thankful to God
Tenday, Tendae, Tendaa, Tendaye

Tender (American) One who is sensitive; young and vulnerable
Tendere, Tendera, Tenderia, Tenderre, Tenderiya

Teranika (Gaelic) Victory of the earth
Teranikah, Teranieka, Teraneika, Teraneeka, Teranica, Teranicka, Teranicca, Teraneaka

Teresa (Greek) A harvester
Theresa, Theresah, Theresia, Therese, Thera, Tresa, Tressa, Tressam, Reese, Reza

Terpsichore (Greek) In mythology, the muse of dancing and singing
Terpsichora, Terpsichoria, Terpsichoriya

Terra (Latin) From the earth; in mythology, an earth goddess
Terrah, Terah, Teralyn, Terran, Terena, Terenah, Terenna, Terrena

Terrian (Greek) One who is innocent
Terriane, Terrianne, Terriana, Terianna, Terian, Terianne

Tessa (Greek) Form of Teresa, meaning "a harvester"

Tetsu (Japanese) A strong woman
Tetsue

Tetty (English) Form of Elizabeth, meaning "my God is bountiful; God's promise"
Tettey, Tetti, Tettie, Tettee, Tettea

Tevy (Cambodian) An angel
Tevey, Tevi, Tevie, Tevee, Tevea

Thandiwe (African) The loving one
Thandywe, Thandiewe, Thandeewe, Thandie, Thandi, Thandee, Thandy, Thandey

Thara (Arabic) One who is wealthy; prosperous
Tharah, Tharra, Tharrah, Tharwat

Thelma (Greek) One who is ambitious and willful
Thelmah, Telma, Thelmai, Thelmia, Thelmalina

Thelred (English) One who is well-advised
Thelrede, Thelread, Thelredia, Thelredina, Thelreid, Thelreed, Thelryd

Thema (African) A queen
Themah, Theema, Thyma, Theyma, Theama

Theora (Greek) A watcher
Theorra, Theoria, Theoriya, Theorya

Theta (Greek) Eighth letter of the Greek alphabet
Thetta

Thistle (English) Resembling the prickly, flowered plant
Thistel, Thissle, Thissel

Thomasina (Hebrew) Feminine form of Thomas; a twin
Thomasine, Thomsina, Thomasin, Tomasina, Tomasine, Thomasa, Thomaseena, Thomaseana

Thoosa (Greek) In mythology, a sea nymph
Thoosah, Thoosia, Thoosiah, Thusa, Thusah, Thusia, Thusiah, Thousa

Thorberta (Norse) Brilliance of Thor
Thorbiartr, Thorbertha

Thordia (Norse) Spirit of Thor
Thordiah, Thordis, Tordis, Thordissa, Tordissa, Thoridyss

Thuy (Vietnamese) One who is gentle and pure
Thuye, Thuyy, Thuyye

Thy (Vietnamese / Greek) A poet / one who is untamed
Thye

^**Tia** (Spanish / Greek) An aunt / daughter born to royalty
*Tiah, Tea, Teah, **Tiana**, Teea, Tya, Teeya, Tiia*

Tiberia (Italian) Of the Tiber river
Tiberiah, Tiberiya, Tiberya, Tibeeria, Tibearia, Tibieria, Tibeiria

Tiegan (Aztec) A little princess in a big valley
Tiegann, Tieganne

Tierney (Gaelic) One who is regal; lordly
Tiernie, Tierni, Tiernee, Tierny, Tiernea

Tiffany (Greek) Lasting love
Tiffaney, Tiffani, Tiffanie, Tiffanee, Tifany, Tifaney, Tifanee, Tifani

Timothea (English) Feminine form of Timothy; honoring God
Timotheah, Timothia, Timothya, Timothiya

Tina (English) From the river; also shortened form of names ending in -tina
Tinah, Teena, Tena, Teyna, Tyna, Tinna, Teana

Ting (Chinese) Graceful and slim woman

Tirza (Hebrew) One who is pleasant; a delight
Tirzah

Tisa (African) The ninth-born child
Tisah, Tiza

Tita (Latin) Holding a title of honor
Titah, Teeta, Tyta, Teata

Tivona (Hebrew) Lover of nature
Tivonna, Tivone, Tivonia, Tivoniya

Toan (Vietnamese) Form of An-toan, meaning "safe and secure"
Toane, Toanne

Toinette (French) Form of Antoinette, meaning "praiseworthy"
Toinett, Toinete, Toinet, Toineta, Toinetta, Tola

Toki (Japanese / Korean) One who grasps opportunity; hopeful / resembling a rabbit
Tokie, Toky, Tokey, Tokye, Tokiko, Tokee, Tokea

Tola (Polish / Cambodian) Form of Toinette, meaning "praiseworthy" / born during October
Tolah, Tolla, Tollah

Topanga (Native American) From above or a high place
Topangah

Topaz (Latin) Resembling a yellow gemstone
Topazz, Topaza, Topazia, Topaziya, Topazya, Topazea

Tordis (Norse) A goddess
Tordiss, Tordisse, Tordys, Tordyss, Tordysse

Torny (Norse) New; just discovered
Torney, Tornie, Torni, Torne, Torn, Tornee, Tornea

Torunn (Norse) Thor's love
Torun, Torrun, Torrunn

Tory (American) Form of Victoria, meaning "victorious woman; winner; conqueror"
Torry, Torey, Tori, Torie, Torree, Tauri, Torye, Toya

Tosca (Latin) From the Tuscany region
Toscah, Toscka, Toska, Tosckah, Toskah

Tosha (English) Form of Natasha, meaning "born on Christmas"
Toshah, Toshiana, Tasha, Tashia, Tashi, Tassa

Tourmaline (Singhalese) A stone of mixed colors
Tourmalyne, Tourmalina, Tourmalinia

Tova (Hebrew) One who is well-behaved
Tovah, Tove, Tovi, Toba, Toibe, Tovva

Treasa (Irish) Having great strength
Treasah, Treesa, Treisa, Triesa, Treise, Treese, Toirease

*Trinity (Latin) The holy three
Trinitey, Triniti, Trinitie, Trinitee, Trynity, Trynitey, Tryniti, Trynitie

Trisha (Latin) Form of Patricia, meaning "of noble descent"
Trishah, Trishia, Tricia, Trish, Trissa, Trisa

Trishna (Polish) In mythology, the goddess of the deceased, protector of graves
Trishnah, Trishnia, Trishniah, Trishnea, Trishneah, Trishniya, Trishniyah, Trishnya

Trisna (Indian) The one desired
Trisnah, Trisnia, Trisniah, Trisnea, Trisneah, Trisniya, Trisniyah, Trisnya

Trudy (German) Form of Gertrude, meaning "adored warrior"
Trudey, Trudi, Trudie, Trude, Trudye, Trudee, Truda, Trudia

Trupti (Indian) State of being satisfied
Truptie, Trupty, Truptey, Truptee, Trupte, Truptea

Tryamon (English) In Arthurian legend, a fairy princess
Tryamonn, Tryamonne, Tryamona, Tryamonna

Tryna (Greek) The third-born child
Trynah

Tsifira (Hebrew) One who is crowned
Tsifirah, Tsifyra, Tsiphyra, Tsiphira, Tsipheera, Tsifeera

Tuccia (Latin) A vestal virgin

Tula (Hindi) Balance; a sign of the zodiac
Tulah, Tulla, Tullah

Tullia (Irish) One who is peaceful
Tulliah, Tullea, Tulleah, Tullya, Tulia, Tulea, Tuleah, Tulya

Tusti (Hindi) One who brings happiness and peace
Tustie, Tusty, Tustey, Tustee, Tuste, Tustea

Tutilina (Latin) In mythology, the protector goddess of stored grain
Tutilinah, Tutileena, Tutileana, Tutilyna, Tutileina, Tutiliena, Tutilena, Tutylina

Tuuli (Finnish) Of the wind
Tuulie, Tuulee, Tuula, Tuuly, Tuuley, Tuulea

Tuyet (Vietnamese) Snow white woman
Tuyett, Tuyete, Tuyette, Tuyeta, Tuyetta

Tyler (English) Tiler of roofs

Tyme (English) The aromatic
herb thyme
Time, Thyme, Thime

Tyne (English) Of the river
Tyna

Tyro (Greek) In mythology, a
woman who bore twin sons to
Poseidon

Tzidkiya (Hebrew)
Righteousness of the Lord
Tzidkiyah, Tzidkiyahu

Tzigane (Hungarian) A gypsy
*Tzigan, Tzigain, Tzigaine,
Tzigayne*

U

Uadjit (Egyptian) In mythology, a snake goddess
Ujadet, Uajit, Udjit, Ujadit

Ualani (Hawaiian) Of the
heavenly rain
*Ualanie, Ualany, Ualaney,
Ualanee, Ualanea, Ualania,
Ualana*

Udavine (American) A thriving
woman
*Udavyne, Udavina, Udavyna,
Udevine, Udevyne, Udevina,
Udevyna*

Udele (English) One who is
wealthy; prosperous
*Udelle, Udela, Udella, Udelah,
Udellah, Uda, Udah*

Uela (American) One who is
devoted to God
Uelah, Uella, Uellah

Uganda (African) From the
country in Africa
*Ugandah, Ugaunda,
Ugaundah, Ugawnda,
Ugawndah, Ugonda, Ugondah*

Ugolina (German) Having a
bright spirit; bright mind
*Ugolinah, Ugoleena, Ugoliana,
Ugolyna, Ugoline, Ugolyn,
Ugolyne*

Ulalia (Greek) Form of Eulalia,
meaning "well-spoken"
Ulaliah, Ulalya, Ulalyah

Ulan (African) Firstborn of
twins
Ulann, Ulanne

Ulima (Arabic) One who is
wise and astute
*Ulimah, Ullima, Ulimma,
Uleema, Uleama, Ulyma,
Uleima, Uliema*

Ulla (German) A willful woman
Ullah, Ullaa, Ullai, Ullae

Uma (Hindi) Mother; in mythology, the goddess of beauty and sunlight
Umah, Umma

Umberla (French) Feminine form of Umber; providing shade; of an earth color
Umberlah, Umberly, Umberley, Umberlee, Umberleigh, Umberli, Umberlea, Umberlie

Ummi (African) Born of my mother
Ummie, Ummy, Ummey, Ummee, Umi

Unity (American) Woman who upholds oneness; together-ness
Unitey, Unitie, Uniti, Unitee, Unitea, Unyty, Unytey, Unytie

Ura (Indian) Loved from the heart
Urah, Urra

Ural (Slavic) From the mountains
Urall, Urale, Uralle

Urbai (American) One who is gentle
Urbae, Urbay, Urbaye

Urbana (Latin) From the city; city dweller
Urbanah, Urbanna, Urbane, Urbania, Urbanya, Urbanne

Uriela (Hebrew) The angel of light
Uriella, Urielle, Uriel, Uriele, Uriell

Urta (Latin) Resembling the spiny plant
Urtah

Utah (Native American) People of the mountains; from the state of Utah

Uzoma (African) One who takes the right path
Uzomah, Uzomma, Uzommah

Uzzi (Hebrew / Arabic) God is my strength / a strong woman
Uzzie, Uzzy, Uzzey, Uzzee, Uzi, Uzie, Uzy, Uzey

Vala (German) The chosen one; singled out
Valah, Valla

Valda (Teutonic / German) Spirited in battle / famous ruler
Valdah, Valida, Velda, Vada, Vaida, Vayda, Vaeda

Valdis (Norse) In mythology, the goddess of the dead
Valdiss, Valdys, Valdyss

Valencia (Spanish) One who is powerful; strong; from the city of Valencia
Valenciah, Valyncia, Valencya, Valenzia, Valancia, Valenica, Valanca, Valecia

Valentina (Latin) One who is vigorous and healthy
Valentinah, Valentine, Valenteena, Valenteana, Valentena, Valentyna, Valantina, Valentyne

Valeria (Latin) Form of Valerie, meaning "strong and valiant"
Valara, Valera, Valaria, Valeriana, Veleria, Valora

Valerie (Latin) Feminine form of Valerius; strong and valiant
Valeri, Valeree, Valerey, Valery, Valarie, Valari, Vallery

Vandani (Hindi) One who is honorable and worthy
Vandany, Vandaney, Vandanie, Vandanee, Vandania, Vandanya

Vanessa (Greek) Resembling a butterfly
Vanessah, Vanesa, Vannesa, Vannessa, Vanassa, Vanasa, Vanessia, Vanysa, Yanessa

Vanity (English) Having excessive pride
Vanitey, Vanitee, Vaniti, Vanitie, Vanitty, Vanyti, Vanyty, Vanytie

Vanmra (Russian) A stranger; from a foreign place
Vanmrah

Varda (Hebrew) Resembling a rose
Vardah, Vardia, Vardina, Vardissa, Vardita, Vardysa, Vardyta, Vardit

Varuna (Hindi) Wife of the sea
Varunah, Varuna, Varun, Varunani, Varuni

Vashti (Persian) A lovely woman
Vashtie, Vashty, Vashtey, Vashtee

Vasta (Persian) One who is pretty
Vastah

Vasteen (American) A capable woman
Vasteene, Vastiene, Vastien, Vastein, Vasteine, Vastean, Vasteane

Vasuda (Hindi) Of the earth
Vasudah, Vasudhara,
Vasundhara, Vasudhra,
Vasundhra

Vayu (Hindi) A vital life force;
the air
Vayyu

Vedette (French) From the
guard tower
Vedete, Vedett, Vedet, Vedetta,
Vedeta

Vedi (Sanskrit) Filled with
wisdom
Vedie, Vedy, Vedey, Vedee,
Vedea, Vedeah

Vega (Latin) A falling star
Vegah

Vellamo (Finnish) In mythology, the goddess of the sea
Velamo, Vellammo

Ventana (Spanish) As trans-
parent as a window
Ventanah, Ventanna, Ventane,
Ventanne

Venus (Greek) In mythology, the goddess of love and
beauty
Venis, Venys, Vynys, Venusa,
Venusina, Venusia

Veradis (Latin) One who is
genuine; truthful
Veradise, Veradys, Veradisa,
Verdissa, Veradysa, Veradyssa,
Veradisia, Veraditia

Verda (Latin) Springlike; one
who is young and fresh
Verdah, Verdea, Virida, Verdy,
Verdey, Verde, Verdi, Verdie

Verenase (Swedish) One who
is flourishing
Verenese, Verennase, Vyrenase,
Vyrennase, Vyrenese, Verenace,
Vyrenace

Veronica (Latin) Displaying
her true image
Veronicah, Veronic, Veronicca,
Veronicka, Veronika,
Veronicha, Veronique,
Veranique, Ronni

Vesna (Slavic) Messenger; in
mythology, the goddess of
spring
Vesnah, Vezna, Vesnia, Vesnaa

Vespera (Latin) Evening star;
born in the evening
Vesperah, Vespira, Vespeera,
Vesperia, Vesper

Vevila (Gaelic) Woman with a
melodious voice
Vevilah, Veveela, Vevyla,
Vevilla, Vevylla, Vevylle, Vevyle,
Vevillia

Vibeke (Danish) A small
woman
*Vibekeh, Vibeek, Vibeeke,
Vybeke, Viheke*

Vibhuti (Hindi) Of the sacred
ash; a symbol
Vibuti, Vibhutie, Vibhutee

*Victoria (Latin) Victorious
woman; winner; conqueror
*Victoriah, Victorea, Victoreah,
Victorya, Victorria, Victoriya,
Vyctoria, Victorine, Tory*

Vidya (Indian) Having great
wisdom
Vidyah

Viet (Vietnamese) A woman
from Vietnam
Vyet, Viett, Vyett, Viette, Vyette

Vigilia (Latin) Wakefulness;
watchfulness
*Vigiliah, Vygilia, Vygylia,
Vijilia, Vyjilia*

Vignette (French) From the
little vine
*Vignete, Vignet, Vignetta,
Vignett, Vigneta, Vygnette,
Vygnete, Vygnet*

Vilina (Hindi) One who is
dedicated
*Vilinah, Vileena, Vileana,
Vylina, Vyleena, Vyleana,
Vylyna, Vilinia*

Villette (French) From the
small village
*Vilette, Villete, Vilete, Vilet,
Vilett, Villet, Villett, Vylet*

Vimala (Indian) Feminine
form of Vamal; clean and
pure
Vimalah, Vimalia, Vimalla

Vincentia (Latin) Feminine
form of Vincent; conquerer;
triumphant
*Vincentiah, Vincenta,
Vincensia, Vincenzia,
Vyncentia, Vyncyntia,
Vyncenzia, Vycenzya*

Violet (French) Resembling
the purplish-blue flower
*Violett, Violette, Violete, Vyolet,
Vyolett, Vyolette, Vyolete,
Violeta*

Virginia (Latin) One who is
chaste; virginal; from the state
of Virginia
*Virginiah, Virginnia, Virgenya,
Virgenia, Virgeenia, Virgeena,
Virgena, Ginny*

Virtue (Latin) Having moral
excellence, chastity, and
goodness
*Virtu, Vyrtue, Vyrtu, Vertue,
Vertu*

Viveka (German) Little woman of the strong fortress
Vivekah, Vivecka, Vyveka, Viveca, Vyveca, Vivecca, Vivika, Vivieka

^**Vivian** (Latin) Lively woman
*Viv, Vivi, **Vivienne**, Bibiana*

Vixen (American) A flirtatious woman
Vixin, Vixi, Vixie, Vixee, Vixea, Vixeah, Vixy, Vixey

Vlasta (Slavic) A friendly and likeable woman
Vlastah, Vlastia, Vlastea, Vlastiah, Vlasteah

Voleta (Greek) The veiled one
Voletah, Voletta, Volita, Volitta, Volyta, Volytta, Volet, Volett

Volva (Scandinavian) In mythology, a female shaman
Volvah, Volvya, Volvaa, Volvae, Volvai, Volvay, Volvia

Vondila (African) Woman who lost a child
Vondilah, Vondilla, Vondilya, Vondilia, Vondyla, Vondylya

Vonna (French) Form of Yvonne, meaning "young archer"
Vonnah, Vona, Vonah, Vonnia, Vonnya, Vonia, Vonya, Vonny

Vonshae (American) One who is confident
Vonshay, Vonshaye, Vonshai

Vor (Norse) In mythology, an omniscient goddess
Vore, Vorr, Vorre

Vulpine (English) A cunning woman; like a fox
Vulpyne, Vulpina, Vulpyna

Vyomini (Indian) A gift of the divine
Vyominie, Vyominy, Vyominey, Vyominee, Vyomyni, Vyomyny, Viomini, Viomyni

W

Wafa (Arabic) One who is faithful; devoted
Wafah, Wafaa, Waffa, Wapha, Waffah, Waphah

Wagaye (African) My sense of value; my price
Wagay, Wagai, Wagae

Wainani (Hawaiian) Of the beautiful waters
Wainanie, Wainany, Wainaney, Wainanee, Wainanea, Wainaneah

Wajihah (Arabic) One who is
distinguished; eminent
*Wajiha, Wajeeha, Wajyha,
Wajeehah, Wajyhah, Wajieha,
Wajiehah, Wajeiha*

Wakanda (Native American)
One who possesses magical
powers
*Wakandah, Wakenda,
Wakinda, Wakynda*

Wakeishah (American) Filled
with happiness
*Wakeisha, Wakieshah,
Wakiesha, Wakesha*

Walda (German) One who has
fame and power
*Waldah, Wallda, Walida,
Waldine, Waldina, Waldyne,
Waldyna, Welda*

Walker (English) Walker of the
forests
Wallker, Walkher

Walta (African) One who acts
as a shield
Waltah

Wanetta (English) A pale-
skinned woman
*Wanettah, Wanette, Wannette,
Wannetta, Wonetta, Wonette,
Wonitta, Wonitte*

Wangari (African) Resembling
the leopard
*Wangarie, Wangarri, Wangary,
Wangarey, Wangaria,
Wangaree*

Wanyika (African) Of the bush
*Wanyikka, Wanyicka,
Wanyicca, Wanyica*

Waqi (Arabic) Falling;
swooping
Waqqi

Warma (American) A caring
woman
*Warm, Warme, Warmia,
Warmiah, Warmea, Warmeah*

Warna (German) One who
defends her loved ones
Warnah

Washi (Japanese) Resembling
an eagle
*Washie, Washy, Washey,
Washee, Washea, Washeah*

Waynette (English) One who
makes wagons
*Waynett, Waynet, Waynete,
Wayneta, Waynetta*

Wednesday (American) Born
on a Wednesday
*Wensday, Winsday,
Windnesday, Wednesdae,
Wensdae, Winsdae,
Windnesdae, Wednesdai*

Welcome (English) A welcome guest
Welcom, Welcomme

Wendy (Welsh) Form of Gwendolyn, meaning "one who is fair; of the white ring"
Wendi, Wendie, Wendee, Wendey, Wenda, Wendia, Wendea, Wendya

Wesley (English) From the western meadow
Wesly, Weslie, Wesli, Weslee, Weslia, Wesleigh, Weslea, Weslei

Whisper (English) One who is soft-spoken
Whysper, Wisper, Wysper

Whitley (English) From the white meadow
Whitly, Whitlie, Whitli, Whitlee, Whitleigh, Whitlea, Whitlia, Whitlya

Whitney (English) From the white island
Whitny, Whitnie, Whitni, Whitnee, Whittney, Whitneigh, Whytny, Whytney

Wicapi (Native American) A holy star

Wijida (Arabic) An excited seeker
Wijidah, Weejida, Weejidah, Wijeeda, Wijeedah, Wijyda, Wijydah, Wijieda

Wileen (Teutonic) A firm defender
Wiline, Wilean, Wileane, Wilyn, Wileene, Wilene, Wyleen, Wyline

Wilhelmina (German) Feminine form of Wilhelm; determined protector
Wilhelminah, Wylhelmina, Wylhelmyna, Willemina, Wilhelmine, Wilhemina, Wilhemine, Helma, Ilma

Willa (English) Feminine version of William, meaning "protector"
Willah, Wylla

Willow (English) One who is hoped for; desired
Willo, Willough

Winetta (American) One who is peaceful
Wineta, Wynetta, Wyneta, Winet, Winett, Winette, Wynet, Wynett

Winnielle (African) A victorious woman
Winniell, Winniele, Winniel, Winniella

Winola (German) Gracious and charming friend
Winolah, Wynola, Winolla, Wynolla, Wynolah, Winollah, Wynollah

Winta (African) One who is desired
Wintah, Whinta, Wynta, Whynta, Whintah, Wyntah, Whyntah

Wisconsin (French) Gathering of waters; from the state of Wisconsin
Wisconsyn, Wisconsen

Woody (American) A woman of the forest
Woodey, Woodi, Woodie, Woodee, Woodea, Woodeah, Woods

Wren (English) Resembling a small songbird
Wrenn, Wrene, Wrena, Wrenie, Wrenee, Wreney, Wrenny, Wrenna

Wynda (Scottish) From the narrow passage
Wyndah, Winda, Windah

Xalvadora (Spanish) A savior
Xalvadorah, Xalbadora, Xalbadorah, Xalvadoria, Xalbadoria

Xanadu (African) From the exotic paradise

Xantara (American) Protector of the Earth
Xantarah, Xanterra, Xantera, Xantarra, Xantarrah, Xanterah, Xanterrah

Xaquelina (Galician) Form of Jacqueline, meaning "the supplanter"
Xaqueline, Xaqueleena, Xáquelyna, Xaquelayna, Xaqueleana

Xerena (Latin) Form of Serena, meaning "having a peaceful disposition"
Xerenah, Xerene, Xeren, Xereena, Xeryna, Xereene, Xerenna

Xhosa (African) Leader of a nation
Xosa, Xhose, Xhosia, Xhosah, Xosah

Xiang (Chinese) Having a nice fragrance
Xyang, Xeang, Xhiang, Xhyang, Xheang

Xiao Hong (Chinese) Of the morning rainbow

Xin Qian (Chinese) Happy and beautiful woman

Xinavane (African) A mother;
to propagate
*Xinavana, Xinavania,
Xinavain, Xinavaine,
Xinavaen, Xinavaene*

Xirena (Greek) Form of Sirena,
meaning "enchantress"
*Xirenah, Xireena, Xirina,
Xirene, Xyrena, Xyreena,
Xyrina, Xyryna*

Xi-Wang (Chinese) One with
hope

Xochiquetzal (Aztec)
Resembling a flowery feather;
in mythology, the goddess of
love, flowers, and the earth

Xola (African) Stay in peace
Xolah, Xolia, Xolla, Xollah

Xue (Chinese) Woman of
snow

Y

Yachne (Hebrew) One who is
gracious and hospitable
*Yachnee, Yachney, Yachnie,
Yachni, Yachnea, Yachneah*

Yadra (Spanish) Form of
Madre, meaning "mother"
Yadre, Yadrah

Yaffa (Hebrew) A beautiful
woman
Yaffah, Yaffit, Yafit, Yafeal

Yakini (African) An honest
woman
*Yakinie, Yakiney, Yakiny,
Yackini, Yackinie, Yackiney,
Yackiny, Yakinee*

Yalena (Greek) Form of Helen,
meaning "the shining light"
*Yalenah, Yalina, Yaleena,
Yalyna, Yalana, Yaleana,
Yalane, Yaleene*

Yama (Japanese) From the
mountain
Yamma, Yamah, Yammah

Yamin (Hebrew) Right hand
*Yamine, Yamyn, Yamyne,
Yameen, Yameene, Yamein,
Yameine, Yamien*

Yana (Hebrew) He answers
Yanna, Yaan, Yanah, Yannah

Yanessa (American) Form of
Vanessa, meaning "resem-
bling a butterfly"
*Yanessah, Yanesa, Yannesa,
Yannessa, Yanassa, Yanasa,
Yanessia, Yanysa*

Yanka (Slavic) God is good
Yancka, Yancca, Yankka

Yara (Brazilian) In mythology, the goddess of the river; a mermaid
Yarah, Yarrah, Yarra

Yareli (American) The Lord is my light
Yarelie, Yareley, Yarelee, Yarely, Yaresly, Yarelea, Yareleah

Yaretzi (Spanish) Always beloved
Yaretzie, Yaretza, Yarezita

Yashira (Japanese) Blessed with God's grace
Yashirah, Yasheera, Yashyra, Yashara, Yashiera, Yashierah, Yasheira, Yasheirah

Yashona (Hindi) A wealthy woman
Yashonah, Yashawna, Yashauna, Yaseana, Yashawnah, Yashaunah, Yaseanah

Yasmine (Persian) Resembling the jasmine flower
Yasmin, Yasmene, Yasmeen, Yasmeene, Yasmen, Yasemin, Yasemeen, Yasmyn

Yatima (African) An orphan
Yatimah, Yateema, Yatyma, Yateemah, Yatymah, Yatiema, Yatiemah, Yateima

Yedidah (Hebrew) A beloved friend
Yedida, Yedyda, Yedydah, Yedeeda, Yedeedah

Yeira (Hebrew) One who is illuminated
Yeirah, Yaira, Yeyra, Yairah, Yeyrah

Yenge (African) A hardworking woman
Yenga, Yengeh, Yengah

Yeshi (African) For a thousand
Yeshie, Yeshey, Yeshy, Yeshee, Yeshea, Yesheah

Yessica (Hebrew) Form of Jessica, meaning "the Lord sees all"
Yesica, Yessika, Yesika, Yesicka, Yessicka, Yesyka, Yesiko

Yetta (English) Form of Henrietta, meaning "ruler of the house"
Yettah, Yeta, Yette, Yitta, Yettie, Yetty

Yi Min (Chinese) An intelligent woman

Yi Ze (Chinese) Happy and shiny as a pearl

Yihana (African) One deserving congratulations
Yihanah, Yhana, Yihanna, Yihannah, Yhanah, Yhanna, Yhannah

Yinah (Spanish) A victorious woman
Yina, Yinna, Yinnah

Yitta (Hebrew) One who emanates light
Yittah, Yita, Yitah

Ynes (French) Form of Agnes, meaning "pure; chaste"
Ynez, Ynesita

Yogi (Hindi) One who practices yoga
Yogini, Yoginie, Yogie, Yogy, Yogey, Yogee, Yogea, Yogeah

Yohance (African) A gift from God
Yohanse

Yoki (Native American) Of the rain
Yokie, Yokee, Yoky, Yokey, Yokea, Yokeah

Yolanda (Greek) Resembling the violet flower
Yola, Yolana, Yolandah, Colanda

Yomaris (Spanish) I am the sun
Yomariss, Yomarise, Yomarris

Yon (Korean) Resembling a lotus blossom

Yoruba (African) Woman from Nigeria
Yorubah, Yorubba, Yorubbah

Yoshi (Japanese) One who is respectful and good
Yoshie, Yoshy, Yoshey, Yoshee, Yoshiyo, Yoshiko, Yoshino, Yoshea

Ysabel (Spanish) Form of Isabel, meaning "my God is bountiful; God's promise"
Ysabelle, Ysabela, Ysabele, Ysabell, Ysabella, Ysbel, Ysibel, Ysibela

Ysbail (Welsh) A spoiled girl
Ysbale, Ysbayle, Ysbaile, Ysbayl, Ysbael, Ysbaele

Yue (Chinese) Of the moonlight

Yuette (American) A capable woman
Yuett, Yuete, Yuet, Yueta, Yuetta

Yulan (Spanish) A splendid woman
Yulann

Yuna (African) A gorgeous woman
Yunah, Yunna, Yunnah

Yuta (Hebrew / Japanese) One who is awarded praise / one who is superior
Yutah, Yoota, Yootah

Yvonne (French) Young archer
Yvone, Vonne, Vonna

Zabrina (American) Form of Sabrina, meaning "a legendary princess"
Zabreena, Zabrinah, Zabrinna, Zabryna, Zabryne, Zabrynya, Zabreana, Zabreane

Zachah (Hebrew) Feminine form of Zachary; God is remembered
Zacha, Zachie, Zachi, Zachee, Zachea, Zacheah

Zafara (Hebrew) One who sings
Zaphara, Zafarra, Zapharra, Zafarah, Zafarrah, Zapharah, Zapharrah

Zagir (Armenian) Resembling a flower
Zagiri, Zagirie, Zagiree, Zagirea, Zagireah, Zagiry, Zagirey, Zagira

Zahiya (Arabic) A brilliant woman; radiant
Zahiyah, Zehiya, Zehiyah, Zeheeya, Zaheeya, Zeheeyah, Zaheeyah, Zaheiya

Zahra (Arabic / Swahili) White-skinned / flowerlike
Zahrah, Zahraa, Zahre, Zahreh, Zahara, Zaharra, Zahera, Zahira

Zainab (Arabic) A fragrant flowering plant
Zaynab, Zaenab

Zainabu (Swahili) One who is known for her beauty
Zaynabu, Zaenabu

Zalina (French) Form of Selene, meaning "of the moon"; in mythology Selene was the Greek goddess of the moon
Zalinah, Zaleana, Zaleena, Zalena, Zalyna, Zaleen, Zaleene, Zalene

Zama (Latin) One from the town of Zama
Zamah, Zamma, Zammah

Zambda (Hebrew) One who meditates
Zambdah

Zamella (Zulu) One who strives to succeed
Zamellah, Zamy, Zamie, Zami, Zamey, Zamee, Zamea, Zameah

Zamilla (Greek) Having the strength of the sea
Zamillah, Zamila, Zamilah, Zamylla, Zamyllah, Zamyla, Zamylah

Zamora (Spanish) From the city of Zamora
Zamorah, Zamorrah, Zamorra

Zana (Romanian / Hebrew) In mythology, the three graces / shortened form of Susanna, meaning "lily"
Zanna, Zanah, Zannah

Zane (Scandinavian) One who is bold
Zain, Zaine, Zayn, Zayne, Zaen, Zaene

Zanta (Swahili) A beautiful young woman
Zantah

Zarahlinda (Hebrew) Of the beautiful dawn
Zaralinda, Zaralynda, Zarahlindah, Zaralyndah, Zarahlynda, Zarahlyndah, Zaralenda, Zarahlenda

Zariah (Russian / Slavic) Born at sunrise
Zarya, Zariah, Zaryah

Zarifa (Arabic) One who is successful; moves with grace
Zarifah, Zaryfa, Zaryfah, Zareefa, Zareefah, Zariefa, Zariefah, Zareifa

Zarna (Hindi) Resembling a spring of water
Zarnah, Zarnia, Zarniah

Zarqa (Arabic) Having bluish-green eyes; from the city of Zarqa
Zarqaa

Zaylee (English) A heavenly woman
Zayleigh, Zayli, Zaylie, Zaylea, Zayleah, Zayley, Zayly, Zalee

Zaypana (Tibetan) A beautiful woman
Zaypanah, Zaypo, Zaypanna, Zaypannah

Zaza (Hebrew / Arabic) Belonging to all / one who is flowery
Zazah, Zazu, Zazza, Zazzah, Zazzu

Zdenka (Slovene) Feminine form of Zdenek, meaning "from Sidon"
Zdena, Zdenuska, Zdenicka, Zdenika, Zdenyka, Zdeninka, Zdenynka

Zebba (Persian) A known
beauty
*Zebbah, Zebara, Zebarah,
Zebarra, Zebarrah*

Zelia (Greek / Spanish)
Having great zeal / of the
sunshine
*Zeliah, Zelya, Zelie, Zele,
Zelina, Zelinia*

Zenaida (Greek) White-winged
dove; in mythology, a daugh-
ter of Zeus
*Zenaidah, Zenayda, Zenaide,
Zenayde, Zinaida, Zenina,
Zenna, Zenaydah*

Zenechka (Russian) Form
of Eugenia, meaning "a
well-born woman"

Zenobia (Greek) Child of Zeus
Sinobia

Zephyr (Greek) Of the west
wind
*Zephyra, Zephira, Zephria,
Zephra, Zephyer, Zefiryn,
Zefiryna, Zefyrin*

Zera (Hebrew) A sower of
seeds
*Zerah, Zeria, Zeriah, Zera'im,
Zerra, Zerrah*

Zeraldina (Polish) One who
rules with the spear
*Zeraldinah, Zeraldeena,
Zeraldeenah, Zeraldiena,
Zeraldienah, Zeraldeina,
Zeraldeinah, Zeraldyna*

Zerdali (Turkish) Resembling
the wild apricot
*Zerdalie, Zerdaly, Zerdaley,
Zerdalya, Zerdalia, Zerdalee,
Zerdalea*

Zesta (American) One with
energy and gusto
*Zestah, Zestie, Zestee, Zesti,
Zesty, Zestey, Zestea, Zesteah*

Zetta (Portuguese) Resembling
the rose
Zettah

Zhen (Chinese) One who is
precious and chaste
Zen, Zhena, Zenn, Zhenni

Zhi (Chinese) A woman of
high moral character

Zhong (Chinese) An honorable
woman

Zi (Chinese) A flourishing
young woman

Zia (Arabic) One who
emanates light; splendor
Ziah, Zea, Zeah, Zya, Zyah

Zilias (Hebrew) A shady
woman; a shadow
Zilyas, Zylias, Zylyas

Zillah (Hebrew) The shadowed
one
*Zilla, Zila, Zyla, Zylla, Zilah,
Zylah, Zyllah*

Zilpah (Hebrew) One who
is frail but dignified; in the
Bible, a concubine of Jacob
*Zilpa, Zylpa, Zilpha, Zylpha,
Zylpah, Zilphah, Zylphah*

Zimbab (African) Woman
from Zimbabwe
Zymbab, Zimbob, Zymbob

Zinat (Arabic) A decoration;
graceful beauty
*Zeenat, Zynat, Zienat, Zeinat,
Zeanat*

Zinchita (Incan) One who is
dearly loved
*Zinchitah, Zinchyta,
Zinchytah, Zincheeta,
Zincheetah, Zinchieta,
Zinchietah, Zincheita*

Zintkala Kinyan (Native
American) Resembling a
flying bird
Zintkalah Kinyan

Ziona (Hebrew) One who
symbolizes goodness
Zionah, Zyona, Zyonah

Zipporah (Hebrew) A beauty;
little bird; in the Bible, the
wife of Moses
*Zippora, Ziporah, Zipora,
Zypora, Zyppora, Ziproh,
Zipporia*

Zira (African) The pathway
*Zirah, Zirra, Zirrah, Zyra,
Zyrah, Zyrra, Zyrrah*

Zisel (Hebrew) One who is
sweet
*Zissel, Zisal, Zysel, Zysal,
Zyssel, Zissal, Zyssal*

Zita (Latin / Spanish) Patron
of housewives and servants /
little rose
Zitah, Zeeta, Zyta, Zeetah

Ziwa (Swahili) Woman of the
lake
Ziwah, Zywa, Zywah

Zizi (Hungarian) Dedicated to
God
*Zeezee, Zyzy, Ziezie, Zeazea,
Zeyzey*

Zoa (Greek) One who is full of
life; vibrant

*★**Zoe** (Greek) A life-giving
woman; alive
*Zoee, Zowey, Zowie, Zowe,
Zoelie, Zoeline, Zoelle, **Zoey***

Zofia (Slavic) Form of Sophia,
meaning "wisdom"
*Zofiah, Zophia, Zophiah,
Zophya, Zofie, Zofee, Zofey*

Zora (Slavic) Born at dawn;
aurora
*Zorah, Zorna, Zorra, Zorya,
Zorane, Zory, Zorrah, Zorey*

Zoria (Basque) One who is
lucky
Zoriah

Zoriona (Basque) One who is
happy

Zubeda (Swahili) The best one
Zubedah

Zudora (Arabic) A laborer;
hardworking woman
Zudorah, Zudorra

Zula (African) One who is
brilliant; from the town
of Zula
*Zul, Zulay, Zulae, Zulai,
Zulah, Zulla, Zullah*

Zuni (Native American) One
who is creative
*Zunie, Zuny, Zuney, Zunee,
Zunea, Zuneah*

Zurafa (Arabic) A lovely
woman
*Zurafah, Zirafa, Zirafah,
Ziraf, Zurufa, Zurufah*

Zuri (Swahili / French) A
beauty / lovely and white
*Zurie, Zurey, Zuria, Zuriaa,
Zury, Zuree, Zurya, Zurisha*

Zuwena (African) One who is
pleasant and good
*Zuwenah, Zwena, Zwenah,
Zuwenna, Zuwennah, Zuwyna,
Zuwynah*

Zuyana (Sioux) One who has a
brave heart
Zuyanah, Zuyanna

Zuzena (Basque) One who is
correct
Zuzenah, Zuzenna

Zwi (Scandinavian)
Resembling a gazelle
Zui, Zwie, Zwee, Zwey

Boys

A

Aabha (Indian) One who shines
Abha, Abbha

Aabharan (Hindu) One who is treasured; jewel
Abharan, Abharen, Aabharen, Aabharon

Aaden (Irish) Form of Aidan, meaning "a fiery young man"
Adan, Aden

Aage (Norse) Representative of ancestors
Age, Ake, Aake

Aarif (Arabic) A learned man
Arif, Aareef, Areef, Aareaf, Areaf, Aareif, Areif, Aarief

*Aaron (Hebrew) One who is exalted; from the mountain of strength
Aaran, Aaren, Aarin, Aaro, Aaronas, Aaronn, Aarron, Aaryn, Eron, Aron, Eran

Abdi (Hebrew) My servant
Abdie, Abdy, Abdey, Abdee

Abdul (Arabic) A servant of God
Abdal, Abdall, Abdalla, Abdallah, Abdel, Abdell, Abdella, Abdellah

Abedi (African) One who worships God
Abedie, Abedy, Abedey, Abedee, Abedea

Abednago (Aramaic) Servant of the god of wisdom, Nabu
Abednego

Abejundio (Spanish) Resembling a bee
Abejundo, Abejundeo, Abedjundiyo, Abedjundeyo

^Abel (Hebrew) The life force, breath
Abele, Abell, Abelson, Able, Avel, Avele

Abraham (Hebrew) Father of a multitude; father of nations
Abarran, Avraham, Aberham, Abrahamo, Abrahan, Abrahim, Abram, Abrami, Ibrahim

Abram (Hebrew) Form of Abraham, meaning "father of nations"

Absalom (Hebrew) The father of peace
Absalon, Abshalom, Absolem, Absolom, Absolon, Avshalom, Avsholom

Abu (African) A father
Abue, Aboo, Abou

Abundio (Spanish) A man of
plenty
*Abbondio, Abondio, Aboundio,
Abundo, Abundeo, Aboundeo*

Adael (Hebrew) God witnesses
Adaele, Adayel, Adayele

*Adam (Hebrew) Of the earth
*Ad, Adamo, Adams, Adan,
Adao, Addam, Addams, Addem*

Adamson (English) The son of
Adam
*Adamsson, Addamson,
Adamsun, Adamssun*

Addy (Teutonic) One who is
awe-inspiring
*Addey, Addi, Addie, Addee,
Addea, Adi, Ady, Adie*

Adelpho (Greek) A brotherly
man
*Aldelfo, Adelfus, Adelfio,
Adelphe*

Adil (Arabic) A righteous man;
one who is fair and just
*Adyl, Adiel, Adeil, Adeel, Adeal,
Adyeel*

Aditya (Hindi) Of the sun
*Adithya, Adithyan, Adityah,
Aditeya, Aditeyah*

Adonis (Greek) In mythology,
a handsome young man loved
by Aphrodite
Addonia, Adohnes, Adonys

*Adrian (Latin) A man from
Hadria
*Adrien, Adrain, Adrean,
Adreean, Adreyan, Adreeyan,
Adriaan*

^Adriel (Hebrew) From God's
flock
*Adriell, Adriele, Adryel, Adryell,
Adryele*

Afif (Arabic) One who is
chaste; pure
*Afeef, Afief, Afeif, Affeef, Affif,
Afyf, Afeaf*

Agamemnon (Greek) One who
works slowly; in mythology,
the leader of the Greeks at
Troy
Agamemno, Agamenon

^Ahmad (Arabic) One who
always thanks God; a name of
Muhammed
Ahmed

*Aidan (Irish) A fiery young
man
Aiden, *Aedan, Aeden, Aidano,
Aidyn,* **Ayden**, *Aydin, Aydan*

Aiken (English) Constructed of oak; sturdy
Aikin, Aicken, Aickin, Ayken, Aykin, Aycken, Ayckin

Ainsworth (English) From Ann's estate
Answorth, Annsworth, Ainsworthe, Answorthe, Annsworthe

Ajax (Greek) In mythology, a hero of the Trojan war
Aias, Aiastes, Ajaxx, Ajaxe

Ajit (Indian) One who is invincible
Ajeet, Ajeat, Ajeit, Ajiet, Ajyt

Akiko (Japanese) Surrounded by bright light
Akyko

Akin (African) A brave man; a hero
Akeen, Akean, Akein, Akien, Akyn

Akiva (Hebrew) One who protects or provides shelter
Akyva, Akeeva, Akeava, Akieva, Akeiva, Akeyva

Akmal (Arabic) A perfect man
Aqmal, Akmall, Aqmall, Acmal, Acmall, Ackmal, Ackmall

Alaire (French) Filled with joy
Alair, Alaer, Alaere, Alare, Alayr, Alayre

Alamar (Arabic) Covered with gold
Alamarr, Alemar, Alemarr, Alomar, Alomarr

Alan (German / Gaelic) One who is precious / resembling a little rock
Alain, Alann, Allan, Alson, Allin, Allen, Allyn

Alard (German) Of noble strength
Aliard, Allard, Alliard

Albert (German) One who is noble and bright
Alberto, Albertus, Alburt, Albirt, Aubert, Albyrt, Albertos, Albertino

Alden (English) An old friend
Aldan, Aldin, Aldyn, Aldon, Aldun

Aldo (German) Old or wise one; elder
Aldous, Aldis, Aldus, Alldo, Aldys

Aldred (English) An old advisor
Alldred, Aldraed, Alldraed, Aldread, Alldread

Alejandro (Spanish) Form of Alexander, meaning "a helper and defender of mankind"
Alejandrino, Alejo

*Alex (English) Form of Alexander, meaning "a helper and defender of mankind"
*Aleks, Alecks, Alecs, Allex, Alleks, Allecks, **Alexis***

*Alexander (Greek) A helper and defender of mankind
Alex, Alec, Alejandro, Alaxander, Aleksandar, Aleksander, Aleksandr, Alessandro, Alexzander, Zander

Alfonso (Italian) Prepared for battle; eager and ready
Alphonso, Alphonse, Affonso, Alfons, Alfonse, Alfonsin, Alfonsino, Alfonz, Alfonzo

Ali (Arabic) The great one; one who is exalted
Alie, Aly, Aley, Alee

Alijah (American) Form of Elijah, meaning "Jehovah is my god"

Alon (Hebrew) Of the oak tree
Allona, Allon, Alonn

Alonzo (Spanish) Form of Alfonso, meaning "prepared for battle; eager and ready"
Alonso, Alanso, Alanzo, Allonso, Allonzo, Allohnso, Allohnzo, Alohnso

Aloysius (German) A famous warrior
Ahlois, Aloess, Alois, Aloisio, Aloisius, Aloisio, Aloj, Alojzy

Alpha (Greek) The first-born child; the first letter of the Greek alphabet
Alphah, Alfa, Alfah

Alter (Hebrew) One who is old
Allter, Altar, Alltar

Alton (English) From the old town
Aldon, Aldun, Altun, Alten, Allton, Alltun, Allten

Alvin (English) Friend of the elves
Alven, Alvan, Alvyn

Amani (African / Arabic) One who is peaceful / one with wishes and dreams
Amanie, Amany, Amaney, Amanee, Amanye, Amanea, Amaneah

^Amari (African) Having great strength; a builder
Amare, Amarie, Amaree, Amarea, Amary, Amarey

Amil (Hindi) One who is invaluable
Ameel, Ameal, Ameil, Amiel, Amyl

Amit (Hindi) Without limit;
endless
*Ameet, Ameat, Ameit, Amiet,
Amyt*

Amory (German) Ruler and
lover of one's home
*Aimory, Amery, Amorey,
Amry, Amori, Amorie, Amoree,
Amorea*

Amos (Hebrew) To carry;
hardworking
Amoss, Aymoss, Aymos

Andino (Italian) Form of
Andrew, meaning "one who
is manly; a warrior"
*Andyno, Andeeno, Andeano,
Andieno, Andeino*

Andre (French) Form of
Andrew, meaning "manly,
a warrior"
*Andreas, Andrei, Andrej,
Andres, Andrey*

*Andrew (Greek) One who is
manly; a warrior
*Andy, Aindrea, Andreas, Andie,
Andonia, Andor, Andresj,
Anderson*

Andrik (Slavic) Form of
Andrew, meaning "one who
is manly; a warrior"
*Andric, Andrick, Andryk,
Andryck, Andryc*

*Angel (Greek) A messenger
of God
*Andjelko, Ange, Angelino,
Angell, Angelmo, Angelo, Angie,
Angy*

Angus (Scottish) One force;
one strength; one choice
Aengus, Anngus, Aonghus

Anicho (German) An ancestor
*Anico, Anecho, Aneco, Anycho,
Anyco*

Ankur (Indian) One who is
blossoming; a sapling

Annan (Celtic) From the brook
Anan

Ansley (English) From the
noble's pastureland
*Ansly, Anslie, Ansli, Anslee,
Ansleigh, Anslea, Ansleah,
Anslye*

Antenor (Spanish) One who
antagonizes
*Antener, Antenar, Antenir,
Antenyr, Antenur*

*Anthony (Latin) A flourishing
man; of an ancient Roman
family
*Antal, Antony, Anthoney,
Anntoin, Antin, Anton, Antone,
Antonello, **Antonio***

Antoine (French) Form of Anthony, meaning "a flourishing man; of an ancient Roman family"
Antione, Antjuan, Antuan, Antuwain, Antuwaine, Antuwayne, Antuwon, Antwahn

Antonio (Italian) Form of Anthony, meaning "a flourishing man, from an ancient Roman family"
Antonin, Antonino, Antonius, Antonyo

Ara (Armenian / Latin) A legendary king / of the altar; the name of a constellation
Araa, Aira, Arah, Arae, Ahraya

Aram (Assyrian) One who is exalted
Arram

Arcadio (Greek) From an ideal country paradise
Alcadio, Alcado, Alcedio, Arcadios, Arcadius, Arkadi, Arkadios, Arkadius

Arcelio (Spanish) From the altar of heaven
Arcelios, Arcelius, Aricelio, Aricelios, Aricelius

Archard (German) A powerful holy man
Archerd, Archird, Archyrd

Archelaus (Greek) The ruler of the people
Archelaios, Arkelaos, Arkelaus, Arkelaios, Archelaos

^**Archer** (Latin) A skilled bowman

Ardell (Latin) One who is eager
Ardel, Ardelle, Ardele

Arden (Latin / English) One who is passionate and enthusiastic / from the valley of the eagles
Ardan, Arrden, Arrdan, Ardin, Arrdin, Ard, Ardyn, Arrdyn

Arduino (German) A valued friend
Ardwino, Arrduino, Ardueno

Ari (Hebrew) Resembling a lion or an eagle
Aree, Arie, Aristide, Aristides, Arri, Ary, Arye, Arrie

Ariel (Hebrew) A lion of God
Arielle, Ariele, Ariell, Arriel, Ahriel, Airial, Arieal, Arial

Aries (Latin) Resembling a ram; the first sign of the zodiac; a constellation
Arese, Ariese

Arion (Greek) A poet or musician
Arian, Arien, Aryon

Aristotle (Greek) Of high
quality
Aristotelis, Aristotellis

Arius (Greek) Enduring life;
everlasting; immortal
Areos, Areus, Arios

Arley (English) From the
hare's meadow
*Arlea, Arleigh, Arlie, Arly,
Arleah, Arli, Arlee*

^**Armani** (Persian) One who is
desired

Arnold (German) The eagle
ruler
*Arnaldo, Arnaud, Arnauld,
Arnault, Arnd, Arndt, Arnel,
Arnell*

^**Arthur** (Celtic) As strong as a
bear; a hero
*Aart, Arrt, Art, Artair, Arte,
Arther, Arthor, Arthuro*

Arvad (Hebrew) A wanderer;
voyager
Arpad

Arvin (English) A friend to
everyone
*Arvinn, Arvinne, Arven,
Arvenn, Arvenne, Arvyn,
Arvynn, Arvynne*

Asa (Hebrew) One who heals
others
Asah

Asaph (Hebrew) One who
gathers or collects
*Asaf, Asaphe, Asafe, Asiph,
Asiphe, Asif, Asife*

Ash (English) From the
ash tree
Ashe

Asher (Hebrew) Filled with
happiness
*Ashar, Ashor, Ashir, Ashyr,
Ashur*

Ashley (English) From the
meadow of ash trees
*Ashely, Asheley, Ashelie,
Ashlan, Ashleigh, Ashlen, Ashli,
Ashlie*

Ashton (English) From the
ash-tree town
*Asheton, Ashtun, Ashetun,
Ashtin, Ashetin, Ashtyn,
Ashetyn, Aston*

Aslan (Turkish) Resembling
a lion
Aslen, Azlan, Azlen

Athens (Greek) From the
capital of Greece
*Athenios, Athenius, Atheneos,
Atheneus*

^**Atticus** (Latin) A man from
Athens
*Attikus, Attickus, Aticus,
Atickus, Atikus*

Atwell (English) One who lives at the spring
Attwell, Atwel, Attwel

Aubrey (English) One who rules with elf-wisdom
Aubary, Aube, Aubery, Aubry, Aubury, Aubrian, Aubrien, Aubrion

Auburn (Latin) Having a reddish-brown color
Aubirn, Auburne, Aubyrn, Abern, Abirn, Aburn, Abyrn, Aubern

Audley (English) From the old meadow
Audly, Audleigh, Audlee, Audlea, Audleah, Audli, Audlie

August (Irish) One who is venerable; majestic
Austin, Augustine, Agoston, Aguistin, Agustin, Augustin, Augustyn, Avgustin, Augusteen, Agosteen

*Austin (English) Form of August, meaning "one who is venerable; majestic"
Austen, Austyn, Austan, Auston, Austun

Avery (English) One who is a wise ruler; of the nobility
Avrie, Averey, Averie, Averi, Averee

Aviram (Hebrew) My Father is mighty
Avyram, Avirem, Avyrem

^Axel (German / Latin / Hebrew) Source of life; small oak / axe / peace
Aksel, Ax, Axe, Axell, Axil, Axill, Axl

Aya (Hebrew) Resembling a bird
Ayah

*Ayden (Irish) Form of Aiden, meaning "a fiery young man"

Ayo (African) Filled with happiness
Ayoe, Ayow, Ayowe

Azamat (Arabic) A proud man; one who is majestic

Azi (African) One who is youthful
Azie, Azy, Azey, Azee, Azea

Azmer (Islamic) Resembling a lion
Azmar, Azmir, Azmyr, Azmor, Azmur

B

Baakir (African) The eldest
child
*Baakeer, Baakyr, Baakear,
Baakier, Baakeir*

Bachir (Hebrew) The oldest
son
*Bacheer, Bachear, Bachier,
Bacheir, Bachyr*

Baha (Arabic) A glorious and
splendid man
Bahah

Bailintin (Irish) A valiant man
*Bailinten, Bailentin, Bailenten,
Bailintyn, Bailentyn*

Bain (Irish) A fair-haired man
*Baine, Bayn, Bayne, Baen,
Baene, Bane, Baines, Baynes*

Bajnok (Hungarian) A victorious man
Bajnock, Bajnoc

Bakari (Swahili) One who is
promised
*Bakarie, Bakary, Bakarey,
Bakaree, Bakarea*

Bakhit (Arabic) A lucky man
*Bakheet, Bakheat, Bakheit,
Bakhiet, Bakhyt, Bakht*

Bala (Hindi) One who is
youthful
Balu, Balue, Balou

Balark (Hindi) Born with the
rising sun

Balasi (Basque) One who is
flat-footed
*Balasie, Balasy, Balasey,
Balasee, Balasea*

Balbo (Latin) One who mutters
*Balboe, Balbow, Balbowe,
Ballbo, Balbino, Balbi, Balbie,
Balby*

Baldwin (German) A brave
friend
*Baldwine, Baldwinn,
Baldwinne, Baldwen,
Baldwenn, Baldwenne,
Baldwyn, Baldwynn*

Balint (Latin) A healthy and
strong man
*Balent, Balin, Balen, Balynt,
Balyn*

Balloch (Scottish) From the
grazing land

Bancroft (English) From the
bean field
*Bancrofte, Banfield, Banfeld,
Bankroft, Bankrofte*

Bandana (Spanish) A brightly
colored headwrap
*Bandanah, Bandanna,
Bandannah*

Bandy (American) A fiesty
man
Bandey, Bandi, Bandie,
Bandee, Bandea

Bansi (Indian) One who plays
the flute
Bansie, Bansy, Bansey, Bansee,
Bansea

Bao (Vietnamese / Chinese)
To order / one who is prized

Baqir (Arabic) A learned man
Baqeer, Baqear, Baqier, Baqeir,
Baqyr, Baqer

Barak (Hebrew) Of the light-
ning flash
Barrak, Barac, Barrac, Barack,
Barrack

Baram (Hebrew) The son of
the nation
Barem, Barum, Barom, Barim,
Barym

Bard (English) A minstrel;
a poet
Barde, Bardo

Barden (English) From the
barley valley; from the boar's
valley
Bardon, Bardun, Bardin,
Bardyn, Bardan, Bardene

Bardol (Basque) A farmer
Bardo, Bartol

Bardrick (Teutonic) An axe
ruler
Bardric, Bardrik, Bardryck,
Bardryk, Bardryc, Bardarick,
Bardaric, Bardarik

Barek (Arabic) One who is
noble
Barec, Bareck

Barend (German) The hard
bear
Barende, Barind, Barinde,
Barynd, Barynde

Barnett (English) Of honorable
birth
Barnet, Baronet, Baronett

Baron (English) A title of
nobility
Barron

Barr (English) A lawyer
Barre, Bar

Barra (Gaelic) A fair-haired
man

^**Barrett** (German / English)
Having the strength of a
bear / one who argues
Baret, Barrat, Barratt, Barret,
Barrette

Barry (Gaelic) A fair-haired
man
Barrey, Barri, Barrie,
Barree, Barrea, Barrington,
Barryngton, Barringtun

Bartholomew (Aramaic) The
son of the farmer
*Bart, Bartel, Barth, Barthelemy,
Bartho, Barthold, Bartholoma,
Bartholomaus, Bartlett, Bartol*

Bartlett (French) Form of
Bartholomew, meaning "the
son of the farmer"
*Bartlet, Bartlitt, Bartlit,
Bartlytt, Bartlyt*

Bartley (English) From the
meadow of birch trees
*Bartly, Bartli, Bartlie, Bartlee,
Bartlea, Bartleah, Bartleigh*

Bartoli (Spanish) Form of
Bartholomew, meaning "the
son of the farmer"
*Bartolie, Bartoly, Bartoley,
Bartolee, Bartoleigh, Bartolea,
Bartolo, Bartolio*

Barton (English) From the
barley town
*Bartun, Barten, Bartan, Bartin,
Bartyn*

Barwolf (English) The ax-wolf
Barrwolf, Barwulf, Barrwulf

Basant (Arabic) One who
smiles often
Basante

Bassett (English) A little
person
Baset, Basset, Basett

Basy (American) A homebody
*Basey, Basi, Basie, Basee,
Basea, Basye*

Baurice (American) Form of
Maurice, meaning "a dark-
skinned man; Moorish"
*Baurell, Baureo, Bauricio,
Baurids, Baurie, Baurin*

Bay (Vietnamese / English)
The seventh-born child; born
during the month of July /
from the bay
Baye, Bae, Bai

Beal (French) A handsome
man
Beals, Beale, Beall, Bealle

Beamer (English) One who
plays the trumpet
*Beamor, Beamir, Beamyr,
Beamur, Beamar, Beemer,
Beemar, Beemir*

Beau (French) A handsome
man, an admirer
Bo

Becher (Hebrew) The firstborn
son

Beckett (English) From the
small stream; from the brook
Becket

Bedar (Arabic) One who is
attentive
*Beder, Bedor, Bedur, Bedyr,
Bedir*

Beircheart (Anglo-Saxon) Of the intelligent army

Bela (Slavic) A white-skinned man
Belah, Bella, Bellah

Belden (English) From the beautiful valley
Beldan, Beldon, Beldun, Beldin, Beldyn, Bellden, Belldan, Belldon, Belldun, Belldin, Belldyn

Belen (Greek) Of an arrow
Belin, Belyn, Belan, Belon, Belun

Belindo (English) A handsome and tender man
Belyndo, Belindio, Belyndio, Belindeo, Belyndeo, Belindiyo, Belyndiyo, Belindeyo

Bellarmine (Italian) One who is handsomely armed
Bellarmin, Bellarmeen, Bellarmeene, Bellarmean, Bellarmeane, Bellarmyn, Bellarmyne

Belton (English) From the beautiful town
Bellton, Beltun, Belltun, Belten, Bellten

Belvin (American) Form of Melvin, meaning "a friend who offers counsel"
Belven, Belvyn, Belvon, Belvun, Belvan

Bem (African) A peaceful man

Ben (English) Form of Benjamin, meaning "son of the south; son of the right hand"
Benn, Benni, Bennie, Bennee, Benney, Benny, Bennea, Benno

*Benjamin (Hebrew) Son of the south; son of the right hand
Ben, Benejamen, Beniamino, Benjaman, Benjamen, Benjamino, Benjamon, Benjiman, Benjimen

Bennett (English) Form of Benedict, meaning "one who is blessed"
Benett, Bennet, Benet

^*Bentley (English) From the meadow of bent grass
Bently, Bentleigh, Bentlee, Bentlie

Berdy (German) Having a brilliant mind
Berdey, Berdee, Berdea, Berdi, Berdie

Beresford (English) From the barley ford
Beresforde, Beresfurd, Beresfurde, Beresferd, Beresferde, Berford, Berforde, Berfurd

Berkeley (English) From the meadow of birch trees
Berkely, Berkeli, Berkelie, Berkelea, Berkeleah, Berkelee, Berkeleigh, Berkley

Bernard (German) As strong and brave as a bear
Barnard, Barnardo, Barnhard, Barnhardo, Bearnard, Bernardo, Bernarr, Bernd

Berry (English) Resembling a berry fruit
Berrey, Berri, Berrie, Berree, Berrea

Bert (English) One who is illustrious
Berte, Berti, Bertie, Bertee, Bertea, Berty, Bertey

Bethel (Hebrew) The house of God
Bethell, Bethele, Bethelle, Betuel, Betuell, Betuele, Betuelle

Bevis (Teutonic) An archer
Beviss, Bevys, Bevyss, Beavis, Beaviss, Beavys, Beavyss

Biagio (Italian) One who has a stutter
Biaggio

Birney (English) From the island with the brook
Birny, Birnee, Birnea, Birni, Birnie

Black (English) A dark-skinned man
Blak, Blac, Blacke

Blackwell (English) From the dark spring
Blackwel, Blackwelle, Blackwele

Blade (English) One who wields a sword or knife
Blayd, Blayde, Blaid, Blaide, Blaed, Blaede

Blagden (English) From the dark valley
Blagdon, Blagdan, Blagdun, Blagdin, Blagdyn

Blaine (Scottish / Irish) A saint's servant / a thin man
Blayne, Blane, Blain, Blayn, Blaen, Blaene, Blainy, Blainey

Blaise (Latin / American) One with a lisp or a stutter / a fiery man
Blaze, Blaize, Blaiz, Blayze, Blayz, Blaez, Blaeze

*Blake (English) A dark, handsome man
Blayk, Blayke, Blaik, Blaike, Blaek, Blaeke

Bliss (English) Filled with happiness
Blis, Blyss, Blys

Blondell (English) A fair-haired boy
Blondel, Blondele, Blondelle

Boaz (Hebrew) One who is swift
Boaze, Boas, Boase

Bob (English) Form of Robert, meaning "one who is bright with fame"
Bobbi, Bobbie, Bobby, Bobbey, Bobbee, Bobbea

Bogart (French) One who is strong with the bow
Bogaard, Bogaart, Bogaerd, Bogey, Bogie, Bogi, Bogy, Bogee

Bolivar (Spanish) A mighty warrior
Bolevar, Bolivarr, Bolevarr, Bollivar, Bollivarr, Bollevar, Bollevarr

Bonaventure (Latin) One who undertakes a blessed venture
Bonaventura, Buenaventure, Buenaventura, Bueaventure, Bueaventura

Booker (English) One who binds books; a scribe
Bookar, Bookir, Bookyr, Bookur, Bookor

Bosley (English) From the meadow near the forest
Bosly, Boslee, Boslea, Bosleah, Bosleigh, Bosli, Boslie, Bozley

Boston (English) From the town near the forest; from the city of Boston
Bostun, Bostin, Bostyn, Bosten, Bostan

Boyce (French) One who lives near the forest
Boice, Boyse, Boise

Boyd (Celtic) A blond-haired man
Boyde, Boid, Boide, Boyden, Boydan, Boydin, Boydyn, Boydon

Boynton (Irish) From the town near the river Boyne
Boyntun, Boynten, Boyntin, Boyntan, Boyntyn

Bracken (English) Resembling the large fern
Braken, Brackan, Brakan, Brackin, Brakin, Brackyn

Braddock (English) From the broadly spread oak
Bradock, Braddoc, Bradoc, Braddok, Bradok

Braden (Gaelic / English) Resembling salmon / from the wide valley
Bradan, Bradon, Bradin, Bradyn, Braeden, Brayden

Bradford (English) From the wide ford
Bradforde, Bradferd, Bradferde

Bradley (English) From the wide meadow
Bradly, Bradlea, Bradleah, Bradlee, Bradleigh, Bradli

Brady (Irish) The son of a large-chested man
Bradey, Bradee, Bradea, Bradi, Bradie, Braidy, Braidey, Braidee

Bramley (English) From the wild gorse meadow; from the raven's meadow
Bramly, Bramlee, Bramlea

*****Brandon** (English) From the broom or gorse hill
Brandun, Brandin, Brandyn, Brandan, Branden, Brannon, Brannun, Brannen

Branson (English) The son of Brand or Brandon
Bransun, Bransen, Bransan, Bransin, Bransyn

Brant (English) Steep, tall

^**Brantley** (English) Form of Brant, meaning "steep, tall"
Brantly

Braxton (English) From Brock's town
Braxtun, Braxten, Braxtan, Braxtyn

*****Brayden** (Gaelic / English) Form of Braden, meaning "resembling salmon / from the wide valley"
Braydon, Braydan, Braydin, Braydyn

^**Braylen** (American) Combination of Brayden and Lynn
Braylon

Brendan (Irish) Born to royalty; a prince
Brendano, Brenden, Brendin, Brendon, Brendyn, Brendun

Brennan (Gaelic) A sorrowful man; a teardrop
Brenan, Brenn, Brennen, Brennin, Brennon, Brenin, Brennun, Brennyn

Brent (English) From the hill
Brendt, Brennt, Brentan, Brenten, Brentin, Brenton, Brentun, Brentyn

Brett (Latin) A man from Britain or Brittany
Bret, Breton, Brette, Bretton, Brit, Briton, Britt, Brittain

Brewster (English) One who brews
Brewer, Brewstere

Brian (Gaelic / Celtic) Of noble birth / having great strength
Briano, Briant, Brien, Brion, Bryan, Bryant, Bryen, Bryent

Briar (English) Resembling a thorny plant
Brier, Bryar, Bryer

Brock (English) Resembling a badger
Broc

Broderick (English) From the wide ridge
Broderik, Broderic, Brodrick, Brodryk, Brodyrc, Brodrik, Broderyc, Brodrig

*★**Brody** (Gaelic / Irish) From the ditch
Brodie, Brodey, Brodi, Brodee

Brogan (Gaelic) One who is sturdy
Broggan, Brogen, Broggen, Brogon, Broggon, Brogun, Broggun, Brogin, Broggin, Brogyn

^**Brooks** (English) From the running stream
Brookes

^**Bruce** (Scottish) A man from Brieuse; one who is well-born; from an influential family
Brouce, Brooce, Bruci, Brucie, Brucey, Brucy

Bruno (German) A brown-haired man
Brunoh, Brunoe, Brunow, Brunowe, Bruin, Bruine, Brunon, Brunun

Bryce (Scottish / Anglo-Saxon) One who is speckled / the son of a nobleman
Brice, Bricio, Brizio, Brycio

^★**Bryson** (Welsh) The son of Brice
Brisen, Brysin, Brysun, Brysyn, **Brycen**

Bud (English) One who is brotherly
Budd, Buddi, Buddie, Buddee, Buddey, Buddy

Budha (Hindi) Another name for the planet Mercury
Budhan, Budhwar

Bulat (Russian) Having great strength
Bulatt

Burbank (English) From the riverbank of burrs
Burrbank, Burhbank

Burgess (German) A free citizen of the town
Burges, Burgiss, Burgis, Burgyss, Burgys, Burgeis

Burne (English) Resembling a bear; from the brook; the brown-haired one
Burn, Beirne, Burnis, Byrn, Byrne, Burns, Byrnes

Burnet (French) Having brown hair
Burnett, Burnete, Burnette, Bernet, Bernett, Bernete, Bernette

Burton (English) From the fortified town
Burtun, Burten, Burtin, Burtyn, Burtan

Butler (English) The keeper of the bottles (wine, liquor)
Buttler, Butlar, Butlor, Butlir, Buttlir, Butlyr

Byron (English) One who lives near the cow sheds
Byrom, Beyren, Beyron, Biren, Biron, Buiron, Byram, Byran

C

Cable (French) One who makes rope
Cabel, Caibel, Caible, Caybel, Cayble, Caebel, Caeble, Cabe

Caddis (English) Resembling a worsted fabric
Caddys, Caddiss, Caddice

Cade (English / French) One who is round / of the cask
Caid, Caide, Cayd, Cayde, Caed, Caede

Cadell (Welsh) Having the spirit of battle
Cadel, Caddell, Caddel

Caden (Welsh) Spirit of Battle
Caiden, Cayden

Cadmus (Greek) A man from the east; in mythology, the man who founded Thebes
Cadmar, Cadmo, Cadmos, Cadmuss

Cadogan (Welsh) Having glory and honor during battle
Cadogawn, Cadwgan, Cadwgawn, Cadogaun

Caesar (Latin) An emperor
Caezar, Casar, Cezar, Chezare, Caesarius, Ceasar, Ceazer

Cain (Hebrew) One who wields a spear; something acquired; in the Bible, Adam and Eve's first son who killed his brother Abel
Cayn, Caen, Cane, Caine, Cayne, Caene

Caird (Scottish) A traveling metal worker
Cairde, Cayrd, Cayrde, Caerd, Caerde

Cairn (Gaelic) From the mound of rocks
Cairne, Cairns, Caern, Caerne, Caernes

Caith (Irish) Of the battlefield
Caithe, Cayth, Caythe, Cathe, Caeth, Caethe

Calbert (English) A cowboy
Calberte, Calburt, Calburte, Calbirt, Calbirte, Calbyrt, Calbyrte

Cale (English) Form of Charles, meaning "one who is manly and strong / a free man"
Cail, Caile, Cayl, Cayle, Cael, Caele

*Caleb** (Hebrew) Resembling a dog
Cayleb, Caileb, Caeleb, Calob, Cailob, Caylob, Caelob, Kaleb

Calian (Native American) A warrior of life
Calien, Calyan, Calyen

Callum (Gaelic) Resembling a dove
Calum

Calvin (French) The little bald one
Cal, Calvyn, Calvon, Calven, Calvan, Calvun, Calvino

Camara (African) One who teaches others

Camden (Gaelic) From the winding valley
Camdene, Camdin, Camdyn, Camdan, Camdon, Camdun

Cameo (English) A small, perfect child
Cammeo

*Cameron** (Scottish) Having a crooked nose
Cameren, Cameran, Camerin, Cameryn, Camerun, Camron, Camren, Camran, Tameron

Campbell (Scottish) Having a crooked mouth
Campbel, Cambell, Cambel, Camp, Campe, Cambeul, Cambeull, Campbeul

Candan (Turkish) A sincere man
Canden, Candin, Candyn, Candon, Candun

Cannon (French) An official of the church
Canon, Cannun, Canun, Cannin, Canin

Canyon (Spanish / English) From the footpath / from the deep ravine
Caniyon, Canyun, Caniyun

Capricorn (Latin) The tenth sign of the zodiac; the goat

Cargan (Gaelic) From the small rock
Cargen, Cargon, Cargun, Cargin, Cargyn

Carl (German) Form of Karl, meaning "a free man"
Carel, Carlan, Carle, Carlens, Carlitis, Carlin, Carlo, **Carlos**

*Carlos (Spanish) Form of Karl, meaning "a free man"
Carolos, Carolo, Carlito

Carlsen (Scandinavian) The son of Carl
Carlssen, Carlson, Carlsson, Carlsun, Carllsun, Carlsin, Carllsin, Carlsyn

Carlton (English) From the free man's town
Carltun, Carltown, Carston, Carstun, Carstown, Carleton, Carletun, Carlten

Carmichael (Scottish) A follower of Michael

Carmine (Latin / Aramaic) A beautiful song / the color crimson
Carman, Carmen, Carmin, Carmino, Carmyne, Carmon, Carmun, Carmyn

*Carson (Scottish) The son of a marsh dweller
Carsen, Carsun, Carsan, Carsin, Carsyn

*Carter (English) One who transports goods; one who drives a cart
Cartar, Cartir, Cartyr, Cartor, Cartur, Cartere, Cartier, Cartrell

Cartland (English) From Carter's land
Carteland, Cartlan, Cartlend, Cartelend, Cartlen

Cary (Celtic / Welsh / Gaelic) From the river / from the fort on the hill / having dark features
Carey, Cari, Carie, Caree, Carea, Carry, Carrey, Carri

Case (French) Refers to a chest or box
Cace

Cash (Latin) money

^**Cason** (Greek) A seer
Casen

Cassander (Spanish) A brother of heroes
Casander, Casandro, Cassandro, Casandero

Cassius (Latin) One who is empty; hollow; vain
Cassios, Cassio, Cach, Cache, Cashus, Cashos, Cassian, Cassien

Castel (Spanish) From the castle
Castell, Castal, Castall, Castol, Castoll, Castul, Castull, Castil

Castor (Greek) Resembling a beaver; in mythology, one of the Dioscuri
Castur, Caster, Castar, Castir, Castyr, Castorio, Castoreo, Castoro

Cat (American) Resembling the animal
Catt, Chait, Chaite

Cathmore (Irish) A renowned fighter
Cathmor, Cathemore

Cato (Latin) One who is all-knowing
Cayto, Caito, Caeto

Caton (Spanish) One who is knowledgable
Caten, Catun, Catan, Catin, Catyn

Cavell (Teutonic) One who is bold
Cavel, Cavele, Cavelle

Caxton (English) From the lump settlement
Caxtun, Caxten

Celesto (Latin) From heaven
Célestine, Celestino, Celindo, Celestyne, Celestyno

Cephas (Hebrew) As solid as a rock

Cesar (Spanish) Form of Caesar, meaning "emperor"
Cesare, Cesaro, Cesario

Chad (English) One who is warlike
Chaddie, Chadd, Chadric, Chadrick, Chadrik, Chadryck, Chadryc, Chadryk

Chadwick (English) From Chad's dairy farm
Chadwik, Chadwic, Chadwyck, Chadwyk, Chadwyc

Chai (Hebrew) A giver of life
Chaika, Chaim, Cahyim, Cahyyam

Chalkley (English) From the chalk meadow
Chalkly, Chalkleigh, Chalklee, Chalkleah, Chalkli, Chalklie, Chalklea

Champion (English) A warrior; the victor
Champeon, Champiun, Champeun, Champ

Chan (Spanish / Sanskrit) Form of John, meaning "God is gracious" / a shining man
Chayo, Chano, Chawn, Chaun

Chanan (Hebrew) God is compassionate
Chanen, Chanin, Chanyn, Chanun, Chanon

Chance (English) Having good fortune

^**Chandler** (English) One who makes candles
Chandlar, Chandlor

Chaniel (Hebrew) The grace of God
Chanyel, Chaniell, Chanyell

Channing (French / English) An official of the church / resembling a young wolf
Channyng, Canning, Cannyng

Chao (Chinese) The great one

Chappel (English) One who works in the chapel
Capel, Capell, Capello, Cappel, Chappell

*****Charles** (English / German) One who is manly and strong / a free man
Charls, Chas, Charli, Charlie, Charley, Charly, Charlee, Charleigh, Cale, Chuck, Chick

Charleson (English) The son of Charles
Charlesen, Charlesin, Charlesyn, Charlesan, Charlesun

Charlton (English) From the free man's town
Charleton, Charltun, Charletun, Charleston, Charlestun

Charro (Spanish) A cowboy
Charo

*****Chase** (English) A huntsman
Chace, Chasen, Chayce, Chayse, Chaise, Chaice, Chaece, Chaese

Chatwin (English) A warring friend
Chatwine, Chatwinn, Chatwinne, Chatwen, Chatwenn, Chatwenne, Chatwyn, Chatwynn

Chaviv (Hebrew) One who is
dearly loved
*Chaveev, Chaveav, Chaviev,
Chaveiv, Chavyv, Chavivi,
Chavivie, Chavivy*

Chay (Gaelic) From the fairy
place
Chaye, Chae

Chelsey (English) From the
landing place for chalk
*Chelsee, Chelseigh, Chelsea,
Chelsi, Chelsie, Chelsy, Chelcey,
Chelcy*

Cheslav (Russian) From the
fortified camp
Cheslaw

Chester (Latin) From the camp
of the soldiers
*Chet, Chess, Cheston, Chestar,
Chestor, Chestur, Chestir,
Chestyr*

Chico (Spanish) A boy; a lad

Chien (Vietnamese) A
combative man

Chiron (Greek) A wise tutor
Chyron, Chirun, Chyrun

Chogan (Native American)
Resembling a blackbird
*Chogen, Chogon, Chogun,
Chogin, Chogyn*

Choni (Hebrew) A gracious
man
*Chonie, Chony, Choney,
Chonee, Chonea*

*Christian (Greek) A follower
of Christ
*Chrestien, Chretien, Chris,
Christan, Christer, Christiano,
Cristian*

*Christopher (Greek) One who
bears Christ inside
*Chris, Kit, Christof, Christofer,
Christoffer, Christoforo,
Christoforus, Christoph,
Christophe, Cristopher, Cristofer*

Chuchip (Native American) A
deer spirit

Chuck (English) Form of
Charles, meaning "one who
is manly and strong / a free
man"
*Chucke, Chucki, Chuckie,
Chucky, Chuckey, Chuckee,
Chuckea*

Chul (Korean) One who stands
firm

Chun (Chinese) Born during
the spring

Cid (Spanish) A lord
Cyd

Cillian (Gaelic) One who suffers strife

Ciqala (Native American) The little one

Cirrus (Latin) A lock of hair; resembling the cloud
Cyrrus

Clair (Latin) One who is bright
Clare, Clayr, Claer, Clairo, Claro, Claero

Clancy (Celtic) Son of the red-haired warrior
Clancey, Clanci, Clancie, Clancee, Clancea, Clansey, Clansy, Clansi

Clark (English) A cleric; a clerk
Clarke, Clerk, Clerke, Clerc

Claude (English) One who is lame
Claud, Claudan, Claudell, Claidianus, Claudicio, Claudien, Claudino, Claudio

Clay (English) Of the earth's clay

Clayton (English) From the town settled on clay
Claytun, Clayten, Claytin, Claytyn, Claytan, Cleyton, Cleytun, Cleytan

Cleon (Greek) A well-known man
Cleone, Clion, Clione, Clyon, Clyone

Clifford (English) From the ford near the cliff
Cliff, Clyfford, Cliford, Clyford

Cliffton (English) From the town near the cliff
Cliff, Cliffe, Clyff, Clyffe, Clifft, Clift, Clyfft, Clyft

Clinton (English) From the town on the hill
Clynton, Clintun, Clyntun, Clint, Clynt, Clinte, Clynte

Clive (English) One who lives near the cliff
Clyve, Cleve

Cluny (Irish) From the meadow
Cluney, Cluni, Clunie, Clunee, Clunea, Cluneah

Cobden (English) From the cottage in the valley
Cobdenn, Cobdale, Cobdail, Cobdaile, Cobdell, Cobdel, Cobdayl, Cobdayle

Coby (English) Form of Jacob, meaning "he who supplants"
Cobey

Cody (Irish / English) One who is helpful; a wealthy man / acting as a cushion
Codi, Codie, Codey, Codee, Codeah, Codea, Codier, Codyr

Colbert (French) A famous
and bright man
*Colvert, Culbert, Colburt,
Colbirt, Colbyrt, Colbart,
Culburt, Culbirt*

Colby (English) From the coal
town
*Colbey, Colbi, Colbie, Colbee,
Collby, Coalby, Colbea, Colbeah*

*Cole (English) Having dark
features; having coal-black
hair
*Coley, Coli, Coly, Colie, Colee,
Coleigh, Colea, Colson*

Coleridge (English) From the
dark ridge
Colerige, Colridge, Colrige

Colgate (English) From the
dark gate
*Colegate, Colgait, Colegait,
Colgayt, Colegayt, Colgaet*

Colin (Scottish) A young man;
a form of Nicholas, meaning
"of the victorious people"
*Cailean, Colan, Colyn, Colon,
Colen, Collin, Collan*

Colt (English) A young horse;
from the coal town
Colte

Colter (English) A horse
herdsman
*Coltere, Coltar, Coltor, Coltir,
Coltyr, Coulter, Coultar, Coultir*

*Colton (English) From the
coal town
*Colten, Coltun, Coltan, Coltin,
Coltyn, Coltrain*

Comanche (Native American)
A tribal name
*Comanchi, Comanchie,
Comanchee, Comanchea,
Comanchy, Comanchey*

Comus (Latin) In mythology,
the god of mirth and revelry
Comas, Comis, Comys

Conan (English / Gaelic)
Resembling a wolf / one who
is high and mighty
Conant

Condon (Celtic) A dark,
wise man
*Condun, Condan, Conden,
Condin, Condyn*

Cong (Chinese) A clever man

Conn (Irish) The chief
Con

Connecticut (Native American)
From the place beside the
long river / from the state of
Connecticut

Connery (Scottish) A daring
man
*Connary, Connerie, Conneri,
Connerey, Connarie, Connari,
Connarey, Conary*

*Connor (Gaelic) A wolf lover
*Conor, Conner, Coner, Connar,
Conar, Connur, Conur, Connir,
Conir*

Conroy (Irish) A wise adviser
Conroye, Conroi

Constantine (Latin) One who
is steadfast; firm
Dinos

Consuelo (Spanish) One who
offers consolation
*Consuel, Consuelio, Consueleo,
Consueliyo, Consueleyo*

Conway (Gaelic) The hound
of the plain; from the sacred
river
*Conwaye, Conwai, Conwae,
Conwy*

Cook (English) One who
prepares meals for others
Cooke

Cooney (Irish) A handsome
man
*Coony, Cooni, Coonie, Coonee,
Coonea*

*Cooper (English) One who
makes barrels
*Coop, Coopar, Coopir, Coopyr,
Coopor, Coopur, Coopersmith,
Cupere*

Corbett (French) Resembling
a young raven
*Corbet, Corbete, Corbette,
Corbit, Corbitt, Corbite,
Corbitte*

Corcoran (Gaelic) Having a
ruddy complexion
Cochran

Cordero (Spanish) Resembling
a lamb
*Corderio, Corderiyo, Cordereo,
Cordereyo*

Corey (Irish) From the hollow;
of the churning waters
*Cory, Cori, Corie, Coree, Corea,
Correy, Corry, Corri*

Coriander (Greek) A romantic
man; resembling the spice
*Coryander, Coriender,
Coryender*

Corlan (Irish) One who wields
a spear
*Corlen, Corlin, Corlyn, Corlon,
Corlun*

Corrado (German) A bold
counselor
Corrade, Corradeo, Corradio

Corridon (Irish) One who
wields a spear
*Corridan, Corridun, Corriden,
Corridin, Corridyn*

Cortez (Spanish) A courteous man
Cortes

Cosmo (Greek) The order of the universe
Cosimo, Cosmé, Cosmos, Cosmas, Cozmo, Cozmos, Cozmas

Cotton (American) Resembling or farmer of the plant
Cottin, Cotten, Cottyn, Cottun, Cottan

Courtney (English) A courteous man; courtly
Cordney, Cordni, Cortenay, Corteney, Cortni, Cortnee, Cortneigh, Cortney

Covert (English) One who provides shelter
Couvert

Covey (English) A brood of birds
Covy, Covi, Covie, Covee, Covea, Covvey, Covvy, Covvi

Covington (English) From the town near the cave
Covyngton, Covingtun, Covyngtun

Cox (English) A coxswain
Coxe, Coxi, Coxie, Coxey, Coxy, Coxee, Coxea

Coyle (Irish) A leader during battle
Coyl, Coil, Coile

Craig (Gaelic) From the rocks; from the crag
Crayg, Craeg, Craige, Crayge, Craege, Crage, Crag

Crandell (English) From the valley of cranes
Crandel, Crandale, Crandail, Crandaile, Crandayl, Crandayle, Crandael, Crandaele

Crawford (English) From the crow's ford
Crawforde, Crawferd, Crawferde, Crawfurd, Crawfurde

Creed (Latin) A guiding principle; a belief
Creede, Cread, Creade, Creedon, Creadon, Creedun, Creadun, Creedin

Creek (English) From the small stream
Creeke, Creak, Creake, Creik, Creike

Creighton (Scottish) From the border town
Creightun, Crayton, Craytun, Craiton, Craitun, Craeton, Craetun, Crichton

Crescent (French) One who creates; increasing; growing
Creissant, Crescence, Cressant, Cressent, Crescant

Cruz (Spanish) Of the cross

Cuarto (Spanish) The fourth-born child
Cuartio, Cuartiyo, Cuarteo

Cullen (Gaelic) A good-looking young man
Cullin, Cullyn, Cullan, Cullon, Cullun

Cunningham (Gaelic) Descendant of the chief
Conyngham, Cuningham, Cunnyngham, Cunyngham

Curcio (French) One who is courteous
Curceo

Cuthbert (English) One who is bright and famous
Cuthbeorht, Cuthburt, Cuthbirt, Cuthbyrt

Cyneley (English) From the royal meadow
Cynely, Cyneli, Cynelie, Cynelee, Cynelea, Cyneleah, Cyneleigh

Czar (Russian) An emperor

D

Dacey (Gaelic / Latin) A man from the south / a man from Dacia
Dacy, Dacee, Dacea, Daci, Dacie, Daicey, Daicy

Dack (English) From the French town of Dax
Dacks, Dax

Daedalus (Greek) A craftsman
Daldalos, Dedalus

Dag (Scandinavian) Born during the daylight
Dagney, Dagny, Dagnee, Dagnea, Dagni, Dagnie, Daeg, Dagget

Daijon (American) A gift of hope
Dayjon, Daejon, Dajon

Dainan (Australian) A kind-hearted man
Dainen, Dainon, Dainun, Dainyn, Dainin, Daynan, Daynen, Daynon

Daire (Irish) A wealthy man
Dair, Daere, Daer, Dayr, Dayre, Dare, Dari, Darie

Daivat (Hindi) A powerful man

Dakarai (African) Filled with happiness

Dakota (Native American) A friend to all
Daccota, Dakoda, Dakodah, Dakotah, Dakoeta, Dekota, Dekohta, Dekowta

Dallan (Irish) One who is blind
Dalan, Dallen, Dalen, Dalin, Dallin, Dallyn, Dalyn, Dallon, Dalon, Dallun, Dalun

Dallas (Scottish) From the dales
Dalles, Dallis, Dallys, Dallos

Dalton (English) from the town in the valley
Daltun, Dalten, Daltan, Daltin, Daltyn, Daleten, Dalte, Daulten

Damario (Greek / Spanish) Resembling a calf / one who is gentle
Damarios, Damarius, Damaro, Damero, Damerio, Damereo, Damareo, Damerios

^**Damian** (Greek) One who tames or subdues others
Daemon, Daimen, Daimon, Daman, Damen, Dameon, Damiano, Damianos, **Damon**

Dane (English) A man from Denmark
Dain, Daine, Dayn, Dayne

Danely (Scandinavian) A man from Denmark
Daneley, Daneli, Danelie, Danelee, Daneleigh, Danelea, Daineley, Dainely

Daniachew (African) A mediator

*****Daniel** (Hebrew) God is my judge
Dan, Danal, Daneal, Danek, Danell, Danial, Daniele, Danil, Danilo

Danso (African) A reliable man
Dansoe, Dansow, Dansowe

Dante (Latin) An enduring man; everlasting
Dantae, Dantay, Dantel, Daunte, Dontae, Dontay, Donte, Dontae

Daoud (Arabian) Form of David, meaning "the beloved one"
Daoude, Dawud, Doud, Daud, Da'ud

Daphnis (Greek) In mythology, the son of Hermes
Daphnys

Dar (Hebrew) Resembling a pearl
Darr

Darcel (French) Having dark features
Darcell, Darcele, Darcelle, Darcio, Darceo

Dardanus (Greek) In mythology, the founder of Troy
Dardanio, Dardanios, Dardanos, Dard, Darde

Darek (English) Form of Derek, meaning "the ruler of the tribe"
Darrek, Darec, Darrec, Darreck, Dareck

Darion (Greek) A gift
Darian, Darien, Dariun, Darrion, Darrian, Darrien, Daryon, Daryan

Darius (Greek) A kingly man; one who is wealthy
Darias, Dariess, Dario, Darious, Darrius, Derrius, Derrious, Derrias

Darlen (American) A sweet man; a darling
Darlon, Darlun, Darlan, Darlin, Darlyn

Darnell (English) From the hidden place
Darnall, Darneil, Darnel, Darnele, Darnelle

Darold (English) Form of Harold, meaning "the ruler of an army"
Darrold, Derald, Derrald, Derold, Derrold

Darren (Gaelic / English) A great man / a gift from God
Darran, Darrin, Darryn, Darron, Darrun, Daren, Darin, Daran

Dart (English / American) From the river / one who is fast
Darte, Darrt, Darrte, Darti, Dartie, Dartee, Dartea, Darty

Darvell (French) From the eagle town
Darvel, Darvele, Darvelle

Dasras (Indian) A handsome man

Dasya (Indian) A servant

*David (Hebrew) The beloved one
Dave, Davey, Davi, Davidde, Davide, Davie, Daviel, Davin, Daoud

Davis (English) The son of David
Davies, Daviss, Davys, Davyss

Davu (African) Of the beginning
Davue, Davoo, Davou, Davugh

Dawson (English) The son of David
Dawsan, Dawsen, Dawsin, Dawsun

Dax (French) From the French town Dax
Daxton

Dayton (English) From the sunny town

Deacon (Greek) The dusty one; a servant
Deecon, Deakon, Deekon, Deacun, Deecun, Deakun, Deekun, Deacan

Dean (English) From the valley; a church official
Deane, Deen, Deene, Dene, Deans, Deens, Deani, Deanie

DeAndre (American) A manly man
D'André, DeAndrae, DeAndray, Diandray, Diondrae, Diondray

Dearon (American) One who is much loved
Dearan, Dearen, Dearin, Dearyn, Dearun

Decker (German / Hebrew) One who prays / a piercing man
Deker, Decer, Dekker, Deccer, Deck, Decke

^**Declan** (Irish) The name of a saint

Dedrick (English) Form of Dietrich, meaning "the ruler of the tribe"
Dedryck, Dedrik, Dedryk, Dedric, Dedryc

Deegan (Irish) A black-haired man
Deagan, Degan, Deegen, Deagen, Degen, Deegon, Deagon, Degon

Deinorus (American) A lively man
Denorius, Denorus, Denorios, Deinorius, Deinorios

Dejuan (American) A talkative man
Dejuane, Dewon, Dewonn, Dewan, Dewann, Dwon, Dwonn, Dajuan

Delaney (Irish / French) The dark challenger / from the elder-tree grove
Delany, Delanee, Delanea, Delani, Delanie, Delainey, Delainy, Delaini

Delaware (English) From the state of Delaware
Delawair, Delaweir, Delwayr, Delawayre, Delawaire, Delawaer, Delawaere

Delius (Greek) A man from Delos
Delios, Delos, Delus, Delo

Dell (English) From the small valley
Delle, Del

Delmon (English) A man of the mountain
Delmun, Delmen, Delmin, Delmyn, Delmont, Delmonte, Delmond, Delmonde

Delsi (American) An easygoing guy
Delsie, Delsy, Delsey, Delsee, Delsea, Delci, Delcie, Delcee

Delvin (English) A godly friend
Delvinn, Delvinne, Delvyn, Delvynn, Delvynne, Delven, Delvenn, Delvenne

Demarcus (American) The son of Marcus
DeMarcus, DaMarkiss, DeMarco, Demarkess, DeMarko, Demarkus, DeMarques, DeMarquez

Dembe (African) A peaceful man
Dembi, Dembie, Dembee, Dembea, Dembey, Demby

Denali (American) From the national park
Denalie, Denaly, Denaley, Denalee, Denalea, Denaleigh

Denley (English) From the meadow near the valley
Denly, Denlea, Denleah, Denlee, Denleigh, Denli, Denlie

Denman (English) One who lives in the valley
Denmann, Denmin, Denmyn, Denmen, Denmon, Denmun

Dennis (French) A follower of Dionysus
Den, Denies, Denis, Dennes, Dennet, Denney, Dennie, Denys, Dennys

Dennison (English) The son of Dennis
Denison, Dennisun, Denisun, Dennisen, Denisen, Dennisan, Denisan

Deo (Greek) A godly man

Deonte (French) An outgoing man
Deontay, Deontaye, Deontae, Dionte, Diontay, Diontaye, Diontae

Deotis (American) A learned man; a scholar
Deotiss, Deotys, Deotyss, Deotus, Deotuss

Derek (English) The ruler of the tribe
Dereck, Deric, Derick, Derik, Deriq, Derk, Derreck, Derrek, Derrick

Dervin (English) A gifted
friend
*Dervinn, Dervinne, Dervyn,
Dervynn, Dervynne, Dervon,
Dervan, Dervun*

Deshan (Hindi) Of the nation
Deshal, Deshad

Desiderio (Latin) One who is
desired; hoped for
*Derito, Desi, Desideratus,
Desiderios, Desiderius,
Desiderus, Dezi, Diderot*

Desmond (Gaelic) A man
from South Munster
*Desmonde, Desmund,
Desmunde, Dezmond,
Dezmonde, Dezmund,
Dezmunde, Desmee*

Desperado (Spanish) A
renegade

Destin (French) Recognizing
one's certain fortune; fate
*Destyn, Deston, Destun, Desten,
Destan*

Destrey (American) A cowboy
*Destry, Destree, Destrea, Destri,
Destrie*

Deutsch (German) A German

Devanshi (Hindi) A divine
messenger
*Devanshie, Devanshy,
Devanshey, Devanshee*

Devante (Spanish) One who
fights wrongdoing

Deverell (French) From the
riverbank
*Deverel, Deveral, Deverall,
Devereau, Devereaux, Devere,
Deverill, Deveril*

Devlin (Gaelic) Having fierce
bravery; a misfortunate man
*Devlyn, Devlon, Devlen,
Devlan, Devlun*

Devon (English) From the
beautiful farmland; of the
divine
*Devan, Deven, Devenn, Devin,
Devonn, Devone, Deveon,
Devonne*

Dewitt (Flemish) A blond-
haired man
*DeWitt, Dewytt, DeWytt,
Dewit, DeWit, Dewyt, DeWyt*

^**Dexter** (Latin) A right-handed
man; one who is skillful
*Dextor, Dextar, Dextur, Dextir,
Dextyr, Dexton, Dextun,
Dexten*

Dhyanesh (Indian) One who
meditates
*Dhianesh, Dhyaneshe,
Dhianeshe*

Dice (American) A gambling
man
Dyce

Dichali (Native American) One
who talks a lot
*Dichalie, Dichaly, Dichaley,
Dichalee, Dichalea, Dichaleigh*

*★**Diego** (Spanish) Form of
James, meaning "he who
supplants"
Dyego, Dago

Diesel (American) Having
great strength
Deisel, Diezel, Deizel, Dezsel

Dietrich (German) The ruler of
the tribe
Dedrick

Digby (Norse) From the town
near the ditch
*Digbey, Digbee, Digbea, Digbi,
Digbie*

Diji (African) A farmer
Dijie, Dijee, Dijea, Dijy, Dijey

Dillon (Gaelic) Resembling a
lion; a faithful man
*Dillun, Dillen, Dillan, Dillin,
Dillyn, Dilon, Dilan, Dilin*

Dino (Italian) One who wields
a little sword
*Dyno, Dinoh, Dynoh, Deano,
Deanoh, Deeno, Deenoh, Deino*

Dinos (Greek) Form of
Constantine, meaning "one
who is steadfast; firm"
*Dynos, Deanos, Deenos, Deinos,
Dinose, Dinoz*

Dins (American) One who
climbs to the top
Dinz, Dyns, Dynz

Dionysus (Greek) The god of
wine and revelry
*Dion, Deion, Deon, Deonn,
Deonys, Deyon, Diandre*

Dior (French) The golden one
*D'Or, Diorr, Diorre, Dyor,
Deor, Dyorre, Deorre*

Diron (American) Form of
Darren, meaning "a great
man / a gift from God"
*Dirun, Diren, Diran, Dirin,
Diryn, Dyron, Dyren*

Dixon (English) The son of
Dick
*Dixen, Dixin, Dixyn, Dixan,
Dixun*

Doane (English) From the
rolling hills
Doan

Dobber (American) An inde-
pendent man
*Dobbar, Dobbor, Dobbur,
Dobbir, Dobbyr*

Dobbs (English) A fiery man
Dobbes, Dobes, Dobs

Domevlo (African) One who
doesn't judge others
Domivlo, Domyvlo

Domingo (Spanish) Born on a Sunday
Domyngo, Demingo, Demyngo

*Dominic (Latin) A lord
Demenico, Dom, Domenic, Domenico, Domenique, Domini, Dominick, Dominico

Domnall (Gaelic) A world ruler
Domhnall, Domnull, Domhnull

Don (Scottish) Form of Donald, meaning "ruler of the world"
Donn, Donny, Donney, Donnie, Donni, Donnee, Donnea, Donne

Donald (Scottish) Ruler of the world
Don, Donold, Donuld, Doneld, Donild, Donyld

Donato (Italian) A gift from God

Donovan (Irish) A brown-haired chief
Donavan, Donavon, Donevon, Donovyn

Dor (Hebrew) Of this generation
Doram, Doriel, Dorli, Dorlie, Dorlee, Dorlea, Dorleigh, Dorly

Doran (Irish) A stranger; one who has been exiled
Doren, Dorin, Doryn

Dorsey (Gaelic) From the fortress near the sea
Dorsy, Dorsee, Dorsea, Dorsi, Dorsie

Dost (Arabic) A beloved friend
Doste, Daust, Dauste, Dawst, Dawste

Dotson (English) The son of Dot
Dotsen, Dotsan, Dotsin, Dotsyn, Dotsun, Dottson, Dottsun, Dottsin

Dove (American) A peaceful man
Dovi, Dovie, Dovy, Dovey, Dovee, Dovea

Drade (American) A serious-minded man
Draid, Draide, Drayd, Drayde, Draed, Draede, Dradell, Dradel

Drake (English) Resembling a dragon
Drayce, Drago, Drakie

Drew (Welsh) One who is wise
Drue, Dru

Driscoll (Celtic) A media-tor; one who is sorrowful; a messenger
Dryscoll, Driscol, Dryscol, Driskoll, Dryskoll, Driskol, Dryskol, Driskell

Druce (Gaelic / English) A wise man; a druid / the son of Drew
Drews, Drewce, Druece, Druse, Druson, Drusen

Drummond (Scottish) One who lives on the ridge
Drummon, Drumond, Drumon, Drummund, Drumund, Drummun

Duane (Gaelic) A dark or swarthy man
Dewain, Dewayne, Duante, Duayne, Duwain, Duwaine, Duwayne, Dwain

Dublin (Irish) From the capital of Ireland
Dublyn, Dublen, Dublan, Dublon, Dublun

Duc (Vietnamese) One who has upstanding morals

Due (Vietnamese) A virtuous man

Duke (English) A title of nobility; a leader
Dooke, Dook, Duki, Dukie, Dukey, Duky, Dukee, Dukea

Dumi (African) One who inspires others
Dumie, Dumy, Dumey, Dumee, Dumea

Dumont (French) Man of the mountain
Dumonte, Dumount, Dumounte

Duncan (Scottish) A dark warrior
Dunkan, Dunckan, Dunc, Dunk, Dunck

Dundee (Scottish) From the town on the Firth of Tay
Dundea, Dundi, Dundie, Dundy, Dundey

Dung (Vietnamese) A brave man; a heroic man

Dunton (English) From the town on the hill
Duntun, Dunten, Duntan, Duntin, Duntyn

Durin (Norse) In mythology, one of the fathers of the dwarves
Duryn, Duren, Duran, Duron, Durun

Durjaya (Hindi) One who is difficult to defeat

Durrell (English) One who is strong and protective
Durrel, Durell, Durel

Dustin (English / German) From the dusty area / a courageous warrior
Dustyn, Dusten, Dustan, Duston, Dustun, Dusty, Dustey, Dusti

Duvall (French) From the valley
Duval, Duvale

Dwade (English) A dark traveler
Dwaid, Dwaide, Dwayd, Dwayde, Dwaed, Dwaede

Dwight (Flemish) A white- or blond-haired man
Dwite, Dwhite, Dwyght, Dwighte

Dyami (Native American) Resembling an eagle
Dyamie, Dyamy, Dyamey, Dyamee, Dyamea, Dyame

Dyer (English) A creative man
Dier, Dyar, Diar, Dy, Dye, Di, Die

*****Dylan** (Welsh) Son of the sea
Dyllan, Dylon, Dyllon, Dylen, Dyllen, Dylun, Dyllun, Dylin

Dzigbode (African) One who is patient

E

Eagan (Irish) A fiery man
Eegan, Eagen, Eegen, Eagon, Eegon, Eagun, Eegun

Eagle (Native American) Resembling the bird
Eegle, Eagel, Eegel

Eamon (Irish) Form of Edmund, meaning "a wealthy protector"
Eaman, Eamen, Eamin, Eamyn, Eamun, Eamonn, Eames, Eemon

Ean (Gaelic) Form of John, meaning "God is gracious"
Eion, Eyan, Eyon, Eian

Earl (English) A nobleman
Earle, Erle, Erl, Eorl

Easey (American) An easy-going man
Easy, Easi, Easie, Easee, Easea, Eazey, Eazy, Eazi

Eastman (English) A man from the east
East, Easte, Eeste

^**Easton** (English) Eastern place
Eastan, Easten, Eastyn

Eckhard (German) Of the brave sword point
Eckard, Eckardt, Eckhardt, Ekkehard, Ekkehardt, Ekhard, Ekhardt

Ed (English) Form of Edward, meaning "a wealthy protector"
Edd, Eddi, Eddie, Eddy, Eddey, Eddee, Eddea, Edi

Edan (Celtic) One who is full of fire
Edon, Edun

Edbert (English) One who is prosperous and bright
Edberte, Edburt, Edburte, Edbirt, Edbirte, Edbyrt, Edbyrte

Edenson (English) Son of Eden
Eadenson, Edensun, Eadensun, Edinson

Edgar (English) A powerful and wealthy spearman
Eadger, Edgardo, Edghur, Edger

Edison (English) Son of Edward
Eddison, Edisun, Eddisun, Edisen, Eddisen, Edisyn, Eddisyn, Edyson

Edlin (Anglo-Saxon) A wealthy friend
Edlinn, Edlinne, Edlyn, Edlynn, Edlynne, Eadlyn, Eadlin, Edlen

Edmund (English) A wealthy protector
Ed, Eddie, Edmond, Eamon

Edom (Hebrew) A red-haired man
Edum, Edam, Edem, Edim, Edym

Edred (Anglo-Saxon) A king
Edread, Edrid, Edryd

Edward (English) A wealthy protector
Ed, Eadward, Edik, Edouard, Eduard, Eduardo, Edvard, Edvardas, Edwardo

Edwardson (English) The son of Edward
Edwardsun, Eadwardsone, Eadwardsun

Edwin (English) A wealthy friend
Edwinn, Edwinne, Edwine, Edwyn, Edwynn, Edwynne, Edwen, Edwenn

Effiom (African) Resembling a crocodile
Efiom, Effyom, Efyom, Effeom, Efeom

Efigenio (Greek) Form of Eugene, meaning "a well-born man"
Ephigenio, Ephigenios, Ephigenius, Efigenios

Efrain (Spanish) Form of Ephraim, meaning "one who is fertile; productive"
Efraine, Efrayn, Efrayne, Efraen, Efraene, Efrane

Efrat (Hebrew) One who is honored
Efratt, Ephrat, Ephratt

Egesa (Anglo-Saxon) One who creates terror
Egessa, Egeslic, Egeslick, Egeslik

Eghert (German) An intelligent man
Egherte, Eghurt, Eghurte, Eghirt, Eghirte, Eghyrt

Egidio (Italian) Resembling a young goat
Egydio, Egideo, Egydeo, Egidiyo, Egydiyo, Egidius

Eilert (Scandinavian) Of the hard point
Elert, Eilart, Elart, Eilort, Elort, Eilurt, Elurt, Eilirt

Eilon (Hebrew) From the oak tree
Eilan, Eilin, Eilyn, Eilen, Eilun

Einar (Scandinavian) A leading warrior
Einer, Ejnar, Einir, Einyr, Einor, Einur, Ejnir, Ejnyr

Einri (Teutonic) An intelligent man
Einrie, Einry, Einrey, Einree, Einrea

Eisig (Hebrew) One who laughs often
Eisyg

Eladio (Spanish) A man from Greece
Eladeo, Eladiyo, Eladeyo

Elbert (English / German) A well-born man / a bright man
Elberte, Elburt, Elburte, Elbirt, Elbirte, Ethelbert, Ethelburt, Ethelbirt

Eldan (English) From the valley of the elves

Eldon (English) From the sacred hill
Eldun

Eldorado (Spanish) The golden man

Eldred (English) An old, wise advisor
Eldrid, Eldryd, Eldrad, Eldrod, Edlrud, Ethelred

Eldrick (English) An old, wise ruler
Eldrik, Eldric, Eldryck, Eldryk, Eldryc, Eldrich

Eleazar (Hebrew) God will
help
*Elazar, Eleasar, Eliezer,
Elazaro, Eleazaro, Elazer*

*Eli (Hebrew) One who has
ascended; my God on High
Ely

Eliachim (Hebrew) God will
establish
*Eliakim, Elyachim, Elyakim,
Eliakym*

Elian (Spanish) A spirited man
*Elyan, Elien, Elyen, Elion,
Elyon, Eliun, Elyun*

Elias (Hebrew) Form of Elijah,
meaning "Jehovah is my god"
Eliyas

Elihu (Hebrew) My God is He
Elyhu, Elihue, Elyhue

*Elijah (Hebrew) Jehovah is
my God
*Elija, Eliyahu, Eljah, Elja,
Elyjah, Elyja, Elijuah, Elyjuah*

Elimu (African) Having
knowledge of science
*Elymu, Elimue, Elymue,
Elimoo, Elymoo*

Elisha (Hebrew) God is my
salvation
*Elisee, Eliseo, Elisher, Eliso,
Elisio, Elysha, Elysee, Elyseo*

Elliott (English) Form of
Elijah, meaning "Jehovah is
my God"
Eliot, Eliott, Elliot, Elyot

Ellory (Cornish) Resembling
a swan
*Ellorey, Elloree, Ellorea, Ellori,
Ellorie, Elory, Elorey*

Ellsworth (English) From the
nobleman's estate
*Elsworth, Ellswerth, Elswerth,
Ellswirth, Elswirth, Elzie*

Elman (English) A nobleman
Elmann, Ellman, Ellmann

Elmo (English / Latin) A
protector / an amiable man
Elmoe, Elmow, Elmowe

Elmot (American) A lovable
man
Elmott, Ellmot, Ellmott

Elof (Swedish) The only heir
*Eluf, Eloff, Eluff, Elov, Ellov,
Eluv, Elluv*

Elois (German) A famous
warrior
Eloys, Eloyis, Elouis

Elpidio (Spanish) A fearless
man; having heart
*Elpydio, Elpideo, Elpydeo,
Elpidios, Elpydios, Elpidius*

Elroy (Irish / English) A red-haired young man / a king
Elroi, Elroye, Elric, Elryc, Elrik, Elryk, Elrick, Elryck

Elston (English) From the nobleman's town
Ellston, Elstun, Ellstun, Elson, Ellson, Elsun, Ellsun

Elton (English) From the old town
Ellton, Eltun, Elltun, Elten, Ellten, Eltin, Elltin, Eltyn

Eluwilussit (Native American) A holy man

Elvey (English) An elf warrior
Elvy, Elvee, Elvea, Elvi, Elvie

Elvis (Scandinavian) One who is wise
Elviss, Elvys, Elvyss

Elzie (English) Form of Ellsworth, meaning "from the nobleman's estate"
Elzi, Elzy, Elzey, Elzee, Elzea, Ellzi, Ellzie, Ellzee

Emest (German) One who is serious
Emeste, Emesto, Emestio, Emestiyo, Emesteo, Emesteyo, Emo, Emst

Emil (Latin) One who is eager; an industrious man
Emelen, Emelio, Emile, Emilian, Emiliano, Emilianus, Emilio, Emilion

Emiliano (Spanish) Form of Emil, meaning "one who is eager"

Emmanuel (Hebrew) God is with us
Manuel, Manny, Em, Eman, Emmannuel

^**Emmett** (German) A universal man
Emmet, Emmit, Emmitt, Emmot

Emrys (Welsh) An immortal man

Enapay (Native American) A brave man
Enapaye, Enapai, Enapae

Enar (Swedish) A great warrior
Ener, Enir, Enyr, Enor, Enur

Engelbert (German) As bright as an angel
Englebert, Englbert, Engelburt, Engleburt, Englburt, Englebirt, Engelbirt, Englbirt

Enoch (Hebrew) One who is dedicated to God
Enoc, Enok, Enock

Enrique (Spanish) The ruler of the estate
Enrico, Enriko, Enricko, Enriquez, Enrikay, Enreekay, Enrik, Enric

Enyeto (Native American) One who walks like a bear

^**Enzo** (Italian) The ruler of the estate
Enzio, Enzeo, Enziyo, Enzeyo

Eoin Baiste (Irish) Refers to John the Baptist

Ephraim (Hebrew) One who is fertile; productive
Eff, Efraim, Efram, Efrem, Efrain

Eric (Scandinavian) Ever the ruler
Erek, Erich, Erick, Erik, Eriq, Erix, Errick, Eryk

Ernest (English) One who is sincere and determined; serious
Earnest, Ernesto, Ernestus, Ernst, Erno, Ernie, Erni, Erney

Eron (Spanish) Form of Aaron, meaning "one who is exalted"
Erun, Erin, Eran, Eren, Eryn

Errigal (Gaelic) From the small church
Errigel, Errigol, Errigul, Errigil, Errigyl, Erigal, Erigel, Erigol

Erskine (Gaelic) From the high cliff
Erskin, Erskyne, Erskyn, Erskein, Erskeine, Erskien, Erskiene

Esam (Arabic) A safeguard
Essam

Esben (Scandinavian) Of God
Esbin, Esbyn, Esban, Esbon, Esbun

Esmé (French) One who is esteemed
Esmay, Esmaye, Esmai, Esmae, Esmeling, Esmelyng

Esmun (American) A kind man
Esmon, Esman, Esmen, Esmin, Esmyn

Esperanze (Spanish) Filled with hope
Esperance, Esperence, Esperenze, Esperanzo, Esperenzo

Estcott (English) From the eastern cottage
Estcot

Esteban (Spanish) One who is crowned in victory
Estebon, Estevan, Estevon, Estefan, Estefon, Estebe, Estyban, Estyvan

*Ethan (Hebrew) One who is
firm and steadfast
*Ethen, Ethin, Ethyn, Ethon,
Ethun, Eitan, Etan, Eithan*

Ethanael (American) God has
given me strength
*Ethaniel, Ethaneal, Ethanail,
Ethanale*

Ethel (Hebrew) One who is
noble
Ethal, Etheal

Etlelooaat (Native American)
One who shouts

Eudocio (Greek) One who is
respected
*Eudoceo, Eudociyo, Eudoceyo,
Eudoco*

*Eugene (Greek) A well-born
man
*Eugean, Eugenie, Ugene,
Efigenio, Gene, **Owen***

Eulogio (Greek) A reasonable
man
*Eulogiyo, Eulogo, Eulogeo,
Eulogeyo*

Euodias (Greek) Having good
fortune
Euodeas, Euodyas

Euphemios (Greek) One who
is well-spoken
*Eufemio, Eufemius, Euphemio,
Eufemios, Euphemius,
Eufemius*

Euphrates (Turkish) From the
great river
*Eufrates, Euphraites, Eufraites,
Euphraytes, Eufraytes*

Eusebius (Greek) One who is
devout
*Esabio, Esavio, Esavius, Esebio,
Eusabio, Eusaio, Eusebio,
Eusebios*

Eustace (Greek) Having an
abundance of grapes
*Eustache, Eustachios,
Eustachius, Eustachy,
Eustaquio, Eustashe, Eustasius,
Eustatius*

*Evan (Welsh) Form of John,
meaning "God is gracious"
*Evann, Evans, Even, Evin,
Evon, Evyn, Evian, Evien*

Evander (Greek) A benevolent
man
*Evandor, Evandar, Evandir,
Evandur, Evandyr*

Everett (English) Form of
Everhard, meaning "as strong
as a bear"

Evett (American) A bright man
*Evet, Evatt, Evat, Evitt, Evit,
Evytt, Evyt*

Eyal (Hebrew) Having great
strength

Eze (African) A king

Ezeji (African) The king of
yams
Ezejie, Ezejy, Ezejey, Ezejee,
Ezejea

Ezekiel (Hebrew) Strengthened
by God
Esequiel, Ezechiel, Eziechiele,
Eziequel, Ezequiel, Ezekial,
Ezekyel, Esquevelle, Zeke

F

Factor (English) A business-
man
Facter, Factur, Factir, Factyr,
Factar

Fairbairn (Scottish) A fair-
haired boy
Fayrbairn, Faerbairn,
Fairbaern, Fayrbaern,
Faerbaern, Fairbayrn,
Fayrbayrn, Faerbayrn

Fairbanks (English) From the
bank along the path
Fayrbanks, Faerbanks,
Farebanks

Faisal (Arabic) One who is
decisive; resolute
Faysal, Faesal, Fasal, Feisal,
Faizal, Fasel, Fayzal, Faezal

Fakhir (Arabic) A proud man
Fakheer, Fakhear, Fakheir,
Fakhier, Fakhyr, Faakhir,
Faakhyr, Fakhr

Fakih (Arabic) A legal expert
Fakeeh, Fakeah, Fakieh,
Fakeih, Fakyh

Falco (Latin) Resembling a
falcon; one who works with
falcons
Falcon, Falconer, Falconner,
Falk, Falke, Falken, Falkner,
Faulconer

Fam (American) A family-
oriented man

Fang (Scottish) From the
sheep pen
Faing, Fayng, Faeng

Faraji (African) One who
provides consolation
Farajie, Farajy, Farajey,
Farajee, Farajea

Fardoragh (Irish) Having dark
features

Fargo (American) One who is
jaunty
Fargoh, Fargoe, Fargouh

Farha (Arabic) Filled with
happiness
Farhah, Farhad, Farhan,
Farhat, Farhani, Farhanie,
Farhany, Farhaney

Fariq (Arabic) One who holds rank as lieutenant general
Fareeq, Fareaq, Fareiq, Farieq, Faryq, Farik, Fareek, Fareak

Farnell (English) From the fern hill
Farnel, Farnall, Farnal, Fernauld, Farnauld, Fernald, Farnald

Farold (English) A mighty traveler
Farould, Farald, Farauld, Fareld

Farran (Irish / Arabic / English) Of the land / a baker / one who is adventurous
Fairran, Fayrran, Faerran, Farren, Farrin, Farron, Ferrin, Ferron

Farrar (English) A blacksmith
Farar, Farrer, Farrier, Ferrar, Ferrars, Ferrer, Ferrier, Farer

Farro (Italian) Of the grain
Farroe, Faro, Faroe, Farrow, Farow

Fatik (Indian) Resembling a crystal
Fateek, Fateak, Fatyk, Fatiek, Fateik

Faust (Latin) Having good luck
Fauste, Faustino, Fausto, Faustos, Faustus, Fauston, Faustin, Fausten

Fawcett (American) An audacious man
Fawcet, Fawcette, Fawcete, Fawce, Fawci, Fawcie, Fawcy, Fawcey

Fawwaz (Arabic) A successful man
Fawaz, Fawwad, Fawad

Fay (Irish) Resembling a raven
Faye, Fai, Fae, Feich

Februus (Latin) A pagan god

Fedor (Russian) A gift from God
Faydor, Feodor, Fyodor, Fedyenka, Fyodr, Fydor, Fjodor

Feechi (African) One who worships God
Feechie, Feechy, Feechey, Feechee, Feachi, Feachie

Feivel (Hebrew) The brilliant one
Feival, Feivol, Feivil, Feivyl, Feivul, Feiwel, Feiwal, Feiwol

Felim (Gaelic) One who is always good
Felym, Feidhlim, Felimy, Felimey, Felimee, Felimea, Felimi, Felimie

Felipe (Spanish) Form of Phillip, meaning "one who loves horses"
Felippe, Filip, Filippo, Fillip, Flip, Fulop, Fullop, Fulip

Felix (Latin) One who is happy and prosperous

Felton (English) From the town near the field
Feltun, Felten, Feltan, Feltyn, Feltin

Fenn (English) From the marsh
Fen

Ferdinand (German) A courageous voyager
Ferdie, Ferdinando, Fernando

Fergus (Gaelic) The first and supreme choice
Fearghas, Fearghus, Feargus, Fergie, Ferguson, Fergusson, Furgus, Fergy

Ferrell (Irish) A brave man; a hero
Ferell, Ferel, Ferrel

Fiacre (Celtic) Resembling a raven
Fyacre, Fiacra, Fyacra, Fiachra, Fyachra, Fiachre, Fyachre

Fielding (English) From the field
Fieldyng, Fielder, Field, Fielde, Felding, Feldyng, Fields

Fiero (Spanish) A fiery man
Fyero

Finbar (Irish) A fair-haired man
Finnbar, Finnbarr, Fionn, Fionnbharr, Fionnbar, Fionnbarr, Fynbar, Fynnbar

Finch (English) Resembling the small bird
Fynch, Finche, Fynche, Finchi, Finchie, Finchy, Finchey, Finchee

Fineas (Egyptian) A dark-skinned man
Fyneas, Finius, Fynius

Finian (Irish) A handsome man; fair
Finan, Finnian, Fionan, Finien, Finnien, Finghin, Finneen, Fineen

Finn (Gaelic) A fair-haired man
Fin, Fynn, Fyn, Fingal, Fingall

^**Finnegan** (Irish) A fair-haired man
Finegan, Finnegen, Finegen, Finnigan, Finigan

Finnley (Gaelic) A fair-haired hero
Findlay, Findley, Finly, Finlay, Finlee, Finnly, Finnley

Fiorello (Italian) Resembling a little flower
Fiorelo, Fiorelio, Fioreleo, Fiorellio, Fiorelleo

Fisher (English) A fisherman
Fischer, Fysher

Fitch (English) Resembling an
ermine
*Fytch, Fich, Fych, Fitche,
Fytche*

Fitzgerald (English) The son of
Gerald
Fytzgerald

Flann (Irish) One who has a
ruddy complexion
*Flan, Flainn, Flannan,
Flannery, Flanneri, Flannerie,
Flannerey*

Fletcher (English) One who
makes arrows
Fletch, Fletche, Flecher

Flynn (Irish) One who has a
ruddy complexion
*Flyn, Flinn, Flin, Flen, Flenn,
Floinn*

Fogarty (Irish) One who has
been exiled
*Fogartey, Fogartee, Fogartea,
Fogarti, Fogartie, Fogerty,
Fogertey, Fogerti*

Foley (English) A creative man
Foly, Folee, Foli, Folie

Folker (German) A guardian of
the people
*Folkar, Folkor, Folkur, Folkir,
Folkyr, Folke, Folko, Folkus*

Fonso (German) Form of
Alfonso, meaning "prepared
for battle; eager and ready"
*Fonzo, Fonsie, Fonzell, Fonzie,
Fonsi, Fonsy, Fonsey, Fonsee*

Fontaine (French) From the
water source
*Fontayne, Fontaene, Fontane,
Fonteyne, Fontana, Fountain*

Ford (English) From the river
crossing
*Forde, Forden, Fordan, Fordon,
Fordun, Fordin, Fordyn, Forday*

Fouad (Arabic) One who
has heart
Fuad

Francisco (Spanish) A man
from France
*Francesco, Franchesco,
Fransisco*

Frank (Latin) Form of Francis,
meaning "a man from
France; one who is free"
Franco, Frankie

Fred (German) Form of
Frederick, meaning "a
peaceful ruler"
*Freddi, Freddie, Freddy,
Freddey, Freddee, Freddea,
Freddis, Fredis*

Frederick (German) A peaceful ruler
Fred, Fredrick, Federico, Federigo, Fredek, Frederic, Frederich, Frederico, Frederik, Fredric

Freeborn (English) One who was born a free man
Freeborne, Freebourn, Freebourne, Freeburn, Freeburne, Free

Fremont (French) The protector of freedom
Freemont, Fremonte

Frigyes (Hungarian) A mighty and peaceful ruler

Frode (Norse) A wise man
Froad, Froade

Froyim (Hebrew) A kind man
Froiim

Fructuoso (Spanish) One who is fruitful
Fructo, Fructoso, Fructuso

Fu (Chinese) A wealthy man

Fudail (Arabic) Of high moral character
Fudaile, Fudayl, Fudayle, Fudale, Fudael, Fudaele

Fulbright (English) A brilliant man
Fullbright, Fulbrite, Fullbrite, Fulbryte, Fullbryte, Fulbert, Fullbert

Fulki (Indian) A spark
Fulkie, Fulkey, Fulky, Fulkee, Fulkea

Fullerton (English) From Fuller's town
Fullertun, Fullertin, Fullertyn, Fullertan, Fullerten

Fursey (Gaelic) The name of a missionary saint
Fursy, Fursi, Fursie, Fursee, Fursea

Fyfe (Scottish) A man from Fifeshire
Fife, Fyffe, Fiffe, Fibh

Fyren (Anglo-Saxon) A wicked man
Fyrin, Fyryn, Fyran, Fyron, Fyrun

G

Gabai (Hebrew) A delightful man

Gabbana (Italian) A creative man
Gabbanah, Gabana, Gabanah, Gabbanna, Gabanna

Gabbo (English) To joke or scoff
Gabboe, Gabbow, Gabbowe

Gabor (Hebrew) God is my strength
Gabur, Gabar, Gaber, Gabir, Gabyr

Gabra (African) An offering
Gabre

*Gabriel (Hebrew) A hero of God
Gabrian, Gabriele, Gabrielli, Gabriello, Gaby, Gab, Gabbi, Gabbie

Gad (Hebrew / Native American) Having good fortune / from the juniper tree
Gadi, Gadie, Gady, Gadey, Gadee, Gadea

Gadiel (Arabic) God is my fortune
Gadiell, Gadiele, Gadielle, Gaddiel, Gaddiell, Gadil, Gadeel, Gadeal

Gaffney (Irish) Resembling a calf
Gaffny, Gaffni, Gaffnie, Gaffnee, Gaffnea

Gage (French) Of the pledge
Gaige, Gaege, Gauge

Gahuj (African) A hunter

Gair (Gaelic) A man of short stature
Gayr, Gaer, Gaire, Gayre, Gaere, Gare

Gaius (Latin) One who rejoices
Gaeus

Galal (Arabic) A majestic man
Galall, Gallal, Gallall

Galbraith (Irish) A foreigner; a Scot
Galbrait, Galbreath, Gallbraith, Gallbreath, Galbraithe, Gallbraithe, Galbreathe, Gallbreathe

Gale (Irish / English) A foreigner / one who is cheerful
Gail, Gaill, Gaille, Gaile, Gayl, Gayle, Gaylle, Gayll

Galen (Greek) A healer; one who is calm
Gaelan, Gaillen, Galan, Galin, Galyn, Gaylen, Gaylin, Gaylinn

Gali (Hebrew) From the fountain
Galie, Galy, Galey, Galee, Galea, Galeigh

Galip (Turkish) A victorious man
Galyp, Galup, Galep, Galap, Galop

Gallagher (Gaelic) An eager
helper
*Gallaghor, Gallaghar,
Gallaghur, Gallaghir, Gallaghyr,
Gallager, Gallagar, Gallagor*

Galt (English) From the high,
wooded land
Galte, Gallt, Gallte

Galtero (Spanish) Form
of Walter, meaning "the
commander of the army"
*Galterio, Galteriyo, Galtereo,
Galtereyo, Galter, Galteros,
Galterus, Gualterio*

Gamaliel (Hebrew) God's
reward
*Gamliel, Gamalyel, Gamlyel,
Gamli, Gamlie, Gamly,
Gamley, Gamlee*

Gameel (Arabic) A handsome
man
*Gameal, Gamil, Gamiel,
Gameil, Gamyl*

Gamon (American) One who
enjoys playing games
*Gamun, Gamen, Gaman,
Gamin, Gamyn, Gammon,
Gammun, Gamman*

Gan (Chinese) A wanderer

Gandy (American) An
adventurer
*Gandey, Gandi, Gandie,
Gandee, Gandea*

Gann (English) One who
defends with a spear
Gan

Gannon (Gaelic) A fair-
skinned man
*Gannun, Gannen, Gannan,
Gannin, Gannyn, Ganon,
Ganun, Ganin*

Garcia (Spanish) One who is
brave in battle
*Garce, Garcy, Garcey, Garci,
Garcie, Garcee, Garcea*

Gared (English) Form of
Gerard, meaning "one who is
mighty with a spear"
*Garad, Garid, Garyd, Garod,
Garud*

Garman (English) A spearman
*Garmann, Garmen, Garmin,
Garmon, Garmun, Garmyn,
Gar, Garr*

Garrett (English) Form of
Gerard, meaning "one who is
mighty with a spear"
*Garett, Garret, Garretson, Garritt,
Garrot, Garrott, Gerrit, Gerritt*

Garrison (French) Prepared
Garris, Garrish, Garry, Gary

Garson (English) The son of
Gar (Garrett, Garrison, etc.)
*Garrson, Garsen, Garrsen,
Garsun, Garrsun, Garsone,
Garrsone*

Garth (Scandinavian) The keeper of the garden
Garthe, Gart, Garte

Garvey (Gaelic) A rough but peaceful man
Garvy, Garvee, Garvea, Garvi, Garvie, Garrvey, Garrvy, Garrvee

Garvin (English) A friend with a spear
Garvyn, Garven, Garvan, Garvon, Garvun

Gary (English) One who wields a spear
Garey, Gari, Garie, Garea, Garee, Garry, Garrey, Garree

Gassur (Arabic) A courageous man
Gassor, Gassir, Gassyr, Gassar, Gasser

Gaston (French) A man from Gascony
Gastun, Gastan, Gasten, Gascon, Gascone, Gasconey, Gasconi, Gasconie

Gate (American) One who is close-minded
Gates, Gait, Gaite, Gaits

*Gavin (Welsh) A little white falcon
Gavan, Gaven, Gavino, Gavyn, Gavynn, Gavon, Gavun, Gavyno

Gazali (African) A mystic
Gazalie, Gazaly, Gazaley, Gazalee, Gazalea, Gazaleigh

Geirleif (Norse) A descendant of the spear
Geirleaf, Geerleif, Geerleaf

Geirstein (Norse) One who wields a rock-hard spear
Geerstein, Gerstein

Gellert (Hungarian) A mighty soldier
Gellart, Gellirt, Gellyrt, Gellort, Gellurt

Genaro (Latin) A dedicated man
Genaroh, Genaroe, Genarow, Genarowe

Gene (English) Form of Eugene, meaning "a well-born man"
Genio, Geno, Geneo, Gino, Ginio, Gineo

Genet (African) From Eden
Genat, Genit, Genyt, Genot, Genut

Genoah (Italian) From the city of Genoa
Genoa, Genovise, Genovize

Geoffrey (English) Form of
Jeffrey, meaning "a man of
peace"
*Geffrey, Geoff, Geoffery,
Geoffroy, Geoffry, Geofrey,
Geofferi, Geofferie*

George (Greek) One who
works the earth; a farmer
*Georas, Geordi, Geordie, Georg,
Georges, Georgi, Georgie,
Georgio, Yegor, Jurgen, Joren*

Gerald (German) One who
rules with the spear
*Jerald, Garald, Garold, Gearalt,
Geralde, Geraldo, Geraud,
Gere, Gerek*

Gerard (French) One who is
mighty with a spear
*Gerord, Gerrard, Gared,
Garrett*

Geremia (Italian) Form of
Jeremiah, meaning "one who
is exalted by the Lord"
*Geremiah, Geremias, Geremija,
Geremiya, Geremyah,
Geramiah, Geramia*

Germain (French / Latin) A
man from Germany / one
who is brotherly
*Germaine, German, Germane,
Germanicus, Germano,
Germanus, Germayn,
Germayne*

Gerry (German) Short form of
names beginning with Ger-,
such as Gerald or Gerard
*Gerrey, Gerri, Gerrie, Gerrea,
Gerree*

Gershom (Hebrew) One who
has been exiled
*Gersham, Gershon, Gershoom,
Gershem, Gershim, Gershym,
Gershum, Gersh*

Getachew (African) Their
master

Ghazi (Arabic) An invader; a
conqueror
*Ghazie, Ghazy, Ghazey,
Ghazee, Ghazea*

Ghoukas (Armenian) Form of
Lucas, meaning "a man from
Lucania"
Ghukas

Giancarlo (Italian) One who is
gracious and mighty
Gyancarlo

^Gideon (Hebrew) A mighty
warrior; one who fells trees
*Gideone, Gidi, Gidon, Gidion,
Gid, Gidie, Gidy, Gidey*

Gilam (Hebrew) The joy of the
people
*Gylam, Gilem, Gylem, Gilim,
Gylim, Gilym, Gylym, Gilom*

Gilbert (French / English) Of the bright promise / one who is trustworthy
Gib, Gibb, Gil, Gilberto, Gilburt, Giselbert, Giselberto, Giselbertus

Gildas (Irish / English) One who serves God / the golden one
Gyldas, Gilda, Gylda, Gilde, Gylde, Gildea, Gyldea, Gildes

Giles (Greek) Resembling a young goat
Gyles, Gile, Gil, Gilles, Gillis, Gilliss, Gyle, Gyl

Gill (Gaelic) A servant
Gyll, Gilly, Gilley, Gillee, Gillea, Gilli, Gillie, Ghill

Gillivray (Scottish) A servant of God
Gillivraye, Gillivrae, Gillivrai

Gilmat (Scottish) One who wields a sword
Gylmat, Gilmet, Gylmet

Gilmer (English) A famous hostage
Gilmar, Gilmor, Gilmur, Gilmir, Gilmyr, Gillmer, Gillmar, Gillmor

Gilon (Hebrew) Filled with joy
Gilun, Gilen, Gilan, Gilin, Gilyn, Gilo

Ginton (Arabic) From the garden
Gintun, Gintan, Ginten, Gintin, Gintyn

Giovanni (Italian) Form of John, meaning "God is gracious"
Geovani, Geovanney, Geovanni, Geovanny, Geovany, Giannino, Giovan, Giovani, Yovanny

Giri (Indian) From the mountain
Girie, Giry, Girey, Giree, Girea

Girvan (Gaelic) The small rough one
Gyrvan, Girven, Gyrven, Girvin, Gyrvin, Girvyn, Gyrvyn, Girvon

Giulio (Italian) One who is youthful
Giuliano, Giuleo

Giuseppe (Italian) Form of Joseph, meaning "God will add"
Giuseppi, Giuseppie, Giuseppy, Giuseppee, Giuseppea, Giuseppey, Guiseppe, Guiseppi

Gizmo (American) One who is playful
Gismo, Gyzmo, Gysmo, Gizmoe, Gismoe, Gyzmoe, Gysmoe

Glade (English) From the clearing in the woods
Glayd, Glayde, Glaid, Glaide, Glaed, Glaede

Glaisne (Irish) One who is calm; serene
Glaisny, Glaisney, Glaisni, Glaisnie, Glaisnee, Glasny, Glasney, Glasni

Glasgow (Scottish) From the city in Scotland
Glasgo

Glen (Gaelic) From the secluded narrow valley
Glenn, Glennard, Glennie, Glennon, Glenny, Glin, Glinn, Glyn

Glover (English) One who makes gloves
Glovar, Glovir, Glovyr, Glovur, Glovor

Gobind (Sanskrit) The cow finder
Gobinde, Gobinda, Govind, Govinda, Govinde

Goby (American) An audacious man
Gobi, Gobie, Gobey, Gobee, Gobea

Godfrey (German) God is peace
Giotto, Godefroi, Godfry, Godofredo, Goffredo, Gottfrid, Gottfried, Godfried

Godfried (German) God is peace
Godfreed, Gjord

Gogo (African) A grandfatherly man

Goldwin (English) A golden friend
Goldwine, Goldwinn, Goldwinne, Goldwen, Goldwenn, Goldwenne, Goldwyn, Goldwynn

Goode (English) An upstanding man
Good, Goodi, Goodie, Goody, Goodey, Goodee, Goodea

Gordon (Gaelic) From the great hill; a hero
Gorden, Gordin, Gordyn, Gordun, Gordan, Gordi, Gordie, Gordee

Gormley (Irish) The blue spearman
Gormly, Gormlee, Gormlea, Gormleah, Gormleigh, Gormli, Gormlie, Gormaly

Goro (Japanese) The fifth-born child

Gotzon (Basque) A heavenly messenger; an angel

Gower (Welsh) One who is pure; chaste
Gwyr, Gowyr, Gowir, Gowar, Gowor, Gowur

Gozal (Hebrew) Resembling a baby bird
Gozall, Gozel, Gozell, Gozale, Gozele

Grady (Gaelic) One who is famous; noble
Gradey, Gradee, Gradea, Gradi, Gradie, Graidy, Graidey, Graidee

Graham (English) From the gravelled area; from the gray home
Graem

Grand (English) A superior man
Grande, Grandy, Grandey, Grandi, Grandie, Grandee, Grandea, Grander

Granger (English) A farmer
Grainger, Graynger, Graenger, Grange, Graynge, Graenge, Grainge, Grangere

Grant (English) A tall man; a great man
Grante, Graent

Granville (French) From the large village
Granvylle, Granvil, Granvyl, Granvill, Granvyll, Granvile, Granvyle, Grenvill

Gray (English) A gray-haired man
Graye, Grai, Grae, Greye, Grey, Graylon, Graylen, Graylin

^***Grayson** (English) The son of a gray-haired man
*Graysen, Graysun, Graysin, **Greyson**, Graysan, Graison, Graisun, Graisen*

Greenwood (English) From the green forest
Greenwode

Gregory (Greek) One who is vigilant; watchful
Greg, Greggory, Greggy, Gregori, Gregorie, Gregry, Grigori

Gremian (Anglo-Saxon) One who enrages others
Gremien, Gremean, Gremyan

Gridley (English) From the flat meadow
Gridly, Gridlee, Gridlea, Gridleah, Gridleigh, Gridli, Gridlie

Griffin (Latin) Having a
hooked nose
*Griff, Griffen, Griffon, Gryffen,
Gryffin, Gryphen*

Griffith (Welsh) A mighty chief
Griffyth, Gryffith, Gryffyth

Grimsley (English) From the
dark meadow
*Grimsly, Grimslee, Grimslea,
Grimsleah, Grimsleigh,
Grimsli, Grimslie*

Griswold (German) From the
gray forest
*Griswald, Gryswold, Gryswald,
Greswold, Greswald*

Guban (African) One who has
been burnt
*Guben, Gubin, Gubyn, Gubon,
Gubun*

Guedado (African) One who is
unwanted

Guerdon (English) A warring
man
*Guerdun, Guerdan, Guerden,
Guerdin, Guerdyn*

Guido (Italian) One who acts
as a guide
*Guidoh, Gwedo, Gwido,
Gwydo, Gweedo*

Guillaume (French) Form of
William, meaning "the deter-
mined protector"
*Gillermo, Guglielmo,
Guilherme, Guillermo, Gwillyn,
Gwilym, Guglilmo*

Gulshan (Hindi) From the
gardens

Gunner (Scandinavian) A bold
warrior
*Gunnar, Gunnor, Gunnur,
Gunnir, Gunnyr*

Gunnolf (Norse) A warrior
wolf
Gunolf, Gunnulf, Gunulf

Gur (Hebrew) Resembling a
lion cub
*Guryon, Gurion, Guriel,
Guriell, Guryel, Guryell, Guri,
Gurie*

Gurpreet (Indian) A devoted
follower
*Gurpreat, Gurpriet, Gurpreit,
Gurprit, Gurpryt*

Guru (Indian) A teacher; a religious head

Gurutz (Basque) Of the holy
cross
Guruts

Gus (German) A respected
man; one who is exalted
Guss

Gustav (Scandinavian) Of the staff of the gods
Gus, Gustave, Gussie, Gustaf, Gustof, Tavin

Gusty (American) Of the wind; a revered man
Gustey, Gustee, Gustea, Gusti, Gustie, Gusto

Guwayne (American) Form of Wayne, meaning "one who builds wagons"
Guwayn, Guwain, Guwaine, Guwaen, Guwaene, Guwane

Gwalchmai (Welsh) A battle hawk

Gwandoya (African) Suffering a miserable fate

Gwydion (Welsh) In mythology, a magician
Gwydeon, Gwydionne, Gwydeonne

Gylfi (Scandinavian) A king
Gylfie, Gylfee, Gylfea, Gylfi, Gylfie, Gylphi, Gylphie, Gylphey

Gypsy (English) A wanderer; a nomad
Gipsee, Gipsey, Gipsy, Gypsi, Gypsie, Gypsey, Gypsee, Gipsi

H

Habimama (African) One who believes in God
Habymama

Hadden (English) From the heather-covered hill
Haddan, Haddon, Haddin, Haddyn, Haddun

Hadriel (Hebrew) The splendor of God
Hadryel, Hadriell, Hadryell

Hadwin (English) A friend in war
Hadwinn, Hadwinne, Hadwen, Hadwenn, Hadwenne, Hadwyn, Hadwynn, Hadwynne

Hafiz (Arabic) A protector
Haafiz, Hafeez, Hafeaz, Hafiez, Hafeiz, Hafyz, Haphiz, Haaphiz

Hagar (Hebrew) A wanderer

Hagen (Gaelic) One who is youthful
Haggen, Hagan, Haggan, Hagin, Haggin, Hagyn, Haggyn, Hagon

Hagop (Armenian) Form of James, meaning "he who supplants"
Hagup, Hagap, Hagep, Hagip, Hagyp

Hagos (African) Filled with happiness

Hahnee (Native American) A beggar
Hahnea, Hahni, Hahnie, Hahny, Hahney

Haim (Hebrew) A giver of life
Hayim, Hayyim

Haines (English) From the vined cottage; from the hedged enclosure
Haynes, Haenes, Hanes, Haine, Hayne, Haene, Hane

Hajari (African) One who takes flight
Hajarie, Hajary, Hajarey, Hajaree, Hajarea

Haji (African) Born during the hajj
Hajie, Hajy, Hajey, Hajee, Hajea

Hakan (Norse / Native American) One who is noble / a fiery man

Hakim (Arabic) One who is wise; intelligent
Hakeem, Hakeam, Hakeim, Hakiem, Hakym

Hal (English) A form of Henry, meaning "the ruler of the house"; a form of Harold, meaning "the ruler of an army"

Halford (English) From the hall by the ford
Hallford, Halfurd, Hallfurd, Halferd, Hallferd

Halil (Turkish) A beloved friend
Haleel, Haleal, Haleil, Haliel, Halyl

Halla (African) An unexpected gift
Hallah, Hala, Halah

Hallberg (Norse) From the rocky mountain
Halberg, Hallburg, Halburg

Halle (Norse) As solid as a rock

Halley (English) From the hall near the meadow
Hally, Halli, Hallie, Halleigh, Hallee, Halleah, Hallea

Halliwell (English) From the holy spring
Haligwell

Hallward (English) The guardian of the hall
Halward, Hallwerd, Halwerd, Hallwarden, Halwarden, Hawarden, Haward, Hawerd

Hamid (Arabic / Indian) A praiseworthy man / a beloved friend
Hameed, Hamead, Hameid, Hamied, Hamyd, Haamid

Hamidi (Swahili) One who is commendable
Hamidie, Hamidy, Hamidey, Hamidee, Hamidea, Hamydi, Hamydie, Hamydee

Hamilton (English) From the flat-topped hill
Hamylton, Hamiltun, Hamyltun, Hamilten, Hamylten, Hamelton, Hameltun, Hamelten

Hamlet (German) From the little home
Hamlett, Hammet, Hammett, Hamnet, Hamnett, Hamlit, Hamlitt, Hamoelet

Hammer (German) One who makes hammers; a carpenter
Hammar, Hammor, Hammur, Hammir, Hammyr

Hampden (English) From the home in the valley
Hampdon, Hampdan, Hampdun, Hampdyn, Hampdin

Hancock (English) One who owns a farm
Hancok, Hancoc

Hanford (English) From the high ford
Hanferd, Hanfurd, Hanforde, Hanferde, Hanfurde

Hanisi (Swahili) Born on a Thursday
Hanisie, Hanisy, Hanisey, Hanisee, Hanisea, Hanysi, Hanysie, Hanysy

Hank (English) Form of Henry, meaning "the ruler of the house"
Hanke, Hanks, Hanki, Hankie, Hankee, Hankea, Hanky, Hankey

Hanley (English) From the high meadow
Hanly, Hanleigh, Hanleah, Hanlea, Hanlie, Hanli

Hanoch (Hebrew) One who is dedicated
Hanock, Hanok, Hanoc

Hanraoi (Irish) Form of Henry, meaning "the ruler of the house"

Hansraj (Hindi) The swan king

Hardik (Indian) One who has heart
Hardyk, Hardick, Hardyck, Hardic, Hardyc

Hare (English) Resembling a rabbit

Harence (English) One who is swift
Harince, Harense, Harinse

Hari (Indian) Resembling a lion
Harie, Hary, Harey, Haree, Harea

Harim (Arabic) A superior man
Hareem, Haream, Hariem, Hareim, Harym

Harkin (Irish) Having dark red hair
Harkyn, Harken, Harkan, Harkon, Harkun

Harlemm (American) A soulful man
Harlam, Harlom, Harlim, Harlym, Harlem

Harlow (English) From the army on the hill
Harlowe, Harlo, Harloe

Harold (Scandinavian) The ruler of an army
Hal, Harald, Hareld, Harry, Darold

Harper (English) One who plays or makes harps
Harpur, Harpar, Harpir, Harpyr, Harpor, Hearpere

Harrington (English) From Harry's town; from the herring town
Harringtun, Harryngton, Harryngtun, Harington, Haringtun, Haryngton, Haryntun

Harrison (English) The son of Harry
Harrisson, Harris, Harriss, Harryson

Harshad (Indian) A bringer of joy
Harsh, Harshe, Harsho, Harshil, Harshyl, Harshit, Harshyt

Hartford (English) From the stag's ford
Harteford, Hartferd, Harteferd, Hartfurd, Hartefurd, Hartforde, Harteforde, Hartferde

Haru (Japanese) Born during the spring

Harvey (English / French) One who is ready for battle / a strong man
Harvy, Harvi, Harvie, Harvee, Harvea, Harv, Harve, Hervey

Hasim (Arabic) One who is decisive
Haseem, Haseam, Hasiem, Haseim, Hasym

Haskel (Hebrew) An intelligent man
Haskle, Haskell, Haskil, Haskill, Haske, Hask

Hasso (German) Of the sun
Hassoe, Hassow, Hassowe

Hassun (Native American) As solid as a stone

Hastiin (Native American) A man

Hastin (Hindi) Resembling an elephant
Hasteen, Hastean, Hastien, Hastein, Hastyn

Hawes (English) From the hedged place
Haws, Hayes, Hays, Hazin, Hazen, Hazyn, Hazon, Hazan

Hawiovi (Native American) One who descends on a ladder
Hawiovie, Hawiovy, Hawiovey, Hawiovee, Hawiovea

Hawkins (English) Resembling a small hawk
Haukins, Hawkyns, Haukyn

Hawthorne (English) From the hawthorn tree
Hawthorn

*Hayden** (English) From the hedged valley
Haydan, Haydon, Haydun, Haydin, Haydyn, Haden, Hadan, Hadon

Haye (Scottish) From the stockade
Hay, Hae, Hai

Hazaiah (Hebrew) God will decide
Hazaia, Haziah, Hazia

Hazleton (English) From the hazel-tree town
Hazelton, Hazletun, Hazelton, Hazleten, Hazelten

Heath (English) From the untended land of flowering shrubs
Heathe, Heeth, Heethe

Heaton (English) From the town on high ground
Heatun, Heeton, Heetun, Heaten, Heeten

Heber (Hebrew) A partner or companion
Heeber, Hebar, Heebar, Hebor, Heebor, Hebur, Heebur, Hebir

Hector (Greek) One who is steadfast; in mythology, the prince of Troy
Hecter, Hekter, Heckter

Helio (Greek) Son of the sun
Heleo, Helios, Heleos

Hem (Indian) The golden son

Hemendu (Indian) Born
beneath the golden moon
Hemendue, Hemendoo

Hemi (Maori) Form of James,
meaning "he who supplants"
*Hemie, Hemy, Hemee, Hemea,
Hemey*

Henderson (Scottish) The son
of Henry
*Hendrie, Hendries, Hendron,
Hendri, Hendry, Hendrey,
Hendree, Hendrea*

Hendrick (English) Form of
Henry, meaning "the ruler of
the house"
*Hendryck, Hendrik, Hendryk,
Hendric, Hendryc*

Henley (English) From the
high meadow
*Henly, Henleigh, Henlea,
Henleah, Henlee, Henli, Henlie*

*Henry (German) The ruler of
the house
*Hal, Hank, Harry, Henny,
Henree, Henri, Hanraoi,
Hendrick*

Heraldo (Spanish) Of the
divine

Hercules (Greek) In mythol-
ogy, a son of Zeus who pos-
sessed superhuman strength
*Herakles, Hercule, Herculi,
Herculie, Herculy, Herculey,
Herculee*

Herman (German) A soldier
*Hermon, Hermen, Hermun,
Hermin, Hermyn, Hermann,
Hermie*

Herne (English) Resembling
a heron
Hern, Hearn, Hearne

Hero (Greek) The brave
defender
Heroe, Herow, Herowe

Hershel (Hebrew) Resembling
a deer
*Hersch, Herschel, Herschell,
Hersh, Hertzel, Herzel, Herzl,
Heschel*

Herwin (Teutonic) A friend of
war
*Herwinn, Herwinne, Herwen,
Herwenn, Herwenne, Herwyn,
Herwynn, Herwynne*

Hesed (Hebrew) A kind man

Hesutu (Native American) A
rising yellow-jacket nest
Hesutou, Hesoutou

Hewson (English) The son of
Hugh
Hewsun

Hiawatha (Native American)
He who makes rivers
*Hiawathah, Hyawatha,
Hiwatha, Hywatha*

Hickok (American) A famous
frontier marshal
*Hickock, Hickoc, Hikock,
Hikoc, Hikok, Hyckok,
Hyckock, Hyckoc*

Hidalgo (Spanish) The noble
one
Hydalgo

Hideaki (Japanese) A clever
man; having wisdom
*Hideakie, Hideaky, Hideakey,
Hideakee, Hideakea*

Hieronim (Polish) Form of
Jerome, meaning "of the
sacred name"
*Hieronym, Hieronymos,
Hieronimos, Heronim,
Heronym, Heronymos,
Heronimos*

Hietamaki (Finnish) From the
sand hill
*Hietamakie, Hietamaky,
Hietamakey, Hietamakee,
Hietamakea*

Hieu (Vietnamese) A pious
man

Hikmat (Islamic) Filled with
wisdom
Hykmat

Hildefuns (German) One who
is ready for battle
Hildfuns, Hyldefuns, Hyldfuns

Hillel (Hebrew) One who is
praised
*Hyllel, Hillell, Hyllell, Hilel,
Hylel, Hilell, Hylell*

Hiranmay (Indian) The golden
one
*Hiranmaye, Hiranmai,
Hiranmae, Hyranmay,
Hyranmaye, Hyranmai,
Hyranmae*

Hiroshi (Japanese) A generous
man
*Hiroshie, Hiroshy, Hiroshey,
Hiroshee, Hiroshea, Hyroshi,
Hyroshie, Hyroshey*

Hirsi (African) An amulet
*Hirsie, Hirsy, Hirsey, Hirsee,
Hirsea*

Hisoka (Japanese) One who is
secretive
*Hysoka, Hisokie, Hysokie,
Hisoki, Hysoki, Hisokey,
Hysokey, Hisoky*

Hitakar (Indian) One who
wishes others well
Hitakarin, Hitakrit

Hobart (American) Form of Hubert, meaning "having a shining intellect"
Hobarte, Hoebart, Hoebarte, Hobert, Hoberte, Hoburt, Hoburte, Hobirt

Hohberht (German) One who is high and bright
Hohbert, Hohburt, Hohbirt, Hohbyrt, Hoh

Holcomb (English) From the deep valley
Holcom, Holcombe

Holden (English) From a hollow in the valley
Holdan, Holdyn, Holdon

Holland (American) From the Netherlands
Hollend, Hollind, Hollynd, Hollande, Hollende, Hollinde, Hollynde

Hollis (English) From the holly tree
Hollys, Holliss, Hollyss, Hollace, Hollice, Holli, Hollie, Holly

Holman (English) A man from the valley
Holmann, Holmen, Holmin, Holmyn, Holmon, Holmun

Holt (English) From the forest
Holte, Holyt, Holyte, Holter, Holtar, Holtor, Holtur, Holtir

Honaw (Native American) Resembling a bear
Honawe, Honau

Hondo (African) A warring man
Hondoh, Honda, Hondah

Honesto (Spanish) One who is honest
Honestio, Honestiyo, Honesteo, Honesteyo, Honestoh

Honon (Native American) Resembling a bear
Honun, Honen, Honan, Honin, Honyn

Honovi (Native American) Having great strength
Honovie, Honovy, Honovey, Honovee, Honovea

Honza (Czech) A gift from God

Horsley (English) From the horse meadow
Horsly, Horslea, Horsleah, Horslee, Horsleigh, Horsli, Horslie

Horst (German) From the thicket
Horste, Horsten, Horstan, Horstin, Horstyn, Horston, Horstun, Horstman

Hoshi (Japanese) Resembling a star
Hoshiko, Hoshyko, Hoshie, Hoshee, Hoshea, Hoshy, Hoshey

Hototo (Native American) One who whistles; a warrior spirit that sings

Houston (Gaelic / English) From Hugh's town / from the town on the hill
Huston, Houstyn, Hustin, Husten, Hustin, Houstun

Howard (English) The guardian of the home
Howerd, Howord, Howurd, Howird, Howyrd, Howi, Howie, Howy

Howi (Native American) Resembling a turtle dove

Hrothgar (Anglo-Saxon) A king
Hrothgarr, Hrothegar, Hrothegarr, Hrothgare, Hrothegare

Hubert (German) Having a shining intellect
Hobart, Huberte, Huburt, Huburte, Hubirt, Hubirte, Hubyrt, Hubyrte, Hubie, Uberto

Hudson (English) The son of Hugh; from the river
Hudsun, Hudsen, Hudsan, Hudsin, Hudsyn

Hugin (Norse) A thoughtful man
Hugyn, Hugen, Hugan, Hugon, Hugun

Humam (Arabic) A generous and brave man

Hungan (Haitian) A spirit master or priest
Hungen, Hungon, Hungun, Hungin, Hungyn

Hungas (Irish) A vigorous man

*Hunter (English) A great huntsman and provider
Huntar, Huntor, Huntur, Huntir, Huntyr, Hunte, Hunt, Hunting

Husky (American) A big man; a manly man
Huski, Huskie, Huskey, Huskee, Huskea, Husk, Huske

Huslu (Native American) Resembling a hairy bear
Huslue, Huslou

Husto (Spanish) A righteous man
Hustio, Husteo, Hustiyo, Husteyo

Huynh (Vietnamese) An older brother

Iakovos (Hebrew) Form of Jacob, meaning "he who supplants"
Iakovus, Iakoves, Iakovas, Iakovis, Iakovys

*Ian** (Gaelic) Form of John, meaning "God is gracious"
Iain, Iaine, Iayn, Iayne, Iaen, Iaene, Iahn

Iavor (Bulgarian) From the sycamore tree
Iaver, Iavur, Iavar, Iavir, Iavyr

^**Ibrahim** (Arabic) Form of Abraham, meaning "father of a multitude; father of nations"
Ibraheem, Ibraheim, Ibrahiem, Ibraheam, Ibrahym

Ichabod (Hebrew) The glory has gone
Ikabod, Ickabod, Icabod, Ichavod, Ikavod, Icavod, Ickavod, Icha

Ichtaca (Nahuatl) A secretive man
Ichtaka, Ichtacka

Ida (Anglo-Saxon) A king
Idah

Idi (African) Born during the holiday of Idd
Idie, Idy, Idey, Idee, Idea

Ido (Arabic / Hebrew) A mighty man / to evaporate
Iddo, Idoh, Iddoh

Idris (Welsh) An eager lord
Idrys, Idriss, Idrisse, Idryss, Idrysse

Iefan (Welsh) Form of John, meaning "God is gracious"
Iefon, Iefen, Iefin, Iefyn, Iefun, Ifan, Ifon, Ifen

Ifor (Welsh) An archer
Ifore, Ifour, Ifoure

Igasho (Native American) A wanderer
Igashoe, Igashow, Igashowe

Ignatius (Latin) A fiery man; one who is ardent
Ignac, Ignace, Ignacio, Ignacius, Ignatious, Ignatz, Ignaz, Ignazio

Igor (Scandinavian / Russian) A hero / Ing's soldier
Igoryok

Ihit (Indian) One who is honored
Ihyt, Ihitt, Ihytt

Ihsan (Arabic) A charitable man
Ihsann, Ihsen, Ihsin, Ihsyn, Ihson, Ihsun

Ike (Hebrew) Form of Isaac,
meaning "full of laughter"
Iki, Ikie, Iky, Ikey, Ikee, Ikea

^Iker (Basque) A visitor
Ikar, Ikir, Ikyr, Ikor, Ikur

Ilario (Italian) A cheerful man
*Ilareo, Ilariyo, Ilareyo, Ilar,
Ilarr, Ilari, Ilarie, Ilary*

Ilhuitl (Nahuatl) Born during
the daytime

Illanipi (Native American) An
amazing man
*Illanipie, Illanipy, Illanipey,
Illanipee, Illanipea*

Iluminado (Spanish) One who
shines brightly
*Illuminado, Iluminato,
Illuminato, Iluminados,
Iluminatos, Illuminados,
Illuminatos*

Imaran (Indian) Having great
strength
*Imaren, Imaron, Imarun,
Imarin, Imaryn*

Inaki (Basque) An ardent man
*Inakie, Inaky, Inakey, Inakee,
Inakea, Inacki, Inackie,
Inackee*

Ince (Hungarian) One who
is innocent
Inse

Indiana (English) From the
land of the Indians; from the
state of Indiana
Indianna, Indyana, Indyanna

Ingemar (Scandinavian) The
son of Ing
*Ingamar, Ingemur, Ingmar,
Ingmur, Ingar, Ingemer,
Ingmer*

Inger (Scandinavian) One who
is fertile
Inghar, Ingher

Ingo (Scandinavian / Danish)
A lord / from the meadow
Ingoe, Ingow, Ingowe

Ingram (Scandinavian) A raven
of peace
*Ingra, Ingrem, Ingrim, Ingrym,
Ingrum, Ingrom, Ingraham,
Ingrahame, Ingrams*

Iniko (African) Born during
troubled times
*Inicko, Inico, Inyko, Inycko,
Inyco*

Iranga (Sri Lankan) One who
is special

Irenbend (Anglo-Saxon) From
the iron bend
Ironbend

Irwin (English) A friend of the
wild boar
*Irwinn, Irwinne, Irwyn, Irwynne,
Irwine, Irwen, Irwenn, Irwenne*

*Isaac (Hebrew) Full of
laughter
*Ike, Isaack, Isaak, Isac, Isacco,
Isak, Issac, Itzak*

*Isaiah (Hebrew) God is my
salvation
*Isa, Isaia, Isais, Isia, Isiah,
Issiah, Izaiah, Iziah*

Iseabail (Hebrew) One who is
devoted to God
*Iseabaile, Iseabayl, Iseabyle,
Iseabael, Iseabaele*

Isham (English) From the iron
one's estate
*Ishem, Ishom, Ishum, Ishim,
Ishym, Isenham*

Isidore (Greek) A gift of Isis
*Isador, Isadore, Isidor, Isidoro,
Isidorus, Isidro*

Iskander (Arabic) Form of
Alexander, meaning "a helper
and defender of mankind"
*Iskinder, Iskandar, Iskindar,
Iskynder, Iskyndar, Iskender,
Iskendar*

Israel (Hebrew) God perse-
veres
Israeli, Israelie, Isreal, Izrael

Istvan (Hungarian) One who
is crowned
*Istven, Istvin, Istvyn, Istvon,
Istvun*

Iulian (Romanian) A youthful
man
Iulien, Iulio, Iuleo

Ivan (Slavic) Form of John,
meaning "God is gracious"
*Ivann, Ivanhoe, Ivano, Iwan,
Iban, Ibano, Ivanti, Ivantie*

Ives (Scandinavian) The
archer's bow; of the yew wood
*Ivair, Ivar, Iven, Iver, Ivo, Ivon,
Ivor, Ivaire*

Ivy (English) Resembling the
evergreen vining plant
Ivee, Ivey, Ivie, Ivi, Ivea

Iyar (Hebrew) Surrounded by
light
Iyyar, Iyer, Iyyer

J

Ja (Korean / African) A handsome man / one who is mag-
netic

Jabari (African) A valiant man
*Jabarie, Jabary, Jabarey,
Jabaree, Jabarea*

Jabbar (Indian) One who
consoles others
Jabar

Jabin (Hebrew) God has built; one who is perceptive

Jabon (American) A fiesty man
Jabun, Jabin, Jabyn, Jaben, Jaban

^**Jace** (Hebrew) God is my salvation
Jacen, Jacey, Jacian, Jacy, Jaice, Jayce, Jaece, Jase

Jacinto (Spanish) Resembling a hyacinth
Jacynto, Jacindo, Jacyndo, Jacento, Jacendo, Jacenty, Jacentey, Jacentee

*****Jack** (English) Form of John, meaning "God is gracious"
Jackie, Jackman, Jacko, Jacky, Jacq, Jacqin, Jak, Jaq

*****Jackson** (English) The son of Jack or John
Jacksen, Jacksun, Jacson, Jakson, Jaxen, Jaxon, Jaxun, Jaxson

*****Jacob** (Hebrew) He who supplants
Jake, James, Kuba, Iakovos, Yakiv, Yankel, Yaqub, Jaco, Jacobo, Jacobi, Jacoby, Jacobie, Jacobey, Jacobo

Jacoby (Hebrew) Form of Jacob, meaning "he who supplants"

Jadal (American) One who is punctual
Jadall, Jadel, Jadell

Jade (Spanish) Resembling the green gemstone
Jadee, Jadie, Jayde, Jaden

^***Jaden** (Hebrew / English) One who is thankful to God; God has heard / form of Jade, meaning "resembling the green gemstone"
Jaiden, Jadyn, Jaeden, Jaidyn, Jayden, Jaydon

Jagan (English) One who is self-confident
Jagen, Jagin, Jagyn, Jagon, Jagun, Jago

Jahan (Indian) Man of the world
Jehan, Jihan, Jag, Jagat, Jagath

Jaidayal (Indian) The victory of kindness
Jadayal, Jaydayal, Jaedayal

Jaime (Spanish) Form of James, meaning "he who supplants"
Jamie, Jaimee, Jaimey, Jaimi, Jaimie, Jaimy, Jamee

Jaimin (French) One who is loved
Jaimyn, Jamin, Jamyn, Jaymin, Jaymyn, Jaemin, Jaemyn

Jairdan (American) One who enlightens others
Jardan, Jayrdan, Jaerdan, Jairden, Jarden, Jayrden, Jaerden

Jaja (African) A gift from God

Jajuan (American) One who loves God

Jake (English) Form of Jacob, meaning "he who supplants"
Jaik, Jaike, Jayk, Jayke, Jakey, Jaky

Jakome (Basque) Form of James, meaning "he who supplants"
Jackome, Jakom, Jackom, Jacome

^**Jalen** (American) One who heals others; one who is tranquil
*Jaylon, Jaelan, Jalon, Jaylan, **Jaylen**, Jalan, **Jaylin***

Jamal (Arabic) A handsome man
Jamail, Jahmil, Jam, Jamaal, Jamy, Jamar

Jamar (American) Form of Jamal, meaning "a handsome man"
Jamarr, Jemar, Jemarr, Jimar, Jimarr, Jamaar, Jamari, Jamarie

***James** (Hebrew) Form of Jacob, meaning "he who supplants"
Jaimes, Jaymes, Jame, Jaym, Jaim, Jaem, Jaemes, Jamese, Jim, Jaime, Diego, Hagop, Hemi, Jakome

^**Jameson** (English) The son of James
*Jaimison, Jamieson, Jaymeson, **Jamison**, Jaimeson, Jaymison, Jaemeson, Jaemison*

Jamin (Hebrew) The right hand of favor
Jamian, Jamiel, Jamon, Jaymin, Jaemin, Jaymon

Janesh (Hindi) A leader of the people
Janeshe

Japa (Indian) One who chants
Japeth, Japesh, Japendra

Japheth (Hebrew) May he expand; in the Bible, one of Noah's sons
Jaypheth, Jaepheth, Jaipheth, Jafeth, Jayfeth

Jarah (Hebrew) One who is as sweet as honey
Jarrah, Jara, Jarra

Jared (Hebrew) Of the descent; descending
Jarad, Jarod, Jarrad, Jarryd, Jarred, Jarrod, Jaryd, Jerod, Jerrad, Jered

Jarman (German) A man from Germany
Jarmann, Jerman, Jermann

Jaron (Israeli) A song of rejoicing
Jaran, Jaren, Jarin, Jarran, Jarren, Jarrin, Jarron, Jaryn

Jaroslav (Slavic) Born with the beauty of spring
Jaroslaw

Jarrett (English) One who is strong with the spear
Jaret, Jarret, Jarrott, Jerett, Jarritt, Jaret

*****Jason** (Hebrew / Greek) God is my salvation / a healer; in mythology, the leader of the Argonauts
Jacen, Jaisen, Jaison, Jasen, Jasin, Jasun, Jayson, Jaysen

Jaspar (Persian) One who holds the treasure
Jasper, Jaspir, Jaspyr, Jesper, Jespar, Jespir, Jespyr

Jatan (Indian) One who is nurturing

Javan (Hebrew) Man from Greece; in the Bible, Noah's grandson
Jayvan, Jayven, Jayvon, Javon, Javern, Javen

Javier (Spanish) The owner of a new house
Javiero

Jax (American) Form of Jackson, meaning "son of Jack or John"

Jay (Latin / Sanskrit) Resembling a jaybird / one who is victorious
Jae, Jai, Jaye, Jayron, Jayronn, Jey

^Jayce (American) Form of Jason, meaning "God is my salvation"
Jayse, Jace, Jase

Jean (French) Form of John, meaning "God is gracious"
Jeanne, Jeane, Jene, Jeannot, Jeanot

Jedidiah (Hebrew) One who is loved by God
Jedadiah, Jedediah, Jed, Jedd, Jedidiya, Jedidiyah, Jedadia, Jedadiya

Jeffrey (English) A man of peace
Jeff, Geoffrey, Jeffery, Jeffree

Jelani (African) One who is mighty; strong
Jelanie, Jelany, Jelaney, Jelanee, Jelanea

Jennett (Hindi) One who is heaven-sent
Jenett, Jennet, Jenet, Jennitt, Jenitt, Jennit, Jenit

Jerald (English) Form of Gerald, meaning "one who rules with the spear"
Jeraldo, Jerold, Jerrald, Jerrold

*Jeremiah (Hebrew) One who is exalted by the Lord
Jeremia, Jeremias, Jeremija, Jeremiya, Jeremyah, Jeramiah, Jeramia, Jerram, Geremia

Jeremy (Hebrew) Form of Jeremiah, meaning "one who is exalted by the Lord"
Jeramey, Jeramie, Jeramy, Jerami, Jereme, Jeromy

Jermaine (French / Latin) A man from Germany / one who is brotherly
Jermain, Jermane, Jermayne, Jermin, Jermyn, Jermayn, Jermaen, Jermaene

Jerome (Greek) Of the sacred name
Jairome, Jeroen, Jeromo, Jeronimo, Jerrome, Jerom, Jerolyn, Jerolin, Hieronim

Jerram (Hebrew) Form of Jeremiah, meaning "one who is exalted by the Lord"
Jeram, Jerrem, Jerem, Jerrym, Jerym

Jesimiel (Hebrew) The Lord establishes
Jessimiel

Jesse (Hebrew) God exists; a gift from God; God sees all
Jess, Jessey, Jesiah, Jessie, Jessy, Jese, Jessi, Jessee

*Jesus (Hebrew) God is my salvation
*Jesous, Jesues, **Jesús**, Xesus*

Jett (English) Resembling the jet-black lustrous gemstone
Jet, Jette

Jibril (Arabic) Refers to the archangel Gabriel
Jibryl, Jibri, Jibrie, Jibry, Jibrey, Jibree

Jim (English) Form of James, meaning "he who supplants"
Jimi, Jimmee, Jimmey, Jimmie, Jimmy, Jimmi, Jimbo

Jimoh (African) Born on a Friday
Jymoh, Jimo, Jymo

Jivan (Hindi) A giver of life
Jivin, Jiven, Jivyn, Jivon

Joab (Hebrew) The Lord is my father
Joabb, Yoav

Joachim (Hebrew) One who is established by God; God will judge
Jachim, Jakim, Joacheim, Joaquim, Joaquin, Josquin, Joakim, Joakeen

Joe (English) Form of Joseph, meaning "God will add"
Jo, Joemar, Jomar, Joey, Joie, Joee, Joeye

Joel (Hebrew) Jehovah is God; God is willing

Johan (German) Form of John, meaning "God is gracious"

*John (Hebrew) God is gracious; in the Bible, one of the Apostles
***Sean, Jack, Juan,** Ian, Ean, **Evan,** Giovanni, Hanna, Hovannes, Iefan, Ivan, Jean, Xoan, Yochanan, Yohan, Johnn, Johnny, Jhonny*

Jonah (Hebrew) Resembling a dove; in the Bible, the man swallowed by a whale

Jonas (Greek) Form of Jonah, meaning "resembling a dove"

*Jonathan (Hebrew) A gift of God
Johnathan, Johnathon, Jonathon, Jonatan, Jonaton, Jonathen, Johnathen, Jonaten, Yonatan

*Jordan (Hebrew) Of the down-flowing river; in the Bible, the river where Jesus was baptized
Johrdan, Jordain, Jordaine, Jordane, Jordanke, Jordann, Jorden, Jordaen

Jorge (Spanish) Form of George, meaning "one who works the earth; a farmer"

*Jose (Spanish) Form of Joseph, meaning "God will add"
José, Joseito, Joselito

*Joseph (Hebrew) God will add
*Joe, Guiseppe, Yosyp, Jessop, Jessup, Joop, Joos, **José,** Jose, Josef, Joseito*

*Joshua (Hebrew) God is salvation
Josh, Joshuah, Josua, Josue, Joushua, Jozua, Joshwa, Joshuwa

*Josiah (Hebrew) God will help
Josia, Josias, Joziah, Jozia, Jozias

Journey (American) One who likes to travel
Journy, Journi, Journie, Journee, Journye, Journea

*Juan (Spanish) Form of John, meaning "God is gracious"
Juanito, Juwan, Jwan

Judah (Hebrew) One who praises God
Juda, Jude, Judas, Judsen, Judson, Judd, Jud

Jude (Latin) Form of Judah, meaning "one who praises God"

*Julian (Greek) The child of Jove; one who is youthful
Juliano, Julianus, Julien, Julyan, Julio, Jolyon, Jullien, Julen

Julius (Greek) One who is youthful
Juleus, Yuliy

Juma (African) Born on a Friday
Jumah

Jumbe (African) Having great strength
Jumbi, Jumbie, Jumby, Jumbey, Jumbee

Jumoke (African) One who is dearly loved
Jumok, Jumoak

Jun (Japanese) One who is obedient

Junaid (Arabic) A warrior
Junaide, Junayd, Junayde

Jung (Korean) A righteous man

Jurgen (German) Form of George, meaning "one who works the earth; a farmer"
Jorgen, Jurgin, Jorgin

Justice (English) One who upholds moral rightness and fairness
Justyce, Justiss, Justyss, Justis, Justus, Justise

*Justin (Latin) One who is just and upright
Joost, Justain, Justan, Just, Juste, Justen, Justino, Justo

Justinian (Latin) An upright ruler
Justinien, Justinious, Justinius, Justinios, Justinas, Justinus

K

Kabir (Indian) A spiritual leader
Kabeer, Kabear, Kabier, Kabeir, Kabyr, Kabar

Kabonesa (African) One who is born during difficult times

Kacancu (African) The first-born child
Kacancue, Kakancu, Kakancue, Kacanku, Kacankue

Kacey (Irish) A vigilant man; one who is alert
Kacy, Kacee, Kacea, Kaci, Kacie, Kasey, Kasy, Kasi

Kachada (Native American) A white-skinned man

Kaden (Arabic) A beloved companion
Kadan, Kadin, Kadon, Kaidan, Kaiden, Kaidon, Kaydan, **Kayden**

Kadmiel (Hebrew) One who stands before God
Kamiell

Kaemon (Japanese) Full of joy; one who is right-handed
Kamon, Kaymon, Kaimon

Kagen (Irish) A fiery man; a thinker
Kaigen, Kagan, Kaigan, Kaygen, Kaygan, Kaegen, Kaegan

Kahoku (Hawaiian) Resembling a star
Kahokue, Kahokoo, Kahokou

Kai (Hawaiian / Welsh / Greek) Of the sea / the keeper of the keys / of the earth
Kye

Kaimi (Hawaiian) The seeker
Kaimie, Kaimy, Kaimey, Kaimee, Kaimea

Kalama (Hawaiian) A source of light
Kalam, Kalame

Kale (English) Form of Charles, meaning "one who is manly and strong / a free man"

Kaleb (Hebrew) Resembling an aggressive dog
Kaileb, Kaeleb, Kayleb, Kalob, Kailob, Kaelob

Kalidas (Hindi) A poet or musician; a servant of Kali
Kalydas

Kalki (Indian) Resembling a white horse
Kalkie, Kalky, Kalkey, Kalkee, Kalkea

Kalkin (Hindi) The tenth-born child
Kalkyn, Kalken, Kalkan, Kalkon, Kalkun

^**Kamden** (English) From the winding valley
Kamdun, Kamdon, Kamdan, Kamdin, Kamdyn

Kane (Gaelic) The little warrior
Kayn, Kayne, Kaen, Kaene, Kahan, Kahane

Kang (Korean) A healthy man

Kano (Japanese) A powerful man
Kanoe, Kanoh

Kantrava (Indian) Resembling a roaring animal

Kaper (American) One who is capricious
Kahper, Kapar, Kahpar

Kapono (Hawaiian) A righteous man

Karcsi (French) A strong, manly man
Karcsie, Karcsy, Karcsey, Karcsee, Karcsea

Karl (German) A free man
Carl, Karel, Karlan, Karle, Karlens, Karli, Karlin, Karlo, Karlos

Karman (Gaelic) The lord of the manor
Karmen, Karmin, Karmyn, Karmon, Karmun

^**Karson** (Scottish) Form of Carson, meaning son of a marsh dweller
Karsen

^**Karter** (English) Form of Carter, meaning one who drives a cart

Kashvi (Indian) A shining man
Kashvie, Kashvy, Kashvey, Kashvee, Kashvea

Kasib (Arabic) One who is fertile
Kaseeb, Kaseab, Kasieb, Kaseib, Kasyb

Kasim (Arabic) One who is divided
Kassim, Kaseem, Kasseem, Kaseam, Kasseam, Kasym, Kassym

Kasimir (Slavic) One who demands peace
Kasimeer, Kasimear, Kasimier, Kasimeir, Kasimyr, Kaz, Kazimierz

Kason (Basque) Protected by a helmet
Kasin, Kasyn, Kasen, Kasun, Kasan

Katzir (Hebrew) The harvester
Katzyr, Katzeer, Katzear, Katzier, Katzeir

Kaushal (Indian) One who is skilled
Kaushall, Koshal, Koshall

Kazim (Arabic) An even-tempered man
Kazeem, Kazeam, Kaziem, Kazeim, Kazym

Keahi (Hawaiian) Of the flames
Keahie, Keahy, Keahey, Keahee, Keahea

Kealoha (Hawaiian) From the bright path
Keeloha, Kieloha

Kean (Gaelic / English) A warrior / one who is sharp
Keane, Keen, Keene, Kein, Keine, Keyn, Keyne, Kien

Keandre (American) One who is thankful
Kiandre, Keandray, Kiandray, Keandrae, Kiandrae, Keandrai, Kiandrai

Keanu (Hawaiian) Of the mountain breeze
Keanue, Kianu, Kianue, Keanoo, Kianoo, Keanou

Keaton (English) From the town of hawks
Keatun, Keeton, Keetun, Keyton, Keytun

Kedar (Arabic) A powerful man
Keder, Kedir, Kedyr, Kadar, Kader, Kadir, Kadyr

Kefir (Hebrew) Resembling a young lion
Kefyr, Kefeer, Kefear, Kefier, Kefeir

Keegan (Gaelic) A small and fiery man
Kegan, Keigan, Keagan, Keagen, Keegen

Keith (Scottish) Man from the forest
Keithe, Keath, Keathe, Kieth, Kiethe, Keyth, Keythe, Keithen

Kellach (Irish) One who suffers strife during battle
Kelach, Kellagh, Kelagh, Keallach

^**Kellen** (Gaelic / German) One who is slender / from the swamp
Kellan, *Kellon, Kellun, Kellin*

Kelley (Celtic / Gaelic) A warrior / one who defends
Kelly, Kelleigh, Kellee, Kellea, Kelleah, Kelli, Kellie

Kendi (African) One who is much loved
Kendie, Kendy, Kendey, Kendee, Kendea

Kendrick (English / Gaelic) A royal ruler / the champion
Kendric, Kendricks, Kendrik, Kendrix, Kendryck, Kenrick, Kenrik, Kenricks

Kenley (English) From the king's meadow
Kenly, Kenlee, Kenleigh, Kenlea, Kenleah, Kenli, Kenlie

Kenn (Welsh) Of the bright waters

Kennedy (Gaelic) A helmeted chief
Kennedi, Kennedie, Kennedey, Kennedee, Kennedea, Kenadie, Kenadi, Kenady

Kenneth (Irish) Born of the fire; an attractive man
Kennet, Kennett, Kennith, Kennit, Kennitt

Kent (English) From the edge or border
Kentt, Kennt, Kentrell

Kenton (English) From the king's town
Kentun, Kentan, Kentin, Kenten, Kentyn

Kenyon (Gaelic) A blond-haired man
Kenyun, Kenyan, Kenyen, Kenyin

Kepler (German) One who makes hats
Keppler, Kappler, Keppel, Keppeler

Kerbasi (Basque) A warrior
Kerbasie, Kerbasee, Kerbasea, Kerbasy, Kerbasey

Kershet (Hebrew) Of the rainbow

Kesler (American) An energetic man; one who is independent
Keslar, Keslir, Keslyr, Keslor, Keslur

Keung (Chinese) A universal spirit

*Kevin** (Gaelic) A beloved and handsome man
Kevyn, Kevan, Keven, Keveon, Kevinn, Kevion, Kevis, Kevon

Khairi (Swahili) A kingly man
Khairie, Khairy, Khairey, Khairee, Khairea

Khalon (American) A strong warrior
Khalun, Khalen, Khalan, Khalin, Khalyn

Khayri (Arabic) One who is charitable
Khayrie, Khayry, Khayrey, Khayree, Khayrea

Khouri (Arabic) A spiritual man; a priest
Khourie, Khoury, Khourey, Khouree, Kouri, Kourie, Koury, Kourey

Khushi (Indian) Filled with happiness
Khushie, Khushey, Khushy, Khushee

306 • THE 2014 BABY NAMES ALMANAC

Kibbe (Native American) A
nocturnal bird
Kybbe

Kibo (African) From the highest mountain peak
Keybo, Keebo, Keabo, Keibo, Kiebo

Kidd (English) Resembling a
young goat
Kid, Kydd, Kyd

Kiefer (German) One who
makes barrels
*Keefer, Keifer, Kieffer, Kiefner,
Kieffner, Kiefert, Kuefer, Kueffner*

^Kieran (Gaelic) Having dark
features; the little dark one
*Keiran, Keiron, Kernan, Kieren,
Kiernan, Kieron, Kierren, Kierrien,
Kierron, Keeran, Keeron, Keernan,
Keeren, Kearan, Kearen,
Kearon, Kearnan*

Kim (Vietnamese) As precious
as gold
Kym

Kimoni (African) A great man
*Kimonie, Kimony, Kimoney,
Kimonee, Kymoni, Kymonie,
Kymony, Kymoney*

Kincaid (Celtic) The leader
during battle
*Kincade, Kincayd, Kincayde,
Kincaide, Kincaed, Kincaede,
Kinkaid, Kinkaide*

Kindin (Basque) The fifth-born
child
*Kinden, Kindan, Kindyn,
Kindon, Kindun*

Kindle (American) To set
aflame
Kindel, Kyndle, Kyndel

King (English) The royal ruler
Kyng

Kingston (English) From the
king's town
Kingstun, Kinston, Kindon

Kinnard (Irish) From the tall
hill
*Kinard, Kinnaird, Kinaird,
Kynnard, Kynard, Kynnaird,
Kynaird*

Kinsey (English) The victori-
ous prince
*Kynsey, Kinsi, Kynsi, Kinsie,
Kynsie, Kinsee, Kynsee, Kinsea*

Kione (African) One who has
come from nowhere

Kioshi (Japanese) One who is
quiet
*Kioshe, Kioshie, Kioshy,
Kioshey, Kioshee, Kyoshi,
Kyoshe, Kyoshie*

Kipp (English) From the small
pointed hill
*Kip, Kipling, Kippling, Kypp,
Kyp, Kiplyng, Kipplyng, Kippi*

Kiri (Vietnamese) Resembling the mountains
Kirie, Kiry, Kirey, Kiree, Kirea

Kirk (Norse) A man of the church
Kyrk, Kerk, Kirklin, Kirklyn

Kirkland (English) From the church's land
Kirklan, Kirklande, Kyrkland, Kyrklan, Kyrklande

Kirkley (English) From the church's meadow
Kirkly, Kirkleigh, Kirklea, Kirkleah, Kirklee, Kirkli, Kirklie

Kit (English) Form of Christopher, meaning "one who bears Christ inside"
Kitt, Kyt, Kytt

Kitchi (Native American) A brave young man
Kitchie, Kitchy, Kitchey, Kitchee, Kitchea

Kitoko (African) A handsome man
Kytoko

Kivi (Finnish) As solid as stone
Kivie, Kivy, Kivey, Kivee, Kivea

Knight (English) A noble solidier
Knights

^**Knox** (English) From the rounded hill

Knud (Danish) A kind man
Knude

Kobe (African / Hungarian) Tortoise / Form of Jacob, meaning "he who supplants"
Kobi, Koby

Kody (English) One who is helpful
Kodey, Kodee, Kodea, Kodi, Kodie

Koen (German) An honest advisor
Koenz, Kunz, Kuno

Kohana (Native American / Hawaiian) One who is swift / the best

Kohler (German) One who mines coal
Koler

Kojo (African) Born on a Monday
Kojoe, Koejo, Koejoe

Koka (Hawaiian) A man from Scotland

^**Kolton** (American) Form of Colton, meaning from the coal town
Kolten, Koltan

Konane (Hawaiian) Born beneath the bright moon
Konain, Konaine, Konayn, Konayne, Konaen, Konaene

Konnor (English) A wolf lover; one who is strong-willed
Konnur, Konner, Konnar, Konnir, Konnyr

Koofrey (African) Remember me
Koofry, Koofri, Koofrie, Koofree

Kordell (English) One who makes cord
Kordel, Kord, Kordale

Koresh (Hebrew) One who digs in the earth; a farmer
Koreshe

Kory (Irish) From the hollow; of the churning waters
Korey, Kori, Korie, Koree, Korea, Korry, Korrey, Korree

Kozma (Greek) One who is decorated
Kozmah

Kozue (Japanese) Of the tree branches
Kozu, Kozoo, Kozou

Kraig (Gaelic) From the rocky place; as solid as a rock
Kraige, Krayg, Krayge, Kraeg, Kraege, Krage

Kramer (German) A shop-keeper
Kramar, Kramor, Kramir, Kramur, Kramyr, Kraymer, Kraimer, Kraemer

Krany (Czech) A man of short stature
Kraney, Kranee, Kranea, Krani, Kranie

Krikor (Armenian) A vigilant watchman
Krykor, Krikur, Krykur

Kristian (Scandinavian) An annointed Christian
Kristan, Kristien, Krist, Kriste, Krister, Kristar, Khristian, Khrist

Kristopher (Scandinavian) A follower of Christ
Khristopher, Kristof, Kristofer, Kristoff, Kristoffer, Kristofor, Kristophor, Krystof

Kuba (Polish) Form of Jacob, meaning "he who supplants"
Kubas

Kuckunniwi (Native American) Resembling a little wolf
Kukuniwi

Kuleen (Indian) A high-born man
Kulin, Kulein, Kulien, Kulean, Kulyn

Kumar (Indian) A prince;
a male child

Kuri (Japanese) Resembling
a chestnut
*Kurie, Kury, Kurey, Kuree,
Kurea*

Kuron (African) One who gives
thanks
*Kurun, Kuren, Kuran, Kurin,
Kuryn*

Kurt (German) A brave
counselor
Kurte

Kushal (Indian) A talented
man; adroit
Kushall

Kwaku (African) Born on a
Wednesday
*Kwakue, Kwakou, Kwako,
Kwakoe*

Kwan (Korean) Of a bold
character
Kwon

Kwintyn (Polish) The fifth-
born child
*Kwentyn, Kwinton, Kwenton,
Kwintun, Kwentun, Kwintan,
Kwentan, Kwinten*

Kyle (Gaelic) From the narrow
channel
*Kile, Kiley, Kye, Kylan, Kyrell,
Kylen, Kily, Kili*

Kylemore (Gaelic) From the
great wood
Kylmore, Kylemor, Kylmor

Kyrone (English) Form of
Tyrone, meaning "from
Owen's land"
*Kyron, Keirohn, Keiron,
Keirone, Keirown, Kirone*

L

Lacey (French) Man from
Normandy; as delicate as lace
Lacy, Laci, Lacie, Lacee, Lacea

Lachlan (Gaelic) From the land
of lakes
*Lachlen, Lachlin, Lachlyn,
Locklan, Locklen, Locklin,
Locklyn, Loklan*

Lachman (Gaelic) A man from
the lake
*Lachmann, Lockman,
Lockmann, Lokman, Lokmann,
Lakman, Lakmann*

Ladan (Hebrew) One who is
alert and aware
*Laden, Ladin, Ladyn, Ladon,
Ladun*

Ladd (English) A servant;
a young man
*Lad, Laddey, Laddie, Laddy,
Laddi, Laddee, Laddea, Ladde*

Ladislas (Slavic) A glorious
ruler
*Lacko, Ladislaus, Laslo, Laszlo,
Lazlo, Ladislav, Ladislauv,
Ladislao*

Lagrand (American) A
majestic man
Lagrande

Laibrook (English) One who
lives on the road near the
brook
*Laebrook, Laybrook, Laibroc,
Laebroc, Laybroc, Laibrok,
Laebrok, Laybrok*

Laird (Scottish) The lord of the
manor
*Layrd, Laerd, Lairde, Layrde,
Laerde*

Laken (American) Man from
the lake
*Laike, Laiken, Laikin, Lakin,
Lakyn, Lakan, Laikyn, Laeken*

Lalam (Indian) The best
Lallam, Lalaam, Lallaam

Lam (Vietnamese) Having a
full understanding

Laman (Arabic) A bright and
happy man
Lamaan, Lamann, Lamaann

Lamar (German / French)
From the renowned land / of
the sea
*Lamarr, Lamarre, Lemar,
Lemarr*

Lambert (Scandinavian) The
light of the land
*Lambart, Lamberto, Lambirt,
Landbert, Lambirto, Lambrecht,
Lambret, Lambrett*

Lambi (Norse) In mythology,
the son of Thorbjorn
*Lambie, Lamby, Lambey,
Lambe, Lambee*

Lameh (Arabic) A shining man

Lamorak (English) In
Arthurian legend, the brother
of Percival
*Lamerak, Lamurak, Lamorac,
Lamerac, Lamurac, Lamorack,
Lamerack, Lamurack*

Lance (English) Form of
Lancelot, meaning an
attendant, a knight of the
Round Table

Lander (English) One who
owns land
*Land, Landers, Landis, Landiss,
Landor, Lande, Landry, Landri*

Landon (English) From the
long hill
*Landyn, Landan, Landen,
Landin, Lando, Langdon,
Langden, Langdan*

Lane (English) One who takes the narrow path
Laine, Lain, Laen, Laene, Layne, Layn

Langhorn (English) Of the long horn
Langhorne, Lanhorn, Lanhorne

Langilea (Polynesian) Having a booming voice, like thunder
Langileah, Langilia, Langiliah

Langston (English) From the tall man's town
Langsten, Langstun, Langstown, Langstin, Langstyn, Langstan, Langton, Langtun

Langundo (Native American / Polynesian) A peaceful man / one who is graceful

Langworth (English) One who lives near the long paddock
Langworthe, Lanworth, Lanworthe

Lanier (French) One who works with wool

Lantos (Hungarian) One who plays the lute
Lantus

Lapidos (Hebrew) One who carries a torch
Lapydos, Lapidot, Lapydot, Lapidoth, Lapydoth, Lapidus, Lapydus

Laquinton (American) Form of Quinton, meaning "from the queen's town or settlement"
Laquinntan, Laquinnten, Laquinntin, Laquinnton, Laquintain, Laquintan, Laquintyn, Laquintynn

Lar (Anglo-Saxon) One who teaches others

Larson (Scandinavian) The son of Lawrence
Larsan, Larsen, Larsun, Larsin, Larsyn

Lasalle (French) From the hall
Lasall, Lasal, Lasale

Lashaun (American) An enthusiastic man
Lashawn, Lasean, Lashon, Lashond

Lassit (American) One who is open-minded
Lassyt, Lasset

Lathan (American) Form of Nathan, meaning "a gift from God"
Lathen, Lathun, Lathon, Lathin, Lathyn, Latan, Laten, Latun

Latimer (English) One who serves as an interpreter
Latymer, Latimor, Latymor, Latimore, Latymore, Lattemore, Lattimore

Latty (English) A generous
man
*Lattey, Latti, Lattie, Lattee,
Lattea*

Laurian (English) One who
lives near the laurel trees
*Laurien, Lauriano, Laurieno,
Lawrian, Lawrien, Lawriano,
Lawrieno*

Lave (Italian) Of the burning
rock
Lava

Lawford (English) From the
ford near the hill
*Lawforde, Lawferd, Lawferde,
Lawfurd, Lawfurde*

Lawler (Gaelic) A soft-spoken
man; one who mutters
*Lauler, Lawlor, Loller, Lawlar,
Lollar, Loller, Laular, Laulor*

Lawley (English) From the
meadow near the hill
*Lawly, Lawli, Lawlie, Lawleigh,
Lawlee, Lawlea, Lawleah*

Lawrence (Latin) Man from
Laurentum; crowned with
laurel
*Larance, Laranz, Larenz,
Larrance, Larrence, Larrens,
Larrey, Larry*

Laziz (Arabic) One who is
pleasant
*Lazeez, Lazeaz, Laziez,
Lazeiz, Lazyz*

Leaman (American) A
powerful man
*Leeman, Leamon, Leemon,
Leamond, Leamand*

Lear (Greek) Of the royalty
Leare, Leer, Leere

Leather (American) As tough
as hide
Lether

Leavitt (English) A baker
*Leavit, Leavytt, Leavyt, Leavett,
Leavet*

Leben (English) Filled with
hope

Lech (Slavic) In mythology, the
founder of the Polish people
Leche

Ledyard (Teutonic) The
protector of the nation
Ledyarde, Ledyerd, Ledyerde

Lee (English) From the
meadow
Leigh, Lea, Leah, Ley

Leeto (African) One who
embarks on a journey
Leato, Leito, Lieto

Legend (American) One who is memorable
Legende, Legund, Legunde

Leighton (English) From the town near the meadow
Leightun, Layton, Laytun, Leyton, Leytun

Lekhak (Hindi) An author
Lekhan

Leland (English) From the meadow land

Lema (African) One who is cultivated
Lemah, Lemma, Lemmah

Lemon (American) Resembling the fruit
Lemun, Lemin, Lemyn, Limon, Limun, Limin, Limyn, Limen

Len (Native American) One who plays the flute

Lencho (African) Resembling a lion
Lenchos, Lenchio, Lenchiyo, Lencheo, Lencheyo

Lennon (English) Son of love
Lennan

Lennor (English) A courageous man

Lennox (Scottish) One who owns many elm trees
Lenox, Lenoxe, Lennix, Lenix, Lenixe

Lensar (English) One who stays with his parents
Lenser, Lensor, Lensur

Lenton (American) A pious man
Lentin, Lentyn, Lentun, Lentan, Lenten, Lent, Lente

Leo (Latin) Having the strength of a lion
Lio, Lyo, Leon

Leon (Greek) Form of Leo, meaning "resembling a lion"

Leonard (German) Having the strength of a lion
Len, Lenard, Lenn, Lennard, Lennart, Lennerd, Leonardo

Leor (Latin) One who listens well
Leore

Lerato (Latin) The song of my soul
Leratio, Lerateo

Leron (French / Arabic) The circle / my song
Lerun, Leran, Leren, Lerin, Leryn

Leroy (French) The king
Leroi, Leeroy, Leeroi, Learoy, Learoi

*Levi (Hebrew) We are united as one; in the Bible, one of Jacob's sons
Levie, Levin, Levyn, Levy, Levey, Levee

Li (Chinese) Having great strength

*Liam (Gaelic) Form of William, meaning "the determined protector"

Lian (Chinese) Of the willow

Liang (Chinese) A good man
Lyang

Lidmann (Anglo-Saxon) A man of the sea; a sailor
Lidman, Lydmann, Lydman

Lif (Scandinavian) An energetic man; lively

Lihau (Hawaiian) A spirited man

Like (Asian) A soft-spoken man
Lyke

Lilo (Hawaiian) One who is generous
Lylo, Leelo, Lealo, Leylo, Lielo, Leilo

Lincoln (English) From the village near the lake
Lincon, Lyncon, Linc, Lynk, Lync

Lindford (English) From the linden-tree ford
Linford, Lindforde, Linforde, Lyndford, Lynford, Lyndforde, Lynforde

Lindhurst (English) From the village by the linden trees
Lyndhurst, Lindenhurst, Lyndenhurst, Lindhirst, Lindherst, Lyndhirst, Lyndherst, Lindenhirst

Lindley (English) From the meadow of linden trees
Lindly, Lindleigh, Lindlea, Lindleah, Lindlee, Lindli

Lindman (English) One who lives near the linden trees
Lindmann, Lindmon

Line (English) From the bank

Lipût (Hungarian) A brave young man

Lisimba (African) One who has been attacked by a lion
Lisymba, Lysimba, Lysymba

Liu (Asian) One who is quiet; peaceful

Llewellyn (Welsh) Resembling a lion
Lewellen, Lewellyn, Llewellen, Llewelyn, Llwewellin, Llew, Llewe, Llyweilun

Lochan (Hindi / Irish) The eyes / one who is lively

*Logan (Gaelic) From the little hollow
Logann, Logen, Login, Logyn, Logenn, Loginn, Logynn

Lolonyo (African) The beauty of love
Lolonyio, Lolonyeo, Lolonio, Lolonea

Loman (Gaelic) One who is small and bare
Lomann, Loeman, Loemann

Lombard (Latin) One who has a long beard
Lombardi, Lombardo, Lombardie, Lombardy, Lombardey, Lombardee

London (English) From the capital of England
Lundon, Londen, Lunden

Lonzo (Spanish) One who is ready for battle
Lonzio, Lonzeo

Lootah (Native American) Refers to the color red
Loota, Loutah, Louta, Lutah, Luta

Lorcan (Irish) The small fierce one
Lorcen, Lorcin, Lorcyn, Lorcon, Lorcun, Lorkan, Lorken, Lorkin

Lord (English) One who has authority and power
Lorde, Lordly, Lordley, Lordlee, Lordlea, Lordleigh, Lordli, Lordlie

Lore (Basque / English) Resembling a flower / form of Lawrence, meaning "man from Laurentum; crowned with laurel"
Lorea

Lorimer (Latin) One who makes harnesses
Lorrimer, Lorimar, Lorrimar, Lorymar, Lorrymar, Lorymer, Lorrymer

Louis (German) A famous warrior
Lew, Lewes, Lewis, Lodewick, Lodovico, Lou, Louie, Lucho, **Luis**

Luba (Yugoslavian) One who loves and is loved
Lubah

*Lucas (English) A man from Lucania
Lukas, Loucas, Loukas, Luckas, Louckas, Lucus, Lukus, Ghoukas

Lucian (Latin) Surrounded by light
Luciano, Lucianus, Lucien, Lucio, Lucjan, Lukianos, Lukyan, Luce

Lucky (English) A fortunate man
Luckey, Luckee, Luckea, Lucki, Luckie

Ludlow (English) The ruler of the hill
Ludlowe

*Luis (Spanish) Form of Louis, meaning "a famous warrior"
Luiz

*Luke (Greek) A man from Lucania
Luc, Luken

Lunt (Scandinavian) From the grove
Lunte

Luthando (Latin) One who is dearly loved

Luther (German) A soldier of the people
Louther, Luter, Luthero, Lutero, Louthero, Luthus, Luthas, Luthos

Lux (Latin) A man of the light
Luxe, Luxi, Luxie, Luxee, Luxea, Luxy, Luxey

Ly (Vietnamese) A reasonable man

Lynn (English) A man of the lake
Linn, Lyn, Lynne, Linne

M

Maahes (Egyptian) Resembling a lion

Mac (Gaelic) The son of Mac (Macarthur, Mackinley, etc.)
Mack, Mak, Macky, Macki, Mackie, Mackee, Mackea

Macadam (Gaelic) The son of Adam
Macadhamh, MacAdam, McAdam, MacAdhamh

Macallister (Gaelic) The son of Alistair
MacAlister, McAlister, McAllister, Macalister

Macardle (Gaelic) The son of great courage
MacArdle, McCardle, Macardell, MacArdell, McCardell

Macartan (Gaelic) The son of
Artan
*MacArtan, McArtan,
Macarten, MacArten, McArten*

Macarthur (Gaelic) The son of
Arthur
*MacArthur, McArthur,
Macarther, MacArther,
McArther*

Macauslan (Gaelic) The son of
Absalon
*MacAuslan, McAuslan,
Macauslen, MacAuslen,
McAuslen*

Maccoll (Gaelic) The son of
Coll
McColl, Maccoll, MacColl

Maccrea (Gaelic) The son of
grace
*McCrea, Macrae, MacCrae,
MacCray, MacCrea*

Macedonio (Greek) A man
from Macedonia
*Macedoneo, Macedoniyo,
Macedoneyo*

Macgowan (Gaelic) The son of
a blacksmith
*MacGowan, Magowan,
McGowan, McGowen,
McGown, MacCowan,
MacCowen*

Machau (Hebrew) A gift from
God

Machenry (Gaelic) The son of
Henry
MacHenry, McHenry

Machk (Native American)
Resembling a bear

Macintosh (Gaelic) The son of
the thane
*MacIntosh, McIntosh,
Macintoshe, MacIntoshe,
McIntoshe, Mackintosh,
MacKintosh*

Mackay (Gaelic) The son of
fire
*MacKay, McKay, Mackaye,
MacKaye, McKaye*

Mackinley (Gaelic) The son of
the white warrior
*MacKinley, McKinley,
MacKinlay, McKinlay,
Mackinlay, Mackinlie,
MacKinlie*

Macklin (Gaelic) The son of
Flann
*Macklinn, Macklyn, Macklynn,
Macklen, Macklenn*

Maclaine (Gaelic) The son of
John's servant
*MacLaine, Maclain, MacLain,
Maclayn, McLaine, McLain,
Maclane, MacLane*

Macleod (Gaelic) The son of
the ugly one
*MacLeod, McLeod, McCloud,
MacCloud*

Macmurray (Gaelic) The son
of Murray
*MacMurray, McMurray,
Macmurra, MacMurra*

Macnab (Gaelic) The son of
the abbot
MacNab, McNab

Macon (English / French)
To make / from the city in
France
*Macun, Makon, Makun,
Maken, Mackon, Mackun*

Macqueen (Gaelic) The son of
the good man
MacQueen, McQueen

Macrae (Gaelic) The son of
Ray
*MacRae, McRae, Macray,
MacRay, McRay, Macraye,
MacRaye, McRaye*

Madden (Pakistani) One who
is organized; a planner
*Maddon, Maddan, Maddin,
Maddyn, Maddun, Maden,
Madon, Madun*

Maddox (Welsh) The son of
the benefactor
Madox, Madocks, Maddocks

Madhur (Indian) A sweet man

Magee (Gaelic) The son of
Hugh
*MacGee, McGee, MacGhee,
Maghee*

Maguire (Gaelic) The son of
the beige one
*Magwire, MacGuire, McGuire,
MacGwire, McGwire*

Magus (Latin) A sorcerer
*Magis, Magys, Magos, Magas,
Mages*

Mahan (American) A cowboy
*Mahahn, Mahen, Mayhan,
Maihan, Maehan, Mayhen,
Maihen, Maehen*

Mahant (Indian) Having a
great soul
Mahante

Mahatma (Hindi) Of great
spiritual development

Mahfouz (Arabic) One who is
protected
*Mafouz, Mahfooz, Mafooz,
Mahfuz, Mafuz*

Mahkah (Native American) Of
the earth
Mahka, Makah, Maka

Mahmud (Arabic) One who is
praiseworthy
*Mahmood, Mahmoud,
Mehmood, Mehmud, Mehmoud*

Mailhairer (French) An ill-fated man

Maimon (Arabic) One who is dependable; having good fortune
Maymon, Maemon, Maimun, Maymun, Maemun, Mamon, Mamun

Maitland (English) From the meadow land
Maytland, Maetland, Maitlande, Maytlande, Maetlande

Majdy (Arabic) A glorious man
Majdey, Majdi, Majdie, Majdee, Majdea

Makaio (Hawaiian) A gift from God

Makena (Hawaiian) Man of abundance
Makenah

Makin (Arabic) Having great strength
Makeen, Makean, Makein, Makien, Makyn

Makis (Hebrew) A gift from God
Madys, Makiss, Makyss, Makisse, Madysse

Malachi (Hebrew) A messenger of God
Malachie, Malachy, Malaki, Malakia, Malakie, Malaquias, Malechy, Maleki

Malawa (African) A flourishing man

Malcolm (Gaelic) Follower of St. Columbus
Malcom, Malcolum, Malkolm, Malkom, Malkolum

Mali (Indian) A ruler; the firstborn son
Malie, Maly, Maley, Malee, Malea

Mamoru (Japanese) Of the earth
Mamorou, Mamorue, Mamorew, Mamoroo

Manchester (English) From the city in England
Manchestar, Manchestor, Manchestir, Manchestyr, Manchestur

Mandan (Native American) A tribal name
Manden, Mandon, Mandun, Mandin, Mandyn

Mandhatri (Indian) A prince; born to royalty
Mandhatrie, Mandhatry, Mandhatrey, Mandhatree, Mandhatrea

Mani (African) From the mountain
Manie, Many, Maney, Manee, Manea

Manjit (Indian) A conqueror of the mind; having great knowledge
Manjeet, Manjeat, Manjeit, Manjiet, Manjyt

Manley (English) From the man's meadow; from the hero's meadow
Manly, Manli, Manlie, Manlea, Manleah, Manlee, Manleigh

Manmohan (Indian) A handsome and pleasing man
Manmohen, Manmohin, Manmohyn

Mannheim (German) From the hamlet in the swamp
Manheim

Mano (Hawaiian) Resembling a shark
Manoe, Manow, Manowe

Manohar (Indian) A delightful and captivating man
Manoharr, Manohare

Mansel (English) From the clergyman's house
Mansle, Mansell, Mansele, Manselle, Manshel, Manshele, Manshell, Manshelle

Mansfield (English) From the field near the small river
Mansfeld, Maunfield, Maunfeld

Manton (English) From the man's town; from the hero's town
Mantun, Manten, Mannton, Manntun, Mannten

Manu (African) The second-born child
Manue, Manou, Manoo

Manuel (Spanish) Form of Emmanuel, meaning "God is with us"
Manuelo, Manuello, Manolito, Manolo, Manollo, Manny, Manni

Manya (Indian) A respected man
Manyah

Manzo (Japanese) The third son with ten-thousand-fold strength

Mar (Spanish) Of the sea
Marr, Mare, Marre

Marcel (French) The little warrior
Marceau, Marcelin, Marcellin, Marcellino, Marcell, Marcello, Marcellus, Marcelo

Marcus (Latin) Form of Mark, meaning "dedicated to Mars, the god of war"
Markus, Marcas, Marco, Markos

Mariatu (African) One who is pure; chaste
Mariatue, Mariatou, Mariatoo

Marid (Arabic) A rebellious man
Maryd

Mario (Latin) A manly man
Marius, Marios, Mariano, Marion, Mariun, Mareon

Mark (Latin) Dedicated to Mars, the god of war
Marc, Markey, Marky, Marki, Markie, Markee, Markea, Markov

Marmion (French) Our little one
Marmyon, Marmeon

Marsh (English) From the marshland
Marshe

Marshall (French / English) A caretaker of horses / a steward
Marchall, Marischal, Marischall, Marschal, Marshal, Marshell, Marshel, Marschall

Marston (English) From the town near the marsh
Marstun, Marsten, Marstin, Marstyn, Marstan

Martin (Latin) Dedicated to Mars, the god of war
Martyn, Mart, Martel, Martell, Marten, Martenn, Marti, Martie

Marvin (Welsh) A friend of the sea
Marvinn, Marvinne, Marven, Marvenn, Marvenne, Marvyn, Marvynn, Marvynne, Mervin

Maryland (English) Honoring Queen Mary; from the state of Maryland
Mariland, Maralynd, Marylind, Marilind

Masanao (Japanese) A good man

Masao (Japanese) A righteous man

***Mason** (English) One who works with stone
Masun, Masen, Masan, Masin, Masyn, Masson, Massun, Massen

Masselin (French) A young Thomas
Masselyn, Masselen, Masselan, Masselon, Masselun, Maselin, Maselyn, Maselon

Masura (Japanese) A good
destiny
Masoura

Mataniah (Hebrew) A gift
from God
*Matania, Matanya,
Matanyahu, Mattania,
Mattaniah, Matanyah*

Matata (African) One who
causes trouble

Matin (Arabic) Having great
strength
*Maten, Matan, Matyn, Maton,
Matun*

Matisse (French) One who is
gifted
*Matiss, Matysse, Matyss,
Matise, Matyse*

Matlock (American) A rancher
Matlok, Matloc

^**Matteo** (Italian) Form of
Matthew, meaning "a gift
from God"
Mateo

*****Matthew** (Hebrew) A gift
from God
*Matt, Mathew, Matvey,
Mateas, Mattix, Madteos,
Matthias, Mat, Mateo, Matteo,
Mateus*

Matunde (African) One who is
fruitful
Matundi, Matundie

Matvey (Russian) Form of
Matthew, meaning "a gift
from God"
*Matvy, Matvee, Matvea, Matvi,
Matvie, Motka, Matviyko*

Matwau (Native American)
The enemy

Maurice (Latin) A dark-
skinned man; Moorish
*Maurell, Maureo, Mauricio,
Maurids, Maurie, Maurin,
Maurio, Maurise, Baurice*

^**Maverick** (English) An
independent man; a non-
conformist
*Maveric, Maverik, Mavrick,
Mavric, Mavrik*

*****Max** (English) Form of
Maxwell, meaning from
Mack's spring

^**Maximilian** (Latin) The
greatest
*Max, Macks, Maxi, Maxie,
Maxy, Maxey, Maxee, Maxea,
Maximiliano*

Maxfield (English) From
Mack's field
Mackfield, Maxfeld, Macksfeld

Maxwell (English) From
Mack's spring
*Maxwelle, Mackswell, Maxwel,
Mackswel, Mackwelle, Maxwill,
Maxwille, Mackswill*

Mayer (Latin / German / Hebrew) A large man / a farmer / one who is shining bright
Maier, Mayar, Mayor, Mayir, Mayur, Meyer, Meir, Myer

Mayfield (English) From the strong one's field
Mayfeld, Maifield, Maifeld, Maefield, Maefeld

Mayo (Gaelic) From the yew tree plain
Mayoe, Maiyo, Maeyo, Maiyoe, Maeyoe, Mayoh, Maioh

Mccoy (Gaelic) The son of Coy
McCoy

McKenna (Gaelic) The son of Kenna; to ascend
McKennon, McKennun, McKennen, McKennan

Mckile (Gaelic) The son of Kyle
McKile, Mckyle, McKyle, Mackile, Mackyle, MacKile, MacKyle

Medad (Hebrew) A beloved friend
Meydad

Medgar (German) Having great strength
Medgarr, Medgare, Medgard, Medárd

Medwin (German) A strong friend
Medwine, Medwinn, Medwinne, Medwen, Medwenn, Medwenne, Medwyn, Medwynn

Meged (Hebrew) One who has been blessed with goodness

Mehdi (Arabian) One who is guided
Mehdie, Mehdy, Mehdey, Mehdee, Mehdea

Mehetabel (Hebrew) One who is favored by God
Mehetabell, Mehitabel, Mehitabell, Mehytabel, Mehytabell

Meilyr (Welsh) A regal ruler

Meinrad (German) A strong counselor
Meinred, Meinrod, Meinrud, Meinrid, Meinryd

Meka (Hawaiian) Of the eyes
Mekah

Melancton (Greek) Resembling a black flower
Melankton, Melanctun, Melanktun, Melancten, Melankten, Melanchton, Melanchten, Melanchthon

Mele (Hawaiian) One who is happy

Melesio (Spanish) An attentive man; one who is careful
Melacio, Melasio, Melecio, Melicio, Meliseo, Milesio

Meletius (Greek) A cautious man
Meletios, Meletious, Meletus, Meletos

Meli (Native American) One who is bitter
Melie, Mely, Meley, Melee, Melea, Meleigh

Melker (Swedish) A king
Melkar, Melkor, Melkur, Melkir, Melkyr

Melton (English) From the mill town
Meltun, Meltin, Meltyn, Melten, Meltan

Melville (English) From the mill town
Melvill, Melvil, Melvile, Melvylle, Melvyll, Melvyl, Melvyle

Melvin (English) A friend who offers counsel
Melvinn, Melvinne, Melven, Melvenn, Melvenne, Melvyn, Melvynn, Melvynne, Belvin

Memphis (American) From the city in Tennessee
Memfis, Memphys, Memfys, Memphus, Memfus

Menachem (Hebrew) One who provides comfort
Menaheim, Menahem, Menachim, Menachym, Menahim, Menahym, Machum, Machem

Menassah (Hebrew) A forgetful man
Menassa, Menass, Menas, Menasse, Menasseh

Menefer (Egyptian) Of the beautiful city
Menefar, Menefir, Menefyr, Menefor, Menefur

Menelik (African) The son of a wise man
Menelick, Menelic, Menelyk, Menelyck, Menelyc

Merewood (English) From the forest with the lake
Merwood, Merewode, Merwode

Merlin (Welsh) Of the sea fortress; in Arthurian legend, the wizard and mentor of King Arthur
Merlyn, Merlan, Merlon, Merlun, Merlen, Merlinn, Merlynn, Merlonn

Merrill (English) Of the shining sea
Meril, Merill, Merrel, Merrell, Merril, Meryl, Merryll, Meryll

Merton (English) From the town near the lake
Mertun, Mertan, Merten, Mertin, Mertyn, Murton, Murtun, Murten

Mervin (Welsh) Form of Marvin, meaning "a friend of the sea"
Mervinn, Mervinne, Mervyn, Mervynn, Mervynne, Merven, Mervenn, Mervenne

Meshach (Hebrew) An enduring man
Meshack, Meshac, Meshak, Meeshach, Meeshack, Meeshak, Meeshac

Mhina (African) One who is delightful
Mhinah, Mheena, Mheenah, Mheina, Mheinah, Mhienah, Mhienah, Mhyna

Micah (Hebrew) Form of Michael, meaning "who is like God?"
Mica, Mycah

*Michael (Hebrew) Who is like God?
*Makai, Micael, Mical, Micha, Michaelangelo, Michail, Michal, Micheal, **Miguel**, Mick*

Mick (English) Form of Michael, meaning "who is like God?"
Micke, Mickey, Micky, Micki, Mickie, Mickee, Mickea, Mickel

Mieko (Japanese) A bright man

Miguel (Portuguese / Spanish) Form of Michael, meaning "who is like God?"
Migel, Myguel

Milan (Latin) An eager and hardworking man
Mylan

Miles (German / Latin) One who is merciful / a soldier
Myles, Miley, Mily, Mili, Milie, Milee

Milford (English) From the mill's ford
Millford, Milfurd, Millfurd, Milferd, Millferd, Milforde, Millforde, Milfurde

Miller (English) One who works at the mill
Millar, Millor, Millur, Millir, Millyr, Myller, Millen, Millan

^Milo (German) Form of Miles, meaning "one who is merciful"
Mylo

Milson (English) The son of
Miles
*Milsun, Milsen, Milsin, Milsyn,
Milsan*

Mimir (Norse) In mythology, a
giant who guarded the well of
wisdom
*Mymir, Mimeer, Mimyr,
Mymeer, Mymyr, Meemir,
Meemeer, Meemyr*

Miner (Latin / English) One
who works in the mines / a
youth
*Minor, Minar, Minur, Minir,
Minyr*

Mingan (Native American)
Resembling a gray wolf
*Mingen, Mingin, Mingon,
Mingun, Mingyn*

Minh (Vietnamese) A clever
man

Minster (English) Of the
church
*Mynster, Minstar, Mynstar,
Minstor, Mynstor, Minstur,
Mynstur, Minstir*

Miracle (American) An act of
God's hand
*Mirakle, Mirakel, Myracle,
Myrakle*

Mirage (French) An illusion
Myrage

Mirumbi (African) Born
during a period of rain
*Mirumbie, Mirumby,
Mirumbey, Mirumbee,
Mirumbea*

Missouri (Native American)
From the town of large
canoes; from the state of
Missouri
*Missourie, Mizouri, Mizourie,
Missoury, Mizoury, Missuri,
Mizuri, Mizury*

Mitchell (English) Form of
Michael, meaning "who is
like God?"
*Mitch, Mitchel, Mytch,
Mitchum, Mytchill, Mitcham*

Mitsu (Japanese) Of the light
Mytsu, Mitsue, Mytsue

Mochni (Native American)
Resembling a talking bird
*Mochnie, Mochny, Mochney,
Mochnee, Mochnea*

Modesty (Latin) One who is
without conceit
*Modesti, Modestie, Modestee,
Modestus, Modestey, Modesto,
Modestio, Modestine*

Mogens (Dutch) A powerful
man
*Mogen, Mogins, Mogin,
Mogyns, Mogyn, Mogan,
Mogans*

Mohajit (Indian) A charming man
Mohajeet, Mohajeat, Mohajeit, Mohajiet, Mohajyt

Mohammed (Arabic) One who is greatly praised; the name of the prophet and founder of Islam
Mahomet, Mohamad, Mohamed, Mohamet, Mohammad, Muhammad, Muhammed, Mehmet

Mohave (Native American) A tribal name
Mohav, Mojave

Mojag (Native American) One who is never quiet

Molan (Irish) The servant of the storm
Molen

Momo (American) A warring man

Mona (African) A jealous man
Monah

Mongo (African) A well-known man
Mongoe, Mongow, Mongowe

Mongwau (Native American) Resembling an owl

Monroe (Gaelic) From the mouth of the river Roe
Monro, Monrow, Monrowe, Munro, Munroe, Munrow, Munrowe

Montenegro (Spanish) From the black mountain

Montgomery (French) From Gomeric's mountain
Monty, Montgomerey, Montgomeri, Montgomerie, Montgomeree, Montgomerea

Monty (English) Form of Montgomery, meaning "from Gomeric's mountain"
Montey, Monti, Montie, Montee, Montea, Montes, Montez

Moon (American) Born beneath the moon; a dreamer

Mooney (Irish) A wealthy man
Moony, Mooni, Moonie, Maonaigh, Moonee, Moonea, Moone

Moose (American) Resembling the animal; a big, strong man
Moos, Mooze, Mooz

Moran (Irish) A great man
Morane, Morain, Moraine, Morayn, Morayne, Moraen, Moraene

Morathi (African) A wise man
Morathie, Morathy, Morathey,
Morathee, Morathea

Moreland (English) From the
moors
Moorland, Morland

Morley (English) From the
meadow on the moor
Morly, Morleigh, Morlee,
Morlea, Morleah, Morli,
Morlie, Moorley

Morpheus (Greek) In mythology, the god of dreams
Morfeus, Morphius, Mofius

Mortimer (French) Of the still
water; of the dead sea
Mortymer, Morty, Mortey,
Morti, Mortie, Mortee, Mortea,
Mort, Morte

Moses (Hebrew) A savior; in
the Bible, the leader of the
Israelites; drawn from the
water
Mioshe, Mioshye, Mohsen,
Moke, Moise, Moises, Mose,
Moshe

Mostyn (Welsh) From the
mossy settlement
Mostin, Mosten, Moston,
Mostun, Mostan

Moswen (African) A light-
skinned man
Moswenn, Moswenne, Moswin,
Moswinn, Moswinne, Moswyn,
Moswynn, Moswynne

Moubarak (Arabian) One who
is blessed
Mubarak, Moobarak

Mounafes (Arabic) A rival

Muhannad (Arabic) One who
wields a sword
Muhanned, Muhanad,
Muhaned, Muhunnad,
Muhunad, Muhanned,
Muhaned

Mukhtar (Arabic) The chosen
one
Muktar

Mukisa (Ugandan) Having
good fortune
Mukysa

Mulcahy (Irish) A war chief
Mulcahey, Mulcahi, Mulcahie,
Mulcahee, Mulcahea

Mundhir (Arabic) One who
cautions others
Mundheer, Mundhear,
Mundheir, Mundhier,
Mundhyr

Murdock (Scottish) From the sea
Murdok, Murdoc, Murdo, Murdoch, Murtagh, Murtaugh, Murtogh, Murtough

Murfain (American) Having a warrior spirit
Murfaine, Murfayn, Murfayne, Murfaen, Murfaene, Murfane

Muriel (Gaelic) Of the shining sea
Muryel, Muriell, Muryell, Murial, Muriall, Muryal, Muryall, Murell

Murphy (Gaelic) A warrior of the sea
Murphey, Murphee, Murphea, Murphi, Murphie, Murfey, Murfy, Murfee

Murray (Gaelic) The lord of the sea
Murrey, Murry, Murri, Murrie, Murree, Murrea, Murry

Murron (Celtic) A bitter man
Murrun, Murren, Murran, Murrin, Murryn

Murtadi (Arabic) One who is content
Murtadie, Murtady, Murtadey, Murtadee, Murtadea

Musad (Arabic) One who is lucky
Musaad, Mus'ad

Mushin (Arabic) A charitable man
Musheen, Mushean, Mushein, Mushien, Mushyn

Muskan (Arabic) One who smiles often
Musken, Muskon, Muskun, Muskin, Muskyn

Muslim (Arabic) An adherent of Islam
Muslym, Muslem, Moslem, Moslim, Moslym

Mustapha (Arabic) The chosen one
Mustafa, Mostapha, Mostafa, Moustapha, Moustafa

Muti (Arabic) One who is obedient
Mutie, Muty, Mutey, Mutee, Mutea, Muta

Myron (Greek) Refers to myrrh, a fragrant oil
Myrun, Myran, Myren, Myrin, Myryn, Miron, Mirun, Miran

Mystique (French) A man with an air of mystery
Mystic, Mistique, Mysteek, Misteek, Mystiek, Mistiek, Mysteeque, Misteeque

N

Nabendu (Indian) Born beneath the new moon
Nabendue, Nabendoo, Nabendou

Nabhi (Indian) The best
Nabhie, Nabhy, Nabhey, Nabhee, Nabhea

Nabhomani (Indian) Of the sun
Nabhomanie, Nabhomany, Nabhomaney, Nabhomanee, Nabhomanea

Nabil (Arabic) A highborn man
Nabeel, Nabeal, Nabeil, Nabiel, Nabyl

Nabu (Babylonian) In mythology, the god of writing and wisdom
Nabue, Naboo, Nabo, Nebo, Nebu, Nebue, Neboo

Nachshon (Hebrew) An adventurous man; one who is daring
Nachson

Nadav (Hebrew) A generous man
Nadaav

Nadif (African) One who is born between seasons
Nadeef, Nadief, Nadeif, Nadyf, Nadeaf

Nadim (Arabic) A beloved friend
Nadeem, Nadeam, Nadiem, Nadeim, Nadym

Naftali (Hebrew) A struggling man; in the Bible, one of Jacob's sons
Naphtali, Naphthali, Neftali, Nefthali, Nephtali, Nephthali, Naftalie, Naphtalie

Nagel (German) One who makes nails
Nagle, Nagler, Naegel, Nageler, Nagelle, Nagele, Nagell

Nahir (Hebrew) A clear-headed and bright man
Naheer, Nahear, Naheir, Nahier, Nahyr, Naher

Nahum (Hebrew) A compassionate man
Nahom, Nahoum, Nahoom, Nahuem

Naji (Arabic) One who is safe
Najea, Naje, Najee, Najie, Najy, Najey, Nanji, Nanjie

Najib (Arabic) Of noble descent; a highborn man
Najeeb, Najeab, Najeib, Najieb, Najyb, Nageeb, Nageab, Nagyb

Nally (Irish) A poor man
*Nalley, Nalli, Nallie, Nallee,
Nallea, Nalleigh*

Namir (Israeli) Resembling a
leopard
*Nameer, Namear, Namier,
Nameir, Namyr*

Nandan (Indian) One who is
pleasing
*Nanden, Nandin, Nandyn,
Nandon, Nandun*

Naotau (Indian) Our new son
Naotou

Napier (French / English) A
mover / one who takes care of
the royal linens
Neper

Napoleon (Italian / German)
A man from Naples / son of
the mists
*Napolean, Napolion,
Napoleone, Napoleane,
Napolione*

Narcissus (Greek) Resembling
a daffodil; self-love; in mythology, a youth who fell in love
with his reflection
*Narciso, Narcisse, Narkissos,
Narses, Narcisus, Narcis,
Narciss*

Naresh (Indian) A king
Nareshe, Natesh, Nateshe

Nasih (Arabic) One who
advises others
Nasyh

Natal (Spanish) Born at
Christmastime
*Natale, Natalino, Natalio,
Natall, Natalle, Nataleo, Natica*

*Nathan (Hebrew) Form of
Nathaniel, meaning "a gift
from God"
*Nat, Natan, Nate, Nathen,
Nathon, Nathin, Nathyn,
Nathun, Lathan*

*Nathaniel (Hebrew) A gift
from God
*Nathan, Natanael, Nataniel,
Nathanael, Nathaneal,
Nathanial, Nathanyal,
Nathanyel, Nethanel*

Nature (American) An
outdoorsy man
Natural

Navarro (Spanish) From the
plains
*Navaro, Navarrio, Navario,
Navarre, Navare, Nabaro,
Nabarro*

Naveed (Persian) Our best
wishes
*Navead, Navid, Navied,
Naveid, Navyd*

Nazim (Arabian) Of a soft
breeze
*Nazeem, Nazeam, Naziem,
Nazeim, Nazym*

Nebraska (Native American)
From the flat water land;
from the state of Nebraska

Neckarios (Greek) Of the
nectar; one who is immortal
*Nectaire, Nectarios, Nectarius,
Nektario, Nektarius, Nektarios,
Nektaire*

Neelotpal (Indian) Resembling
the blue lotus
*Nealotpal, Nielotpal, Neilotpal,
Nilothpal, Neelothpal*

Negm (Arabian) Resembling
a star

Nehal (Indian) Born during a
period of rain
Nehall, Nehale, Nehalle

Nehemiah (Hebrew) God
provides comfort
*Nehemia, Nechemia,
Nechemiah, Nehemya,
Nehemyah, Nechemya,
Nechemyah*

Neil (Gaelic) The champion
*Neal, Neale, Neall, Nealle,
Nealon, Neel, Neilan, Neile*

Neirin (Irish) Surrounded by
light
*Neiryn, Neiren, Neerin, Neeryn,
Neeren*

Nelek (Polish) Resembling a
horn
Nelec, Neleck

Nelson (English) The son of
Neil; the son of a champion
*Nealson, Neilson, Neillson,
Nelsen, Nilson, Nilsson, Nelli,
Nellie*

Neptune (Latin) In mythology,
god of the sea
*Neptun, Neptoon, Neptoone,
Neptoun, Neptoune*

Neroli (Italian) Resembling an
orange blossom
*Nerolie, Neroly, Neroley,
Neroleigh, Nerolea, Nerolee*

Nevan (Irish) The little saint
Naomhan

Neville (French) From the new
village
*Nev, Nevil, Nevile, Nevill,
Nevylle, Nevyl, Nevyle, Nevyll*

Newcomb (English) From the
new valley
*Newcom, Newcome, Newcombe,
Neucomb, Neucombe, Neucom,
Neucome*

Newlin (Welsh) From the new pond
Newlinn, Newlyn, Newlynn, Neulin, Neulinn, Neulyn, Neulynn

Newman (English) A new-comer
Newmann, Neuman, Neumann

Nhat (Vietnamese) Having a long life
Nhatt, Nhate, Nhatte

Niaz (Persian) A gift
Nyaz

Nibaw (Native American) One who stands tall
Nybaw, Nibau, Nybau

^*Nicholas** (Greek) Of the victorious people
Nick, Nicanor, Niccolo, Nichol, Nicholai, Nicholaus, Nikolai, Nicholl, Nichols, Colin, Nicolas, **Nico**

Nick (English) Form of Nicholas, meaning "of the victorious people"
Nik, Nicki, Nickie, Nickey, Nicky, Nickee, Nickea, Niki

Nickler (American) One who is swift
Nikler, Nicler, Nyckler, Nykler, Nycler

Nicomedes (Greek) One who thinks of victory
Nikomedes, Nicomedo, Nikomedo

Nihal (Indian) One who is content
Neehal, Neihal, Niehal, Neahal, Neyhal, Nyhal

Nihar (Indian) Covered with the morning's dew
Neehar, Niehar, Neihar, Neahar, Nyhar

Nikan (Persian) One who brings good things
Niken, Nikin, Nikyn, Nikon, Nikun

Nikshep (Indian) One who is treasured
Nykshep

Nikunja (Indian) From the grove of trees

Nino (Italian / Spanish) God is gracious / a young boy
Ninoshka

Nirad (Indian) Of the clouds
Nyrad

Niran (Thai) The eternal one
Nyran, Niren, Nirin, Niryn, Niron, Nirun, Nyren, Nyrin

Nirav (Indian) One who is quiet
Nyrav

Nirbheet (Indian) A fearless man
Nirbhit, Nirbhyt, Nirbhay, Nirbhaye, Nirbhai, Nirbhae

Niremaan (Arabic) One who shines as brightly as fire
Nyremaan, Nireman, Nyreman

Nishan (Armenian) A sign or symbol

Nishok (Indian) Filled with happiness
Nyshok, Nishock, Nyshock

Nissan (Hebrew) A miracle child
Nisan

Niyol (Native American) Of the wind

Njord (Scandinavian) A man from the north
Njorde, Njorth, Njorthe

*Noah (Hebrew) A peaceful wanderer
Noa

Nodin (Native American) Of the wind
Nodyn, Noden, Nodan, Nodon, Nodun

*Nolan (Gaelic) A famous and noble man; a champion of the people
Nolen, Nolin, Nolon, Nolun, Nolyn, Noland, Nolande

North (English) A man from the north
Northe

Northcliff (English) From the northern cliff
Northcliffe, Northclyf, Northclyff, Northclyffe

Norval (Scottish) From the northern valley
Norvall, Norvale, Norvail, Norvaile, Norvayl, Norvayle, Norvael, Norvaele

Norward (English) A guardian of the north
Norwarde, Norwerd, Norwerde, Norwurd, Norwurde

Noshi (Native American) A fatherly man
Noshie, Noshy, Noshey, Noshee, Noshea, Nosh, Noshe

Notaku (Native American) Resembling a growling bear
Notakou, Notakue, Notakoo

Nuhad (Arabic) A brave young man
Nuehad, Nouhad, Neuhad

Nukpana (Native American) An evil man
Nukpanah, Nukpanna, Nukpannah, Nuckpana, Nucpana

Nulte (Irish) A man from Ulster
Nulti, Nultie, Nulty, Nultey, Nultee, Nultea

Nuncio (Spanish) A messenger
Nunzio

Nuriel (Hebrew) God's light
Nuriell, Nuriele, Nurielle, Nuryel, Nuryell, Nuryele, Nuryelle, Nooriel

Nuru (African) My light
Nurue, Nuroo, Nurou, Nourou, Nooroo

Nyack (African) One who is persistent
Niack, Nyak, Niak, Nyac, Niac

Nye (English) One who lives on the island
Nyle, Nie, Nile

O

Obedience (American) A well-behaved man
Obediance, Obedyence, Obedeynce

Oberon (German) A royal bear; having the heart of a bear
Oberron

Obert (German) A wealthy and bright man
Oberte, Oberth, Oberthe, Odbart, Odbarte, Odbarth, Odbarthe, Odhert

Ochi (African) Filled with laughter
Ochie, Ochee, Ochea, Ochy, Ochey

Odam (English) A son-in-law
Odom, Odem, Odum

Ode (Egyptian / Greek) Traveler of the road / a lyric poem

Oded (Hebrew) One who is supportive and encouraging

Oder (English) From the river
Odar, Odir, Odyr, Odur

Odin (Norse) In mythology, the supreme deity
Odyn, Odon, Oden, Odun

Odinan (Hungarian) One who is wealthy and powerful
Odynan, Odinann, Odynann

Odion (African) The first-born of twins
Odiyon, Odiun, Odiyun

Odissan (African) A wanderer; traveler
Odyssan, Odisan, Odysan, Odissann, Odyssann, Odisann, Odysann

Ofir (Hebrew) The golden son
Ofeer, Ofear, Ofyr, Ofier, Ofeir, Ofer

Ogaleesha (Native American) A man wearing a red shirt
Ogaleasha, Ogaleisha, Ogaleysha, Ogalesha, Ogaliesha, Ogalisha

Oghe (Irish) One who rides horses
Oghi, Oghie, Oghee, Oghea, Oghy, Oghey

Oguz (Hungarian) An arrow
Oguze, Oguzz, Oguzze

Ohanko (Native American) A reckless man
Ohankio, Ohankiyo

Ojaswit (Indian) A powerful and radiant man
Ojaswyt, Ojaswin, Ojaswen, Ojaswyn, Ojas

Okal (African) To cross
Okall

Okan (Turkish) Resembling a horse
Oken, Okin, Okyn

Okapi (African) Resembling an animal with a long neck
Okapie, Okapy, Okapey, Okapee, Okapea, Okape

Okechuku (African) Blessed by God

Oki (Japanese) From the center of the ocean
Okie, Oky, Okey, Okee, Okea

Oklahoma (Native American) Of the red people; from the state of Oklahoma

Oktawian (African) The eighth-born child
Oktawyan, Oktawean, Octawian, Octawyan, Octawean

Olaf (Scandinavian) The remaining of the ancestors
Olay, Ole, Olef, Olev, Oluf, Uolevi

Olafemi (African) A lucky young man
Olafemie, Olafemy, Olafemey, Olafemee, Olafemea

Oleg (Russian) One who is holy
Olezka

*Oliver (Latin) From the olive tree
Oliviero, Olivero, Olivier, Oliviero, Olivio, Ollie

Olney (English) From the loner's field
Olny, Olnee, Olnea, Olni, Olnie, Ollaneg, Olaneg

Olujimi (African) One who is close to God
Olujimie, Olujimy, Olujimey, Olujimee, Olujimea

Olumide (African) God has arrived
Olumidi, Olumidie, Olumidy, Olumidey, Olumidee, Olumidea, Olumyde, Olumydi

Omar (Arabic) A flourishing man; one who is well-spoken
Omarr, Omer

Omeet (Hebrew) My light
Omeete, Omeit, Omeite, Omeyt, Omeyte, Omit, Omeat, Omeate

Omega (Greek) The last great one; the last letter of the Greek alphabet
Omegah

Onaona (Hawaiian) Having a pleasant scent

Ond (Hungarian) The tenth-born child
Onde

Ondrej (Czech) A manly man
Ondrejek, Ondrejec, Ondrousek, Ondravsek

Onkar (Indian) The purest one
Onckar, Oncar, Onkarr, Onckarr, Oncarr

Onofrio (Italian) A defender of peace
Onofre, Onofrius, Onophrio, Onophre, Onfrio, Onfroi

Onslow (Arabic) From the hill of the enthusiast
Onslowe, Ounslow, Ounslowe

Onyebuchi (African) God is in everything
Onyebuchie, Onyebuchy, Onyebuchey, Onyebuchee, Onyebuchea

Oqwapi (Native American) Resembling a red cloud
Oqwapie, Oqwapy, Oqwapey, Oqwapee, Oqwapea

Oram (English) From the enclosure near the riverbank
Oramm, Oraham, Orahamm, Orham, Orhamm

Ordell (Latin) Of the beginning
Ordel, Ordele, Ordelle, Orde

Ordway (Anglo-Saxon) A fighter armed with a spear
Ordwaye, Ordwai, Ordwae

Oren (Hebrew / Gaelic) From the pine tree / a pale-skinned man
Orenthiel, Orenthiell, Orenthiele, Orenthielle, Orenthiem, Orenthium, Orin

Orion (Greek) A great hunter

Orleans (Latin) The golden child
Orlean, Orleane, Orleens, Orleen, Orleene, Orlins, Olryns, Orlin

Orly (Hebrew) Surrounded by light
Orley, Orli, Orlie, Orlee, Orleigh, Orlea

Ormod (Anglo-Saxon) A sorrowful man

Ormond (English) One who defends with a spear / from the mountain of bears
Ormonde, Ormund, Ormunde, Ormemund, Ormemond, Ordmund, Ordmunde, Ordmond

Ornice (Irish / Hebrew) A pale-skinned man / from the cedar tree
Ornyce, Ornise, Orynse, Orneice, Orneise, Orniece, Orniese, Orneece

Orris (Latin) One who is inventive
Orriss, Orrisse, Orrys, Orryss, Orrysse

Orson (Latin) Resembling a bear; raised by a bear
Orsen, Orsin, Orsini, Orsino, Orsis, Orsonio, Orsinie, Orsiny

Orth (English) An honest man
Orthe

Orton (English) From the settlement by the shore
Ortun, Oraton, Oratun

Orville (French) From the gold town
Orvell, Orvelle, Orvil, Orvill, Orvele, Orvyll, Orvylle, Orvyl

Orwel (Welsh) Of the horizon
Orwell, Orwele, Orwelle

Os (English) The divine

Osborn (Norse) A bear of God
Osborne, Osbourn, Osbourne, Osburn, Osburne

Oscar (English / Gaelic) A spear of the gods / a friend of deer
Oskar, Osker, Oscer, Osckar, Oscker, Oszkar, Oszcar

Osher (Hebrew) A man of good fortune

Osias (Greek) Salvation
Osyas

Osileani (Polynesian) One who talks a lot
Osileanie, Osileany, Osileaney, Osileanee, Osileanea

Oswald (English) The power of God
Oswalde, Osvald, Osvaldo, Oswaldo, Oswell, Osvalde, Oswallt, Osweald

Oswin (English) A friend of God
Oswinn, Oswinne, Oswen, Oswenn, Oswenne, Oswyn, Oswynn, Oswynne

Othniel (Hebrew) God's lion
Othniell, Othnielle, Othniele, Othnyel, Othnyell, Othnyele, Othnyelle

Otmar (Teutonic) A famous warrior
Otmarr, Othmar, Othmarr, Otomar, Ottomar

Otoahhastis (Native American) Resembling a tall bull

Ottokar (German) A spirited warrior
Otokar, Otokarr, Ottokarr, Ottokars, Otokars, Ottocar, Otocar, Ottocars

Ouray (Native American) The arrow
Ouraye, Ourae, Ourai

Ourson (French) Resembling a little bear
Oursun, Oursoun, Oursen, Oursan, Oursin, Oursyn

Ovid (Latin) A shepherd; an egg
Ovyd, Ovidio, Ovido, Ovydio, Ovydo, Ovidiu, Ovydiu, Ofydd

*****Owen** (Welsh / Gaelic) Form of Eugene, meaning "a well-born man" / a youthful man
Owenn, Owenne, Owin, Owinn, Owinne, Owyn, Owynn, Owynne

Oxton (English) From the oxen town
Oxtun, Oxtown, Oxnaton, Oxnatun, Oxnatown

Oz (Hebrew) Having great strength
Ozz, Ozzi, Ozzie, Ozzy, Ozzey, Ozzee, Ozzea, Ozi

Ozni (Hebrew) One who knows God
Oznie, Ozny, Ozney, Oznee, Oznea

Ozuru (Japanese) Resembling a stork
Ozurou, Ozourou, Ozuroo, Ozooroo

P

Paavo (Finnish) Form of Paul, meaning "a small or humble man"
Paaveli

Pace (Hebrew / English) Refers to Passover / a peaceful man
Paice, Payce, Paece, Pacey, Pacy, Pacee, Paci, Pacie

Pacho (Spanish) An independent man; one who is free

Pachu'a (Native American) Resembling a water snake

Paco (Spanish) A man from France
Pacorro, Pacoro, Paquito

Padgett (French) One who strives to better himself
Padget, Padgette, Padgete, Padgeta, Padgetta, Padge, Paget, Pagett

Padman (Indian) Resembling the lotus
Padmann

Padruig (Scottish) Of the royal family

Paine (Latin) Man from the country; a peasant
Pain, Payn, Payne, Paen, Paene, Pane, Paien

Palamedes (English) In Arthurian legend, a knight
Palomydes, Palomedes, Palamydes, Palsmedes, Palsmydes, Pslomydes

Palban (Spanish) A blond-haired man
Palben, Palbin, Palbyn, Palbon, Palbun

Paley (English) Form of Paul, meaning "a small or humble man"
Paly, Pali, Palie, Palee, Palea

Palladin (Greek) Filled with wisdom
Palladyn, Palladen, Palladan, Paladin, Paladyn, Paladen, Paladan

Palmer (English) A pilgrim bearing a palm branch
Pallmer, Palmar, Pallmar, Palmerston, Palmiro, Palmeero, Palmeer, Palmire

Pan (Greek) In mythology, god of the shepherds
Pann

Panama (Spanish) From the canal

Pancho (Spanish) A man from France

Pankaj (Indian) Resembling the lotus flower

Panya (African) Resembling a mouse
Panyah

Panyin (African) The first-born of twins
Panyen

Paras (Hindi) A touchstone
Parasmani, Parasmanie, Parasmany, Parasmaney, Parasmanee

*****Parker** (English) The keeper of the park
Parkar, Parkes, Parkman, Park

Parley (Scottish) A reluctant man
Parly, Parli, Parlie, Parlee, Parlea, Parle

Parmenio (Spanish) A studious man; one who is intelligent
Parmenios, Parmenius

Parounag (Armenian) One who is thankful

Parrish (Latin) Man of the church
Parish, Parrishe, Parishe, Parrysh, Parysh, Paryshe, Parryshe, Parisch

Parry (Welsh) The son of Harry
Parrey, Parri, Parrie, Parree, Parrea

Parthenios (Greek) One who is pure; chaste
Parthenius

Parthik (Greek) One who is pure; chaste
Parthyk, Parthick, Parthyck, Parthic, Parthyc

Pascal (Latin) Born during Easter
Pascale, Pascalle, Paschal, Paschalis, Pascoe, Pascual, Pascuale, Pasqual

Patamon (Native American) Resembling a tempest
Patamun, Patamen, Pataman, Patamyn, Patamin

Patch (American) Form of Peter, meaning "as solid and strong as a rock"
Pach, Patche, Patchi, Patchie, Patchy, Patchey, Patchee

Patrick (Latin) A nobleman; patrician
Packey, Padric, Pat, Patrece, Patric, Patrice, Patreece, Patricio

Patton (English) From the town of warriors
Paten, Patin, Paton, Patten, Pattin, Paddon, Padden, Paddin

Patwin (Native American) A manly man
Patwinn, Patwinne, Patwyn, Patwynne, Patwynn, Patwen, Patwenn, Patwenne

Paul (Latin) A small or humble man
Pauley, Paulie, Pauly, Paley, Paavo

Paurush (Indian) A courageous man
Paurushe, Paurushi, Paurushie, Paurushy, Paurushey, Paurushee

Pavanjit (Indian) Resembling the wind
Pavanjyt, Pavanjeet, Pavanjeat, Pavanjete

Paxton (English) From the peaceful town
Packston, Paxon, Paxten, Paxtun, Packstun, Packsten

Pazel (Hebrew) God's gold; treasured by God
Pazell, Pazele, Pazelle

Pearroc (English) Man of the forest
Pearoc, Pearrok, Pearok, Pearrock, Pearock

Pecos (American) From the river; a cowboy
Pekos, Peckos

Pedro (Spanish) Form of Peter, meaning "as solid and strong as a rock"
Pedrio, Pepe, Petrolino, Piero, Pietro

Pelham (English) From the house of furs; from Peola's home
Pellham, Pelam, Pellam

Pell (English) A clerk or one who works with skins
Pelle, Pall, Palle

Pelon (Spanish) Filled with joy
Pellon

Pelton (English) From the town by the lake
Pellton, Peltun, Pelltun, Peltan, Pelltan, Pelten, Pellten, Peltin

Penda (African) One who is dearly loved
Pendah, Penha, Penhah

Penley (English) From the enclosed meadow
Penly, Penleigh, Penli, Penlie, Penlee, Penlea, Penleah, Pennley

Penrod (German) A respected commander

Pentele (Hungarian) A merciful man
Pentelle, Pentel, Pentell

Penuel (Hebrew) The face of God
Penuell, Penuele, Penuelle

Percival (French) One who can pierce the vale"
Purcival, Percy, Percey, Perci, Percie, Percee, Percea, Persy, Persey, Persi

Peregrine (Latin) One who travels; a wanderer
Perry, Perree, Perrea, Perri, Perrie, Perregrino

Perez (Hebrew) To break through
Peretz

Pericles (Greek) One who is in excess of glory
Perricles, Perycles, Perrycles, Periclees, Perriclees, Peryclees, Perryclees, Periclez

Perk (American) One who is cheerful and jaunty
Perke, Perky, Perkey, Perki, Perkie, Perkee, Perkea

Perkinson (English) The son of Perkin; the son of Peter
Perkynson

Perseus (Greek) In mythology, son of Zeus who slew Medusa
Persius, Persyus, Persies, Persyes

Perth (Celtic) From the thorny thicket
Perthe, Pert, Perte

Perye (English) From the pear tree

Peter (Greek) As solid and strong as a rock
Peder, Pekka, Per, Petar, Pete, Peterson, Petr, Petre, Pierce, Patch, Pedro

Petuel (Hindi) The Lord's vision
Petuell, Petuele, Petuelle

Peyton (English) From the village of warriors
Payton, Peytun, Paytun, Peyten, Payten, Paiton, Paitun, Paiten

Pharis (Irish) A heroic man
Pharys, Pharris, Pharrys

Phex (American) A kind man
Phexx

Philemon (Hebrew) A loving man
Phylemon, Philimon, Phylimon, Philomon, Phylomon, Philamon, Phylamon

Philetus (Greek) A collector
Phyletus, Philetos, Phyletos

Phillip (Greek) One who loves horses
Phil, Philip, Felipe, Filipp, Phillie, Philly

Philo (Greek) One who loves and is loved

Phoebus (Greek) A radiant man
Phoibos

Phomello (African) A successful man
Phomelo

Phong (Vietnamese) Of the wind

Phuc (Vietnamese) One who is blessed
Phuoc

Picardus (Hispanic) An adventurous man
Pycardus, Picardos, Pycardos, Picardas, Pycardas, Picardis, Pycardis, Picardys

Pickworth (English) From the woodcutter's estate
Pikworth, Picworth, Pickworthe, Pikworthe, Picworthe

Pierce (English) Form of Peter, meaning "as solid and strong as a rock"
Pearce, Pears, Pearson, Pearsson, Peerce, Peirce, Pierson, Piersson

Pin (Vietnamese) Filled with joy
Pyn

Pio (Latin) A pious man
Pyo, Pios, Pius, Pyos, Pyus

Pirro (Greek) A red-haired man
Pyrro

Pitney (English) From the island of the stubborn man
Pitny, Pitni, Pitnie, Pitnee, Pitnea, Pytney, Pytny, Pytni

Pittman (English) A laborer
Pyttman, Pitman, Pytman

Plantagenet (French) Resembling the broom flower

Poetry (American) A romantic man
Poetrey, Poetri, Poetrie, Poetree, Poetrea, Poet, Poete

Pollux (Greek) One who is crowned
Pollock, Pollok, Polloc, Pollack, Polloch

Polo (African) Resembling an alligator
Poloe, Poloh

Ponce (Spanish) The fifth-born child
Ponse

Pongor (Hungarian) A mighty man
Pongorr, Pongoro, Pongorro

Poni (African) The second-born son
Ponni, Ponie, Ponnie, Pony, Ponny, Poney, Ponney, Ponee

Pons (Latin) From the bridge
Pontius, Ponthos, Ponthus

Poornamruth (Indian) Full of sweetness
Pournamruth

Poornayu (Indian) Full of life; blessed with a full life
Pournayu, Poornayou, Pournayou, Poornayue, Pournayue

Porat (Hebrew) A productive man

Porfirio (Greek) Refers to a purple coloring
Porphirios, Prophyrios, Porfiro, Porphyrios

Powhatan (Native American) From the chief's hill

Prabhakar (Hindu) Of the sun

Prabhat (Indian) Born during the morning

Pragun (Indian) One who is straightforward; honest

Pramod (Indian) A delightful young man

Pranit (Indian) One who is humble; modest
Pranyt, Praneet, Praneat

Prasad (Indian) A gift from God

Prashant (Indian) One who is peaceful; calm
Prashante, Prashanth, Prashanthe

Pratap (Hindi) A majestic man

Pravat (Thai) History

Prem (Indian) An affectionate man

Prentice (English) A student; an apprentice
Prentyce, Prentise, Prentyse, Prentiss, Prentis

Prescott (English) From the priest's cottage
Prescot, Prestcot, Prestcott, Preostcot

Preston (English) From the priest's town
Prestin, Prestyn, Prestan, Prestun, Presten, Pfeostun

Prewitt (French) A brave young one
Prewet, Prewett, Prewit, Pruitt, Pruit, Pruet, Pruett

Prine (English) One who surpasses others
Pryne

Prometheus (Greek) In mythology, he stole fire from the heavens and gave it to man
Promitheus, Promethius, Promithius

Prop (American) A fun-loving man
Propp, Proppe

Prosper (Latin) A fortunate man
Prospero, Prosperus

Pryderi (Celtic) Son of the sea
Pryderie, Prydery, Pryderey, Pryderee, Pryderea

Prydwen (Welsh) A handsome man
Prydwenn, Prydwenne, Prydwin, Prydwinne, Prydwinn, Prydwyn, Prydwynn, Prydwynne

Pullman (English) One who works on a train
Pulman, Pullmann, Pulmann

Pyralis (Greek) Born of fire
Pyraliss, Pyralisse, Pyralys, Pyralyss, Pyralysse, Pyre

Q

Qabil (Arabic) An able-bodied man
Qabyl, Qabeel, Qabeal, Qabeil, Qabiel

Qadim (Arabic) From an ancient family
Qadeem, Qadiem, Qadeim, Qadym, Qadeam

Qaiser (Arabic) A king; a ruler
Qeyser

Qamar (Arabic) Born beneath the moon
Qamarr, Quamar, Quamarr

Qimat (Hindi) A highly valued man
Qymat

Qing (Chinese) Of the deep water
Qyng

Quaashie (American) An ambitious man
Quashie, Quashi, Quashy, Quashey, Quashee, Quashea, Quaashi, Quaashy

Quaddus (American) A bright man
Quadus, Quaddos, Quados

Quade (Latin) The fourth-born child
Quadrees, Quadres, Quadrys, Quadries, Quadreis, Quadreys, Quadreas, Quadrhys

Quaid (Irish) Form of Walter, meaning "the commander of the army"
Quaide, Quayd, Quayde, Quaed, Quaede

Quashawn (American) A tenacious man
Quashaun, Quasean, Quashon, Quashi, Quashie, Quashee, Quashea, Quashy

Qued (Native American) Wearing a decorated robe

Quentin (Latin) The fifth-born child
Quent, Quenten, Quenton, Quentun, Quentan, Quentyn, Quente, Qwentin

Quick (American) One who is fast; a witty man
Quik, Quicke, Quic

Quillan (Gaelic) Resembling a cub
Quilan, Quillen, Quilen, Quillon, Quilon

Quilliam (Gaelic) Form of William, meaning "the determined protector"
Quilhelm, Quilhelmus, Quilliams, Quilliamson

Quimby (Norse) From the woman's estate
Quimbey, Quimbee, Quimbea, Quimbi, Quimbie

Quincy (English) The fifth-born child; from the fifth son's estate
Quincey, Quinci, Quincie, Quincee, Quinncy, Quinnci, Quyncy, Quyncey

Quinlan (Gaelic) A strong and healthy man
Quindlan, Quinlen, Quindlen, Quinian, Quinlin, Quindlin, Quinlyn, Quindlyn

Quinn (Gaelic) One who provides counsel; an intelligent man
Quin, Quinne, Qwinn, Quynn, Qwin, Quiyn, Quyn, Qwinne

Quintavius (American) The fifth-born child
Quintavios, Quintavus, Quintavies

Quinto (Spanish) The fifth-born child
Quynto, Quintus, Quintos, Quinty, Quinti, Quintie

Quinton (Latin) From the queen's town or settlement
Laquinton

Quintrell (English) An elegant and dashing man
Quintrel, Quintrelle, Quyntrell, Quyntrelle, Quyntrel, Quyntrele, Quintrele

Quirinus (Latin) One who wields a spear
Quirinos, Quirynus, Quirynos, Quirinius, Quirynius

Quito (Spanish) A lively man
Quyto, Quitos, Quytos

Quoc (Vietnamese) A patriot
Quok, Quock

Qutub (Indian) One who is tall

R

Rabbaanee (African) An easy-going man

Rabbi (Hebrew) The master

Rach (African) Resembling a frog

Radames (Egyptian) A hero
Radamays, Radamayes, Radamais, Radamaise

Radford (English) From the red ford
Radforde, Radferd, Radfurd, Radferde, Radfurde

Rafael (Spanish) Form of Raphael, meaning "one who is healed by God"
Raphael, Raphaello, Rafaello

Rafe (Irish) A tough man
Raffe, Raff, Raf, Raif, Rayfe, Raife, Raef, Raefe

Rafi (Arabic) One who is exalted
Rafie, Rafy, Rafey, Rafea, Rafee, Raffi, Raffie, Raffy

Rafiki (African) A gentle friend
Rafikie, Rafikea, Rafikee, Rafiky, Rafikey

Rafiya (African) A dignified man
Rafeeya, Rafeaya, Rafeiya, Rafieya

Raghib (Arabic) One who is desired
Ragheb, Ragheeb, Ragheab, Raghyb, Ragheib, Raghieb

Ragnar (Norse) A warrior who places judgment
Ragnor, Ragner, Ragnir, Ragnyr, Ragnur, Regnar

Rahim (Arabic) A compassionate man
Rahym, Raheim, Rahiem, Raheem, Raheam

Raiden (Japanese) In mythology, the god of thunder and lightning
Raidon, Rayden, Raydon, Raeden, Raedon, Raden

Raimi (African) A compassionate man
Raimie, Raimy, Raimey, Raimee, Raimea

Rajab (African) A glorified man

Rajan (Indian) A king
Raj, Raja, Rajah

Rajarshi (Indian) The king's sage
Rajarshie, Rajarshy, Rajarshey, Rajarshee, Rajarshea

Rajesh (Hindi) The king's rule

Rajit (Indian) One who is decorated
Rajeet, Rajeit, Rajiet, Rajyt, Rajeat

Rajiv (Hindi) To be striped
Rajyv, Rajeev, Rajeav

Ralph (English) Wolf counsel
Ralf, Ralphe, Ralfe, Ralphi, Ralphie, Ralphee, Ralphea, Ralphy, Raoul

Ram (Hebrew / Sanskrit) A superior man / one who is pleasing
Rahm, Rama, Rahma, Ramos, Rahmos, Ramm

Rambert (German) Having great strength; an intelligent man
Ramberte, Ramberth, Ramberthe, Ramburt

Rami (Arabic) A loving man
Ramee, Ramea, Ramie, Ramy, Ramey

Ramiro (Portuguese) A famous counselor; a great judge
Ramyro, Rameero, Rameyro, Ramirez, Ramyrez, Rameerez

Ramsey (English) From the raven island; from the island of wild garlic
Ramsay, Ramsie, Ramsi, Ramsee, Ramsy, Ramsea, Ramzy, Ramzey

Rand (German) One who shields others
Rande

Randall (German) The wolf shield
Randy, Randal, Randale, Randel, Randell, Randl, Randle, Randon, Rendall

Randolph (German) The wolf shield
Randy, Randolf, Ranolf, Ranolph, Ranulfo, Randulfo, Randwulf, Ranwulf, Randwolf

Randy (English) Form of Randall or Randolph, meaning "the wolf shield"
Randey, Randi, Randie, Randee, Randea

Rang (English) Resembling a raven
Range

Rangey (English) From raven's island
Rangy, Rangi, Rangie, Rangee, Rangea

Rangle (American) A cowboy
Rangel

Ranjan (Indian) A delightful boy

Raoul (French) Form of Ralph, meaning "wolf counsel"
Raoule, Raul, Roul, Rowl, Raule, Roule, Rowle

Raqib (Arabic) A glorified man
Raqyb, Raqeeb, Raqeab, Rakib, Rakeeb, Rakeab, Rakyb

Rashard (American) A good-hearted man
Rasherd, Rashird, Rashurd, Rashyrd

Rashaun (American) Form of Roshan, meaning "born during the daylight"
Rashae, Rashane, Rashawn, Rayshaun, Rayshawn, Raishaun, Raishawn, Raeshaun

Ratul (Indian) A sweet man
Ratule, Ratoul, Ratoule, Ratool, Ratoole

Raulo (Spanish) One who is wise
Rawlo

Ravi (Hindi) From the sun
Ravie, Ravy, Ravey, Ravee, Ravea

Ravid (Hebrew) A wanderer; one who searches
Ravyd, Raveed, Ravead, Raviyd, Ravied, Raveid

Ravindra (Indian) The strength of the sun
Ravyndra

Ravinger (English) One who lives near the ravine
Ravynger

Rawlins (French) From the renowned land
Rawlin, Rawson, Rawlinson, Rawlings, Rawling, Rawls, Rawl, Rawle

Ray (English) Form of Raymond, meaning "a wise protector"
Rae, Rai, Rayce, Rayder, Rayse, Raye, Rayford, Raylen

Rayfield (English) From the field of roe deer
Rayfeld

Rayhurn (English) From the roe deer's stream
Rayhurne, Rayhorn, Rayhorne, Rayhourn, Rayhourne

Raymond (German) A wise protector
Ray, Raemond, Raemondo, Raimond, Raimondo, Raimund, Raimundo, Rajmund, Ramon

Rebel (American) An outlaw
Rebell, Rebele, Rebelle, Rebe, Rebbe, Rebbi, Rebbie, Rebbea

Redwald (English) Strong counsel
Redwalde, Raedwalde, Raedwald

Reeve (English) A bailiff
Reve, Reave, Reeford, Reeves, Reaves, Reves, Reaford

Regal (American) Born into royalty
Regall

Regan (Gaelic) Born into royalty; the little ruler
Raegan, Ragan, Raygan, Reganne, Regann, Regane, Reghan, Reagan

Regenfrithu (English) A peaceful raven

Reggie (Latin) Form of Reginald, meaning "the king's advisor"
Reggi, Reggy, Reggey, Reggea, Reggee, Reg

Reginald (Latin) The king's advisor
Reggie, Reynold, Raghnall, Rainault, Rainhold, Raonull, Raynald, Rayniero, Regin, Reginaldo

Regine (French) One who is artistic
Regeen, Regeene, Regean, Regeane, Regein, Regeine, Regien, Regiene

^**Reid** (English) A red-haired man; one who lives near the reeds
Read, Reade, Reed, Reede, Reide, Raed

Reilly (Gaelic) An outgoing man
Reilley, Reilli, Reillie, Reillee, Reilleigh, Reillea

^**Remington** (English) From
the town of the raven's family
*Remyngton, Remingtun,
Remyngtun*

Renweard (Anglo-Saxon) The
guardian of the house
Renward, Renwarden, Renwerd

Renzo (Japanese) The third-
born son

Reuben (Hebrew) Behold, a
son!
*Reuban, Reubin, Reuven,
Rouvin, Rube, Ruben, Rubin,
Rubino*

Rev (American) One who is
distinct
*Revv, Revin, Reven, Revan,
Revyn, Revon, Revun*

Rex (Latin) A king
Reks, Recks, Rexs

Rexford (English) From the
king's ford
*Rexforde, Rexferd, Rexferde,
Rexfurd, Rexfurde*

Reynold (English) Form of
Reginald, meaning "the
king's advisor"
*Reynald, Reynaldo, Reynolds,
Reynalde, Reynolde*

Rhett (Latin) A well-spoken
man
Rett, Rhet

^**Rhys** (Welsh) Having great
enthusiasm for life

Richard (English) A powerful
ruler
*Rick, Rich, Ricard, Ricardo,
Riccardo, Richardo, Richart,
Richerd, Rickard, Rickert*

Richmond (French / German)
From the wealthy hill / a
powerful protector
*Richmonde, Richmund,
Richmunde*

Rick (English) Form of
Richard, meaning "a powerful
ruler"
*Ric, Ricci, Ricco, Rickie, Ricki,
Ricky, Rico, Rik*

Rickward (English) A strong
protector
*Rickwerd, Rickwood, Rikward,
Ricward, Rickweard, Rikweard,
Ricweard*

Riddock (Irish) From the
smooth field
*Ridock, Riddoc, Ridoc,
Ryddock, Rydock, Ryddoc,
Rydoc, Ryddok*

Ridgeway (English) One who
lives on the road near the
ridge
Rydgeway, Rigeway, Rygeway

Rigg (English) One who lives near the ridge
Rig, Ridge, Rygg, Ryg, Rydge, Rige, Ryge, Riggs

Riley (English) From the rye clearing
Ryly, Ryli, Rylie, Rylee, Ryleigh, Rylea, Ryleah

Riordain (Irish) A bright man
Riordane, Riordayn, Riordaen, Reardain, Reardane, Reardayn, Reardaen

Riordan (Gaelic) A royal poet; a bard or minstrel
Riorden, Rearden, Reardan, Riordon, Reardon

Ripley (English) From the noisy meadow
Riply, Ripleigh, Ripli, Riplie, Riplea, Ripleah, Riplee, Rip

Rishley (English) From the untamed meadow
Rishly, Rishli, Rishlie, Rishlee, Rishlea, Rishleah, Rishleigh

Rishon (Hebrew) The first-born son
Ryshon, Rishi, Rishie, Rishea, Rishee, Rishy, Rishey

Risley (English) From the brushwood meadow
Risly, Risli, Rislie, Risleigh, Rislea, Risleah, Rislee

Riston (English) From the brushwood settlement
Ryston, Ristun, Rystun

Ritter (German) A knight
Rytter, Ritt, Rytt

River (American) From the river
Ryver, Rivers, Ryvers

Roald (Norse) A famous ruler
Roal

Roam (American) One who wanders, searches
Roami, Roamie, Roamy, Roamey, Roamea, Roamee

Roark (Gaelic) A champion
Roarke, Rorke, Rourke, Rork, Rourk, Ruark, Ruarke

*****Robert** (German) One who is bright with fame
Bob, Rupert, Riobard, Roban, Robers, Roberto, Robertson, Robartach

Rochester (English) From the stone fortress

Rockford (English) From the rocky ford
Rockforde, Rokford, Rokforde, Rockferd, Rokferd, Rockfurd, Rokfurd

Roderick (German) A famous
ruler
*Rod, Rodd, Roddi, Roddie,
Roddy, Roddee, Roddea*

Rodney (German / English)
From the famous one's island /
from the island's clearing
Rodny, Rodni, Rodnie

Rogelio (Spanish) A famous
soldier
*Rogelo, Rogeliyo, Rogeleo,
Rogeleyo, Rojelio, Rojeleo*

Roland (German) From the
renowned land
*Roeland, Rolando, Roldan,
Roley, Rollan, Rolland, Rollie,
Rollin*

Roman (Latin) A citizen of
Rome
Romain, Romaine, Romeo

Romeo (Italian) Traveler to
Rome

Ronald (Norse) The king's
advisor
*Ranald, Renaldo, Ronal,
Ronaldo, Rondale, Roneld,
Ronell, Ronello*

^**Ronan** (Gaelic) Resembling a
little seal

Rong (Chinese) Having glory

Rook (English) Resembling a
raven
Rooke, Rouk, Rouke, Ruck, Ruk

Rooney (Gaelic) A red-haired
man
*Roony, Rooni, Roonie, Roonea,
Roonee, Roon, Roone*

Roosevelt (Danish) From the
field of roses
Rosevelt

Roper (English) One who
makes rope
Rapere

Rory (Gaelic) A red-haired
man
*Rori, Rorey, Rorie, Rorea,
Roree, Rorry, Rorrey, Rorri*

Roshan (Hindi) Born during
the daylight
Rashaun

Roslin (Gaelic) A little red-
haired boy
*Roslyn, Rosselin, Rosslyn,
Rozlin, Rozlyn, Rosling,
Rozling*

Roswald (German) Of the
mighty horses
Rosswald, Roswalt, Rosswalt

Roswell (English) A fascinat-
ing man
*Rosswell, Rozwell, Roswel,
Rozwel*

Roth (German) A red-haired
man
Rothe

Rousseau (French) A little red-
haired boy
*Roussell, Russo, Rousse,
Roussel, Rousset, Rousskin*

Rowdy (English) A boisterous
man
*Rowdey, Rowdi, Rowdie,
Rowdee, Rowdea*

Roy (Gaelic / French) A red-
haired man / a king
Roye, Roi, Royer, Ruy

Royce (German / French) A
famous man / son of the king
Roice, Royse, Roise

Ruadhan (Irish) A red-haired
man; the name of a saint
*Ruadan, Ruadhagan,
Ruadagan*

Ruarc (Irish) A famous ruler
*Ruarck, Ruarcc, Ruark,
Ruarkk, Ruaidhri, Ruaidri*

Rubio (Spanish) Resembling
a ruby

Rudeger (German) A friendly
man
*Rudegar, Rudger, Rudgar,
Rudiger, Rudigar*

Rudolph (German) A famous
wolf
*Rodolfo, Rodolph, Rodolphe,
Rodolpho, Rudy, Rudey, Rudi,
Rudie*

Rudyard (English) From the
red paddock

Rufus (Latin) A red-haired
man
Ruffus, Rufous, Rufino

Ruiz (Spanish) A good friend

Rujul (Indian) An honest man
*Rujool, Rujoole, Rujule, Rujoul,
Rujoule*

Rumford (English) From the
broad ford
*Rumforde, Rumferd, Rumferde,
Rumfurd*

Rupert (English) Form of
Robert, meaning "one who is
bright with fame"
Ruprecht

Rushford (English) From the
ford with rushes
*Rusheford, Rushforde,
Rusheforde, Ryscford*

Russell (French) A little red-
haired boy
*Russel, Roussell, Russ, Rusel,
Rusell*

Russom (African) The chief;
the boss
Rusom, Russome, Rusome

Rusty (English) One who
has red hair or a ruddy
complexion
*Rustey, Rusti, Rustie, Rustee,
Rustea, Rust, Ruste, Rustice*

Rutherford (English) From the
cattle's ford
*Rutherfurd, Rutherferd,
Rutherforde, Rutherfurde*

*Ryan (Gaelic) The little ruler;
little king
*Rian, Rien, Rion, Ryen, Ryon,
Ryun, Rhyan, Rhyen*

Ryder (English) An accom-
plished horseman
*Rider, Ridder, Ryden, Rydell,
Rydder*

Ryker (Danish) Form of
Richard, meaning "a powerful
ruler"
Riker

Rylan (English) Form of
Ryland, meaning "from the
place where rye is grown"
Ryelan, Ryle

^Ryland (English) From the
place where Rye is grown

Saarik (Hindi) Resembling a
small songbird
*Saarick, Saaric, Sarik, Sarick,
Saric, Saariq, Sareek, Sareeq*

Saber (French) Man of the
sword
Sabere, Sabr, Sabre

Sabir (Arabic) One who is
patient
*Sabyr, Sabeer, Sabear, Sabeir,
Sabier, Sabri, Sabrie, Sabree*

Saddam (Arabic) A powerful
ruler; the crusher
Saddum, Saddim, Saddym

Sadiq (Arabic) A beloved
friend
*Sadeeq, Sadyq, Sadeaq, Sadeek,
Sadeak, Sadyk, Sadik*

Saga (American) A storyteller
Sago

Sagar (Indian / English) A
king / one who is wise
Saagar, Sagarr, Saagarr

Sagaz (Spanish) One who is
clever
Sagazz

Sagiv (Hebrew) Having great strength
Sagev, Segiv, Segev

Sahaj (Indian) One who is natural

Saieshwar (Hindi) A well-known saint
Saishwar

Sailor (American) Man who sails the seas
Sailer, Sailar, Saylor, Sayler, Saylar, Saelor

Saith (English) One who is well-spoken
Saithe, Sayth, Saythe, Saeth, Saethe, Sath, Sathe

Sajal (Indian) Resembling a cloud
Sajall, Sajjal, Sajjall

Sajan (Indian) One who is dearly loved
Sajann, Sajjan, Sajjann

Saki (Japanese) One who is cloaked
Sakie, Saky, Sakey, Sakee, Sakea

Salaam (African) Resembling a peach

Salehe (African) A good man
Saleh, Salih

Salim (Arabic) One who is peaceful
Saleem, Salem, Selim

Salute (American) A patriotic man
Saloot, Saloote, Salout

Salvador (Spanish) A savior
Sal, Sally, Salvadore, Xalvador

Samanjas (Indian) One who is proper

Samarth (Indian) A powerful man; one who is efficient
Samarthe

Sameen (Indian) One who is treasured
Samine, Sameene, Samean, Sameane, Samyn, Samyne

Sami (Arabic) One who has been exalted
Samie, Samy, Samey, Samee, Samea

Sammohan (Indian) An attractive man

Sampath (Indian) A wealthy man
Sampathe, Sampat

Samson (Hebrew) As bright as the sun; in the Bible, a man with extraordinary strength
Sampson, Sansom, Sanson, Sansone

*Samuel** (Hebrew) God has heard
Sam, Sammie, Sammy, Samuele, Samuello, Samwell, Samuelo, Sammey

Samuru (Japanese) The name of God

Sandburg (English) From the sandy village
Sandbergh, Sandberg, Sandburgh

Sandon (English) From the sandy hill
Sanden, Sandan, Sandun, Sandyn, Sandin

Sanford (English) From the sandy crossing
Sandford, Sanforde, Sandforde, Sanfurd, Sanfurde, Sandfurd, Sandfurde

Sang (Vietnamese) A bright man
Sange

Sanjiro (Japanese) An admirable man
Sanjyro

Sanjiv (Indian) One who lives a long life
Sanjeev, Sanjyv, Sanjeiv, Sanjiev, Sanjeav, Sanjivan

Sanorelle (American) An honest man
Sanorell, Sanorel, Sanorele

Santana (Spanish) A saintly man
Santanna, Santanah, Santannah, Santa

Santiago (Spanish) Refers to St. James

Santo (Italian) A holy man
Sante, Santino, Santos, Santee, Santi, Santie, Santea, Santy

Sapan (Indian) A dream or vision
Sapann

Sar (Anglo-Saxon) One who inflicts pain
Sarlic, Sarlik

Sarbajit (Indian) The conqueror
Sarbajeet, Sarbajyt, Sarbajeat, Sarbajet, Sarvajit, Sarvajeet, Sarvajyt, Sarvajeat

Sarojin (Hindu) Resembling a lotus
Saroj

Sarosh (Persian) One who prays
Saroshe

Satayu (Hindi) In Hinduism, the brother of Amavasu and Vivasu
Satayoo, Satayou, Satayue

Satoshi (Japanese) Born from the ashes
Satoshie, Satoshy, Satoshey, Satoshee, Satoshea

Satparayan (Indian) A good-natured man

Saturn (Latin) In mythology, the god of agriculture
Saturnin, Saturno, Saturnino

Satyankar (Indian) One who speaks the truth
Satyancar, Satyancker

Saville (French) From the willow town
Savil, Savile, Savill, Savyile, Savylle, Savyle, Sauville, Sauvile

Savir (Indian) A great leader
Savire, Saveer, Saveere, Savear, Saveare, Savyr, Savyre

Sawyer (English) One who works with wood
Sayer, Saer

Saxon (English) A swordsman
Saxen, Saxan, Saxton, Saxten, Saxtan

Sayad (Arabic) An accomplished hunter

Scadwielle (English) From the shed near the spring
Scadwyelle, Scadwiell, Scadwyell, Scadwiel, Scadwyel, Scadwiele, Scadwyele

Scand (Anglo-Saxon) One who is disgraced
Scande, Scandi, Scandie, Scandee, Scandea

Sceotend (Anglo-Saxon) An archer

Schaeffer (German) A steward
Schaffer, Shaeffer, Shaffer, Schaeffur, Schaffur, Shaeffur, Shaffur

Schelde (English) From the river
Shelde

Schneider (German) A tailor
Shneider, Sneider, Snider, Snyder

Schubert (German) One who makes shoes
Shubert, Schuberte, Shuberte, Schubirt, Shubirt, Schuburt, Shuburt

Scirocco (Italian) Of the warm wind
Sirocco, Scyrocco, Syrocco

Scott (English) A man from Scotland
Scot, Scottie, Scotto, Scotty, Scotti, Scottey, Scottee, Scottea

Scowyrhta (Anglo-Saxon) One who makes shoes

Seabury (English) From the village by the sea
Seaburry, Sebury, Seburry, Seaberry, Seabery, Seberry

Seaman (English) A mariner

Sean (Irish) Form of John, meaning "God is gracious"
Shaughn, Shawn, Shaun, Shon, Shohn, Shonn, Shaundre, Shawnel

Seanachan (Irish) One who is wise

Seanan (Hebrew / Irish) A gift from God / an old, wise man
Sinon, Senen, Siobhan

*Sebastian (Greek) The revered one
Sabastian, Seb, Sebastiano, Sebastien, Sebestyen, Sebo, Sebastyn, Sebestyen

Sedgwick (English) From the place of sword grass
Sedgewick, Sedgewyck, Sedgwyck, Sedgewic, Sedgewik, Sedgwic, Sedgwik, Sedgewyc

Seerath (Indian) A great man
Seerathe, Searath, Searathe

Sef (Egyptian) Son of yesterday
Sefe

Seferino (Greek) Of the west wind
Seferio, Sepherino, Sepherio, Seferyno, Sepheryno

Seignour (French) Lord of the house

Selas (African) Refers to the Trinity
Selassi, Selassie, Selassy, Selassey, Selassee, Selassea

Selestino (Spanish) One who is heaven-sent
Selestyno, Selesteeno, Selesteano

Sellers (English) One who dwells in the marshland
Sellars, Sellurs, Sellirs, Sellyrs

Seminole (Native American) A tribal name
Semynole

Seppanen (Finnish) A black-smith
Sepanen, Seppenen, Sepenen, Seppanan, Sepanan

September (American) Born in the month of September
Septimber, Septymber, Septemberia, Septemberea

Septimus (Latin) The seventh-born child
Septymus

Seraphim (Hebrew) The burning ones; heavenly winged angels
Sarafino, Saraph, Serafin, Serafino, Seraph, Seraphimus, Serafim

Sereno (Latin) One who is calm; tranquil

Serfati (Hebrew) A man from France
Sarfati, Serfatie, Sarfatie, Serfaty, Sarfaty, Serfatey, Sarfatey, Serfatee

Sergio (Latin) An attendant; a servant
Seargeoh, Serge, Sergei, Sergeo, Sergey, Sergi, Sergios, Sergiu

Seth (Hebrew) One who has been appointed
Sethe, Seath, Seathe, Zeth

Seung (Korean) A victorious successor

Seven (American) Refers to the number; the seventh-born child
Sevin, Sevyn

Sewati (Native American) Resembling a bear claw
Sewatie, Sewaty, Sewatey, Sewatee, Sewatea

Sexton (English) The church's custodian
Sextun, Sextan, Sextin, Sextyn

Seymour (French) From the French town of Saint Maur
Seamore, Seamor, Seamour, Seymore

Shaan (Hebrew) A peaceful man

Shade (English) A secretive man
Shaid, Shaide, Shayd, Shayde, Shaed, Shaede

Shadi (Persian / Arabic) One who brings happiness and joy / a singer
Shadie, Shady, Shadey

Shadrach (Hebrew) Under the command of the moon god Aku
Shadrack, Shadrick, Shad

Shah (Persian) The king

Shai (Hebrew) A gift from God

Shail (Indian) A mountain rock
Shaile, Shayl, Shayle, Shael, Shaele, Shale

Shaka (African) A tribal leader
Shakah

Shakir (Arabic) One who is grateful
Shakeer, Shaqueer, Shakier, Shakeir, Shakear, Shakar, Shaker, Shakyr

Shane (English) Form of John, meaning "God is gracious"
Shayn, Shayne, Shaine, Shain

Shannon (Gaelic) Having ancient wisdom
Shanan, Shanen, Shannan, Shannen, Shanon

Shardul (Indian) Resembling a tiger
Shardule, Shardull, Shardulle

Shashi (Indian) Of the moonbeam
Shashie, Shashy, Shashey, Shashee, Shashea, Shashhi

Shavon (American) One who is open-minded
Shavaughn, Shavonne, Shavaun, Shovon, Shovonne, Shovaun

Shaw (English) From the woodland
Shawe

Shaykeen (American) A successful man
Shaykean, Shaykein, Shakeyn, Shakine

Shea (Gaelic) An admirable man / from the fairy fortress
Shae, Shai, Shay, Shaye, Shaylon, Shays

Sheen (English) A shining man
Sheene, Shean, Sheane

Sheffield (English) From the crooked field
Sheffeld

Sheldon (English) From the steep valley
Shelden, Sheldan, Sheldun, Sheldin, Sheldyn, Shel

Shelley (English) From the meadow's ledge
Shelly, Shelli, Shellie, Shellee, Shellea, Shelleigh, Shelleah

Shelton (English) From the farm on the ledge
Shellton, Sheltown, Sheltun, Shelten, Shelny, Shelney, Shelni, Shelnie

Shem (Hebrew) Having a well-known name

Shepherd (English) One who herds sheep
Shepperd, Shep, Shepard, Shephard, Shepp, Sheppard

Sheridan (Gaelic) A seeker
Sheredan, Sheridon, Sherridan, Seireadan, Sheriden, Sheridun, Sherard, Sherrard

Sherlock (English) A fair-haired man
Sherlocke, Shurlock, Shurlocke

Sherman (English) One who cuts wool cloth
Shermon, Scherman, Schermann, Shearman, Shermann, Sherm, Sherme

Sherrerd (English) From the open field
Shererd, Sherrard, Sherard

Shields (Gaelic) A faithful protector
Sheelds, Shealds

Shikha (Indian) A fiery man
Shykha

Shiloh (Hebrew) He who was sent
Shilo, Shyloh, Shylo

Shing (Chinese) A victorious man
Shyng

Shino (Japanese) A bamboo stem
Shyno

Shipton (English) From the ship town; from the sheep town

Shiro (Japanese) The fourth-born son
Shyro

Shorty (American) A man who is small in stature
Shortey, Shorti, Shortie, Shortee, Shortea

Shreshta (Indian) The best; one who is superior

Shubhang (Indian) A handsome man

Shuraqui (Arabic) A man from the east

Siamak (Persian) A bringer of joy
Syamak, Siamack, Syamack, Siamac, Syamac

Sidor (Russian) One who is talented
Sydor

Sierra (Spanish) From the jagged mountain range
Siera, Syerra, Syera, Seyera, Seeara

Sigehere (English) One who is victorious
Sygehere, Sigihere, Sygihere

Sigenert (Anglo-Saxon) A king
Sygenert, Siginert, Syginert

Sigmund (German) The victorious protector
Siegmund, Sigmond, Zsigmond, Zygmunt

Sihtric (Anglo-Saxon) A king
Sihtrik, Sihtrick, Syhtric, Syhtrik, Syhtrick, Sihtryc, Sihtryk, Sihtryck

Sik'is (Native American) A friendly man

Silas (Latin) Form of Silvanus, meaning "a woodland dweller"

Silny (Czech) Having great strength
Silney, Silni, Silnie, Silnee, Silnea

Simbarashe (African) The power of God
Simbarashi, Simbarashie, Simbarashy, Simbarashey, Simbarashee

Simcha (Hebrew) Filled with joy
Symcha, Simha, Symha

Simmons (Hebrew) The son of Simon
Semmes, Simms, Syms, Simmonds, Symonds, Simpson, Symms, Simson

Simon (Hebrew) God has heard
Shimon, Si, Sim, Samien, Semyon, Simen, Simeon, Simone

Sinai (Hebrew) From the clay desert

Sinclair (English) Man from Saint Clair
Sinclaire, Sinclare, Synclair, Synclaire, Synclare

Singer (American) A vocalist
Synger

Sion (Armenian) From the fortified hill
Sionne, Syon, Syonne

Sirius (Greek) Resembling the brightest star
Syrius

Siyavash (Persian) One who owns black horses
Siyavashe

Skerry (Norse) From the rocky island
Skereye, Skerrey, Skerri, Skerrie, Skerree, Skerrea

Slade (English) Son of the valley
Slaid, Slaide, Slaed, Slaede, Slayd, Slayde

Sladkey (Slavic) A glorious man
Sladky, Sladki, Sladkie, Sladkee, Sladkea

Smith (English) A blacksmith
Smyth, Smithe, Smythe, Smedt, Smid, Smitty, Smittee, Smittea

Snell (Anglo-Saxon) One who is bold
Snel, Snelle, Snele

Solange (French) An angel of the sun

Solaris (Greek) Of the sun
*Solarise, Solariss, Solarisse,
Solarys, Solaryss, Solarysse,
Solstice, Soleil*

Somer (French) Born during
the summer
*Somers, Sommer, Sommers,
Sommar, Somar*

Somerset (English) From the
summer settlement
*Sommerset, Sumerset,
Summerset*

Songaa (Native American)
Having great strength
Songan

Sophocles (Greek) An ancient
playwright
Sofocles

Sorley (Irish) Of the summer
vikings
*Sorly, Sorlee, Sorlea, Sorli,
Sorlie*

Soumil (Indian) A beloved
friend
*Soumyl, Soumille, Soumylle,
Soumill, Soumyll*

Southern (English) Man from
the south
Sothern, Suthern

Sovann (Cambodian) The
golden son
Sovan, Sovane

Spark (English / Latin) A
gallant man / to scatter
*Sparke, Sparki, Sparkie,
Sparky, Sparkey, Sparkee,
Sparkea*

Spencer (English) One who
dispenses provisions
Spenser

Squire (English) A knight's
companion; the shield-bearer
*Squier, Squiers, Squires,
Squyre, Squyres*

Stanford (English) From the
stony ford
*Standford, Standforde,
Standforde, Stamford*

Stanhope (English) From the
stony hollow
Stanhop

Stanton (English) From the
stone town
*Stantown, Stanten, Staunton,
Stantan, Stantun*

Stark (German) Having great
strength
Starke, Starck, Starcke

Stavros (Greek) One who is
crowned

Steadman (English) One who
lives at the farm
*Stedman, Steadmann,
Stedmann, Stedeman*

Steed (English) Resembling a stallion
Steede, Stead, Steade

Stephen (Greek) Crowned with garland
Staffan, Steba, Steben, Stefan, Stefano, Steffan, Steffen, Steffon, Steven, Steve

Sterling (English) One who is highly valued
Sterlyng, Stirling, Sterlyn

Stian (Norse) A voyager; one who is swift
Stig, Styg, Stygge, Stieran, Steeran, Steeren, Steeryn, Stieren

Stilwell (Anglo-Saxon) From the quiet spring
Stillwell, Stilwel, Stylwell, Styllwell, Stylwel, Stillwel

Stobart (German) A harsh man
Stobarte, Stobarth, Stobarthe

Stockley (English) From the meadow of tree stumps
Stockly, Stockli, Stocklie, Stocklee, Stockleigh

Storm (American) Of the tempest; stormy weather; having an impetuous nature
Storme, Stormy, Stormi, Stormie, Stormey, Stormee, Stormea

Stowe (English) A secretive man
Stow, Stowey, Stowy, Stowee, Stowea, Stowi, Stowie

Stratford (English) From the street near the river ford
Strafford, Stratforde, Straford, Strafforde, Straforde

Stratton (Scottish) A homebody
Straton, Stratten, Straten, Strattan, Stratan, Strattun, Stratun

Strider (English) A great warrior
Stryder

Striker (American) An aggressive man
Strike, Stryker, Stryke

Struthers (Irish) One who lives near the brook
Struther, Sruthair, Strother, Strothers

Stuart (English) A steward; the keeper of the estate
Steward, Stewart, Stewert, Stuert, Stu, Stew

Suave (American) A smooth and sophisticated man
Swave

Subhi (Arabic) Born during
the early morning hours
*Subhie, Subhy, Subhey,
Subhee, Subhea*

Suffield (English) From the
southern field
Suffeld, Suthfeld, Suthfield

Sullivan (Gaelic) Having dark
eyes
Sullavan, Sullevan, Sullyvan

Sully (English) From the
southern meadow
*Sulley, Sulli, Sullie, Sulleigh,
Sullee, Sullea, Sulleah, Suthley*

Sultan (African / American) A
ruler / one who is bold
*Sultane, Sulten, Sultun, Sulton,
Sultin, Sultyn*

Suman (Hindi) A wise man

Sundiata (African) Resembling
a hungry lion
*Sundyata, Soundiata,
Soundyata, Sunjata*

Sundown (American) Born at
dusk
Sundowne

Su'ud (Arabic) One who has
good luck
Suoud

Swahili (Arabic) Of the coastal
people
*Swahily, Swahiley, Swahilee,
Swahiley, Swaheeli, Swaheelie,
Swaheely, Swaheeley*

Sylvester (Latin) Man from the
forest
*Silvester, Silvestre, Silvestro,
Sylvestre, Sylvestro, Sly,
Sevester, Seveste*

Syon (Indian) One who is
followed by good fortune

Szemere (Hungarian) A man
of small stature
*Szemir, Szemeer, Szemear,
Szemyr*

T

Tabari (Arabic) A famous his-
torian
*Tabarie, Tabary, Tabarey,
Tabaree, Tabarea*

Tabbai (Hebrew) A well-
behaved boy
Tabbae, Tabbay, Tabbaye

Tabbart (German) A brilliant
man
*Tabbert, Tabart, Tabert,
Tahbert, Tahberte*

Tacari (African) As strong as a
warrior
*Tacarie, Tacary, Tacarey,
Tacaree, Tacarea*

Tadao (Japanese) One who is
satisfied

Tadeusuz (Polish) One who is
worthy of praise
Tadesuz

Tadi (Native American) Of the
wind
*Tadie, Tady, Tadey, Tadee,
Tadea*

Tadzi (American / Polish)
Resembling the loon / one
who is praised
*Tadzie, Tadzy, Tadzey, Tadzee,
Tadzea*

Taft (French / English) From
the homestead / from the
marshes
Tafte

Taggart (Gaelic) Son of a
priest
*Taggert, Taggort, Taggirt,
Taggyrt*

Taghee (Native American) A
chief
*Taghea, Taghy, Taghey, Taghi,
Taghie*

Taheton (Native American)
Resembling a hawk

Tahoe (Native American)
From the big water
Taho

Tahoma (Native American)
From the snowy mountain peak
*Tehoma, Tacoma, Takoma,
Tohoma, Tocoma, Tokoma,
Tekoma, Tecoma*

Taishi (Japanese) An ambi-
tious man
*Taishie, Taishy, Taishey,
Taishee, Taishea*

Taj (Indian) One who is
crowned
Tahj, Tajdar

Tajo (Spanish) Born during
the daytime

Taksony (Hungarian) One
who is content; well-fed
*Taksoney, Taksoni, Taksonie,
Taksonee, Taksonea, Tas*

Talasi (Native American)
Resembling a cornflower
*Talasie, Talasy, Talasey,
Talasee, Talasea*

Talford (English) From the
high ford
Talforde, Tallford, Tallforde

Talfryn (Welsh) From the high
hill
*Talfrynn, Talfrin, Talfrinn,
Talfren, Talfrenn, Tallfryn,
Tallfrin, Tallfren*

Talmai (Hebrew) From the furrows
Talmae, Talmay, Talmaye

Talmon (Hebrew) One who is oppressed
Talman, Talmin, Talmyn, Talmen

Talo (Finnish) From the homestead

Tam (Vietnamese / Hebrew) Having heart / one who is truthful

Taman (Hindi) One who is needed

Tamarius (American) A stubborn man
Tamarias, Tamarios, Tamerius, Tamerias, Tamerios

Tameron (American) Form of Cameron, meaning "having a crooked nose"
Tameren, Tameryn, Tamryn, Tamerin, Tamren, Tamrin, Bamron

Tammany (Native American) A friendly chief
Tammani, Tammanie, Tammaney, Tammanee, Tammanea

Tanafa (Polynesian) A drumbeat

Taneli (Hebrew) He will be judged by God
Tanelie, Tanely, Taneley, Tanelee, Tanelea

Tanish (Indian) An ambitious man
Tanishe, Taneesh, Taneeshe, Taneash, Taneashe, Tanysh, Tanyshe

Tanjiro (Japanese) The prized second-born son
Tanjyro

Tank (American) A man who is big and strong
Tankie, Tanki, Tanky, Tankey, Tankee, Tankea

Tanner (English) One who makes leather
Tannere, Tannor, Tannar, Tannir, Tannyr, Tannur, Tannis

Tannon (German) From the fir tree
Tannan, Tannen, Tannin, Tansen, Tanson, Tannun, Tannyn

Tano (Ghanese) From the river
Tanu

Tao (Chinese) One who will have a long life

Taos (Spanish) From the city in New Mexico

Tapani (Hebrew) A victorious man
Tapanie, Tapany, Tapaney, Tapanee, Tapanea

Tapko (American) Resembling an antelope

Tappen (Welsh) From the top of the cliff
Tappan, Tappon, Tappin, Tappyn, Tappun

Taran (Gaelic) Of the thunder
Taren, Taron, Tarin, Taryn, Tarun

Taranga (Indian) Of the waves

Taregan (Native American) Resembling a crane
Taregen, Taregon, Taregin, Taregyn

Tarit (Indian) Resembling lightning
Tarite, Tareet, Tareete, Tareat, Tareate, Taryt, Taryte

Tarn (Norse) From the mountain pool

Tarquin (Latin) One who is impulsive
Tarquinn, Tarquinne, Tarquen, Tarquenn, Tarquenne, Tarquyn, Tarquynn, Tarquynne

Tarrant (American) One who upholds the law
Tarrent, Tarrint, Tarrynt, Tarront, Tarrunt

Tarun (Indian) A youthful man
Taroun, Taroon, Tarune, Taroune, Taroone

Tashi (Tibetan) One who is prosperous
Tashie, Tashy, Tashey, Tashee, Tashea

^**Tate** (English) A cheerful man; one who brings happiness to others
Tayt, Tayte, Tait, Taite, Taet, Taete

Tausiq (Indian) One who provides strong backing
Tauseeq, Tauseaq, Tausik, Tauseek, Tauseak

Tavaris (American) Of misfortune; a hermit
Tavarius, Tavaress, Tavarious, Tavariss, Tavarous, Tevarus, Tavorian, Tavarian

Tavas (Hebrew) Resembling a peacock

Tavi (Aramaic) A good man
Tavie, Tavy, Tavey, Tavee, Tavea

Tavin (German) Form of Gustav, meaning "of the staff of the gods"
Tavyn, Taven, Tavan, Tavon, Tavun, Tava, Tave

Tawa (Native American) Born beneath the sun
Tawah

Tay (Scottish) From the river
Taye, Tae, Tai

Taylor (English) Cutter of cloth, one who alters garments

Teagan (Gaelic) A handsome man
Teegan, Teygan, Tegan, Teigan

Ted (English) Form of Theodore, meaning "a gift from God"
Tedd, Teddy, Teddi, Teddie, Teddee, Teddea, Teddey, Tedric

Tedmund (English) A protector of the land
Tedmunde, Tedmond, Tedmonde, Tedman, Theomund, Theomond, Theomunde, Theomonde

Teetonka (Native American) One who talks too much
Teitonka, Tietonka, Teatonka, Teytonka

Tegene (African) My protector
Tegeen, Tegeene, Tegean, Tegeane

Teiji (Japanese) One who is righteous
Teijo

Teilo (Welsh) A saintly man

Teka (African) He has replaced

Tekeshi (Japanese) A formidable and brave man
Tekeshie, Tekeshy, Tekeshey, Tekeshee, Tekeshea

Telly (Greek) The wisest man
Telley, Tellee, Tellea, Telli, Tellie

Temman (Anglo-Saxon) One who has been tamed

Temple (Latin) From the sacred place
Tempel, Templar, Templer, Templo

Teneangopte (Native American) Resembling a high-flying bird

Tennant (English) One who rents
Tennent, Tenant, Tenent

Tennessee (Native American) From the state of Tennessee
Tenese, Tenesee, Tenessee, Tennese, Tennesee, Tennesse

Teon (Anglo-Saxon) One who harms others

Teris (Irish) The son of
Terence
*Terys, Teriss, Teryss, Terris,
Terrys, Terriss, Terryss*

^**Terrance** (Latin) From an
ancient Roman clan
*Tarrants, Tarrance, Tarrence,
Tarrenz, Terencio, Terance,
Terrence, Terrey, Terry*

Terrian (American) One who is
strong and ambitious
Terrien, Terriun, Terriyn

Terron (English) Form of
Terence, meaning "from an
ancient Roman clan"
Tarran, Tarren, Tarrin

Teshi (African) One who is full
of laughter
*Teshie, Teshy, Teshey, Teshee,
Teshea*

Tessema (African) One to
whom people listen

Tet (Vietnamese) Born on
New Year's

Teteny (Hungarian) A
chieftain

Teva (Hebrew) A natural man
Tevah

Texas (Native American) One
of many friends; from the
state of Texas
Texus, Texis, Texes, Texos, Texys

Teyrnon (Celtic) A regal man
*Teirnon, Tayrnon, Tairnon,
Taernon, Tiarchnach, Tiarnach*

Thabo (African) Filled with
happiness

Thackary (English) Form of
Zachary, meaning "the Lord
remembers"
*Thackery, Thakary, Thakery,
Thackari, Thackarie,
Thackarey, Thackaree,
Thackarea*

Thaddeus (Aramaic) Having
heart
*Tad, Tadd, Taddeo, Taddeusz,
Thad, Thadd, Thaddaios,
Thaddaos*

Thandiwe (African) One who
is dearly loved
*Thandie, Thandi, Thandy,
Thandey, Thandee, Thandea*

Thang (Vietnamese) One who
is victorious

Thanus (American) One who
owns land

Thao (Vietnamese) One who is
courteous

Thatcher (English) One who
fixes roofs
*Thacher, Thatch, Thatche,
Thaxter, Thacker, Thaker,
Thackere, Thakere*

Thayer (Teutonic) Of the nation's army

Theodore (Greek) A gift from God
Ted, Teddy, Teddie, Theo, Theodor

Theron (Greek) A great hunter
Therron, Tharon, Theon, Tharron

Theseus (Greek) In mythology, hero who slew the Minotaur
Thesius, Thesyus

Thinh (Vietnamese) A prosperous man

*__Thomas__ (Aramaic) One of twins
Tam, Tamas, Tamhas, Thom, Thomason, Thomson, Thompson, Tomas

Thor (Norse) In mythology, god of thunder
Thorian, Thorin, Thorsson, Thorvald, Tor, Tore, Turo, Thorrin

Thorburn (Norse) Thor's bear
Thorburne, Thorbern, Thorberne, Thorbjorn, Thorbjorne, Torbjorn, Torborg, Torben

Thormond (Norse) Protected by Thor
Thormonde, Thormund, Thormunde, Thurmond, Thurmonde, Thurmund, Thurmunde, Thormun

Thorne (English) From the thorn bush
Thorn

Thornycroft (English) From the field of thorn bushes
Thornicroft, Thorneycroft, Thorniecroft, Thorneecroft, Thorneacroft

Thuong (Vietnamese) One who loves tenderly

Thurston (English) From Thor's town; Thor's stone
Thorston, Thorstan, Thorstein, Thorsten, Thurstain, Thurstan, Thursten, Torsten

Thuy (Vietnamese) One who is kind

Tiassale (African) It has been forgotten

Tiberio (Italian) From the Tiber river
Tibero, Tyberio, Tybero, Tiberius, Tiberios, Tyberius, Tyberios

Tibor (Slavic) From the sacred place

Tiburon (Spanish) Resembling a shark

Tiernan (Gaelic) Lord of the manor
Tiarnan, Tiarney, Tierney, Tierny, Tiernee, Tiernea, Tierni, Tiernie

Tilian (Anglo-Saxon) One who strives to better himself
Tilien, Tiliun, Tilion

Tilon (Hebrew) A generous man
Tilen, Tilan, Tilun, Tilin, Tilyn

Tilton (English) From the fertile estate
Tillton, Tilten, Tillten, Tiltan, Tilltan, Tiltin, Tilltin, Tiltun

Timir (Indian) Born in the darkness
Timirbaran

Timothy (Greek) One who honors God
Tim, Timmo, Timmothy, Timmy, Timo, Timofei, Timofeo

Tin (Vietnamese) A great thinker

Tino (Italian) A man of small stature
Teeno, Tieno, Teino, Teano, Tyno

Tip (American) A form of Thomas, meaning "one of twins"
Tipp, Tipper, Tippy, Tippee, Tippea, Tippey, Tippi, Tippie

Tisa (African) The ninth-born child
Tisah, Tysa, Tysah

^**Titus** (Greek / Latin) Of the giants / a great defender
Tito, Titos, Tytus, Tytos, Titan, Tytan, Tyto

Toa (Polynesian) A brave-hearted woman

Toan (Vietnamese) One who is safe
Toane

Tobias (Hebrew) The Lord is good
Toby

Todd (English) Resembling a fox
Tod

Todor (Bulgarian) A gift from God
Todos, Todros

Tohon (Native American) One who loves the water

Tokala (Native American) Resembling a fox
Tokalo

Tomer (Hebrew) A man of tall stature
Tomar, Tomur, Tomir, Tomor, Tomyr

Tomi (Japanese / African) A wealthy man / of the people
Tomie, Tomee, Tomea, Tomy, Tomey

Tonauac (Aztec) One who possesses the light

Torger (Norse) The power of Thor's spear
Thorger, Torgar, Thorgar, Terje, Therje

Torht (Anglo-Saxon) A bright man
Torhte

Torin (Celtic) One who acts as chief
Toran, Torean, Toren, Torion, Torran, Torrian, Toryn

Tormaigh (Irish) Having the spirit of Thor
Tormey, Tormay, Tormaye, Tormai, Tormae

Torr (English) From the tower
Torre

Torrence (Gaelic) From the little hills
Torence, Torrance, Torrens, Torrans, Toran, Torran, Torrin, Torn, Torry

Torry (Norse / Gaelic) Refers to Thor / form of Torrence, meaning "from the little hills"
Torrey, Torree, Torrea, Torri, Torrie, Tory, Torey, Tori

Toshiro (Japanese) One who is talented and intelligent
Toshihiro

Tostig (English) A well-known earl
Tostyg

Toviel (Hebrew) The Lord is good
Toviell, Toviele, Tovielle, Tovi, Tovie, Tovee, Tovea, Tovy

Toyo (Japanese) A man of plenty

Tracy (Gaelic) One who is warlike
Tracey, Traci, Tracie, Tracee, Tracea, Treacy, Trace, Tracen

Travis (French) To cross over
Travys, Traver, Travers, Traviss, Trevis, Trevys, Travus, Traves

Treffen (German) One who socializes
Treffan, Treffin, Treffon, Treffyn, Treffun

Tremain (Celtic) From the town built of stone
Tramain, Tramaine, Tramayne, Tremaine, Tremayne, Tremaen, Tremaene, Tramaen

Tremont (French) From the three mountains
Tremonte, Tremount, Tremounte

Trenton (English) From the town near the rushing rapids
Trent, Trynt, Trenten, Trentyn

Trevin (English) From the fair town
Trevan, Treven, Trevian, Trevion, Trevon, Trevyn, Trevonn

Trevor (Welsh) From the large village
Trefor, Trevar, Trever, Treabhar, Treveur, Trevir, Trevur

Trey (English) The third-born child
Tre, Trai, Trae, Tray, Traye, Trayton, Treyton, Trayson

Trigg (Norse) One who is truthful
Trygg

Tripp (English) A traveler
Trip, Trypp, Tryp, Tripper, Trypper

Tripsy (American) One who enjoys dancing
Tripsey, Tripsee, Tripsea, Tripsi, Tripsie

*****Tristan** (Celtic) A sorrowful man; in Arthurian legend, a knight of the Round Table
Trystan, Tris, Tristam, Tristen, Tristian, Tristin, Triston, Tristram

Trocky (American) A manly man
Trockey, Trocki, Trockie, Trockee, Trockea

Trong (Vietnamese) One who is respected

Troy (Gaelic) Son of a foot-soldier
Troye, Troi

Trumbald (English) A bold man
Trumbold, Trumbalde, Trumbolde

Trygve (Norse) One who wins with bravery

Tse (Native American) As solid as a rock

Tsidhqiyah (Hebrew) The Lord is just
Tsidqiyah, Tsidhqiya, Tsdqiya

Tsubasa (Japanese) A winged
being
Tsubasah, Tsubase, Tsubaseh

Tucker (English) One who
makes garments
*Tuker, Tuckerman, Tukerman,
Tuck, Tuckman, Tukman,
Tuckere, Toukere*

Tuketu (Native American)
Resembling a running bear
*Tuketue, Tuketoo, Tuketou,
Telutci, Telutcie, Telutcy,
Telutcey, Telutcee*

Tulsi (Indian) A holy man
*Tulsie, Tulsy, Tulsey, Tulsee,
Tulsea*

Tumaini (African) An optimist
*Tumainie, Tumainee,
Tumainy, Tumainey, Tumayni,
Tumaynie, Tumaynee,
Tumayney*

Tunde (African) One who
returns
*Tundi, Tundie, Tundee,
Tundea, Tundy, Tundey*

Tunleah (English) From the
town near the meadow
*Tunlea, Tunleigh, Tunly,
Tunley, Tunlee, Tunli, Tunlie*

Tupac (African) A messenger
warrior
Tupack, Tupoc, Tupock

Turfeinar (Norse) In mythol-
ogy, the son of Rognvald
*Turfaynar, Turfaenar,
Turfanar, Turfenar, Turfainar*

Tushar (Indian) Of the snow
Tusharr, Tushare

Tusita (Chinese) One who is
heaven-sent

Twrgadarn (Welsh) From the
strong tower

Txanton (Basque) Form
of Anthony, meaning "a
flourishing man; of an
ancient Roman family"
*Txantony, Txantoney,
Txantonee, Txantoni,
Txantonie, Txantonea*

Tybalt (Latin) He who sees the
truth
Tybault, Tybalte, Tybaulte

Tye (English) From the
fenced-in pasture
Tyg, Tyge, Tie, Tigh, Teyen

Tyfiell (English) Follower of
the god Tyr
Tyfiel, Tyfielle, Tyfiele

*Tyler (English) A tiler of roofs
*Tilar, Tylar, Tylor, Tiler, Tilor,
Ty, Tye, Tylere*

Typhoon (Chinese) Of the great wind
Tiphoon, Tyfoon, Tifoon, Typhoun, Tiphoun, Tyfoun, Tifoun

Tyrone (French) From Owen's land
Terone, Tiron, Tirone, Tyron, Ty, Kyrone

Tyson (French) One who is high-spirited; fiery
Thyssen, Tiesen, Tyce, Tycen, Tyeson, Tyssen, Tysen, Tysan

U

U (Korean) A kind and gentle man

Uaithne (Gaelic) One who is innocent; green
Uaithn, Uaythne, Uaythn, Uathne, Uathn, Uaethne, Uaethn

Ualan (Scottish) Form of Valentine, meaning "one who is strong and healthy"
Ualane, Ualayn, Ualayne, Ualen, Ualon

Uba (African) One who is wealthy; lord of the house
Ubah, Ubba, Ubbah

Uberto (Italian) Form of Hubert, meaning "having a shining intellect"
Ulberto, Umberto

Udath (Indian) One who is noble
Udathe

Uddam (Indian) An exceptional man

Uddhar (Indian) One who is free; an independent man
Uddharr, Udhar, Udharr

Udell (English) From the valley of yew trees
Udale, Udel, Udall, Udayle, Udayl, Udail, Udaile, Udele

Udi (Hebrew) One who carries a torch
Udie, Udy, Udey, Udee, Udea

Udup (Indian) Born beneath the moon's light
Udupp, Uddup, Uddupp

Udyan (Indian) Of the garden
Uddyan, Udyann, Uddyann

Ugo (Italian) A great thinker

Uland (English) From the
noble country
*Ulande, Ulland, Ullande,
Ulandus, Ullandus*

Ulhas (Indian) Filled with
happiness
Ulhass, Ullhas, Ullhass

Ull (Norse) Having glory; in
mythology, god of justice and
patron of agriculture
Ulle, Ul, Ule

Ulmer (German) Having the
fame of the wolf
*Ullmer, Ullmar, Ulmarr,
Ullmarr, Ulfmer, Ulfmar,
Ulfmaer*

Ultman (Indian) A godly man
Ultmann, Ultmane

Umrao (Indian) One who is
noble

Unai (Basque) A shepherd
Unay, Unaye, Unae

Unathi (African) God is
with us
*Unathie, Unathy, Unathey,
Unathee, Unathea*

Uncas (Native American)
Resembling a fox
Unkas, Unckas

Ungus (Irish) A vigorous man
Unguss

Unique (American) Unlike
others; the only one
*Unikue, Unik, Uniqui, Uniqi,
Uniqe, Unikque, Unike, Unicke*

Uolevi (Finnish) Form of Olaf,
meaning "the remaining of
the ancestors"
*Uolevie, Uolevee, Uolevy,
Uolevey, Uolevea*

Upchurch (English) From the
upper church
Upchurche

Uranus (Greek) In mythology,
the father of the Titans
*Urainus, Uraynus, Uranas,
Uraynas, Urainas, Uranos,
Uraynos, Urainos*

Uri (Hebrew) Form of Uriah,
meaning "the Lord is my
light"
Urie, Ury, Urey, Uree, Urea

Uriah (Hebrew) The Lord is
my light
*Uri, Uria, Urias, Urija, Urijah,
Uriyah, Urjasz, Uriya*

Urjavaha (Hindu) Of the Nimi
dynasty

Urtzi (Basque) From the sky
*Urtzie, Urtzy, Urtzey, Urtzee,
Urtzea*

Usher (Latin) From the mouth of the river
Ushar, Ushir, Ussher, Usshar, Usshir

Ushi (Chinese) As strong as an ox
Ushie, Ushy, Ushey, Ushee, Ushea

Utah (Native American) People of the mountains; from the state of Utah

Utsav (Indian) Born during a celebration
Utsavi, Utsave, Utsava, Utsavie, Utsavy, Utsavey, Utsavee, Utsavea

Utt (Arabic) One who is kind and wise
Utte

Uzi (Hebrew) Having great power
Uzie, Uzy, Uzey, Uzee, Uzea, Uzzi, Uzzie, Uzzy

Uzima (African) One who is full of life
Uzimah, Uzimma, Uzimmah, Uzyma

Uzziah (Hebrew) The Lord is my strength
Uzzia, Uziah, Uzia, Uzzya, Uzzyah, Uzyah, Uzya, Uzziel

V

Vachel (French) Resembling a small cow
Vachele, Vachell

Vachlan (English) One who lives near water

Vadar (Dutch) A fatherly man
Vader, Vadyr

Vadhir (Spanish) Resembling a rose
Vadhyr, Vadheer

Vadim (Russian) A good-looking man
Vadime, Vadym, Vadyme, Vadeem, Vadeeme

Vaijnath (Hindi) Refers to Lord Shiva
Vaejnath, Vaijnathe, Vaejnathe

Valdemar (German) A well-known ruler
Valdemarr, Valdemare, Valto, Valdmar, Valdmarr, Valdimar, Valdimarr

Valentine (Latin) One who is strong and healthy
Val, Valentin, Valentino, Valentyne, Ualan

Valerian (Latin) One who is strong and healthy
Valerien, Valerio, Valerius, Valery, Valeryan, Valere, Valeri, Valerii

Valin (Hindi) The monkey king

Valle (French) From the glen
Vallejo

Valri (French) One who is strong
Valrie, Valry, Valrey, Valree

Vance (English) From the marshland
Vanse

Vanderveer (Dutch) From the ferry
Vandervere, Vandervir, Vandervire, Vandervyr, Vandervyre

Vandy (Dutch) One who travels; a wanderer
Vandey, Vandi, Vandie, Vandee

Vandyke (Danish) From the dike
Vandike

Vanir (Norse) Of the ancient gods

Varante (Arabic) From the river

Vardon (French) From the green hill
Varden, Verdon, Verdun, Verden, Vardun, Vardan, Verddun, Varddun

Varg (Norse) Resembling a wolf

Varick (German) A protective ruler
Varrick, Warick, Warrick

Varius (Latin) A versatile man
Varian, Varinius

Variya (Hindi) The excellent one

Vasava (Hindi) Refers to Indra

Vashon (American) The Lord is gracious
Vashan, Vashawn, Vashaun, Vashone, Vashane, Vashayn, Vashayne

Vasin (Indian) A great ruler
Vasine, Vaseen, Vaseene, Vasyn, Vasyne

Vasuki (Hindi) In Hinduism, a serpent king
Vasukie, Vasuky, Vasukey, Vasukee, Vasukea

Vasuman (Indian) Son born of fire

Vasyl (Slavic) A king
Vasil, Vassil, Wasyl

Vatsa (Indian) Our beloved son
Vathsa

Vatsal (Indian) One who is affectionate

Velimir (Croatian) One who wishes for great peace
Velimeer, Velimyr, Velimire, Velimeere, Velimyre

Velyo (Bulgarian) A great man
Velcho, Veliko, Velin, Velko

Vere (French) From the alder tree

Verge (Anglo-Saxon) One who owns four acres

Vernon (French) From the alder-tree grove
Vern, Vernal, Vernard, Verne, Vernee, Vernen, Verney, Vernin

Verrill (French) One who is faithful
Verill, Verrall, Verrell, Verroll, Veryl, Veryll, Verol, Verall

Vibol (Cambodian) A man of plenty
Viboll, Vibole, Vybol, Vyboll, Vybole

Victor (Latin) One who is victorious; the champion
Vic, Vick, Victoriano

Vidal (Spanish) A giver of life
Videl, Videlio, Videlo, Vidalo, Vidalio, Vidas

Vidar (Norse) Warrior of the forest; in mythology, a son of Odin
Vidarr

Vien (Vietnamese) One who is complete; satisfied

Vincent (Latin) One who prevails; the conqueror
Vicente, Vicenzio, Vicenzo, Vin, Vince, Vincens, Vincente, Vincentius

Viorel (Romanian) Resembling the bluebell
Viorell, Vyorel, Vyorell

Vipin (Indian) From the forest
Vippin, Vypin, Vypyn, Vyppin, Vyppyn, Vipyn, Vippyn

Vipul (Indian) A man of plenty
Vypul, Vipull, Vypull, Vipool, Vypool

Virag (Hungarian) Resembling a flower

Virgil (Latin) The staff-bearer
Verge, Vergil, Vergilio, Virgilio, Vergilo, Virgilo, Virgilijus

Virginius (Latin) One who is pure; chaste
Virginio, Virgino

Vitéz (Hungarian) A courageous warrior

Vito (Latin) One who gives life
*Vital, Vitale, Vitalis, Vitaly,
Vitas, Vitus, Vitali, Vitaliy, Vid*

Vitus (Latin) Giver of life
Wit

Vladimir (Slavic) A famous
prince
*Vladamir, Vladimeer,
Vladimyr, Vladimyre,
Vladamyr, Vladamyre,
Vladameer, Vladimer*

Vladislav (Slavic) One who
rules with glory

Volodymyr (Slavic) To rule
with peace
Wolodymyr

Vulcan (Latin) In mythology,
the god of fire
Vulkan, Vulckan

Vyacheslav (Russian) Form
of Wenceslas, meaning "one
who receives more glory"

W

Wade (English) To cross the
river ford
*Wayde, Waid, Waide, Waddell,
Wadell, Waydell, Waidell, Waed*

Wadley (English) From the
meadow near the ford
*Wadly, Wadlee, Wadli, Wadlie,
Wadleigh*

Wadsworth (English) From the
estate near the ford
*Waddsworth, Wadsworthe,
Waddsworthe*

Wafi (Arabic) One who is
trustworthy
*Wafie, Wafy, Wafey, Wafee,
Wafiy, Wafiyy*

Wahab (Indian) A big-hearted
man

Wainwright (English) One who
builds wagons
*Wainright, Wainewright,
Wayneright, Waynewright,
Waynwright*

Wakil (Arabic) A lawyer; a
trustee
*Wakill, Wakyl, Wakyle,
Wakeel, Wakeele*

Wakiza (Native American) A
desperate fighter
*Wakyza, Wakeza, Wakieza,
Wakeiza*

Walbridge (English) From the
Welshman's bridge
*Wallbridge, Walbrydge,
Wallbrydge*

Waljan (Welsh) The chosen
one
*Walljan, Waljen, Walljen,
Waljon, Walljon*

Walker (English) One who
trods the cloth
Walkar, Walkir, Walkor

Wallace (Scottish) A Welshman,
a man from the South
*Wallach, Wallas, Wallie,
Wallis, Wally, Wlash, Welch*

Walter (German) The com-
mander of the army
*Walther, Walt, Walte, Walder,
Wat, Wouter, Wolter, Woulter,
Galtero, Quaid*

Wamblee (Native American)
Resembling an eagle
*Wambli, Wamblie, Wambly,
Wambley, Wambleigh,
Wamblea*

Wanikiy (Native American) A
savior
*Wanikiya, Wanikie, Wanikey,
Waniki, Wanikee*

Wanjala (African) Born during
a famine
Wanjalla, Wanjal, Wanjall

Warford (English) From the
ford near the weir
*Warforde, Weirford, Weirforde,
Weiford, Weiforde*

Warley (English) From the
meadow near the weir
*Warly, Warleigh, Warlee,
Warlea, Warleah, Warli,
Warlie, Weirley*

Warner (German) Of the
defending army
*Werner, Wernher, Warnher,
Worner, Wornher*

Warra (Aboriginal) Man of the
water
Warrah, Wara, Warah

Warren (English / German)
From the fortress

Warrick (English) Form of
Varick, meaning "a protective
ruler"
*Warrik, Warric, Warick,
Warik, Waric, Warryck,
Warryk, Warryc*

Warrigal (Aboriginal) One who
is wild
*Warrigall, Warigall, Warigal,
Warygal, Warygall*

Warwick (English) From the
farm near the weir
Warwik, Warwyck, Warwyk

Wasswa (African) The first-
born of twins
Waswa, Wasswah, Waswah

Wasyl (Ukrainian) Form of
Vasyl, meaning "a king"
Wasyle, Wasil, Wasile

Watson (English) The son of Walter
Watsin, Watsen, Watsan, Watkins, Watckins, Watkin, Watckin, Wattekinson

Waylon (English) From the roadside land

Wayne (English) One who builds wagons
Wain, Wanye, Wayn, Waynell, Waynne, Guwayne

Webster (English) A weaver
Weeb, Web, Webb, Webber, Weber, Webbestre, Webestre, Webbe

Wei (Chinese) A brilliant man; having great strength

Wenceslas (Polish) One who receives more glory
Wenceslaus, Wenzel, Vyacheslav

Wendell (German) One who travels; a wanderer
Wendel, Wendale, Wendall, Wendele, Wendal, Windell, Windel, Windal

Wesley (English) From the western meadow
Wes, Wesly, Wessley, Westleigh, Westley, Wesli, Weslie, Wesleigh

Westby (English) From the western farm
Westbey, Wesby, Wesbey, Westbi, Wesbi, Westbie, Wesbie, Westbee

Weston (English) From the western town

Whit (English) A white-skinned man
White, Whitey, Whitt, Whitte, Whyt, Whytt, Whytte, Whytey

Whitby (English) From the white farm
Whitbey, Whitbi, Whitbie, Whitbee, Whytbey, Whytby, Whytbi, Whytbie

Whitfield (English) From the white field
Whitfeld, Whytfield, Whytfeld, Witfield, Witfeld, Wytfield, Wytfeld

Whitley (English) From the white meadow
Whitly, Whitli, Whitlie, Whitlee, Whitleigh, Whytley, Whytly, Whytli

Whitman (English) A white-haired man
Whitmann, Witman, Witmann, Whitmane, Witmane, Whytman, Whytmane, Wytman

Wildon (English) From the wooded hill
Willdon, Wilden, Willden

Wiley (English) One who is crafty; from the meadow by the water
Wily, Wileigh, Wili, Wilie, Wilee, Wylie, Wyly, Wyley

Wilford (English) From the willow ford
Willford, Wilferd, Willferd, Wilf, Wielford, Weilford, Wilingford, Wylingford

*William (German) The determined protector
Wilek, Wileck, Wilhelm, Wilhelmus, Wilkes, Wilkie, Wilkinson, Will, Guillaume, Quilliam

Willow (English) Of the willow tree
Willowe, Willo, Willoe

Wilmer (German) A strong-willed and well-known man
Wilmar, Wilmore, Willmar, Willmer, Wylmer, Wylmar, Wyllmer, Wyllmar

Winston (English) Of the joy stone; from the friendly town
Win, Winn, Winsten, Winstonn, Wynstan, Wynsten, Wynston, Winstan

Winthrop (English) From the friendly village
Winthrope, Wynthrop, Wynthrope, Winthorp, Wynthorp

Winton (English) From the enclosed pastureland
Wintan, Wintin, Winten, Wynton, Wyntan, Wyntin, Wynten

Wirt (Anglo-Saxon) One who is worthy
Wirte, Wyrt, Wyrte, Wurt, Wurte

Wit (Polish) Form of Vitus, meaning "giver of life"
Witt

Wlodzimierz (Polish) To rule with peace
Wlodzimir, Wlodzimerz

Wolfric (German) A wolf ruler
Wolfrick, Wolfrik, Wulfric, Wulfrick, Wulfrik, Wolfryk, Wolfryck, Wolfryc

Wolodymyr (Ukrainian) Form of Volodymyr, meaning "to rule with peace"
Wolodimyr, Wolodimir, Wolodymeer, Wolodimeer

Woorak (Aboriginal) From the plains
Woorack, Woorac

*Wyatt (English) Having the strength of a warrior
Wyat, Wyatte, Wyate, Wiatt, Wiatte, Wiat, Wiate, Wyeth

Wyndham (English) From the windy village
Windham

Xakery (American) Form of Zachery, meaning "the Lord remembers"
Xaccary, Xaccery, Xach, Xacharie, Xachery, Xack, Xackarey, Xackary

Xalvador (Spanish) Form of Salvador, meaning "a savior"
Xalvadore, Xalvadoro, Xalvadorio, Xalbador, Xalbadore, Xalbadorio, Xalbadoro, Xabat

Xannon (American) From an ancient family
Xanon, Xannen, Xanen, Xannun, Xanun

Xanthus (Greek) A blond-haired man
Xanthos, Xanthe, Xanth

*Xavier (Basque / Arabic) Owner of a new house / one who is bright
Xaver, Xever, Xabier, Xaviere, Xabiere, Xaviar, Xaviare, Xavior

Xenocrates (Greek) A foreign ruler

Xesus (Galician) Form of Jesus, meaning "God is my salvation"

Xoan (Galician) Form of John, meaning "God is gracious"
Xoane, Xohn, Xon

Xue (Chinese) A studious young man

Yael (Israeli) Strength of God
Yaele

Yagil (Hebrew) One who rejoices, celebrates
Yagill, Yagyl, Yagylle

Yahto (Native American) Having blue eyes; refers to the color blue
Yahtoe, Yahtow, Yahtowe

Yahweh (Hebrew) Refers to God
Yahveh, Yaweh, Yaveh, Yehowah, Yehweh, Yehoveh

Yakiv (Ukrainian) Form of Jacob, meaning "he who supplants"
Yakive, Yakeev, Yakeeve, Yackiv, Yackeev, Yakieve, Yakiev, Yakeive

Yakout (Arabian) As precious as a ruby

Yale (Welsh) From the fertile upland
Yayle, Yayl, Yail, Yaile

Yanai (Aramaic) God will answer
Yanae, Yana, Yani

Yankel (Hebrew) Form of Jacob, meaning "he who supplants"
Yankell, Yanckel, Yanckell, Yankle, Yanckle

Yaotl (Aztec) A great warrior
Yaotyl, Yaotle, Yaotel, Yaotyle

Yaphet (Hebrew) A handsome man
Yaphett, Yapheth, Yaphethe

Yaqub (Arabic) Form of Jacob, meaning "he who supplants"
Ya'qub, Yaqob, Yaqoub

Yardley (English) From the fenced-in meadow
Yardly, Yardleigh, Yardli, Yardlie, Yardlee, Yardlea, Yarley, Yarly

Yaromir (Russian) Form of Jaromir, meaning "from the famous spring"
Yaromire, Yaromeer, Yaromeere, Yaromyr, Yaromyre

Yas (Native American) Child of the snow

Yasahiro (Japanese) One who is peaceful and calm

Yasin (Arabic) A wealthy man
Yasine, Yaseen, Yaseene, Yasyn, Yasyne, Yasien, Yasiene, Yasein

Yasir (Arabic) One who is well-off financially
Yassir, Yasser, Yaseer, Yasr, Yasyr, Yassyr, Yasar, Yassar

Yegor (Russian) Form of George, meaning "one who works the earth; a farmer"
Yegore, Yegorr, Yegeor, Yeorges, Yeorge, Yeorgis

Yehonadov (Hebrew) A gift from God
Yehonadav, Yehonedov, Yehonedav, Yehoash, Yehoashe, Yeeshai, Yeeshae, Yishai

Yenge (African) A hard-working man
Yengi, Yengie, Yengy, Yengey, Yengee

Yeoman (English) A man-servant
Youman, Yoman

Yestin (Welsh) One who is just and fair
Yestine, Yestyn, Yestyne

Yigil (Hebrew) He shall be redeemed
Yigile, Yigyl, Yigyle, Yigol, Yigole, Yigit, Yigat

Yishachar (Hebrew) He will be rewarded
Yishacharr, Yishachare, Yissachar, Yissachare, Yisachar, Yisachare

Yiska (Native American) The night has gone

Yngve (Scandinavian) Refers to the god Ing

Yo (Cambodian) One who is honest

Yoav (Hebrew) Form of Joab, meaning "the Lord is my father"
Yoave, Yoavo, Yoavio

Yochanan (Hebrew) Form of John, meaning "God is gracious"
Yochan, Yohannan, Yohanan, Yochannan

Yohan (German) Form of John, meaning "God is gracious"
Yohanan, Yohann, Yohannes, Yohon, Yohonn, Yohonan

Yonatan (Hebrew) Form of Jonathan, meaning "a gift of God"
Yonaton, Yohnatan, Yohnaton, Yonathan, Yonathon, Yoni, Yonie, Yony

Yong (Korean) One who is courageous

York (English) From the yew settlement
Yorck, Yorc, Yorke

Yosyp (Ukrainian) Form of Joseph, meaning "God will add"
Yosip, Yosype, Yosipe

Yovanny (English) Form of Giovanni, meaning "God is gracious"
Yovanni, Yovannie, Yovannee, Yovany, Yovani, Yovanie, Yovanee

Yukon (English) From the settlement of gold
Youkon, Yucon, Youcon, Yuckon, Youckon

Yuliy (Russian) Form of Julius, meaning "one who is youthful"
Yuli, Yulie, Yulee, Yuleigh, Yuly, Yuley, Yulika, Yulian

Yuudai (Japanese) A great hero
Yudai, Yuudae, Yudae, Yuuday, Yuday

Yves (French) A young archer
Yve, Yvo, Yvon, Yvan, Yvet, Yvete

Zabian (Arabic) One who worships celestial bodies
Zabion, Zabien, Zaabian

Zabulon (Hebrew) One who is exalted
Zabulun, Zabulen

Zacchaeus (Hebrew) Form of Zachariah, meaning "The Lord remembers"
Zachaeus, Zachaios, Zaccheus, Zackaeus, Zacheus, Zackaios, Zaccheo

Zachariah (Hebrew) The Lord remembers
Zacaria, Zacarias, Zaccaria, Zaccariah, Zachaios, Zacharia, Zacharias, Zacherish

★Zachary (Hebrew) Form of Zachariah, meaning "the Lord remembers"
Zaccary, Zaccery, Zach, Zacharie, Zachery, Zack, Zackarey, Zackary, Thackary, Xakery

Zaci (African) In mythology, the god of fatherhood

Zaden (Dutch) A sower of seeds
Zadin, Zadan, Zadon, Zadun, Zede, Zeden, Zedan

Zadok (Hebrew) One who is righteous; just
Zadoc, Zaydok, Zadock, Zaydock, Zaydoc, Zaidok, Zaidock, Zaidoc

Zador (Hungarian) An ill-tempered man
Zador, Zadoro, Zadorio

Zafar (Arabic) The conquerer; a victorious man
Zafarr, Zaffar, Zhafar, Zhaffar, Zafer, Zaffer

Zahid (Arabic) A pious man
*Zahide, Zahyd, Zahyde,
Zaheed, Zaheede, Zaheide,
Zahiede, Zaheid*

Zahir (Arabic) A radiant and
flourishing man
*Zahire, Zahireh, Zahyr,
Zahyre, Zaheer, Zaheere,
Zaheir, Zahier*

Zahur (Arabic) Resembling a
flower
*Zahure, Zahureh, Zhahur,
Zaahur*

Zale (Greek) Having the
strength of the sea
*Zail, Zaile, Zayl, Zayle, Zael,
Zaele*

Zamir (Hebrew) Resembling a
songbird
*Zamire, Zameer, Zameere,
Zamyr, Zamyre, Zameir,
Zameire, Zamier*

Zander (Slavic) Form of
Alexander, meaning "a helper
and defender of mankind"
*Zandros, Zandro, Zandar,
Zandur, Zandre*

Zane (English) form of John,
meaning "God is gracious"
Zayne, Zayn, Zain, Zaine

Zareb (African) The protector;
guardian
*Zarebb, Zaareb, Zarebe,
Zarreb, Zareh, Zaareh*

Zared (Hebrew) One who has
been trapped
*Zarede, Zarad, Zarade,
Zaared, Zaarad*

Zasha (Russian) A defender of
the people
*Zashah, Zosha, Zoshah,
Zashiya, Zoshiya*

^**Zayden** (Arabic) Form of
Zayd, meaning "To become
greater, to grow"
Zaiden

Zeke (English) Form of
Ezekiel, meaning "strength-
ened by God"
Zekiel, Zeek, Zeeke, Zeeq

Zene (African) A handsome
man
Zeene, Zeen, Zein, Zeine

Zereen (Arabic) The golden
one
*Zereene, Zeryn, Zeryne, Zerein,
Zereine, Zerrin, Zerren, Zerran*

Zeroun (Armenian) One who
is respected for his wisdom
Zeroune, Zeroon, Zeroone

Zeth (English) Form of Seth, meaning "one who has been appointed"
Zethe

Zion (Hebrew) From the citadel
Zionn, Zione, Zionne

Ziv (Hebrew) A radiant man
Zive, Ziiv, Zivi, Zivie, Zivee, Zivy, Zivey

Ziyad (Arabic) One who betters himself; growth
Ziad

Zlatan (Croatian) The golden son
Zlattan, Zlatane, Zlatann, Zlatain, Zlatayn, Zlaten, Zlaton, Zlatin

Zoltan (Hungarian) A kingly man; a sultan
Zoltann, Zoltane, Zoltanne, Zsolt, Zsoltan

Zorion (Basque) Filled with happiness
Zorian, Zorien

Zoticus (Greek) Full of life
Zoticos, Zoticas

Zsigmond (Hungarian) Form of Sigmund, meaning "the victorious protector"
Zsigmund, Zsigmonde, Zsigmunde, Zsig, Zsiga

Zubair (Arabic) One who is pure
Zubaire, Zubayr, Zubayre, Zubar, Zubarr, Zubare, Zubaer

Zuberi (African) Having great strength
Zuberie, Zubery, Zuberey, Zuberee, Zubari, Zubarie, Zubary, Zubarey

Zubin (English) One with a toothy grin
Zubine, Zuben, Zuban, Zubun, Zubbin

Zuzen (Basque) One who is just and fair
Zuzenn, Zuzan, Zuzin

Zvonimir (Croatian) The sound of peace
Zvonimirr, Zvonimeer

My Favorite Names

My Favorite Names